VPL

the complete
fisherman's handbook

the complete
fisherman's handbook

A comprehensive guide to coarse fishing, sea angling and game fishing

tony miles, martin ford and peter gathercole
consultant editor: bruce vaughan

southwater

This edition is published by Southwater

Southwater is an imprint of Anness Publishing Ltd
Hermes House, 88–89 Blackfriars Road, London SE1 8HA
tel. 020 7401 2077; fax 020 7633 9499; info@anness.com

© Anness Publishing Ltd 1999, 2003

This edition distributed in the UK by The Manning Partnership Ltd, 6 The Old Dairy, Melcombe Road, Bath BA2 3LR;
tel. 01225 478 444; fax 01225 478 440; sales@manning-partnership.co.uk

This edition distributed in the USA and Canada by National Book Network, 4720 Boston Way, Lanham, MD 20706;
tel. 301 459 3366; fax 301 459 1705; www.nbnbooks.com

This edition distributed in Australia by Pan Macmillan Australia, Level 18, St Martins Tower, 31 Market St, Sydney, NSW 2000;
tel. 1300 135 113; fax 1300 135 103; customer.service@macmillan.com.au

This edition distributed in New Zealand by The Five Mile Press (NZ) Ltd, PO Box 33–1071 Takapuna, Unit 11/101–111 Diana Drive,
Glenfield, Auckland 10; tel. (09) 444 4144; fax (09) 444 4518; fivemilenz@clear.net.nz

A CIP catalogue record for this book is available from the British Library.

Publisher: Joanna Lorenz
Project Editor: Doreen Palamartschuk
Editor: Anthony Atha
Designer: James Lawrence
Photography: Sue Ford, Peter Gathercole
Illustrators: Mike Atkinson (species), Dave Batten (rigs and diagrams) and Penny brown (knots)
Editorial Reader: Kate Henderson
Indexer: Ann Barrett
Production Controller: Wendy Lawson

Previously published as: *The Practical Fishing Encyclopedia*

1 3 5 7 9 10 8 6 4 2

Publisher's Note

This book is intended as a source of information
on angling. Neither the author nor the publisher
can be held responsible for any specific
individual's reactions, harmful effects or claims
arising from the use of the general data and
suggestions it contains. The use of any
information contained in this book is entirely at
the reader's own risk.

Contents

Foreword

LEFT: A reservoir angler casts out towards the dying ripple as the sun sets.

BOTTOM: Lily pads, favourite haunts of perch and pike.

There has, without question, never been a better time to go fishing than the present. Our waterways are becoming cleaner, fish are growing bigger, the number of fisheries is increasing and the quality of fishing tackle available is constantly improving and competitively priced.

In the past, many country rivers were badly polluted by industry and outdated sewage works, which resulted in them flowing either totally devoid of life of any kind or, at best, providing a very harsh existence for those fish and other aquatic creatures hardy enough to survive in them. It used to be said in the 1950s and 60s that it was possible to develop a photographic negative by dipping it into certain reaches of the rivers Thames and Trent! Certainly anyone unfortunate enough to fall into them was immediately whisked off to hospital for a thorough check-up.

Coupled with this depressing state of affairs came the added problem that many river authorities ripped the heart out of numerous waters under their jurisdiction. The drainage engineers they employed demanded that work should be done to ensure that any rainwater entering a river system was flushed away to the sea as rapidly as possible. Not only did this dredging work ruin many once-beautiful waterways, but the effect of straightening and levelling also eliminated the numerous slacks and eddies off the main current which were havens for fry and small fish in times of high water. In turn, this was made worse by the effects of flash flooding caused by the rapid draining.

How times have changed. Today, much heavy industry has disappeared and its passing has greatly benefited the rivers; while the relatively recently formed water authorities have invested large sums of money in completely rebuilding or vastly improving sewage works throughout the country.

So rivers that for years have been devoid of aquatic life are now thriving ecosystems, and even species such as trout and salmon are beginning to be spotted in rivers

that run through urban areas that were once industrial heartlands. Thankfully, some water authorities have now admitted to the disastrous effect that some dredging schemes had on many waterways, and they are trying to turn back the clock by creating new special havens for small fish out of the main flow.

While all this is excellent news for fish and anglers, it is has proved an extremely costly exercise and one that would have been totally unnecessary if only many rivers had been left alone, in their original state, all those years ago.

Since the mid-twentieth century, thousands of water-filled pits have been created across the country as a result of the insatiable demand for sand and gravel by the construction and road industries. This phenomenon has hugely benefited anglers, because many of these pits have been landscaped and converted into first-class fisheries that are very well stocked. Additionally, reservoirs have also proliferated in the past few decades,

The extensive canal system of Britain has always been a favourite with anglers and many more miles of canal, that had become weed-choked and unfishable, have been restored and opened up to anglers (and the boating fraternity) in recent years.

Finally, the advent of the "set-aside policy" in agriculture has resulted in many landowners converting areas of farmland into ponds and lakes. A large proportion of these instant fisheries has been generously stocked and provides a totally new and additional facility for anglers right across the country.

Fish are undoubtedly becoming bigger, too. There would seem to be no one obvious reason for this phenomenon; rather it is a combination of factors. The upshot is that anglers today have the chance of catching fish of a bigger size than at any other time.

In carp fishing, during the 1990s, numerous fish over 40 lb (18.14 kg) and 50 lb (22.68 kg) were landed, while Dick Walker's record 44 lb (19.96 kg) common carp,

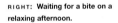

RIGHT: **Waiting for a bite on a relaxing afternoon.**

as the growing population's need for a ready supply of drinking water has grown. Many of these reservoirs are open to anglers as well as other water enthusiasts and they are stocked with a variety of species including trout, which has produced a boom in fly fishing for high-quality browns and rainbows, once regarded as the preserve of the rich and famous only.

caught in 1953, stood unchallenged for 25 years before it was finally beaten. Tench, too, once thought big at 5 lb (2.27 kg) are now caught regularly in double figure weight. Chub and barbel are two other species that have fared particularly well in recent years with more 6–7 lb (2.72–3.18 kg) chub and big double-figure barbel being caught than ever before.

Perch suffered terribly through disease during the 1970s and 80s, but are back to their peak with numerous specimens in the 3–4 lb (1.36–1.81 kg) bracket being caught every year.

One suggestion is that global warming is the key to fish growing bigger – milder winters and hotter summers producing faster growth rates – while further evidence for this theory is provided by the increasing number of exotic marine species that are turning up at coasts with each passing year.

A further possibility is that anglers themselves are partly responsible: the wide use of highly nutritious baits may actually contribute to the fish gaining weight. Poor spawning is another hypothesis frequently propounded and is one that certainly holds true for many sand and gravel pits. While rich in weed and invertebrate life, providing cover and food for the fish that live in them, many pits are deep and thus offer few suitable spawning sites. As a consequence, spawning is low, resulting in few fish being present and therefore little competition for the abundantly available food supply. In short, the fish that are present wax fat. There is, however, one cloud on this horizon: the plight of the salmon and sea trout, the two main migratory fish in the British Isles. There is no doubt that the population of both species has declined in the last years and both have suffered from a combination of loss of habitat and netting on the high seas. Strenuous efforts are being

made by fishery owners and official bodies to remedy this. It is the duty of all anglers to support these efforts, for the loss of either species would be a tragedy.

On a happier note, in terms of range and quality, fishing tackle has made a quantum leap forward over the past few decades, and it is difficult to see how many items could be improved upon. Moreover, prices have never been cheaper, thus widening availability.

Rods and reels have been developed to perform a whole host of specific functions, including casting way beyond the 100 metre mark on lakes and 200 metres down on the beach. Co-polymer lines boasting diameters half those of conventional monofilament have proved

LEFT: Fishing over rocks and rough ground – a good place to catch bass, conger eels or dogfish.

ABOVE: Netting a fish on a boat fishing expedition.

their worth beyond any doubt, while the newly arrived fluorocarbon lines, which are virtually invisible in water, are set to make a similar impact.

Chemically sharpened hooks are highly superior to the old ground-point models and have become standard. Ancillary equipment, such as electronic alarms, bite indicators and rod rests, even angler's shelters, chairs and waterproof clothing, have all increased in sophistication and quality of manufacture, and in many cases will last through a lifetime of angling.

However, the best tackle in the world would not alone guarantee success on the bank. Fortunately, though, for today's angler there has never been so much help at hand in terms of the books, magazines and

LEFT: An Orkney boat pulled up on the shore of a small Highland loch. Often such lochs hold unexpectedly good trout.

videos on all aspects of fishing that are readily available. Tackle dealers, too, should not be forgotten for most are a mine of knowledge and experience built up over many years and are only too pleased to assist newcomers to the sport or those wishing to progress.

Yet, despite all the help and information that is available to anglers of all abilities today, it is vitally important not to become a textbook or video expert. While it is unquestionably a good idea to take advice and learn from the experts – both on and off the printed page and on film – it is essential to use these tips as a stimulus to getting out on the bank and enjoying the thrill of fishing first hand and for learning the art of angling. Anything in life that is worked for ultimately proves more satisfying.

The three authors of this book are all acknowledged experts in their respective fields of coarse, sea and game fishing, and have drawn upon a wealth of experience gleaned from years of fishing at home and abroad. Their collective efforts have resulted in a volume that is both wide ranging and impressive in its coverage, as well as being lavishly illustrated.

No one, from the total novice to the angler wishing to hone his or her skills, could fail to be stimulated by the information contained in this book and, as a result, would undoubtedly go on to become a better angler.

RIGHT: A salmon river in ideal water.

Coarse Fishing

Many people have a problem with the term "coarse fishing". It implies that there is something rather uncouth or unsophisticated about the pastime or even the anglers who pursue it. People have claimed that the term came about because trout and salmon, the main game fish, were delicacies on the table, while freshwater fish such as roach, bream and chub are coarse tasting and unpleasant to eat. Others claim it was because the best trout and salmon fishing in England was the preserve of the rich, although everyone could always fish for trout in Scotland.

Fortunately today all anglers are united with the common goals of unpolluted rivers and ethical angling practices. There has seldom been a better time to be a coarse fisher: modern tackle is vastly improved, waters are better managed, fishing is increasingly popular and records are constantly being broken.

Introduction

The term "coarse fishing" is misleading: there is nothing coarse about this sport. Great skill and finesse are required to capture these fish. Techniques have to be refined and refined again to deceive these wily creatures. The delicacy of presentation required to tempt a crucian carp is almost indescribable; the many hours of inactivity required to catch a big bream or catfish stretches the angler's patience to the very limit. Compared with these species, trout can be easy to catch. As far as fighting ability is concerned, which is probably where the "game" of "game fishing" originated, coarse fish also compare well. Salmon fight powerfully, but pound for pound they certainly fight no harder than carp or barbel, and they fight with far less intelligence. Salmon tend to go off very strongly, but often in a straight line as far and fast as possible. Carp and barbel, on the other hand, are wilier: they are looking for that snag, the bolt hole where they can tangle the line and break free. Thankfully today, the divisions between game fishing and coarse fishing are disappearing as more anglers become all-rounders and realize that each fish has its own individual merit.

The Pleasure Angler

There are three broad sub-divisions among coarse anglers. There are those who will fish for anything that comes along. They seldom compete in matches and would never dream of sitting out all night in winter on a desolate Fenland drain in the hope of a giant zander. They are "pleasure anglers", a misnomer as all anglers get pleasure from the sport.

The Match Angler

Although not all anglers start out this way, there are those who will be drawn to the drug of competition with other anglers. They may have started by taking part in club matches and realized that rivalry with other anglers gave that extra enjoyment to their fishing. Just as there are different levels of skill and commitment to the sport among pleasure anglers, so there are among the match anglers. Some are content to remain as good club-match anglers while others aspire to the heights of competition. These are the people who have honed their skills to razor sharpness by fishing against the clock. At the very pinnacle

BELOW: **The witching hour. The angler waits as the sun sinks away in the west. Dusk and dawn are often the best times to fish.**

of the match scene there is an ever-growing body of professional anglers who consistently pit their skills against the best in the world, including men such as Tom Pickering, and triple world champions Bob Nudd and Alan Scotthorne.

The Specimen Hunter

Lastly, there are the big-fish specialists, the specimen hunters. These are the anglers who have evolved in the opposite direction to the match anglers. Rather than catch small to average fish more quickly than others, the big-fish angler deliberately slows down his or her catch rate and targets the bigger-than-average specimen. This angler will happily go hours, days, weeks or even months in the dedicated pursuit of a monster and is no longer fishing in a haphazard manner but with clear and unambiguous goals.

In the 1960s anglers realized that exchange of information was valuable, and small groups of like-minded individuals banded together to form specimen groups, in which ideas were shared. The specimen group movement advanced the pursuit of deliberately targeting big fish by perhaps decades, in just a few years.

Nowadays, there is much information available to the angler through excellent specialist magazines and television programmes. Match anglers and top specimen hunters are frequently sponsored by tackle and bait manufacturers to promote the sport, and this has increased the profile of the sport.

The Diversity of Coarse Fishing

There should be no artificial divisions between these branches of coarse fishing for it is an incredibly diverse and complex sport. There are dozens of different techniques for catching each species, and methods vary from water to water. Specialist approaches may have to be made to cope with hot or icy weather, low water or floods, high winds or darkness.

And then there are sub-divisions in each technique. Are you going to float fish for specimen roach or average roach, or speed fish for small roach in a match? If you speed fish in a match, do you use rod and line, or a pole or a whip? If a pole is the choice, do you use a wire-stemmed or a carbon-stemmed float?

Perhaps you fish for big carp and are not sure whether you should fish on the bottom or on the top, or in the margins or at range. If you fish on the bottom do you use sweetcorn or boilies, and do you fish the boilies hard on the bottom or popped up? What about loose feeding? If a boilie is the chosen hookbait, do you feed boilies by catapult or stringer? Or do you not use boilies at all, preferring trout pellets in a PVA bag? The number of individual techniques that could be discussed runs into hundreds of permutations.

For the beginner this diversity can be confusing, but in time much will become clear. You will learn as you go along and it is a great mistake to let the technicalities put you off at the outset. Angling is the greatest of all sports. It is a huge challenge, brings you close to nature, and provides hours of happiness and enjoyment. It is a vast subject and consequently there are omissions as there is simply not room to cover all topics in detail.

Tackle and Equipment

There is a bewildering variety of tackle, bait and equipment available, most of it of excellent quality. Where specific manufacturers have been mentioned in this book, it is only because their equipment has been used and tested at firsthand. It does not mean that other manufacturers do not market products of equal quality, and you should always seek advice from a local tackle dealer.

TOP: Trotting a swim for roach in high water in early winter. These are good conditions, and the angler may expect a good bag.

LEFT: A weed raft in a small overgrown river in high summer – a likely place for fish.

Species

Barbel *(Barbus barbus)*

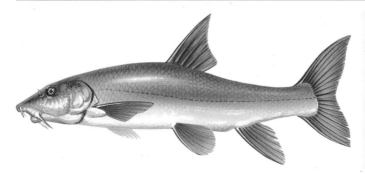

Current Record
British **17 lb 1 oz (7.739 kg)**

Season
June to March.

Distribution
Most prolific in rivers of southern
England and Yorkshire.

Natural Diet
Bottom feeders taking any creatures
living in the gravel.

Top Spots
River Severn, Great Ouse, Hampshire
Avon and Wensum.

Top Tip
Fish with big, smelly baits in a warm
winter flood, when barbel are at their
fighting best.

Recognition

The streamlined torpedo shape and
paddle-like coral-pink fins make the
barbel one of the most easily
recognizable fish in our rivers. The
only fish with which it could possibly
be confused is a gudgeon, and then
only if it was just a couple of ounces
in weight. Barbel of this size are
almost never encountered by anglers,
but if they are, the distinguishing
features are that the barbel has a pair
of barbules at the corner of the mouth
and another pair on the snout. In a
gudgeon, there is only a pair at the
corners of the mouth. The colouring
of a gudgeon is also much more
mottled and generally duller.

These distinctive barbules help
the barbel to locate its food, which it
then sucks into a very underslung
mouth, which is ideally adapted for
grubbing around on the river bed. Its
thick, rubbery lips prevent the barbel
from damaging its mouth on sharp
gravel on the river bed. Strangely, for
a bottom-feeding fish and one that
feeds so well and effectively in low
light conditions, the eyes of the barbel
are fairly small in relation to body size
and set high on the head. This tells us
that the barbel relies more on its
barbules to locate its food than it does
on its eyesight. This is borne out, as
one of the best times to catch barbel is
at night, fishing with meat baits.

Habitat and Location

The barbel is a river fish: the modern
trend of stocking these magnificent
creatures in commercial stillwater
fisheries, for which they are not
suited, is abhorrent.

Although originally a dweller of
fast, gravelly rivers, such as the River
Kennet, in which they spawn most
successfully and are very prolific, they
also do very well in more sedate
environments, such as the Great Ouse.
A lower spawning success rate means
that individual barbel in this type of .
river are becoming very big indeed.

Only a generation ago, distribution
of barbel was very uneven, but as the
popularity of the fish has increased,
more and more rivers have been
stocked, so that nowadays most parts
of England and Wales have good
barbel fishing close at hand.

Classic barbel swims will include
beds of ranunculus, commonly called
streamer weed, river bed depressions,
under overhanging trees, and fast
glides including the tail of weirpools.
Big barbel are particularly attracted to
snags, and most rivers will have
swims of this sort, with a resident
barbel population.

LEFT: **Portrait of a big barbel showing the
prominent barbules on the side of the mouth.**

Size

It is very rare for small barbel to feature in anglers' catches, and the usual run of fish from all rivers would be 2–8 lb (0.91–3.62 kg). When they exceed 10 lb (4.54 kg), barbel are considered specimens and most barbel rivers now contain fish of this calibre. In the past few seasons, barbel weights have increased significantly, and where a 12 lb (5.44 kg) fish was once considered exceptional, a barbel now has to exceed 14 lb (6.35 kg) to achieve that accolade. Monster fish over 15 lb (6.80 kg) have been taken from several rivers, and the current record is a fish of 17 lb 1 oz (7.739 kg) from the Great Ouse River in 1999.

ABOVE: Playing a barbel on the River Kennet. The Kennet, the Hampshire Avon and River Thames were traditionally the best barbel waters in the country, but many rivers not previously associated with barbel are now stocked and contain good fish. The River Severn is one of the best examples.

LEFT: The Great Ouse in summer. This water traditionally did not hold barbel as it was not a fast-flowing river, but it has recently become one of the best barbel waters and holds some very large fish.

Behaviour and Feeding Habits

Barbel are avid bottom feeders, summer and winter, although they feed very spasmodically when the water temperature falls below about 4°C (39.2°F). Much of their time is spent browsing the gravel beds, sucking out all the creatures that live there and other food items that have become entrapped. A shoal of barbel will work a gravel run in an upstream direction, and individual fish at the head of the shoal will often turn downstream with a mouthful of food before resuming station at the rear of the shoal. This behaviour is responsible for the characteristic lunging bite often associated with barbel fishing.

Barbel are easily induced to feed by anglers' baits, especially where particle baits are used in quantity.

Hempseed is well known for imparting preoccupied feeding, as are maggots, tares, worms, casters and sweetcorn. Barbel are also lovers of meaty baits such as processed meats and sausage meat.

Barbel feed well both in daylight and at night, but in clear water, in daylight, will often accept particle baits only, spooking badly on large offerings such as luncheon meat. After dark, when they feed entirely by smell and touch, these larger meat baits come into their own.

Warm winter floods are especially reliable conditions for producing good barbel, when the fish are actively searching for food, and mobile meat baits and lobworms are taken avidly. At this time of year, the fish are at peak condition and a good barbel is a worthy adversary for any angler.

ABOVE: Returning a 12 lb (5.44 kg) barbel to the Bristol Avon. Barbel are strong fighters and require sturdy tackle to hold them. If they are exhausted when landed hold them upright in the river, facing upstream until they have fully recovered and are ready to swim away. This principle applies to all fish.

Bream *(Abramis brama)*

Current Record
British **16 lb 9 oz (7.513 kg)**

Season
June to March in rivers, all year in stillwaters.

Distribution
Widespread in all water types except fast chalk streams.

Natural Diet
Water snails, caddis, insect larvae.

Top Spots
The Fens and Norfolk Broads.

Top Tip
Big fish are very nocturnal. Bait the swim in late afternoon and fish the dark hours for a specimen bream.

Recognition

There are two species of bream, bronze and silver; but the main one of interest to anglers is the much larger bronze bream, as silver bream (*Blicca bjoerkna*) has very limited distribution.

Young bronze bream are silvery in appearance with black fins, giving rise to confusion with silver bream, and as it is very slim and plate-like, it has attracted the nickname "skimmer" or "tin-plate bream". Over about 3 lb (1.36 kg) in weight, the colouration changes to greyish brown, although some large fish, particularly from gravel pits, live up to their name in having rich bronze hues, in some cases becoming nearly black.

As the bream grows, it changes shape and becomes deep bodied, hump backed and heavily coated with slime, while the markedly underslung mouth, with telescopic top lip, betrays the fact that the bream is predominantly a bottom feeder.

BELOW: **A good catch of bream taken from the River Shannon in Ireland. Bream are shoal fish and often a number can be caught from one swim. It is essential to groundbait thoroughly before starting to fish.**

RIGHT: A sluice pool on a southern country river. Although bream are not lovers of fast waters, they can be found below shallows and in slack pools on the inside of bends.

Bream has a flat-sided body that is mainly golden brown, and the pectoral and pelvic fins are tinged with red.

If you do catch a fish you think may be a silver bream, particularly in the Eastern counties of England, an easy point of recognition is that the silver bream has 44–48 scales along the lateral line while the true bronze bream has between 51–60 scales.

Habitat and Location

The bream is very widely distributed in Britain, although it is not a lover of fast-flowing rivers. Bream form vast shoals in extensive lakes such as the Norfolk Broads, in water supply reservoirs and in scenic estate lakes. They also thrive in the sedate waters of the Fens and slow-flowing rivers such as those of East Anglia, the Great Ouse and the Thames.

The biggest bream are now to be found in gravel pits, an environment that has seen bream weights increase significantly in the last 20 years.

Although rarely found in heavy flows, big bream do well in rivers such as the Hampshire Avon, where they will congregate in the deeper, slacker pools, on the inside of bends, in the steadier water below broken shallows and in any swims where fast water borders slow. In high or flood water, they are also lovers of sheltered undercuts under high banks.

Size

Bream exhibit wide size differences from water to water, and generally it is accepted that a 10 lb (4.54 kg) fish is a specimen, although many waters do not produce fish of this size. Until the advent of gravel pits, the big reservoirs produced the bigger bream, to over 12 lb (5.44 kg), but pits have now taken over this mantle.

Although some pits have shoals of average to big fish, up to about 13 lb (5.90 kg), it is the few waters with much lower stock density that hold the monsters. These include Queen-ford Lagoon in Oxfordshire and have produced fish up to the current record of 16 lb 9 oz (7.513 kg), taken in 1991.

Behaviour and Feeding Habits

The natural food of bream are bottom-dwelling creatures such as water snails and caddis, as well as large quantities of insect larvae such as bloodworms. The bream's mouth is designed for vacuuming in the bottom debris to locate this food, and this activity often results in muddying of the water and the release of large mats of bubbles, a reliable guide to the presence of a bream shoal. As the fish form large shoals, they are necessarily nomadic, as they quickly exhaust the food supplies in one area. This often leads to their following well-defined feeding lines, known as patrol routes, and in some waters, particularly the meres of Cheshire and Shropshire, anglers have learned to predict the arrival of a bream shoal in a particular area depending on the time of day. This process is helped by the bream's habit of rolling on the surface, or cutting the surface film with its large dorsal fin, just prior to feeding.

Very big bream, particularly fish in gravel pits, have the well-deserved reputation for being one of the most difficult fish to understand and catch. Even when they are located, they are often not susceptible to anglers' baits and it seems certain that for much of the time they are preoccupied by natural foods.

Although bream can be caught at all times, summer or winter, they are not lovers of very cold conditions. The bigger fish are also very nocturnal, especially in gravel pits where it can be rare to catch a bream in daylight.

Carp *(Cyprinus carpio)*

Current Records
British **56 lb 6 oz (25.571 kg)**
World **75 lb 11 oz (35.35 kg)** France

Season
June to March in rivers, all year in stillwaters.

Distribution
Widely distributed throughout Britain in all water types.

Natural Diet
Insect larvae, molluscs. Moths and flies off surface.

Top Spots
Vast number of carp lakes. Redmire and Wraysbury are both famous.

Top Tip
On big stillwaters, fish into the prevailing wind.

Recognition

The carp is the most popular sporting fish in Britain, and the largest of our cyprinids. A true wild carp, which is covered in large, regular brassy scales and has chestnut fins, is lean and muscular, often with a large tail that can give it tremendous acceleration. Although such "wildies" can reach 20 lb (9.07 kg), it is rare for wild carp to exceed 15 lb (6.80 kg).

The deeper-bodied fish, initially produced by selective breeding and which are now superseding the wild strain, grow much larger. There are a number of varieties that the angler may encounter: **common carp**, which are fully scaled; **mirror carp**, which are partially scaled; and **leather carp**, which are virtually without scales, except perhaps a few small ones on the shoulders and back.

Mirror carp themselves have a number of sub-varieties. True mirror carp have a few very large scales irregularly placed over the body. Much more rarely, there are mirror carp in which these scales are placed evenly along the lateral line, and these are known as linear mirrors.

Carp have four barbules, a large one in each corner of the mouth and one much smaller alongside. The long, concave dorsal fin has 20–26 rays and is totally different in shape from that of the much smaller Crucian carp, which has a smaller, convex dorsal fin.

RIGHT: Orchid Lake as night falls. Many small intimate inland lakes such as this are the home of giant carp.

Habitat and Location

Carp is now one of the most widely distributed coarse fish, and does well in all types of water from fast-flowing rivers to stagnant pools. The most popular carp-fishing venues are stillwaters, particularly estate lakes, reservoirs and gravel pits, the latter holding the biggest fish. Favoured habitats will include overhanging marginal trees, beds of lilies, rushes or reeds, and alongside steep or undercut banks. Beds of silt which house bloodworms are also favoured, as are gravel bars in pits. The margins of

offshore islands are very reliable areas, particularly if they are overgrown. Carp are well known for following the wind on large, open waters, and in the absence of other location aids a good rule of thumb when fishing new water is always to fish into the prevailing wind.

Size

These days, most carp waters will hold plenty of fish in excess of 10 lb (4.54 kg), and a 20 lb (9.07 kg) fish is the normally accepted weight for specimen status. However, recent years have seen carp weights increase generally, so that more and more specialists regard a carp of 30 lb (13.61 kg) or even 40 lb (18.14 kg) as the target to aim for. Certainly, there are now plenty of waters holding fish of 40 lb (18.14 kg) or more, making these huge specimens a realistic ambition for the specimen hunter. The present British record is held by a fish of 56 lb 6 oz (25.571 kg) that was taken in 1998 in Wraysbury, Berkshire.

Behaviour and Feeding Habits

The natural food of carp consists of the larvae of gnats and midges, of which the bloodworm is the best known example. It also consumes insects, molluscs and crustacea, as well as quantities of vegetation such as silkweed. In soft-bottomed lakes, the carp uses its large, extendable lips to root deep in the mud to secure its food, creating large volumes of bubbles and coloured water, a very obvious location aid for the angler.

Carp fish are also well known for browsing through marginal rush and reed beds. This causes the characteristic shaking of the plants as the carp force their large bodies through the rushes. Similarly, in soft surface weed, carp browsing underneath give rise to 'tenting', where a ridge of weed is created by the carp's back.

As well as being an avid bottom feeder, carp also feeds off the surface, taking moths and insects as well as floating bread and is often caught on floating baits. A surface-feeding carp is very easy to spot, as it cruises with its back partially out of the water. It is also given to rolling noisily, creating sufficient disturbance to

TOP: A slow-flowing river fringed with weed beds and bordered by willows and poplar. Carp are fond of feeding in marginal rushes on midge larvae.

ABOVE: A pristine common carp, fully scaled, about to be returned to the water.

create a flat spot in the water even when the surface is heavily broken by wind and wave action. Unless it is disturbed, a carp will feed greedily on anglers' baits and will eat almost anything.

Nevertheless, in spite of this happy fact, there is a great mystique about carp fishing, and carp fish are justly famous both for their cunning and great strength.

Catfish *(Silurus glanis)*

Current Records
British **62 lbs (28.12 kg)**
World **72 lb 12 oz (33 kg)** Russia

Season
All year but warmer months best.

Distribution
Uneven but improving rapidly. Isolated catfish waters are to be found all over the country but especially in the south.

Natural Diet
Swan mussels, dead fish, frogs, newts and leeches.

Top Spots
Claydon Lake, Withy Pool, Oak Lodge and Wintons.

Top Tip
Margin fish with smelly baits on humid, warm, overcast nights.

Recognition

The Wels catfish looks just like a giant tadpole and is impossible to confuse with any other fish. It has an elongated muscular body, a small rounded tail that joins the anal fin and runs along the underside of the fish, and a very insignificant dorsal fin. It has a large flat head and a huge mouth with lots of tiny, but sharp, top and bottom teeth that feel like rough Velcro. At the back of the mouth are hard bony plates, used for cracking the shells of mussels and crustacea, or the bones of prey fish. At the top corners of the upper jaw are two very long feelers, or whiskers, with four smaller appendages on the lower jaw, used for finding food. It has highly sensitive scent glands, making it an efficient night feeder despite its tiny eyes. Catfish colouration varies from water to water: those from clear waters can be very dark, sometimes nearly black, and those from murkier waters are often mid-grey or light brown. All catfish have mottled flanks and a creamy white belly.

Habitat and Location

The ideal catfish water is a weedy, overgrown and very rich estate lake, with an abundance of freely spawning prey fish to sustain this king of predators. Possibly the most famous water is Claydon, Buckinghamshire where, despite the good head of big cats in quite a small lake, the number of other fish is quite astonishing. The distribution of catfish in this country is escalating fast as the demand for the fish grows. In most waters, in dull conditions or at night when they are scavenging, catfish forage quite close to the margins. They spend bright daylight hours under any snags in the lake or in depressions in the lake bed.

RIGHT: A giant among catfish. Catfish weighing over 100 lb (45.4 kg) may well exist in this country.

Size

The present British record is 62 lb (28.12 kg) taken in 1997, but in some ways this is very misleading. There have been so many catfish waters created in recent years, stocked with imported fish, that the true potential of homegrown cats may now never be known. Stockings have been both legal and illegal. The largest catfish caught on rod and line in this country exceeded 100 lb (45.36 kg), but as this fish was stocked without the correct documentation it was discounted for record purposes. Most anglers consider a 20 lb (9.07 kg) catfish a specimen and a 30 lb (13.61 kg) fish something quite exceptional.

Behaviour and Feeding Habits

The catfish is an opportunist feeder and the ultimate scavenger. At night it roams the margins, taking swan mussels, dead fish, small mammals, frogs, newts and leeches. Even small water birds are not safe from catfish attack, and there have been several reports of baby coots and moorhens disappearing into that cavernous mouth. As well as very efficiently locating its food by its incredible senses of smell and touch, the catfish also has something else going for it. It is equipped with ultra-sensitive hearing and vibration detection, courtesy of linkage of its swim bladder to the ears via a series of small bones. This gives the cat terrific sound amplification, so that a small fish passing in pitch darkness is effectively ringing a dinner gong for a hungry catfish. Catfish anglers who travel abroad have used this sound amplification ability to their own advantage, where slapping the surface of the water with a flat paddle attracts cats from quite a distance.

Anglers have wide choices of bait, but all successful baits will have

OPPOSITE: A very rich, shallow, estate lake. This type of water is perfect for catfish, and very large fish have been taken there.

RIGHT: A double-figure catfish taken from the lake at Woburn.

either movement or a good smell. Livebaits obviously trigger the reaction to vibration but can be self-defeating if the water contains a large number of pike. Wire traces are not required for cats; in fact their very sensitive whiskers would probably reject this presentation anyway, and it is unethical to fish with this method without wire when pike are about. Obviously, this applies equally to deadbaits. Where pike are not a problem, anglers often use polystyrene balls on the hooklink to keep the bait lively, or two or three small baits on the same hook to create the effect of a shoal. The smellier the bait the better: chopped fish, squid,

fishmeal boilies, spicy sausages, liver chunks and heavily flavoured luncheon meats of a number of varieties have all caught cats.

Despite its powerful dimensions, the catfish is quite a shy biting fish, especially on hard-fished waters, and is intolerant of resistance. It is therefore important to arrange for your tackle to be free running once the bait has been taken. As many catfish waters are quite small and the fish are reliable margin feeders anyway, there is little need for long casting and freelining is a viable method. Where you need lead, say for tethering a legered livebait, make it the minimum possible.

Chub *(Leuciscus cephalus)*

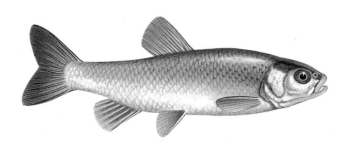

Current Record
British **8 lb 10 oz (3.912 kg)**

Season
June to March on rivers, all year on stillwaters.

Distribution
Widely distributed throughout the country, both in rivers and stillwaters.

Natural Diet
Insects, frogs, crustacea, small fish, spent moths and flies.

Top Spots
Great Ouse, Kennet, Dorset Stour, Hampshire Avon.

Top Tip
Before starting a winter chub session, walk the river and prebait several swims with mashed bread. Fish over this bait with bread flake or crust.

Recognition

The wide, black-edged scales, large mouth adorned with distinctive white lips and the big, blunt head, hence the nickname "loggerhead", make the chub one of the most instantly recognizable of all our coarse fish.

There are, however, two circumstances which make mistakes possible on the bank. The first is hybridization with other species. There have been many cases of chub/roach hybrids reported but these fish have all but the most inexperienced could confuse them with true chub. If you are unsure, the chub has 42–49 scales along the lateral line, and the anal fin has 7–9 branched rays, as has the dorsal.

The most common identification mistakes occur with immature chub, that can be confused with large dace. The clue here is that the anal fin of chub is convex, unlike the markedly concave anal fin of the dace.

Habitat and Location

Although primarily a river fish, the chub does very well indeed in stillwaters, especially gravel pits, where it can grow to large sizes. Big, stillwater chub have earned the reputation as being one of the most difficult specimen fish of all to tempt. Chub are very widely distributed

OPPOSITE TOP: **Stalking chub in high summer. Chub respond well to the floating lure such as a fly, but are easily spooked if you approach carelessly.**

BELOW: **Chub can be caught all the year round. Here the angler is fishing for chub in winter and they can even be caught when there is snow on the ground.**

throughout the rivers of England, Wales and Scotland, although they are not native to Ireland. They thrive in most habitats, from fast shallows to sluggish deeps and are particularly fond of overgrown, neglected streams where they do very well and reach specimen size.

Size

The present chub record is 8 lb 10 oz (3.912 kg), taken in 1994 and is one of the coarse records under threat. The last few years have seen a dramatic increase in average chub weights, with unprecedented numbers of 5–6 lb (2.27–2.72 kg) fish reported to the angling press as well as some of 7 lb (3.18 kg). On most chub rivers, the fish will range from a few ounces to about 5 lb (2.27 kg) – most anglers would call a fish this size a specimen.

Behaviour and Feeding Habits

Chub are one of the most obliging of all fish for anglers, readily eating anything and feeding both in the hottest weather and when it is sub zero. In summer, large natural baits such as big slugs and lobworms are taken with relish, and chub are avid feeders on crustacea such as crayfish,

ABOVE: A nice brace of summer chub caught on slugs. A fresh slug is one of the most popular baits for chub and should be collected at dawn.

small fish, particularly loach, bullheads and minnows, and any insect that might fall from the trees. They particularly love frogs and tadpoles, although these should not be used as bait as there is a general frog shortage in this country. In the evening chub are avid surface feeders, taking spent moths and flies, mayflies being a particular delicacy.

The list of anglers' baits accepted by chub is extensive, and they are as happy accepting single maggots or casters to a feeder rig as they are to

large mouthfuls of cheese paste or luncheon meat. Like barbel, chub are lovers of hempseed and a shoal of chub can be brought to a feeding frenzy over hemp and sweetcorn.

Chub are well known for their caution and are spooked very easily if approached carelessly. This explains their love for quiet, shaded places and densely overgrown stretches. During the winter, chub come to their fighting peak and generally lie in the moderate flows just out of the main push of the current. Even in winter they love a roof over their heads, and their preference for raft swims, where rubbish builds up around draping branches, is well known to all chub anglers.

Unlike roach and barbel, chub do not seem happy in the muddy water of floods and tend not to feed while these conditions persist. It is noticeable that when a chub is caught after prolonged high, dirty water, it will often be thin and anaemic looking. But they make up for their abstinence by going into a feeding binge as the colour clears and the river level begins to fall. A river fining down from a flood is one of the best times of all to be out chub fishing.

Crucian Carp *(Carassius carassius)*

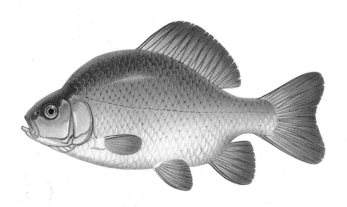

Current Record
British **4 lb 2 oz 8 drm (1.885 kg)**

Season
All year, but warmer months best.

Distribution
Patchy. Mainly found in secluded ponds and estate lakes.

Natural Diet
Shrimps, snails, insect larvae, worms and aquatic vegetation.

Top Spots
Any secluded pond that has not been artificially stocked.

Top Tip
The shyest biting of all fish. Always use the most delicate float arrangement.

Recognition

Crucian carp differ from their larger relatives in having no barbules at the corners of the mouth, a very rounded, tench-like tail and a high convex dorsal. One identifying feature is the number of scales on the lateral line: 31–33 between the upper edge of the gill opening and a point where the tail bends naturally.

Many fish claimed as specimen crucians are in fact either crucian/common carp hybrids or brown goldfish. The problem with both of these variants is that they have no barbules, and most anglers leave it at that. However, both hybrids and brown goldfish have normal, deeply-forked carp tails and markedly long and concave dorsal fins, typical of the big carp species. Everything about the true crucian is rounded. Crucians are short, fully scaled, thickset and with tough, rubbery lips.

Habitat and Location

Crucian carp used to be very wide-spread, especially in the south. They inhabited reservoirs, estate lakes and farm ponds, but unfortunately, largely owing to the growth in popularity of carp fishing, many good crucian waters are now being destroyed because of the regularity of inter-breeding. As with the rudd, the picture is becoming blurred. True crucians are now most likely to be found in undisturbed waters; secluded woodland or farm ponds are the most

OPPOSITE TOP: An undisturbed pond in the country. This type of habitat is an ideal haunt for crucian carp and one of the few remaining locations where true crucians can be caught.

LEFT: A close-up portrait of a crucian carp showing the turned-down mouth, thick, rubbery lips and the rounded, fully scaled, golden-brown body.

BELOW: Netting a crucian carp caught in a reservoir in high summer. Crucians love to feed close to marginal cover and bankside rush beds.

obvious places. They love to feed over fine silty bottoms, close to marginal cover, and are particularly fond of bankside rush beds.

Size

The crucian carp record was vacant until recently. It reflects a ruling that all crucian records prior to July 1998 were unsafe, as the fish were almost certainly either hybrids or brown goldfish. So, a 1 lb (0.45 kg) crucian carp is a specimen and anything approaching 2 lb (0.91 kg) more than likely a hybrid or goldfish.

Behaviour and Feeding Habits

Crucian carp are shoal fish, often moving around in large numbers of mixed sizes. They feed avidly on all the food items appreciated by their larger cousins. Largely vegetarian, their food mainly consists of water plants and vegetable matter, with fresh-water shrimps, snails, blood-worms, insect larvae and worms. Crucians take in mouthfuls of mud or silt and then eject the unwanted material; this creates the characteristic bubbles and mud disturbance on the surface of the water and indicates their presence.

Unlike the larger carp, crucians do not feed much after the first frosts. As they bite delicately, even in warm weather, giving only tiny indications, a crucian bite in cold conditions, when fish are much more lethargic, would be practically undetectable.

The tackle set-up for crucians has to be very delicate to have any chance of registering their interest. They are very intolerant of resistance; even the weight of a shot on a lift float often causes them to reject the bait

LEFT: **The successful angler holds a crucian carp clearly showing the rounded, fully scaled shape of the fish.**

instantaneously. When crucian fishing, always plumb the float accurately to the exact depth. With a crucian bite, the angler needs to know the moment the bait has been moved, by even the tiniest fraction, and then he or she needs to strike immediately. It is a constant source of amazement that if a strike is made straight away at the tiniest of indications the crucian carp will generally be well-hooked in the back of the mouth, but if the bite is left to "develop" into a better indication, nothing happens and you wind in to find the bait gone.

For baits, maggots obviously take crucians, but a favourite bait is a single grain of corn on a size 14 super spade to 2 lb (0.91 kg) line. It pays to trickle corn grains in, perhaps a dozen every 15 minutes, plus a walnut-sized ball of groundbait to keep the fish digging. Crucian carp feed well at night and this is when you can expect better bites. Fishing for them at night with an insert waggler carrying a night light, shotted so that the merest lift or settling is immediately apparent, is the recommended method. The first two hours of darkness are generally the best, and then the hour on either side of dawn.

Dace *(Leuciscus leuciscus)*

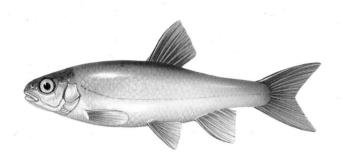

Current Record
British **1 lb 4 oz 4 drm (0.574 kg)**

Season
June to March.

Distribution
Streamy rivers, especially in Wales and southern England.

Natural Diet
Insects and worms. Avid surface feeders on flies and moths.

Top Spot
Hampshire Avon.

Top Tip
Some of the best dace fishing is to be had on cold, frosty days on a clear river, trotting maggots on gossamer tackle.

Recognition

To the inexperienced, a good dace looks for all the world like a small chub, and this has created many problems in angling history with mistaken claims for "record" dace. In overall general shape and streamlined appearance, the two fish are indeed similar in the smaller sizes, although the chub is generally a far chunkier looking character. The acid test distinguishing a dace from a small chub is the anal fin, which in dace is concave while the chub's is convex, or rounded. The overall fin colouration is also more delicate in a dace, being far paler, and varying from light orange to light brown. The head is also a giveaway. The dace looks quite demure, unlike the blunt-headed, aggressive appearance of the chub.

Habitat and Location

Dace are rarely found in stillwaters, unless these are close to river systems that have flooded. They are inhabitants of streamy sections of rivers, although the bigger fish share, with big grayling, an affinity for the deeper, steadier flows where they can be seen dimpling the surface on a summer's afternoon. They also love the fast runs through streamer weed beds on powerful rivers like the Hampshire Avon, where magnificent shoals of good dace are to be found. Where they exist, dace form large shoals that contain fish of all sizes. Dace are widely distributed throughout the rivers of England and Wales, but as with many other coarse fish the better waters are found in the southern counties.

Size

Very few anglers can boast at having caught a dace over 1 lb (0.45 kg) in weight. There is no doubt that a 1 lb (0.45 kg) dace is an enormous fish and any fish of over 12 oz (0.34 kg) must be considered a specimen. Even at that weight, they are rare. The present record, a 1 lb 4 oz 4 dram (0.574 kg) specimen taken in 1960, is an incredible fish, and although a few ounces does not seem much, the dace record remains one of the most difficult of all angling records to crack, a challenge for the specimen hunter.

Behaviour and Feeding Habits

There is nothing complicated about the behaviour of dace. They boldly take up station in large shoals in the main flow, eagerly anticipating anything the current may bring down to them. Nothing seems to disturb their equilibrium for long, even the forays of marauding pike are forgotten quickly. Dace appear to be happy-go-lucky feeders, and it is a pleasing sight to see myriad little bars of silver twisting and turning over the gravel, as they intercept the loose-fed maggots running ahead of the trotting tackle. When there is frantic activity on the shallows from loose feed, this is the time to run a bigger bait down the closest sedate water. Some bigger

LEFT: Dace feed all the year round, and much of the best dace fishing is in winter when the fish are in peak condition. Here an angler is trotting a maggot on a south country river.

ABOVE: A lovely catch of four dace taken trotting with a maggot.

RIGHT: Dace can be caught on the coldest days of the winter even when there is snow on the ground.

BELOW: A weir pool on the Hampshire Avon. This type of water is often the home to a shoal of giant dace.

dace, drawn to the food in the slacker water, have been caught this way.

Dace are far from fussy eaters, and they will accept any of the normal baits used for roach and chub, in appropriately sized mouthfuls. They are particularly fond of surface feeding and take all manner of floating insect life. Fly fishing for dace is good fun, albeit frustrating. If you can connect with one in six offers on the fly from a dace you are a pretty sharp fly angler. Dace take and reject a fly like lightning. They are a good quarry in the winter, especially on a bitterly cold day, when the angler needs some active fishing to keep warm, for they share with grayling the temperament to feed with gusto in chillier weather. Do not shun their small size.

Eel *(Anguilla anguilla)*

Current Record
British **11 lb 2 oz (5.046 kg)**

Season
All year, but warmer months best.

Distribution
Widespread in all types of water.

Natural Diet
Decaying matter, frogs, fish spawn, worms.

Top Spot
Neglected estate lakes where eels have been left to grow undisturbed.

Top Tip
It is best to fish at night in humid, overcast conditions. Thundery weather is excellent for eels. Fish near to snags, which big eels colonize in the same way as conger eels colonize sea wrecks.

Recognition

There is only one species of eel present in British waters, the European eel, that begins its life in the Sargasso sea in the western Atlantic, before being carried to river estuaries by the warm Gulf Stream. From there eels migrate upstream as elvers, many entering stillwaters, where they may become trapped, living for many years. Most eels return to the Sargasso when they become sexually mature to spawn. This may be after about six years, although no one is certain of the exact age. Specimen eels in stillwaters are the ones of most interest to anglers. Around the world there are more than 20 families of eel.

The long, snake-like muscular body and pointed head makes the eel unmistakable, as does the dark back and creamy yellow side and belly. Adult eels possess a long narrow dorsal fin, which travels unbroken around the tail to join the anal fin, creating a very powerful rudder capable of impressive propulsion both backwards and forwards.

One very interesting evolutionary characteristic is the different mouth shape of adult eels: some are very pointed, while others are broad and flat. This suggests an adaptability depending on the diet available: the pointed-head eels possibly feed largely on invertebrates, such as worms, while the broad-headed eels feed on small fish.

Habitat and Location

Of all anglers' quarries, eels are the most nocturnal, spending much of the day resting. They are lovers of cover and will be found in holes, under tree roots and bottom snags of all descriptions. In canals, they love the darkness of bridges, and they are particularly fond of dense weed, where they will be close to a food source as the light begins to fail. A trait the freshwater eel shares with its marine cousin, the conger eel, is its liking for colonizing foreign obstructions on the river or lake bed, such as tree trunks, old cars, bicycles or shopping trolleys.

Although found in all types of water, the specialist eel angler will normally target stillwaters for the larger specimens, particularly neglected estate lakes, large reservoirs and gravel pits. The eels caught in rivers are generally of a smaller average size and very often are just a nuisance to anglers in their search for other species.

Size

Most eel specialists consider any fish over 2 lb (0.91 kg) a worthwhile capture and over 3 lb (1.36 kg) a specimen. When an eel reaches 4 lb (1.81 kg) and over, it is becoming a rare animal, and there are few anglers who can boast an eel of this size among their captures. Fish of 5 lb (2.27 kg) and over are extremely few and far between. This makes the current record of 11 lb 2 oz (5.046 kg), taken in 1978, the more remarkable, and among freshwater fish the eel surely shows the biggest discrepancy between the current record and what is considered a specimen fish. This tends to substantiate the feeling

LEFT: The head of a 6 lb (2.72 kg) eel. Eels of this size are extremely rare.

among many eel specialists that there are far larger eels in Britain than have ever been caught on rod and line. A female eel, trapped in a neglected stillwater and undisturbed by anglers, could live 25 years or more. It is therefore not inconceivable that somewhere in these islands a 20 lb (9.07 kg) eel exists.

Eels and perch have a bone under the gill cover called the operculum. It can be removed from dead fish and read like a tree trunk, as a ring is laid down each year, thus giving the age of the fish. Top eel angler, John Sidley, once killed a 6–7 lb (2.72–3.18 kg) eel to be mounted in a glass case. He had the bone read and discovered that the eel was 68 years old. He vowed never to kill another eel after that.

Behaviour and Feeding Habits

Most of the eel's feeding will be at dusk and through the dark hours, although they are often tempted out of their daytime torpor on rivers if there is a constant stream of maggots drifting downstream from an angler's swimfeeder. As darkness falls, they

TOP: A calm stretch of the Hampshire Avon where a number of big eels have been taken. The majority of large eels are caught from stillwaters where they have been left to grow undisturbed for a number of years.

ABOVE: An angler wrestling with a large eel. Eels can be very difficult to handle when caught, as they scramble up the line. Placing them on newspaper sometimes helps.

emerge from their bolt holes and begin their nocturnal patrol. Eels are very opportunistic feeders, being very catholic in their tastes, and will take all types of animal matter and pungent baits, including frogs, fish spawn, dead fish or offal, and all manner of anglers' baits.

They have a terrific sense of smell, and many modern boilies intended for carp have become much appreciated by eels, greatly to the disgust of carp anglers. They also love maggots, and fishing for other species can become impossible if a carpet of eels moves in.

A big eel will often only feed close to its bolt hole, and anglers target snags deliberately. Once hooked, the fish will try to back into the snag immediately, and strong tackle is needed to counter this initial surge.

As well as taking dead fish off the bottom, eels will take live baits fished off the bottom after dark. Zander anglers on the Fen drains suffer problems with this, both with catching eels accidentally and, more often, by their baits being killed and partially devoured while still on the trace.

Perch *(Perca fluviatilis)*

Recognition

The large mouth, boldly striped flanks, spiked dorsal and crimson fins make the perch the most instantly recognizable fish in British waters, one that cannot be confused with any other. Although one species of perch is found in Britain, the worldwide perch family is extensive, both in fresh and salt water. Interestingly, they all share common features in the double dorsal fin, the first of which is spined, and the presence of spines on the gill covers.

The bold stripes and large eyes provide the best clues to the perch's predatory nature: the first gives the perch the necessary camouflage for stalking its prey and the second confirms that the fish feeds by sight. Whenever I look at a perch, I imagine an aquatic tiger. When threatened, or on the attack, the spiny dorsal is proudly erect, and it is thought that these spines are meant both to intimidate prey fish and protect the perch from larger predators, such as pike or catfish. It is not clear how effective this is, as I have found that in waters where both species are present pike take perch readily without any apparent difficulty.

Current Record
British **5 lb 9 oz (2.523 kg)**

Season
June to March in rivers, all year in stillwaters.

Distribution
Very widespread, perch are found in all waters.

Natural Diet
Fish, crustacea, worms and insect larvae.

Top Spots
For really big perch, reservoirs and gravel pits.

Top Tip
Perch are active feeders at dawn. It is best to start fishing at first light.

Habitat and Location

The perch is one of the most widely distributed species in Britain, thriving in muddy ponds, enormous lochs, stagnant canals and fast chalk streams, and every other type of water imaginable. An interesting fact is that the vast majority of newly flooded waters are first colonized naturally by perch, and this is thought to be caused by their very sticky eggs,

which easily adhere to the feet or feathers of nomadic water birds, thereby transferring the species from water to water.

The large eyes of a perch, adapted for sight feeding in murky conditions, are, by definition, very sensitive to strong light, and this leads to their well-known preference for shaded places, such as overhanging trees, undercut banks, under thick weed rafts and so on. If you include deep water you have all the important clues as to where to look for perch. They are often found at significant depths in stillwaters, and bringing a hooked perch to the surface can often result in what is termed "gassing up". This is because, most unusually, the perch is equipped with a swim bladder minus an air duct, which means that it is able to acclimatize to pressure changes only very gradually. It is the same as a deep-sea diver surfacing too quickly and developing the bends.

Size

The current record is 5 lb 9 oz (2.523 kg) taken from a private lake in Kent, but any perch over 2 lb (0.91 kg) can be considered a very good fish, and a 3 lb (1.36 kg) fish, a specimen. A fish over 4 lb (1.81 kg) remains the unfulfilled dream of many a perch angler, although the recent dramatic upsurge in specimen perch across the country has made the capture of 4 lb

TOP: **A gorgeous perch that clearly shows the huge, spiny, leading dorsal fin. This fish was taken from the Great Ouse on a brisk day in early autumn.**

ABOVE: **Three fine perch that were all caught on a legered lobworm in winter. In the winter months this bait really comes into its own as an attractor for perch.**

OPPOSITE LEFT: **An angler fishing close to the lily pads in summer. Lily pads are favourite haunts for perch, and the angler should fish as close to them as possible.**

(1.81 kg) fish a more realistic target.

The usual size of perch featuring in anglers' catches will be from tiny fish to 1 lb (0.45 kg), and many waters are prolific with fish in the 2–8 oz (50–225 g) range. These can be a nuisance to the angler setting out his stall for worthier quarry. The current record fish was taken in 1985.

Behaviour and Feeding Habits

The perch's aversion to strong light explains why it is an avid feeder in shallow water at dawn in summer, when light levels are low, and why it retreats to deeper quarters when the sun comes up. On gravel shallows on rivers and plateaux in gravel pits, perch are very active, attacking the hordes of fry that have spent the dark hours there. During very bright days, the bulk of a day's feeding will be done during the early hours.

In duller conditions, and during the cooler months, the feeding times are extended, with bottom-dwelling creatures such as crustacea and insect larvae, as well as worms, making up a progressively increasing part of their diet as fry become scarcer. Specimen perch have been taken with full-grown crayfish in their throats.

Perch are cannibalistic; in fact one of the best baits for a specimen fish is a baby perch. Use this knowledge to catch big perch in the summer, by fishing at first light when they are voracious. At this time, if a big perch is present, the small fish keep out of the way.

Perch use their natural camouflage in much the same way as a tiger hides in long grass. A big fish will spend much of its time motionless at the extreme edge of a rush bed, blending in perfectly with the reed stalks, waiting for small fish to swim past and the opportunity to pounce. Again, the angler can take good advantage of this behaviour, and the closer you can manoeuvre your bait to the rush bed, the more perch you will catch.

During cold spells in winter, big perch colonize the deeper areas, and this is when a legered lobworm fished in a deep hole in an estate lake, or presented on a paternoster under a deep undercut on a river bank, really pays dividends.

Pike (*Esox lucius*)

Current Records
British **46 lb 13 oz (21.234 kg)**
World **55 lb 1 oz (25 kg)** Germany

Season
Varies. Some waters all year, rivers June to March, but in some waters October to March only.

Distribution
Widespread in all waters.

Natural Diet
Fish, small mammals, worms.

Top Spots
Trout reservoirs such as Llandegffed, Ardleigh and Ardingley.

Top Tip
Freeze deadbaits individually and straight. They are then easy to use on a cold morning and will provide you with the maximum casting ability.

Recognition

The pike is the largest predatory fish found naturally in Britain. Its colouring is a perfect example of natural camouflage, as it harmonizes with the weeds where pike spend much of their time in ambush. It varies from deep olive on the back, through to a beautifully marbled combination of grey, green and yellow on the flanks, overlaid with a silvery sheen. The dorsal fin is set well back on the body, directly above the anal fin, and together with the large tail, forms a powerful propulsion unit giving the pike incredible acceleration from a standing start.

The head of the pike is unmistakable: long, flattened and equipped with the most fearsomely armed mouth. The upper jaw carries many rows of small, needle-sharp teeth, while the lower jaw has five or six large teeth on each side and rows of smaller ones between. The roof of the mouth and the tongue are also equipped with small teeth, enabling them to seize prey of up to 10–25 per cent of its own body weight.

Habitat and Location

Most rivers, lakes, ponds and pits in Britain contain pike, making the fish one of the most widely distributed. Specimens can as easily be taken from farm ponds as they can from huge Scottish lochs, and to many that is the appeal and mystery of pike fishing.

The pike is by nature a visual hunting predator, using whatever cover or camouflage it can to approach its prey undetected. It will be found lying among tree roots, in rush beds, and in the shadows of trees. It particularly favours depressions in the bed where it can be inconspicuous, both in rivers and stillwaters. Favourite pike hot spots are the natural stream beds in reservoirs, as they are deeper than the surrounding water and the fresh water entering the reservoir creates a current that attracts fish.

In rivers, most fish seek out swims where fast water meets more sedate flows, known as creases. The river pike angler need look no further than a substantial crease swim. A steadier stretch immediately below fast rapids

BELOW: A fine pike caught spinning with a floating plug.

BELOW RIGHT: Spinning for pike off a sluice gate. This is a likely spot for these fish.

Behaviour and Feeding Habits

can also pay dividends. Roach, dace and chub colonize such areas, and the pike follow them.

Size

There has not been the dramatic increase in pike sizes in recent times that has been with tench and bream, and growth rates vary depending on the available food supply. Some of the deep trout reservoirs have certainly seen unprecedented numbers of 30 lb (13.61 kg) fish taken, but the ultimate size fish, with the present record at 46 lb 13 oz (21.23 kg), is no bigger than might have been expected years ago.

The problem with pike is that artificial stocking with big fish rarely succeeds, as it does with carp or catfish, for pike invariably regress in condition when they are stocked. Second, pike do not enjoy pressure. When a large fish is caught, it is rarely allowed to live in peace. Other anglers pursue it, and eventually it will be caught once too often, or be badly hooked, and then it loses weight or dies. A 20 lb (9.07 kg) fish is still a super specimen and a 30 lb (13.61 kg) pike, the fish of a lifetime.

Pike rely on three senses to find their food: their sight when taking live fish, which they do at lightning speed; their sense of smell, for locating dead fish lying on the bottom; and their sensitivity to vibration, for detecting the fluttering distress signals of a wounded or dying fish. It used to be believed that the pike was never a scavenger, but now we know better. In fact, one of the most reliable methods of taking pike is the legered or freelined deadbait. A careful analysis of some records show that the fish caught using deadbaits are a much greater average size than those taken by any other method. All fish tend to get lazier as they get bigger, and a large pike uses a lot less energy taking a chunk of mackerel than it will chasing a sprightly roach.

TOP: Pike anglers afloat at dawn on a reservoir. First light is a favourite time for both fish and angler alike.

RIGHT: Unhooking a pike. Pike have sharp teeth and proper disgorgers are an essential item of equipment for all pike anglers.

Pike are instinctive attackers and can be goaded into action even when they are not hungry. If a noisy fish comes through a pike's field of view, creating a disturbance, the pike will often attack through sheer irritation. This is the basis of pike fishing with plugs, spoons and spinners.

Roach *(Rutilus rutilus)*

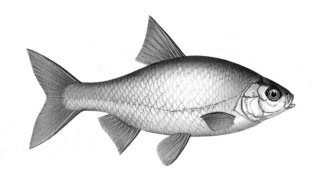

Current Record
British and World **4 lb 3 oz (1.899 kg)**

Season
June to March in rivers, all year in still-waters.

Distribution
Widely distributed in all waters.

Natural Diet
Aquatic insects, snails, worms, caddis, silkweed.

Top Spots
Chalk streams and large reservoirs.

Top Tip
Roach love the coloured water of flooded rivers. Try a big lobworm, upstream legered in a crease off the main flow.

Recognition

In colouring and shape, roach vary considerably between waters. At one extreme, the scales can be almost golden, although this is rare; at the other the roach is bright silver. Golden colouring is more likely to be found in big fish from gravel pits, whereas the bright silver roach is a typical inhabitant of the chalk streams. Generally, the body of a roach varies from blue-green on the back to dull silver flanks and a white belly. The lower fins vary from yellow to bright orange, the latter frequently leading to the common confusion between a true roach and a roach/rudd hybrid. The dorsal and tail fins tend to be reddish brown.

Physical recognition factors are important with big roach because they tend to hybridize with both rudd and bream. A true roach has 9–13 branched rays in the anal fin. This is the acid test between a roach and a roach/bream hybrid: the latter usually has at least 17 rays in the anal fin, and generally duller fins.

Roach/rudd are more difficult to distinguish, but the hybrids tend to have level lips, whereas roach have protruding top lips and rudd protruding bottom lips. The easiest recognition factor, however, is the relative positioning of dorsal and pelvic fins. In a roach, the leading edges of these will be level, whereas in a rudd or roach/rudd the dorsal is set back quite significantly.

Habitat and Location

Roach are very widely distributed throughout the British Isles, thriving in clear, fast rivers, gravel pits, canals, reservoirs and tiny, muddy farm ponds. They can grow to specimen size in all types of water, be it a barren pit or a weed-choked estate lake, so there is always the chance of catching a large fish.

Size

A roach over 2 lb (0.91 kg) is generally considered to be a specimen, and many waters do not hold roach as large as that. They become rarer as they reach 2 lb 8 oz (1.13 kg), and it is exceptional to catch a roach that weighs over 3 lb (1.36 kg). The current British record of 4 lb 3 oz (1.899 kg) was taken from the Dorset Stour in 1990.

Behaviour and Feeding Habits

The diet of roach is very varied, from water plants, aquatic insects and snails through to anglers' baits of all types. They will take bread in all its forms, meat and paste baits, maggots and casters, and large boilies intended for carp. Roach are particularly partial to worms, and a full-sized lobworm is a favourite bait for a big roach in

ABOVE: **A 2 lb (0.91 kg) roach. This is the accepted size for a specimen fish, and many anglers may never catch a roach this size.**

LEFT: **The sun sets on a reservoir that is known to contain giant roach.**

coloured water. Roach are generally
obliging feeders over a wide
temperature range, from a hot
summer's afternoon to a freezing cold
winter's night. Small roach are not
difficult to catch, ranging widely
across all fisheries in large shoals,
mainly in the shallower areas. As they
get bigger they become more inclined
to feed on the bottom, although this
includes the shallows.

A noticeable trait in bigger roach,
possibly due to increased caution, is
that they become more nocturnal in
their feeding habits, coming out to
feed strongly at dusk as light levels
decrease. Even in winter, they can be
reliable night feeders. Big roach also
love coloured water or floods, when
conditions are similarly murky. The
very biggest roach are often solitary
individuals, or members of small
groups, and these tend to favour deep

or steady water. In gravel pits, these
big fish feed avidly over gravel bars,
and over the gravel beds of feeder
streams in reservoirs. Many reservoirs
feature undertows at various points,
caused by a combination of the flow
of the feeder streams, wind action and
pumping, either for domestic water
supply, irrigation or canal top up.

These sub-surface currents are sought
out by big roach.

In rivers, bigger roach also favour
those shaded marginal swims beloved
by chub, such as dense rush beds over
gravel or raft swims under overhanging
trees. They also seek out the gentler
flows just off the main current and can
be found close by in high water.

Rudd (*Scardinius erythropthalmus*)

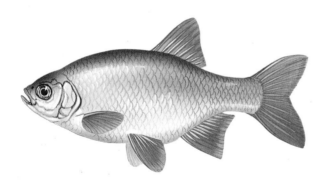

Recognition

Although similar in appearance to the roach, the rudd is much more richly coloured, as it is gold with crimson fins and has a bright yellow eye with a red spot. Although some gravel pit roach are much more deeply coloured than their running-water counterparts, the fins are yellow-orange, quite different to the blood-red of the rudd.

Another distinguishing feature is the prominently protruding bottom lip, marking the fish as a surface feeder, whereas in roach it is the top lip that protrudes. The position of the dorsal fin is another clue as the leading edge is set behind the base of the pelvic fins, whereas in roach the fins are level. Also, rudd display a distinctive pelvic keel, or sharp angle, from the pelvic fins to the tail. The lower body of a roach is altogether more rounded. The main difficulty in recognition comes about because of the rudd's tendency to hybridize, and this unfortunately is rapidly leading to a situation where true rudd are becoming rare. Some roach/rudd hybrids are almost indistinguishable from true rudd and it is extremely difficult for anyone to tell them apart.

Habitat and Location

As rudd are without doubt one of the most beautiful of all fish, it is a great shame that they are not more widely distributed. Unfortunately good waters are rapidly growing fewer in number. There are a number of Cambridge-shire and Bedfordshire gravel pits that contain pure rudd, a handful of waters in the South East and Ireland is still prolific. In all waters, however, particularly if they contain roach, the

Current Record
British **4 lb 8 oz (2.041 kg)**

Season

June to March in all rivers, all year in stillwaters.

Distribution
Patchy, apart from Ireland. In England, neglected estate lakes, farm ponds and eastern-county gravel pits offer the best chances of finding good rudd.

Natural Diet
Avid surface feeder on insects, flies and moths. Also takes nymphs, midwater and insect larvae, and worms from the bottom.

Top Spots
Bedfordshire gravel pits and Irish loughs.

Top Tip
Rudd can feed at any depth in gravel pits. Fish with a slow-sinking leger coupled with a swingtip, so that a slow-sinking bait can be intercepted in midwater.

days of the rudd sadly appear numbered. The only exception is secluded farm ponds, which often contain good rudd and no roach. If you find a water like this, keep it to yourself.

Size

It is doubtful that the present record of 4 lb 8 oz (2.041 kg), taken in 1933, in Thetford, Norfolk, will ever be bettered, not because rudd could not grow beyond that, but because it would be uncertain whether the fish was a hybrid or not. As roach/rudd hybrids grow bigger than either parent species, the record fish committee would have an impossible dilemma with a new claim.

Most rudd waters hold hordes of small fish, up to possibly 2 lb (0.91 kg) or more, while the better waters have a smattering of 3 lb (1.36 kg) rudd. This is the generally accepted measure for a specimen fish.

OPPOSITE: A reedy shallow bay in a secluded pond. Rudd love to feed on the surface, and this is typical rudd territory.

TOP LEFT: A beautiful true rudd taken from a gravel pit.

TOP RIGHT: The River Shannon in Ireland. This is one of the most prolific waters where the angler is likely to catch a true rudd.

LEFT: A roach/rudd hybrid. It is very hard for anyone to tell whether a fish such as this is a hybrid or not.

Behaviour and Feeding Habits

In traditional rudd waters, which include the large, shallow Irish loughs, secluded overgrown estate lakes and farm ponds, the rudd is predominantly a surface feeder, taking all manner of insects from the surface film. They move around in large shoals in big waters and are shy fish, often staying well away from the bank. On the Irish loughs, the method is to pole around the shallow bays very quietly until a shoal of rudd is seen "priming" – breaking the surface. Anchor at least 30 yards upwind and then drift surface baits to them under carp controllers or bubble floats. Big rudd become nervous quickly, and at most two or three fish can be taken before the rest of the shoal move out of range. Then it is a case of upping the anchor and quietly following.

In the more intimate waters, rudd spend much of the daylight basking or feeding in the heavily weeded areas, venturing out as the light fades to feed around the fringes. The exception would be on an overcast, breezy day, when they follow the wind lanes,

picking off nymphs and midge larvae as they become available. Rudd, however, are not exclusively surface feeders, nor are they, as once was thought, only fish of summer.

The advent of gravel pits has shown that rudd are reliable bottom feeders and will take baits in the depths of winter, particularly in the deeper holes. Standard feeder tactics work well, one of the best baits being maggot-flake cocktail. In pits, it is very common to have several tiny fish and then one of 2 lb (0.91 kg) from the same shoal.

For this reason, it is a good idea to bait heavily when bottom feeding. One recommended technique is to use dead maggots or casters to preoccupy the small fish, and then fish over this with two or three grains of corn on a size 10 hook, or a large piece of flake.

Of all specimen fish, predators apart, big rudd are the most prone to feeding midwater, and in deep lakes or pits it is common to find the rudd eight feet down if there is twenty feet of water. Depending on where you find them stationed, they can be fished for with float tackle set at the appropriate depth or by legering a buoyant bait, with the appropriate tail length. A deadly method is to use a buoyant hook bait in conjunction with a swimfeeder loaded with buoyant feed items. After the cast, hook bait and freebies rise at the same rate and you can often catch several rudd quickly using this tactic.

Tench *(Tinca tinca)*

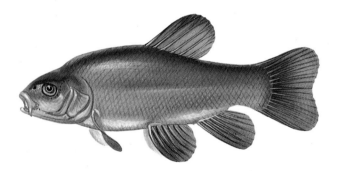

Recognition

The tench is one of the most instantly
recognizable of our coarse fish. It may
vary from olive green to deep bronze,
with a lighter belly. Tench are covered
in tiny scales with a very heavy
mucous covering that gives them a
pleasant satiny feel, quite unlike the
mucous on a bream which comes
away too easily. Tench fins are round
and paddle shaped, the male being
easily identifiable from the female by
its cup-shaped ventral fins, at the
roots of which are solid bands of
muscle. Tench have two small
barbules, one in each corner of the
mouth, and bright red eyes.

Habitat and Location

Tench are very widely distributed
throughout the British Isles, although
they do not inhabit the fast chalk
streams, except in the occasional
sedate backwater. They are primarily
fish of stillwaters or sluggish rivers,
the traditional tench swim being a bed
of lilies as dawn is breaking. They
love to browse the margins,
particularly where there are reed
beds, and stay over the shallows in
early summer, certainly until after
spawning. Tench are one of the later
fish to spawn, sometimes well into
July, but do not seem to suffer loss of
condition as much as other fish.

Gravel pits have provided an
environment in which tench have
done astonishingly well over the past
thirty years.

Size

The size of tench has occupied the
thoughts of many anglers since the
1960s, because of the incredible
transformation that has taken place in
that time, unique among coarse fish.
For a long time, the record stood at 8
lb 8 oz (3.86 kg), a seemingly
unattainable target as a 5 lb (2.27 kg)
fish was very difficult to come by, and
a 6 lb (2.72 kg) tench almost unheard
of. But tench weights have increased
dramatically so that today anglers
regularly make catches that beat the
old record. In any one season,
hundreds of fish over 9 lb (4.08 kg)
are recorded and a fair number over
10 lb (4.54 kg). The current record is
14 lb 7 oz (6.549 kg) and astonishingly
it is viewed as one of the records most
at risk. It is now difficult to pin-point
the size of an average tench, as waters
vary so widely. Certainly, in the
better waters, a tench under 7 lb
(3.18 kg) now hardly warrants a
mention, an incredible situation when
compared to that of a generation ago.

LEFT: Portrait of a 9 lb (4.08 kg) tench
showing the mouth of a bottom feeder and
bright eyes. The size of tench has increased
markedly since the 1960s, and fish such as
this are now relatively common.

Behaviour and Feeding Habits

Although tench will take baits at mid-water and occasional ones are taken off the surface, they are primarily a bottom-feeding fish, moving round in large shoals and browsing areas like a flock of sheep. Their natural food consists of all types of insect larvae, molluscs, crustacea and worms, as well as some water plants, and they are particularly fond of browsing bloodworm beds. In soft-bottomed lakes, they love digging their snouts into soft mud and silt, rooting out their food, and at the same time sending up great clouds of bubbles. These are a classic indicator of tench activity. As tench gill rakers are very fine, bubbles from feeding tench are small and quite distinctive, resembling the froth on a washing up bowl. In these types of waters, where feeding is rich, tench are quite territorial, and their feeding times predictable. Generally early dawn is the best time, gradually tailing off by mid-morning

on a bright day. Large baits are taken confidently at first light; smaller offerings are taken much more circumspectly as the day wears on.

Gravel-pit tench are almost entirely nomadic, as their feeding sites are more widely scattered and probably need to be browsed in rotation. Their feeding times are also less predictable, and they can be caught in the middle of a blazing hot day, when tench of estate lakes are often totally unresponsive. Tench are seldom caught at night – early dawn is definitely the most reliable time.

ABOVE: Creating a new tench swim to be exploited at dawn the following day. It is a good idea to prepare the swim the day before and start fishing for tench at first light.

LEFT: Two massive early-season tench weighing over 9 lb (4.09 kg) each, both caught on maggots. Tench are reliable feeders over beds of particles, and lobworms and maggots are good baits for large tench.

Tench accept the usual range of baits and are particularly reliable feeders over beds of particles, such as casters or hemp. Maggots are a good tench bait and for stalking individual fish, nothing beats a big lobworm.

Tench are fish of the summer, and the first frost signals the end of serious tench fishing. They become semi-dormant and have little interest in feeding except on unusually warm winter days. Anglers that do target winter tench use only tiny baits such as single caster, which the tench take with great delicacy.

Zander *(Stizostedion lucioperca)*

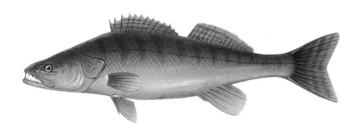

Current Records
British **19 lb 5 oz (8.76 kg)**
World **25 lb 2 oz (11.42 kg) Sweden**

Season
June to March in rivers, all year in stillwaters.

Distribution
Patchy, apart from the fen drain system. Other zander waters include the River Severn and Coombe Abbey Pool.

Natural Diet
Fish.

Top Spots
River Severn, the Fens, Coombe Abbey.

Top Tip
Fresh (not frozen) freshwater baits are best for zander. A good presentation is to fish a small, freshly killed bait popped-up off the bottom.

Recognition

The zander is a member of the pike-perch family, but it is a species in its own right, not a hybrid. It was introduced into this country from Eastern Europe. Streamlined like the pike, it shares many characteristics with the perch, such as the rough, slimeless scales and the double dorsal fin, the front one of which is spined. Like perch, zander are well adapted to feeding in low light conditions and have large eyes for this purpose. Some anglers have said that the huge, unblinking eyes are almost hypnotic! The large mouth is well endowed with small, backward pointing teeth, but the most obvious feature is the two long, front-mounted fangs, designed for stabbing and gripping its prey, which make the zander the vampire of the aquatic world.

Habitat and Location

Although there have been zander in selected fisheries since the 1870s, it was not until the release of 97 fish into the Relief Channel in 1963 that the species flourished and became of general interest to anglers. They rapidly spread through the associated drainage system and into the main River Ouse. The spread of zander still continues unabated, both through natural expansion and through illegal stockings. Some of the waters where the biggest zander are now found, such as the River Severn and Coombe Abbey Pool near Coventry, were originally stocked illegally. Despite this, the distribution of zander through the country is still very haphazard, with a bias towards the eastern counties, although that situation is changing rapidly.

Size

The present record, taken in 1998, is a colossal fish of 19 lb 5 oz (8.76 kg), and zander experts reckon that this could be beaten at any time by the first 20 lb (9.07 kg) fish. The Lower Severn is a short-odds location favourite for this. Generally speaking, most zander run from 2–8 lb (0.91–3.63 kg), and any fish over 10 lb (4.54 kg) is widely accepted as a specimen.

Behaviour and Feeding Habits

Zander feed mostly on small fish, up to perhaps 6 oz (175 g), although big zander have been taken on large baits intended for pike. They are pack hunters, attacking shoals of bait fish en masse and at speed, each shoal of zander comprising similarly sized fish. One of the features of fisheries containing zander is that the fish they prey on form denser and denser shoals for protection, leading to fears that they are being wiped out when in fact they have merely been more concentrated by the predators. As they get bigger, zander, like many other fish, become increasingly isolationist, and if you start catching small zander regularly it is not a good sign if a specimen is your quarry.

Zander share with perch a dislike of sea baits, although the odd big fish has accepted a smelt meant for pike; natural coarse fish, live or dead, are the baits to use. Small deadbaits fished hard on the bottom or livebaits fished

just off bottom are the favoured presentations, and one of the best deadbaits of all is a short eel section. They also share with perch a dislike of resistance, and frequently drop baits if the line is not free running.

The huge eyes give the clue to the preferred hunting conditions of zander, which are in low light. They are very nocturnal feeders in clear water, although high pressure and cold wintry conditions are very unfavourable as they are for many species. Zander are great lovers of brown floodwater, and will feed happily all day in these conditions. Autumn floods seem to be the best times, when they have recovered from spawning and the water temperature remains high after the summer.

The zander packs will obviously be concentrated where their prey fish are to be found, and this will often be around features such as bridges, and in the snaggy margins of stillwaters and around reed beds. The big Coombe fish are taken very close to overhanging foliage.

OPPOSITE: **Fishing for zander close to the margins. Zander hunt by sight and prefer freshwater bait.**

TOP LEFT: **A good zander is displayed.**

TOP RIGHT: **Unhooking a zander carefully.**

RIGHT: **A big zander, hooked at dusk, battles for its freedom.**

Baits and Groundbaits

During the summer months, some of the most effective fishing can be carried out with simple freelining, using natural baits. Natural bait fishing is mobile for the most part, moving from swim to swim, and is a recommended form of fishing for several species.

ABOVE: Cockles, prawns and shrimps all make good baits. They need to be fresh, not preserved, to be effective.

Natural Baits

From time immemorial the traditional bait for many species has been the worm. Worms and maggots are still favourite bait of many anglers, and certainly in the summer, more fish are probably caught on them than on anything else.

Lobworms and Redworms

The lobworm is one of the most universally effective baits, and one of the easiest to obtain. Choose a calm, mild night after steady rain and go on to close-cropped grass about two hours after dark. Use a torch as dim as possible and wear soft-soled shoes. You will see many worms lying completely out of their holes, and many more half in and half out. Grip the body adjacent to where it leaves its hole and pull gently without breaking it. Broken worms do not survive long in a wormery, and a dead worm will lead to the rest of the stock dying quickly. To keep lobs, you can use moist, but not soaking, garden soil. Every few days, place vegetable waste on the soil, and cover with damp sacking. If they are not overcrowded, and kept cool and damp, worms will keep in good condition for months.

The much smaller redworm is another excellent bait. You can ensure a good supply of redworms if you make a compost heap of grass cuttings, leaves, kitchen waste and animal manure in a shaded part of your garden. As the compost rots it becomes full of redworms.

Slugs

For summer chub fishing, the slug is recommended, the bigger and blacker the better. The only problem with slugs is that they can be very uncertain in supply and are difficult to keep fresh for long. It is best to collect them the evening before fishing, or, better still, at dawn on the day itself. On a dewy morning, you will find many slugs in the dampness of bankside vegetation, particularly round the roots of rushes and burdocks. Keep them as fresh as you can in a large bait box, out of the sun, with plenty of damp green stuff such as lettuce leaves to cover them.

ABOVE: Slugs collected early in the morning.

LEFT AND BELOW: Lobworms: both redworms and lobworms keep well in moist soil with some damp moss.

Cockles, Prawns and Shrimps

Prawns and shrimps are terrific baits, their problem being that they are extremely fragile, as well as being expensive. Always buy fresh, shelled cockles from a fish market. Do not buy them preserved or bottled, as they are kept in vinegar for human consumption. These are useless as angling baits.

Maggots and Casters

Maggots and casters (the maggot in its chrysalis stage) are among the most effective baits for all coarse fish, both in summer and winter, and much of their application will be in conjunction with the swimfeeder.

During the summer months maggots and casters are brilliant fished as a mass bait on rivers, when presented as a bunch on a large hook. The swim to select is one with a gentle flow, fairly close in, so the bait will not be unduly dispersed. It is also vitally important to loose feed with a bait dropper. The feed needs to be concentrated on the river bed at the selected fishing position, and the

Redworms

Maggots

ABOVE: All maggots can be dyed, and coloured maggots can be a most effective bait. Here curry powder has been used.

ABOVE: Small baits for summer fishing. Bread tipped with pinkies, sweetcorn, bread flake, a single maggot, casters, redworm and lobworm tail.

ABOVE: Two maggots mounted on a size 16 hook with gossamer monofilament line. Hook maggots through the tough skin at the blunt end and they will stay on the hook.

dropper guarantees this. For maggot fishing, so great is their pulling power, you can use them alone so long as you have sufficient quantity to achieve a level of preoccupation. You would generally need a minimum of half a gallon of maggots to fish this method most effectively. If you are concerned about them crawling away too quickly, they can be scalded or deep frozen before fishing. Dead maggots can be just as effective as live ones when used as loose feed although live maggots for hook baits are recommended.

For most angling applications, there are three important maggots. First, there are the large grubs of the big bluebottle meat fly, the most common hookbait. Pinkies and squatts are the larvae of the greenfly and housefly respectively and although these can be used as hookbaits, they are also widely used as particle attractors in groundbaits or for swimfeeder work.

If using casters, use them in conjunction with hemp, and fish them as you would any other particle bait. The only difference in approach would be that with some particles you should severely restrict the number of free offerings in the hemp, whereas with casters you should use a pint for every four pints of hemp. Obviously, mass baiting with casters alone would be effective, but the limitation to this approach is cost.

Pinkies

ABOVE: The well-prepared angler carries a range of bait and groundbait, including sweetcorn, bread flake, maggots, casters and lobworms.

Processed Baits

There are a number of processed baits available for the angler. One of the most common is bread which is used in several forms.

Bread

The tough crust on the outside of a farmhouse loaf is one of the best bread baits. Buy a fresh loaf from a bakery and if the crust is initially too brittle, seal it in a polythene bag and a few hours later the brittleness will have been replaced by crust so tough you will have trouble tearing it off the loaf. For hookbaits, tear off a piece of this crust, with a good chunk of flake attached, and fold it in half with the crust itself on the outside. Pass the hook through one side of the crust and out the other. When the bread is then released, it springs open on the hook. Thus mounted, you will find that the bait withstands any amount of twitching through the swim.

As well as mashed bread for loose feeding, you can also use handfuls of fresh, squeezed breadcrumbs to keep a swim primed; they disperse rapidly into attractive clouds as soon as they hit the water. For an even finer cloud, with minimal food value, liquidized bread is excellent. Remove the crusts from fresh, sliced bread and liquidize it in a blender. Liquidized bread is good for fishing in conjunction with a feeder, using bread flake hookbaits.

For fishing bread flake, use fresh, medium-sliced white bread. Tear off a strip approximately ½ in (1 cm) wide by 1½ in (4 cm) long and fold it round the hook shank, pinching it in place but leaving the point exposed. Fresh, sliced bread is also useful if you require a bread flake offering on a very small hook, where bread punches come into their own.

Bread is the most versatile bait. A loaf can provide a buoyant, sinking or neutral bait. Alteration of bait size enables the angler to change his presentation in an instant. With crust, increasing the bait size can provide a slow sinking offering, where previously the bait was nailed down to the river bed. With flake, a buoyant offering can be created by squeezing a disc flat on the hook shank. Where conditions are suitable for bread for winter chub, in all but very heavily coloured water, there is no situation where a bread bait can't be adapted to provide the ideal presentation.

Mounting Bread Crust on a Hook

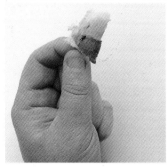

1 Fold a piece of crust in half and pass the hook through both sides.

2 Allow the crust to spring open on the hook.

Mounting Bread Flake on a Hook

1 Fold a strip of flake from a sliced white loaf around the shank of your hook.

2 Squeeze the flake tight, squashing it on the hook, leaving only the point exposed.

ABOVE: Loading a feeder with liquidized bread. A feeder loaded with liquidized bread in this way is most effective when fished with bread flake hookbait.

ABOVE: Bread punches are useful to punch out small flakes of bread.

Sausage

Sausage was a much-used bait for barbel on the River Thames years ago, although many chub, roach and bream were tempted by it. There are two ways of using sausage: either a portion of sausage itself or a paste made of the meat. If using the sausage solely, it is best to use the skinned variety, as the skinless tend to be too soft and fall apart too easily. When using skinned sausages, however, take care to hook them in such a way that the skin does not impede hook penetration.

Sausage correctly mounted on the hook

Luncheon Meats

Luncheon meat is now one of the standard baits for many species, particularly chub and barbel. You can take good chub on all varieties of tinned meats, including luncheon meat, bacon grill, and chopped ham and pork. All these meats can be used successfully straight from the tin, and for chubbing use ¾ in (2 cm) cubes. You must not, however, fall in to the trap of leaving the same bit of meat on the hook all day if there have been no bites. This is a common mistake made by anglers. Most meats of this type, if they have not been specially flavoured, soon lose their natural smells and become bland and unappealing.

If you opt to use a flavoured variety of meat, the base brand does not really matter. The most important factor is the texture and toughness of the meat: it also must be tough enough to withstand casting without flying off the hook.

Many anglers use luncheon meat baits on ridiculously small hooks, and then complain that the meat keeps falling off. If you are going to use ½ in (1 cm) or ¾ in (2 cm) cubes of meat, use a hook matched to the bait, a minimum being a size 6. To hook the meat, push the hook bend through the bait, and then twist and pull the hook

RIGHT: Luncheon meat works well as a bait for many species, particularly chub and barbel, and can be both coloured and flavoured. Use a hook sufficiently large to keep the bait in place when being cast out.

ABOVE: Bread crust mounted on leger tackle. Carp and chub are often caught by fishing with bread baits.

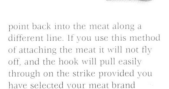

RIGHT: A cube of luncheon meat correctly mounted on a hook.

point back into the meat along a different line. If you use this method of attaching the meat it will not fly off, and the hook will pull easily through on the strike provided you have selected your meat brand correctly.

Spicy Sausage

Sticks of spicy sausage meat, such as pepperami, are readily available from most supermarkets, and are convenient change baits, requiring no preparation and keeping indefinitely if they are in an unopened packet. Break off a chunk, flatten one end to put the hook through and you have a superb bait. As it has a tough skin, you need to pare this away with a sharp knife where the hook is to be inserted. If you wanted to experiment there are a number of other flavoured sausages that could be used as bait.

Mounted spicy sausage

Paste Baits

Paste baits are extremely useful and versatile, and have accounted for numerous fish. There are a number of ready-made pastes available and ones that can be made at home. The easiest to make are bread paste and cheese paste. It is worthwhile making your own paste and taking care to see that it is exactly the right consistency. As you become more practiced, this is easier to achieve.

Bread Paste

Although waning in popularity, bread paste is an excellent bait and much cheaper than high-protein pastes. To prepare bread paste, you need sliced bread, without crusts, at least two days old. Fresh bread makes a lumpy, unappealing paste. Dampen the slices without oversoaking them, and squeeze out as much of the water as possible. Knead the paste in a clean, white cloth. If you knead by hand, the natural retained oil in your skin makes the paste an unappealing, grubby, off-white colour. The end result should be a smooth, white, pliant paste of even consistency.

If you want a variant from the standard bread paste, try adding powdered additives such as custard powder or strawberry blancmange powder. The list of potential flavours available is endless.

Meat Pastes

Meat pastes are superb baits for many species, the most common being made from sausage meat, finely chopped tinned meats or soft pet foods. You can make them up by mixing the soft meat with sausage rusk binder, which is available from butchers. However, you can mix the meat with any bulk binder that takes your fancy, and the delicatessen is full of interesting alternatives for you to try. Three of the most commonly used binders are breadcrumbs, biscuit meal and soya flour.

Cheese Paste

Probably the most common of all orthodox paste baits is cheese paste, which has accounted for numerous chub, barbel, bream, carp, tench and roach. Cheese paste can be made up

RIGHT: A good leather carp that has fallen for some cheese paste. Most cyprinids take paste baits well.

as follows. A 10 oz (284 g) pack of frozen shortcrust pastry is rolled flat, before being smeared with Mature Cheddar flavour. Then you add 6 oz (170 g) of grated mature cheddar and 4 oz (115 g) of finely crumbled Danish Blue cheese. The pastry is then folded over so that the cheese is inside and the whole rolled again. This is repeated constantly until thorough mixing has occurred, when the paste is formed into a large ball and thoroughly kneaded by hand. Put 2 ml of the Mature Cheddar flavouring in a large freezer food bag, put the ball of paste inside, seal the bag and then put it in the freezer until you wish to use it. When it is thawed, the paste has the most appealing texture and consistency, as well as a powerful cheesy aroma.

You can use standard bread paste as the base for your cheese paste, but using the frozen pastry mix is far more convenient and far quicker. It also gives the paste a lovely even texture that is a help when you use it.

During the summer months, when water temperatures are high, you can use cheese on its own, simply moulded into a ball on a large hook. In the winter, however, when the bait would be most used, all cheeses with

the consistency necessary for use on a hook harden considerably in cold water, and this impedes hook penetration. This problem can be overcome by making a paste as described on the opposite page, when the bait remains lovely and soft even in the coldest water.

Hemp Paste

Hemp paste is good for taking barbel and chub, and it is a particularly useful paste to have available as a stand-by. It comes into its own when fishing for these species in any river where there is a troublesome eel population. When plagued with eels, a switch to hemp paste usually solves the problem. For some reason, hemp is the one flavour that eels do not seem to relish.

You can make hemp paste in a similar way to cheese paste, using a base of shortcrust pastry. To make the paste, crush cooked hemp, making sure not to include too much of the liquid. You want the finished product to be a usable paste, and not something too sloppy. Mix the pastry with a little of the crushed hemp at intervals, until the consistency is right. It is easy to make the paste too wet, and then it is useless.

Making Cheese Paste

1 The ingredients: grated cheese, rolled pastry, cheese flavouring and colouring (optional).

2 Smear the pastry with the liquid cheese flavouring and then add the grated cheese and colouring.

3 Fold the pastry up and over the grated cheese. Roll it out again and then repeat the process.

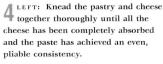

4 LEFT: Knead the pastry and cheese together thoroughly until all the cheese has been completely absorbed and the paste has achieved an even, pliable consistency.

5 RIGHT: The finished paste, ready for the hook, with a portion rolled out as cheese balls. Put a 2 ml of cheese flavouring in a freezer bag and keep the paste in the freezer until you want to use it.

Synthetic Pastes

Commercial boilie mixtures can be used as very successful hookbaits in their soft paste form, although not all boilie mixes are smooth enough to form a paste suitable for a hookbait. Some of the fishmeal mixes are a little coarse in texture, and have to be boiled to work properly, when they are fine. There are many good quality ready-mixed pastes available in tackle shops. As well as fished on their own, they also make good neutral buoyancy cocktails when fished along with bread crust.

Making Synthetic Paste

To make up your own synthetic paste, a strong starting point is a high quality but forgiving base mix, such as 50/50 promix. You then have to decide whether you want to add any more powdered ingredients, such as flavours, colours or sweeteners, or whether those ingredients will be in liquid form.

If you opt for powdered additives, such as curry powder or cheese powder, or natural extracts such as

powdered crab, mussel or nectar, these must be thoroughly mixed with the base mix before adding the mix to the binding liquid.

If based on a balanced 50/50 mixture, pastes can be made successfully with either water or eggs, but if you want the option of a hard-boiled bait as well as a paste, then eggs must be your choice. Even with a soft paste, eggs are recommended, as they give the paste a lovely, pliable, waxy feel.

Beat the eggs thoroughly, add all the other liquids, flavours, oils or enhancers, and then add the powder slowly, mixing thoroughly as you go. Do not be in too much of a hurry. If you pile too much powder in and make the mix too dry initially, there is no way back. When you have a sticky ball of paste still too soft for hookbait, let it rest for five minutes. You will find that the paste tightens up in the air and becomes perfect.

If you plan to freeze the paste it also pays to make it a fraction soft. Pastes tighten up in the freezer. If you do not want the expense of buying

commercially available base mixes, paste baits can be made from a great number of products, such as trout and Koi pellets, or tinned or dry pet foods mixers, all of which are available from many stores and supermarkets.

Ingredients such as tinned pet foods, or tinned fish, are naturally sticky, and simply require a bulk binding agent to produce a workable bait. Kit-Kat chocolate bars mixed with fine breadcrumbs is a well-known example.

If you wish to base your bait on a dry ingredient, such as trout-fry crumb, any ingredients added to the bait must have a glutinous content to bind the powders in with the water or eggs. The simplest material to use is wheat gluten, but you should be careful not to use too much as this results in some very rubbery baits that can be unattractive to the fish.

Baits made with gluten can also be quite chewy, and it can be helpful to add a quantity of a light milk protein or baby milk powder. This balances the ingredients and makes the bait more palatable.

Particle Baits

The preoccupation of fish with large quantities of very small food items is well known, and occurs naturally, for instance when they feed on bloodworm colonies. To obtain the same effect with anglers' baits means saturating a small area with a sufficient quantity of particles so that the fish switch on to them exclusively.

Particle baits are those big enough to be used on their own or with two or three others on a big hook, and include sweetcorn, chick peas, maple peas, peanuts and tiger nuts. Mini-boilies are also considered particles from an angler's point of view.

Cooking Particle Baits

Particle baits must be used responsibly and you must always ensure that seeds, peas, nuts and beans are soaked or cooked well before use, so that they do not swell after they are consumed by fish, thereby causing distress. Cooking also prevents germination of naturally sprouting particles, but you only need to cook for a few minutes after pre-soaking. Overcooking will spoil the bait's attraction and negate the whole point of the exercise. Always keep the baits in the water in which they were prepared, as this maintains and progressively increases the flavour, but be careful to discard if the bait start to smell sour.

Particles can be coloured and flavoured during the soaking and cooking process, by flavouring the water. As many synthetic flavours evaporate during boiling, it is best to stick to natural flavours and syrups, such as maple syrup, molasses, curry sauce or oxtail soup.

Using Sweetcorn

Sweetcorn is one of the most popular particles for many species, and there is little to be said about its preparation. Tins are better than frozen packets, as the sticky liquid enhances the attractiveness of the bait. Sweetcorn, if used in large quantities, is a bait that can become less effective for some species, such as tench, barbel and carp. When this occurs, changing the colour and/or flavour can give the bait a new lease of life. Corn takes flavours well, and a wide range of superb coloured and flavoured corn is available commercially from tackle shops.

Particle Preparation Guide

Tiger nuts, peanuts, cashew nuts, pistachio nuts, maize, red kidney beans

Soak for a minimum of 24 hours, and boil for 30 minutes or pressure cook for 20 minutes.

Tares, lupins, black-eyed beans, tic beans, maple peas, chick-peas, soya beans

Soak for a minimum of 12 hours, and boil for 30 minutes or pressure cook for 20 minutes.

Hemp, dari, buckwheat, groats, rape, rice, wheat, barley, whole oats, millet

Soak for a minimum of 12 hours, then bring to the boil, remove from heat and leave in pan until cool.

Mixed particle feed, moth beans, mung beans

No soaking required. Bring to boil, remove from heat and leave in container for 24 hours.

Sunflower or safflower seeds, crushed hemp, maize flour, trout pellets

No preparation necessary.

ABOVE: This gives some idea of the range of baits required by a professional match angler. If the fish are not attracted by one form of groundbait, they may well be attracted by another, and it can pay to change mixes if your favourite is not successful straight away.

LEFT: Dried and prepared maize (sweetcorn). While it is cheaper to prepare your own in this way, sweetcorn is best used out of a tin, as the sticky liquid seems to add to its attraction. If you wish to flavour sweetcorn, then it is better to start with dried corn so that the flavours can be added as the corn is cooked.

Hempseed, dried and prepared

Crushed tiger nuts, dried and prepared

Uncrushed tiger nuts, dried and prepared

Chickpeas, dried and prepared

Particle feed mass bait, dried and prepared

ABOVE: The most commonly used particle baits shown in their uncooked state on the left and prepared on the right. It is important to prepare all particle bait properly and care should be taken to follow the cooking times given in the table opposite.

Making Different Particle Rigs

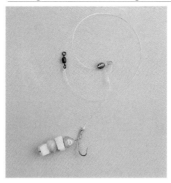

1 A pop-up rig with two kernels of sweetcorn with small pieces of sponge to float the rig off the bottom.

2 A slow-sinking rig mounted with one medium-sized tiger nut to explore various depths.

3 Particle rigs using sweetcorn as the basic ingredient: clockwise from the top; sweetcorn and redworm; dyed sweetcorn grain and maggots; four grains of sweetcorn on a hair rig; sweetcorn and luncheon meat; dyed sweetcorn and bread flake; centre, single grain of sweetcorn with casters.

Mass Baits

It is fairly obvious that you are more likely to create fish preoccupation the more small bait items you have. This points to mass baits, where individual offerings are far smaller than a standard particle such as a grain of corn. The most commonly used mass bait is hempseed, but others such as dari, tares, rice, wheat and pearl barley are also used.

There are two main hookbait choices when fishing over beds of mass bait: either a single large bait, such as a lobworm, or a cluster of the mass bait itself. One example is 20 hemp grains glued to a large hook, or strings of the bait glued to a hair or multiple hairs tied to the hook bend. Two of the better-known examples of using a large bait over a mass bait carpet are luncheon meat over hemp for chub and barbel, or a hookbait of large maggots over a bed of squatts.

One of the best mass baits available is mixed particle feed, from Hinders of Swindon, which is a mixture of many particle attractors. The table for the particle/mass bait preparation is shown opposite. Poorly prepared particles can be lethal to fish, so please take extreme care to follow the instructions given when you are preparing particles for fish.

Deadbaits

Deadbaits of sea fish are mostly used for pike fishing. The most common are herrings, sardines, smelts, sprats and mackerel. Among the best freshwater deadbaits are roach, small chub, an eel or lamprey section, small trout and immature pike. The best large sea baits are half a mackerel or a whole sardine. Sardines in particular are superb, but need to be frozen before casting, as they are very soft and otherwise break apart. In fact, most deadbaits are easier to use when partially frozen, for then they can be cast further. For this reason, a good cool box is an essential part of the pike angler's armoury.

When freezing deadbaits, always freeze them straight, wrapping each individually in a freezer bag or clingfilm. It also pays to cut them into sections before freezing if you intend using half baits. Cutting a frozen mackerel in half on a frosty morning on the river bank is no fun.

Among the freshwater baits, eel and lamprey sections are terrific baits. Eel tends to be best where there is a resident eel population, as the pike will gorge on them. Lamprey, however, is an enigma. Very few inland pike waters will have seen these creatures, and yet they really are superb baits. They are one of the few deadbaits that zander take regularly; they normally show a distinct preference for small livebaits.

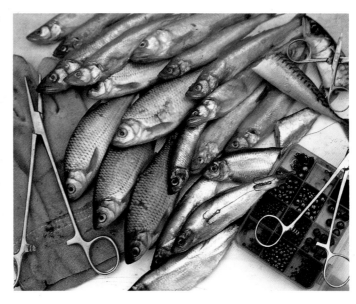

When pike fishing with deadbaits, it is vitally important to carry a range of baits. There are plenty of days when, for instance, mackerel tail fails to produce a run, but smelts will take again and again. On one occasion a few years ago, it was impossible to get a run a half mackerel, but using a sardine would score success. After a few sessions, the runs on the sardine might stop, and it would become necessary to revert to big chunks of mackerel to start catching again. Size

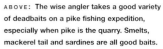

ABOVE: The wise angler takes a good variety of deadbaits on a pike fishing expedition, especially when pike is the quarry. Smelts, mackerel tail and sardines are all good baits.

preference is common particularly when pike are feeding on fry in late autumn. At this time, large baits are often ignored, and you may need to use to small smelts or sprats.

Adding Flavours to Deadbaits

For several years many anglers have been treating deadbaits with various flavours and it can make a significant difference, particularly on big wind-swept stillwaters where sub-surface currents waft the scent trails far and wide. To flavour pike baits pack each bait individually in a sealable sand-wich bag, having first poured a little of the chosen oil into the bag and thoroughly coated the inside walls. The bait is then frozen and the flavour impregnates the surface of the fish.

Before casting, always give the bait a further application with a paint brush, so that as well as being fully flavoured it has an oily surface. This produces a characteristic oil slick on the surface as a pike crushes the bait with its teeth. On a calm day, this gives a very exciting early warning of a take. Try flavouring deadbaits with fish oils such as mackerel, smelt or eel. I have even taken pike on spice- and strawberry-flavoured deadbaits. It sounds all wrong, but it works!

Freshwater Deadbaits

The smaller, freshwater deadbaits, such as minnows, bleak, small roach or bullheads are attractive to zander, perch, eels, catfish, chub and barbel, as well as pike. Even bream and carp may cough up tiny roach when they are caught. In rivers, minnows are a favourite bait for chub, perch and barbel particularly in early season, just after they have finished spawning on the shallows.

Stillwater chub have a tendency to be very predatory and some of the very biggest fish from the Oxford pits, one of the best places for chub, have been caught using a small whole mackerel. More typically, though, big chub are fished for with cubes or strips of mackerel flesh fished with a standard legering rig, although this method is at its most efficient if you use a hair rig, as the firm flesh of the mackerel seriously impedes hook penetration.

TOP: Smaller deadbaits work best for pike when they are feeding on fry. They are also successful with a number of other species, such as perch, catfish and chub.

OPPOSITE: An angler's set up to fish for pike using a deadbait.

Livebait fishing is usually practised for pike, perch, zander and catfish, although the use of live tiny fish, such as minnows, will catch chub and occasionally barbel.

The silvery fish, dace, chub and roach, weighing around 4–6 oz (115–175 g) make the best livebaits, although crucians make excellent pike baits and baby perch are a terrific offering for specimen perch. The biggest problem with livebaiting is catching the bait at the moment when you need it!

BELOW: A small roach makes an excellent livebait for many fish, including pike, perch, catfish and zander.

Boiled Baits

Boiled baits have become one of the standard offerings on many waters today, and there is no doubt they have revolutionized carp fishing. Although most anglers buy commercially produced "boilies", specialists tend to prefer their own mixes in order to maintain a degree of individuality and to ensure that the ingredients and preparation are exactly right.

If you decide to make your own boiled baits, there are two ways of going about it. Either you can add your own ingredients to a commercially available base mix, or you can take the trouble to prepare your own base mix as well. There are commercial base mixes based on bird seeds, mixed ground nuts, fish meals or milk products, or combinations of these. Some of these mixes will be balanced protein, often known as 50/50 mixes, and these contain high protein ingredients on a carbohydrate carrier such as semolina.

Some mixes will be high protein or high nutritional value bases. Other mixes will be intended for long life, others for instant attraction, and some will be more applicable to a particular season of the year. It is therefore important, before you buy your base mix, to discuss with your chosen supplier what you intend to achieve with your particular bait.

If you intend making your own base mix, there are extensive ingredients from which to choose. Find a combination that suits you and stick to it, or you will end up totally confused. Ingredients can include edible casein, sodium and calcium caseinate, lactalbumin, ground nuts of many types, mixed fish meals, soya flour, soya isolate, maize meal, ground bird seeds, rice flour, wheat flour, wheat gluten, oatmeal, ground pet foods and many others. In addition, there are various mineral and protein supplements you can add, such as codlivine, equivite and betaine. It is

possible to control the protein content of your finished base mix by selecting the appropriate ingredients from those available. However, in practice, some theoretical mixes cannot be rolled into usable baits, so experiment with small quantities first.

As a rule of thumb, milk products such as casein, caseinate and lactalbumin are high in protein, as are meat and fish meals. Low protein ingredients include most nut and cereal flours, although soya flour and wheat germ are of medium protein.

Making Boiled Baits

The first step is to mix the dry ingredients thoroughly, including any powdered colours, enhancers, sweeteners and vitamin supplements you have selected as well as the base mix. Second, crack your eggs into a large mixing bowl and beat them before adding any liquid ingredients, then beat the mixture again. The composition of your base mix will

Making and Moulding Boilies

1 The basic ingredients for all boilies are eggs, base mix and whatever flavouring you may choose.

2 Beat the eggs thoroughly and then add the flavouring; do not overdo this, a few drops is usually enough.

3 Mix in the base mix, adding a little at a time until you have achieved a soft, even-textured paste.

4 The finished paste. At this stage it will still be slightly sticky. Allow it to stand between 10–30 minutes to tighten up and become easier to handle.

5 Knead the paste well and roll out into sausages the diameter that you require. Cut them into sections and then roll them into balls.

6 Alternatively, form the boilies into balls with a rolling table. These can be bought commercially and are useful if you are making a large number.

LEFT: Anglers afloat at dawn on a summer's day. Dawn is an excellent time to fish in summer before the water starts to warm up in the sun.

determine how many eggs are required, but you should use about four large eggs to 1 lb (0.45 kg) of dry mix, although you may need as many as six eggs if you are putting together a high protein mix, which will generally be lighter and fluffier than a mix containing balanced proteins.

Add the dry mix slowly to the beaten eggs, thoroughly mixing with a wooden spoon, until a slightly tacky paste has been formed. At this point, rest the paste for about ten minutes and you will find that it tightens into a stiffer mixture that is pliable without sticking to your fingers.

Knead the paste well, and then break it down into conveniently sized lumps and roll it out into sausage shapes of the required diameter. Cut the sausage shape into sections of the required size with a sharp knife and then roll these into balls between the palms of your hands. As an alternative, if you intend fishing home-made boilies extensively, equip yourself with a bait gun and a rolling table, as this makes the laborious job of producing the boilies quicker, easier and faster.

Next "skin" the baits by dropping them into boiling water: generally between one and two minutes is sufficient. It is important that the water continues to boil, so do not make the mistake of trying to boil too many at once. For ⁵⁄₈ in (16 mm) diameter baits, for example, 30 is the maximum number to cook at any one time, and the ideal receptacle is a large chip pan or something similar equipped with a wire basket. For those anglers who plan to make large quantities of home-made boilies the purchase of a specially designed boiler is a godsend, as you can skin large quantities at once. Having removed the baits from the water, allow them to cool and air-dry before attempting to put them into bags.

7 Plunge the balls into boiling water for one or two minutes. Do not let the water go off the boil.

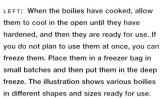

ABOVE: An insulated bag, designed to keep frozen boilies (and other baits) cool during the summer, is an essential item in the angler's list of equipment. It is particularly important if you are on a fishing expedition and do not have the luxury of a deep freeze readily available.

LEFT: When the boilies have cooked, allow them to cool in the open until they have hardened, and then they are ready for use. If you do not plan to use them at once, you can freeze them. Place them in a freezer bag in small batches and then put them in the deep freeze. The illustration shows various boilies in different shapes and sizes ready for use.

A PVA bag rig with boilies and groundbait

Floating Baits

Many fish feed on the surface from time to time and can then be caught on a floating bait. It is always very exciting seeing a fish take a bait from the surface of the water, one of the pleasures of an angler's life.

Boilies

Boilies

Floating boilies, or pop-ups, are effective for any surface-feeding species. They are available commercially, or you can convert your own boilies to floaters by baking them in a hot oven or microwaving them for a short time. Alternatively, mould the paste round a small cork ball before boiling them. When you mount the bait, use a very short hair rig so that the bait is touching the hook shank, or mount the bait in a special bait band sold specifically for surface carp fishing.

Baked boilies – pop-ups

High Protein Floater

A special sponge for surface fishing can be made by using a boilie mix with a double ration of eggs, to produce a runny mixture, and then baking this in the oven just like a normal cake. Different mixes give variations in floater texture: some are very light and open, while others give much denser results. Not all boilie mixes convert successfully to good floating mixes, and you have to go by trial and error.

Pet food mixers

Floating Pet Foods

Pet foods, particularly mixers, are extremely popular for surface fishing. They are a convenient size, visible at range, and retain their buoyancy for a long time. Pet food mixers can simply be glued to the back of the hook shank or fished in conjunction with a bait band. The mixers work best when the fish have been introduced to them for a while by prebaiting and have acquired a taste for them.

Carp pellets

Trout pellets

Koi Pellets and Trout Pellets

Fished in exactly the same way as mixers, Koi and trout pellets are perhaps the ultimate floating bait for many species. Once fish begin feeding on them, they become totally preoccupied and a feeding frenzy can result, until the shoal is spooked by

fish being hooked and landed. As they are smaller than pet food mixers, these pellets are best fished by gluing them to the hook shank.

Breakfast Cereals

Puffed wheat cereals will take surface-feeding fish such as carp, rudd and chub, if you use them in large enough quantities to attain preoccupied feeding. Being very light, they are best used on a calm day. Again, glue them to the hook shank, but as they are much less buoyant than trout pellets, it pays to add a small amount of rig foam to the hook. This prevents a waterlogged bait being dragged under by the weight of the hook.

Bread Crust

This is the most common and versatile floating bait of them all, ideal for both running and still water. In running water, when chub, dace, roach, rudd and possibly carp could be the target, it will be used freelined. For this application, a chunk of the tough crust from the outside of a farmhouse loaf is ideal. For mounting, fold a piece of the crust, flake inwards, pass the hook through the crust and then allow the bait to spring open on the hook. For freelining down a current, fishing with a greased line aids bait presentation by preventing sinking line causing drag.

In stillwaters, crust is often fished anchored in one spot for long periods, and for this application, particularly for big carp, a cube of stale crust, cut from the end of a tin loaf, will float like a cork and be highly visible.

Lobworms

Several years ago it was discovered that if air was injected into a lobworm it could be used on the surface as a bait for chub. This method has been extremely successful and taken many chub since, the bites being very savage. It is particularly deadly as the worm gradually becomes slow sinking as the air slowly leaks out, giving the most natural presentation imaginable.

The slow-sinking lob could be the answer when fish are wary of normal surface baits. You should take immense care when injecting air into lobworms, and always keep the needle well away from your flesh. After use, always replace the needle guard immediately so that you cannot accidentally inject yourself.

Off the-Shelf Baits

If you do not want to make your own boilies and floaters, then you can buy them at your tackle dealer.

Boilies

There are two types of commercially available boiled bait: frozen or shelf-life. As you might expect, the shelf-life varieties contain preservatives to keep them in good condition for long periods or until the packaging is removed. The quality of modern shelf-life boilies has never been higher, and there is no doubting their convenience, especially for the angler travelling abroad, where freezer facilities may be unobtainable.

Commercial boilies come in all sizes from mini baits of 1/4 in (6 mm) diameter to giants of 1 in (25 mm), and they are also available as buoyant baits or pop-ups. There are many top-quality suppliers, whose boilies are all good quality.

Particles

Anyone wanting information on or supply of particle baits need look no further than Hinders of Swindon. They keep all the popular particles, as well as supplying one of the best general mixed particle feeds available.

Most tackle shops sell packets of boiled hempseed and tares, and this is one area where tackle shops provide poor value for money. If you use these seeds in any kind of quantity, buy a sack from a seed supplier or a specialized outlet and prepare the seed yourself. As far as sweetcorn is concerned, you can use tinned corn from supermarkets, but if you wish to use it flavoured, Pescaviva corn, available from good tackle shops, is available in a superb range of flavours and colours, far better than anything you can produce yourself at home.

Groundbaits

There is a very extensive range of groundbaits available to the angler in tackle shops. If you are using pure breadcrumb as your groundbait base, however, try talking to your local bakery. You will often obtain a sackful of breadcrumbs or unsold loaves for a fraction of the normal cost.

Carp Groundbaits

There are now some excellent carp groundbaits available for use with method feeder tactics. There are high-

RIGHT: Effective groundbaiting is essential when fishing for big bream.

quality products available based on finely crushed hemp and other oily particles such as Nutrabaits carpet feed.

Pellets

Another tremendous growth area in groundbaiting is to use pellets, particularly hemp pellets. Some manufacturers produce ball pellets to complement their boilie ranges: the idea is to create a similarly flavoured feed bed around the hookbait.

Base Mixes

There are many tremendous base mixes on the market, some of which are ready to use after adding water or eggs, and some which require the addition of other ingredients. Many of these are proven fish catchers. As well as base mixes, ready-made flavoured pastes in tubs are available from some suppliers. Although good, they sometimes offer poor value for money, as you can make the equivalent bait from a good base mix at a fraction of the cost.

Powders and Bait Soaks

As well as the vast range of flavours and additives now available, particularly successful additives are powdered attractants. Tikka powder and powdered extracts are excellent and catch a lot of fish.

Bait soaks or bait batters are commercially available, the idea being to make the hookbait particularly attractive among its fellows on the lake bed. For the mobile angler, convenient bait enhancement can be provided with spray flavours, and again there are many superb ranges.

ABOVE: A bait rocket with particle bait and boilies.

Swimfeeders and Groundbait

1 Various swimfeeders are designed to allow the chosen groundbait to trickle out at the correct rate.

2 Here a swimfeeder has been filled with fine particle groundbait to be used for bream.

Flavours, Colours, Enhancers and Oils

Although many baits can be modified with common foodstuffs found in all kitchens, such as dipping bread flake in honey, or smearing crust with cheese spread, this section is devoted to those synthetic products used for bait enhancement that are available from tackle shops and bait suppliers.

Flavours

Most commercial flavours come in highly concentrated form, and it is an easy mistake to overdose your baits. This will repel fish rather than attract, as it renders the bait bitter. Very rarely is it recommended to use more than ½ fl oz (5 ml) of flavouring per 1 lb (450 g) weight of synthetic bait, and if you wish to add flavours to orthodox baits such as bread, maggots or luncheon meat, it is better to be sparing, rather than too liberal.

Most manufacturers give instructions on their containers or in brochures on dosage levels that you should follow. Exceeding these levels may give a very short-term attraction for fish, but the bait will soon blow.

For flavouring bread, for crust or flake fishing, put about ½ fl oz (5 ml) of the flavour into a large freezer bag, coat the sides with the liquid, put the loaf inside, then seal and freeze. When the loaf thaws, it sucks in the flavour. You can flavour breadcrumbs and liquidized bread the same way, while mashed bread is treated simply by adding the flavour to the water during the preparation. To flavour maggots, put ½ fl oz (5 ml) of your chosen flavouring in the bottom of a bait box, with a small amount of water to spread the flavour, introduce the maggots and then give the box a vigorous shaking. After a few hours, the box should be dry, as the maggots will have absorbed all the liquid.

It is better to flavour maggots with powdered products, such as turmeric or curry powder, as you get a more even flavour distribution. Sprinkle the powder liberally over the bait and let the maggots continually work through it. Powdered flavours are also useful for coating naturally moist baits such as luncheon meats.

If you wish to use liquid flavours with meats, you can either simply soak or gently fry the meat with the chosen flavour in an old frying pan. Do not fry for too long, however, as one of the attractions of meat is its natural fat content, which will then be lost. A good ploy with luncheon meats is to dampen them with a flavour enhancer, and then coat with a chosen powder. Freezing locks the flavours into the bait and ensures that the bait on your hook will retain its attraction for several hours.

Colours

It is rare that a coloured bait gives any significant advantage over a natural one, and some anglers tend to use colour as a means of identifying different bait batches. Having said that, dark baits can be useful on very bright days in clear water. For instance, barbel have been known to shun pink luncheon meat and then take confidently a piece dyed black, or to take dark red corn after appearing terrified of normal yellow corn.

Some carp anglers swear by brightly coloured baits on dark lake beds, and some pike anglers have great faith in coloured deadbaits. Whatever the truth of the matter, colour will only be significant in water under about six feet deep. At greater depth than that, most colours appear the same.

Enhancers

There are a whole range of flavour enhancers, vitamin supplements, sweeteners, appetite stimulators and bulk food oils, and it is very easy to become confused. They are mainly used with synthetic carp baits, and the best thing to do is to select a small number and try and stick to them.

As with all these types of product, the manufacturer's advice is crucial. As a general guide, add sweeteners

TOP: Dyes for colouring baits. This is really only significant when fishing in shallow water.

LEFT: The range of flavours and additives found in tackle shops can be confusing to the beginner. Choose just a few to start with.

and appetite stimulators to naturally sweeter flavours such as strawberry and molasses, while the sweetener can be substituted with a savoury flavour enhancer when using flavours such as cheese, spice, fish or meat. Many baits, sweet or savoury, are also enhanced by the addition of a little salt in the initial dry mix.

Essential Oils
These oils are highly concentrated natural plant extracts to be used with care and very sparingly. Examples include geranium, peppermint and Mexican onion, and these products are used in concentrations no greater than a few drops per pound of base mix as they are so powerful.

Many carp anglers who prepare baits for long-term use, without that bait blowing, use essential oils on the best quality base mixes, and then keep the recipes strictly to themselves.

TOP: Deadbaits can be both coloured and flavoured and this adds to their attraction.

ABOVE: Colour is a useful way of identifying batches of the same bait. Here cockles have been dyed red, yellow and orange.

Groundbaits and Prebaiting

Groundbaiting means introducing free offerings or a food carpet in a selected area just prior to or during the fishing session, while prebaiting has come to mean the preparatory work carried out hours, days or even weeks before the swim is fished. There are a number of reasons why prebaiting is important. First, it can be used to concentrate fish in the area in which you wish to angle. Second, by allowing the fish time to feed on your bait unmolested, it can make catching the fish easier when you do introduce a baited hook. Lastly, it can wean educated fish on to a bait of your choice, giving you an important edge over other anglers.

Groundbaits

There are endless varieties of groundbaits, varying from fine powdered cereals to mixed particles, or combinations of both. If you wish to stimulate a feeding response to hookbaits, without necessarily feeding the fish, then a pure powdered cloud groundbait is ideal. This would be the common choice for a match angler seeking large numbers of smaller fish. A cloud bait can range from a simple mix of very fine pure breadcrumbs to a complex mixture of meals and attractors designed for specific purposes and different species. Tackle shops are full of products to meet every angling requirement, and you can buy heavy mixes for rivers, light fluffy mixes for canals, bream mixes, carp mixes, and so on.

Specialist anglers seeking bigger fish would more commonly use a combination of meals and particles, particles only or, for carp anglers in the main, beds of boilies. An example of the first category is the tench or bream angler who uses brown breadcrumbs as the bulk carrier, mixed with particle feed such as hemp, corn, rice, pearl barley, casters or maggots. The second category includes the barbel angler preparing a swim with hemp and corn, or the carp angler laying down a bed of tiger nuts.

Mixing powdered groundbaits is critically important, since you want the bait to be neither too sloppy nor too stiff. For bottom-feeding fish in an estate lake, for instance, you want the bait to hit bottom without breaking up, but then quickly disperse into an appealing carpet. For good control of the mixing process place the dry bait in a wide bowl, remove any lumps, and then add the water plus any liquid additives very slowly, mixing as you go, until the required consistency is obtained.

Match anglers use a sponge to sprinkle water evenly over the dry ingredients, and this does give very

Preparing Groundbait

1 The dry ingredients for groundbait. These may include breadcrumbs, particle feed, hemp, sweetcorn and various meals and attractors.

2 Mix dry ingredients together in a bait bowl. Turn the mixture over a number of times to make sure that all the ingredients are evenly distributed.

3 Add water to the mixture. Do this slowly and continue to turn the mixture over as the water is added. It is important to keep an even texture.

7 To bait a swim, take a handful of groundbait and form it into a ball. You may have to add more water to your mixture as the day wears on.

8 The ideal ball is about the size of an orange. Throw it into the water by hand if you are baiting close by. For longer ranges use a bait catapult.

close control. A perfect ball of groundbait should hold together easily without being sticky, but then crumble down into the consistency of damp pastry crumbs. The same bait for river fish could be made slightly stiffer so that, instead of actually breaking up on the river bed, it gives off a constant cloud of attraction which is then washed downstream.

Prebaiting Techniques
Balls of groundbait are generally introduced either by hand or by catapult, and this is where it is important to ensure that the bait does not break up in flight. The more accurate your bait placement, the more efficient your angling. If you have access to a boat or bait boat, your bait can be sloppier, mashed bread for instance, as it will sink straight down to the bottom. For prebaiting particles, if you are baiting

at close range, say with hemp for barbel, the bait dropper is an invaluable aid and allows very accurate placement of the bait. For prebaiting particles at range, the bait rocket or spod is a useful tool. This is a cylinder with buoyancy at the base. It is filled with particles, cast on a strong rod and heavy line, and turns turtle as soon as it hits the water, depositing its load of bait in the required spot.

A similar principle is used with the baiting cone, which is designed to introduce a combination of particles and loose groundbait to the fish. Again, the cone is filled with the particles, the wide top sealed with a groundbait plug, and the lot cast to the desired spot.

For prebaiting with boilies at range, the two most commonly used methods are with the catapult and the throwing stick, although more and

more carp anglers are investing in radio-controlled bait boats for faster baiting at long range. Catapults require little explanation, but the throwing stick is an accurate tool for boilie placement after a little practice. To be proficient, it is vital that your boilies are perfectly round and the same size, or you get baits flying in all directions and to all ranges. This defeats the object of prebaiting, which is to concentrate fish in a fairly tight area. A special rolling table is a help towards achieving this if you are making your boilies at home.

Even pike anglers can employ prebaiting techniques successfully , constantly feeding likely areas with small pieces of fish. It is rarely necessary to bait at range, as big pike are reliable margin feeders, particularly around overgrown banks or in marginal reeds where they lie in wait for their quarry.

4 Keep working the groundbait until you are satisfied that everything is thoroughly mixed and you have achieved the right consistency.

5 The finished mixture should resemble damp crumbs. With experience you will be able to achieve this texture without difficulty.

6 Perfect groundbait should hold together under light pressure but break down easily into light crumbs without lumps when in the water.

9 Using the catapult will enable you to bait at relatively long ranges. As you practise and become more experienced, you will become more accurate and able to achieve greater distance.

Equipment

Before choosing expensive equipment or tackle, such as a fishing rod, be sure that it will perform the task you ask of it and give you pleasure in its use. There are many factors to take into account, such as the species you hope to catch, and the size, the casting weight and distance involved, line strength and so on. Having determined the suitability of the rod, you then need to ask yourself whether its action is to your liking. For example, you may never have been a fan of fast-tapered rods, but if you need to pick up line at long distance in order to set the hook, you have to compromise, and a fast-tapered rod is the best for this.

Rod Actions

There are three types of action. The first, "through action", is where there is a uniformly smooth curve through the blank when playing a fish, and there is no doubt that maximum angling pleasure is to be had with a rod of this type. Where a little more backbone is required, "progressive action" rods come to the fore: with these a modest fish will still give a pleasing bend in the rod but there is a progressive power build-up in the butt to control larger specimens. Lastly, there are "fast taper" rods, that are very stiff in the butt and have very flexible tips. These are designed for ultra-long casting and fast line pick-up.

14 ft (4.27 m) general float trotting rod with centrepin reel

14 ft (4.27 m) carp rod with fixed-spool reel

11 ft (3.35 m) light leger rod with a fixed-spool reel

Type of Fishing	Recommended Rod
	(all progressive action except where stated)
General float trotting	14 ft (4.27 m) Drennan IM9 float rod, 12 oz (0.34 kg) test curve
Float fishing for bigger fish	13 ft (3.96 m) Harrison Supreme Specimen float rod, 1 lb (0.45 kg) test curve
General barbel fishing	TM 11 ft 3 in (3.45 m) Century Pulse Barbel rod, 1 lb 6 oz (0.62 kg) test curve
Upstream barbel fishing	TW 12 ft (3.66 m) Century Pulse Upstreamer rod, 1 lb 12 oz (0.79 kg) test curve
Short/medium-range carp/pike	12 ft (3.66 m) Harrison Supreme carp rods, 2 lb 4 oz (1.02 kg) test curve
Long-range carp	12 ft (3.66 m) Harrison Supremecarp rods, 2 lb 8 oz (1.13 kg) test curve
Pike deadbaiting	13 ft (3.96 m) Century Armalite rod, 3 lb (1.36 kg) test curve
Big chub	11 ft (3.35 m) Century Pulse chub rod, 1 lb 4 oz (0.57 kg) test curve
Light leger, roach, medium chub	11 ft (3.35 m) Shimano Aero Quiver rod, 1 lb (0.45 kg) test curve, through action
Medium/long-range feeder	12 ft (3.66 m) Harrison Supreme feeder rods, 1 lb 8 oz (0.68 kg) test curve

An all-round coarse angler will need several rods in his armoury to deal with different angling circumstances. The list in the table above is recommended, but there are many other excellent manufacturers and rods for the angler to choose from. Buy one rod at a time and expand your range gradually.

The "test curve" is the weight required to pull the tip of the rod to an angle of 90 degrees to the butt. It gives an indication of the weight the rod is capable of casting.

Reels

There are three basic types of reel that any coarse angler needs in his or her fishing bag.

Fixed-spool Reels

These are the most common in popular use. For barbel and tench fishing, feeder work and stillwater float fishing, the Shimano Aero GTM 4010 is a good choice. It has three spools of varying line capacity. The reel features a double handle dyna balance system. This is delightful in use, giving a smooth, vibration-free retrieve. Tapered spools and a two-speed crosswind line lay system ensure that casting is smooth. The GTM 4010 is fitted with a fighting drag system, a two-stage clutch mechanism allowing clutch tension to be varied during a fight.

A delightful little reel to use in conjunction with the Shimano Aero Quivertip rod is the Aero 2000. This is very light, well balanced and has the most delightful clutch.

For carp and pike fishing, where fast runs often take yards of line, the larger GTM 6010, holding a much greater capacity of heavier lines, and which features the baitrunner system is recommended. This allows fast-running fish to take line in free spool manner with the bail arm closed – important in preventing tangles.

Centrepins and Closed-face Reels

Centrepins are usually preferred for trotting, but a closed-face fixed-spool is good if conditions are difficult due to strong winds.

Many anglers use centrepin reels for legering for barbel, using an audible check for bite detection. If you have difficulty casting, Ray Walton markets a centrepin that swivels so it casts like a fixed spool but then reverts to fishing as a traditional centrepin. If you only use the centrepin for legering, this is a good choice.

Multipliers

Where you need a large capacity of heavy line, say for trolling for pike or fishing for big catfish, a multiplier reel is usually best. However, before buying one, ask your tackle dealer for advice.

201 multiplying reel

Centrepin reel

GTM 6010 reel with spare spool

4010 reel

Clothing

The best angling outer garments will be light, comfortable, breathable and yet 100 per cent waterproof.

There is a large range of suits, jackets and trousers, and a bib and brace coupled with the three-quarter jacket gives complete versatility, whatever the weather conditions. A jacket with a detachable hood is recommended. Jackets with a bib and brace are also very convenient. Three-quarter jackets with a separate zip-out quilted lining that can be worn independently, are also available.

Always purchase outer garments at least one size too big, to allow for a one-piece thermal suit or thermal underwear underneath in the depths of winter.

In winter, the body loses heat fastest through the head, hands and feet. Always wear a good hat: a wide-brimmed waterproof trilby, with chin straps, for rain and wind, and a woolly hat or a balaclava for very cold days are well worth the money.

Waterproof jacket and trousers

Fleece hat and gloves with waterproof trilby

Gloves and Waders

Neoprene gloves are some of the warmest angler's gloves available. For mobile fishing, the fingerless gloves are good, while the cut finger variant for more static fishing, say for pike, is appropriate. With these, the whole hand is covered, but for rebaiting the first two fingers and thumb of the glove can be folded back and kept in place by Velcro.

The variety of weather, water and temperature conditions demand a wide selection of footwear for maximum efficiency and comfort. For summer, Derriboots, thigh or chest

Fishing jacket

waders, and for winter thermally lined moonboots or thigh waders are recommended. Neoprene chest waders are also excellent. Several spare pairs of socks, some thermal, should always be to hand, as should a couple of towels. Wet and cold feet in winter is a recipe for misery.

Nets

Landing nets and keepnets should be constructed of the softest material available, thus preventing any damage to fish. For pike, carp, barbel and catfish the Relum Be Safe triangular landing net, with 3 ft (1 m) arms is recommended. For heavy fish, you can use the Relum Springlok system, which allows the mesh frame to be detached or folded back when a fish is landed, thereby taking strain off the handle and making fish carrying easier. The mesh also features weighing straps, to avoid undue handling of the fish, which can be weighed in the net and then released.

There is an option of a mixed mesh, so that a very fine mesh cradle makes up the net base. This is a godsend where hooks are prone to become tangled, for example trebles used in piking. This version is good for stillwaters, but in river work, say for barbel, a plain mesh net is better as the fine variety offers great water resistance in a fair current.

Another option is a net with a telescopic handle, which is useful, as you are often faced with high banks or wide rush margins.

For smaller species, particularly on rivers, spoon-shaped landing nets are preferable as they are less prone to tangling in vegetation. Where spoon landing nets and keepnets are concerned, some of the best products are marketed by Keenets. The big mesh Mega Spoon for mid-size species, such as chub and tench, and a smaller, pan net version with a duplex mesh for roach and rudd are both recommended. Again, it is worth using a telescopic handle, such as a

Wellington boots

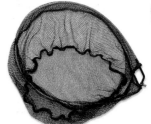

Some of the various types of keepnet that are available.
FAR LEFT: Waterline square keepnet; LEFT: Round keepnet.
ABOVE: Smaller keepnets are suitable for short-term fish retention.

carbon telescopic which extends to 10 ft (3 m). Coupled with a lightweight spoon frame, the whole net is simple to use single-handed. But do not attempt to lift a fish at the end of 10 ft (3 m) of carbon, or you could break the handle. Ship the handle towards you and lift out the fish by grasping the net frame itself.

With regard to keepnets, buy the largest and softest net your budget allows. But use it responsibly, keeping it pegged out in a good depth of water, in uncrowded conditions, and for the minimum time possible.

Weigh Slings, Retention Systems & Unhooking Mats

Most specialist anglers retain a fish they wish to photograph in a carp sack, and there are many excellent products available. The most useful are the sack/weigh sling combinations. They are lightweight, compact and soft enough to stuff into small spaces in seat boxes or rucksacks. Also, always have handy a couple of old guy ropes and bivvy pegs, to ensure a fish can be retained in sufficiently deep water.

Under no circumstances place more than one fish in a keep sack, and when pegging it out in water always ensure that the material is not trapping the fish's gills. In hot weather, particularly where there is only shallow water in the margins, ask yourself whether you should use a sack in the first place. The welfare of the fish should be paramount.

For retaining big fish in running water, make sure that the fish lies with its head upstream and that the sack is not twisting in too strong a flow. A steady throughput of water should be the intention.

Far better, though, in rivers, is a system that can be pegged out into a rigid structure that allows a fish to breath normally and recover properly. The Queenford retention system, a rectangular structure made of very soft sacking material with mesh ends for ease of water flow is recommended. This also has a zip top so that once the sack is in place, it does not need to be disturbed. There are similar pike tubes available commercially.

This idea has now been extended to smaller versions for barbel and large specimens of catfish. Again, the zip top allows ease of access.

It is very important that some fish be retained for a short while to allow them to recover in safety. This is particularly true of barbel that fight themselves to a standstill, and also big bream for which the Queenford system was originally designed.

Unhooking mats are important to use when banks are hard and irregular. This is particularly true of gravel pits. There are many good products about.

ABOVE: An unhooking mat.

ABOVE: A combined sack and weigh sling is essential if you want to weigh your catch without doing any damage to the fish.

Umbrellas and Bivvies

The all-round coarse angler will often require shelter from the elements, and there is much superlative equipment available. Shelters range from the standard umbrella through to the portable detached bungalow. For river fishing, if you are adopting a mobile style, it is better if possible to forego an umbrella, as it discourages moving swims. It is far better to rely on good-quality protective clothing and waterproof luggage.

However, if you intend to spend reasonable time in one swim, an umbrella can provide much greater comfort. For tight swims or on sloping banks, the standard umbrella is fine. If you have a little more room there is a virtually lightweight pop-up bivvy available on the market that erects in about 15 seconds and has sufficient headroom for a seatbox. It has two securing bivvy pegs and special retaining sleeves on the side panels for bivvy poles to give it extra rigidity in rough weather, and two zip-out rear panels to accommodate pole anglers.

For the longer-stay angler on stillwaters, there are many good bivvies. The umbrella/bivvy hybrid, which can be used as an umbrella, is superb when the Velcro-equipped storm sides are added. It is excellent for a short overnight session.

Where a longer stay is planned, and comfort is more of a requirement, one of the new double-skinned super bivvies with built-in groundsheet is

ABOVE: A good modern bivvy protects the angler from the elements.

Folding Chairs and Bedchairs

For long sessions, a low chair is recommended. The most comfortable chairs should be fully sprung and feature high-density foam inserts for total cushioning. As well as seat padding, a good chair might feature generously padded head, leg and arm supports, so preventing the metal frame causing any discomfort. Chair legs should fold flat and be light, making the chairs simple to transport. Each leg should be independently adjustable to cope with uneven banks, and fitted with a non-slip rubber foot.

With all low chairs it is necessary to prevent the feet sinking into very soft mud. The best models feature anti-sink wide feet, which work well most of the time. For those occasions, however, when the banks are very soft, you might want to carry four old carpet tiles to place under the feet, as they keep chairs stable even in boggy conditions.

A lightweight folding chair for the roving angler

For overnight sessions, a bedchair will be required. Better ones fold completely flat, have three sets of adjustable legs for extra stability and a very firm locking mechanism to put the head rest in any position required. This is important as it allows the product to be used as a chair when fishing and then it converts to a bed for sleeping..

Seat Boxes

For very mobile fishing you may prefer a seat box to a chair. This cuts down on the amount of gear to carry. When fishing a swim where continual float casting is required a seat box is often more convenient than a low chair simply because it is higher. In these circumstances, extra comfort and convenience are provided by seat boxes with trays housing all the paraphernalia you are likely to need.

ABOVE: A bedchair is essential for the long-stay angler.

A standard angler's umbrella

the answer. These are available with extended groundsheets into the porch area, side ventilators, mosquito nets, rain skirts, inner and outer doors. Some even have rear doors, clear section windows on the doors, side panels or storm sides. Some bivvies have extended front tunnels to store cooking and lighting equipment, boots and wet clothes.

Hooks

There is a wide choice of hooks and patterns available from many manufacturers. There is simply not enough room to compare each manufacturer's hooks in depth, and for simplicity the hooks discussed all come from Drennan which supplies all the patterns that any angler is likely to require.

There is much debate about the merits of barbed versus barbless, mechanically or chemically sharpened, round bend versus crystal bend, straight point or beak point, and so on. The best advice is to experiment with patterns until you find one that suits the particular style of fishing in which you are engaged. For instance, where you wish to stop a big fish from reaching a snag, a forged beak hook will resist pulling out, whereas you may lose fish after fish on chemically sharpened or barbless patterns. On the other hand, a chemically sharpened pattern such as Super Specialist could be the choice if you want good long-range hooking, where you have room to play the fish without undue pressure.

If you wish to use barbless hooks at all times, Specimen Barbless and Carbon Barbless are excellent. The table at the foot of the page shows the hooks recommended for various fishing styles.

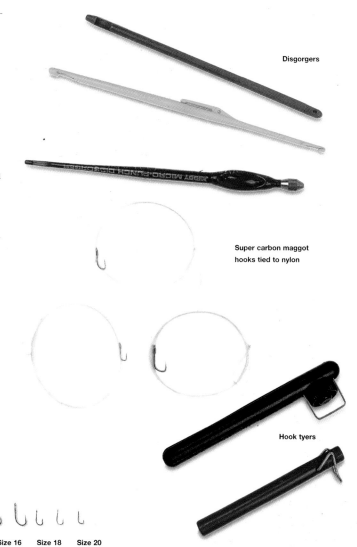

Disgorgers

Super carbon maggot hooks tied to nylon

Hook tyers

Coarse fishing hooks

Size 10   Size 12   Size 14   Size 16   Size 18   Size 20

Size 6 extra strong barbed treble hook

Size 8 extra strong barbed treble hook

Style of Fishing	Hook Choices	Comments
Big Carp	Sizes 2 to 6, beak point, in-curved	Continental boilie
Pike	Sizes 4 to 8, barbed treble hooks	Extra strong
Other species, large baits	Sizes 4 to 8, beak point, in-curved	Continental boilie
General feeder	Sizes 12 to 16, round bend	Carbon specimen
Feeder, strong fish	Sizes 12 to 16, beak point	Super spades
Feeder, roach, dace	Sizes 14 to 18, beak point	Super spades, ready tied
Float fish, flake hookbait	Sizes 8 to 12, crystal bend	Specimen crystal
Float fish, caster hookbait	Sizes 16 or 18, crystal bend	Carbon caster

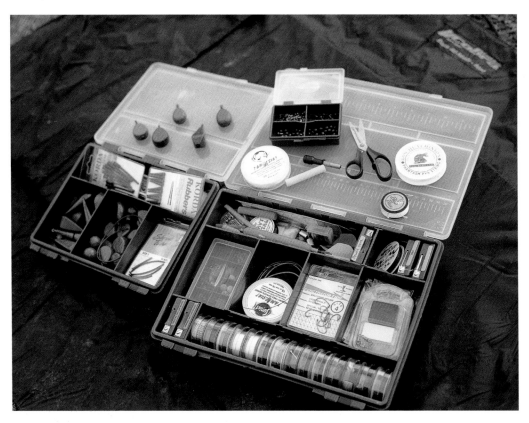

Lines

Modern monofilament lines are a vast improvement on those of even a few years ago. Diameter has decreased and breaking strains increased. Some of the new fluorocarbon lines are now virtually invisible in water

Monofilaments

Whatever main line you use, there is one rule that applies at all times – change your lines regularly. All mono lines deteriorate in time, especially if continually exposed to the sun, and you should renew your lines at least three times a season.

The three monofilament main lines recommended are Drennan Specimen Plus, Berkeley Trilene XT and Sufix Synergy. Specimen Plus is the all-round main line in all breaking strains, but when you require greater abrasion resistance, the Trilene or Sufix lines are excellent.

All three lines are not ideal for hooklinks as they are a little springy. If you require a monofilament hooklink you need more limpness,

and then you might want to switch to Drennan Float Fish or Sufix Ultra Supreme. Anglers who fish for smaller fish will find their low diameters helpful in creating delicate bait presentation. One of the best standard pre-stretched lines with ultra-low diameter is Drennan Double Strength. One of the problems with extra-low diameter pre-stretched lines is that they tend to be a little stiff. A good compromise if you require a little pre-stretch but a line that is ultra limp is extra-soft Trilene XL or Pro Micron.

An exciting development in recent years has been the advent of fluorocarbon lines, which have the same refractive index as water. In other words, they become invisible on immersion. These enable very subtle bait presentations to be made, and the Sufix Invisiline is highly recommended if you are using monofilament links over 4 lb (1.81 kg) breaking strain.

ABOVE: Tackle boxes with compartments for lines, hooks, weights, leads and tools – essential for the serious angler.

Other Hooklink Materials

For most carp and barbel fishing soft braided hooklinks are suitable. Good braids are Drennan Carp Silk and Rod Hutchinson's The Edge. If you are fishing in woody snags, all braids can have a problem if the fibres are continually picked at by wood splinters, progressively weakening the material. Braids are also not ideal if fishing in heavy flows for chub and barbel, particularly upstream where the terminal tackle is constantly on the move, as they tangle very easily. In these situations, you may wish to revert to Drennan solid Dacron. Another alternative is a smoothly coated braid, of which there are many on the market.

Another specialized product from Rod Hutchinson is the Edge Plus, which is a braid with a fine lead core. Using several feet of this above the hooklink ensures that the main line is nailed to the bottom, thereby eliminating the problem of line bites. In barbel fishing, it also keeps the main line below drifting debris.

Super Braids

There is a growing use of ultra-low diameter, high-strength super braids. Many anglers are using these both as main lines and hooklinks, for the advantages of high strength to diameter ratio, zero stretch and good bait presentation. If you adopt this procedure, please be responsible. A 30 lb (13.6 kg) high-strength braid can be as fine as 7 lb (3.18 kg) mono, but a fish running into a snag could get tethered with no way of breaking free. These braids should really be reserved for hooklinks. This gives the advantage of enhanced bait presentation but a main line break will still allow a hooked fish to escape.

There are two basic types of high-strength braid: round or flat section. However, some of the flat varieties are subject to sudden fracture if a wind knot develops. Some are also too stiff, although that does help to overcome the problem that occurs with all braids, that of tangling on the cast. The Sufix Herculine, available in breaking strains from 11 lb (5 kg) upwards, is recommended. This variety has a diameter roughly equivalent to 3 lb (1.36 kg) mono and makes a huge difference if you require fine presentation with a small hook for big powerful fish, such as feeder fishing for tench and barbel. The only problem with Herculine is that, because it is so limp, rigs must be as tangle proof as possible.

Trace Wires

It is a good idea to construct your own pike traces. Use 20 lb (9.07 kg) strand wire and simply twist the swivel and leading treble to the trace with at least a 1 in (2.5 cm) twist. A refinement is strand-coated wire, which is softer and limp to the touch. This is twisted in place in the same way and the plastic coating fused into a solid bond over a low flame. Whatever trace wire you use, make any pike trace at least 20 lb (9.07 kg) in strength and your traces at least 18 in (45 cm) long.

RIGHT: A fully equipped angler approaches the water in high summer. Much modern angling equipment is extremely light and sturdy compared to that available ten or twenty years ago. The important thing in any fishing expedition is not to forget vital equipment, and running through a checklist before you set out is an excellent idea.

ABOVE: Just a few of the lines that are available in any tackle shop. Each one is clearly labelled with the purpose, diameter and breaking strain. Amnesia memory-free lines are being used more and more by all anglers whatever their quarry. The lines do not kink and are a great help in avoiding tangles.

Indicators

There are various ways that anglers go about registering when the fish has taken their bait. Some traditional indicators have been around for centuries; others, such as night floats and electronic alarms, are modern.

Floats

The most traditional bite indicators are floats, which exist in a myriad of different forms, in order to cope with various conditions and angling styles. As with all tackle, good products are available from several manufacturers.

Float design varies to cope with the fishing style involved, and generally those floats used for river work have their body bulk higher on the stem for stability of riding a current, while stillwater floats carry their bulk much lower to minimize the effects of drift. The table offers float choices for various angling circumstances.

Type of Water	Example of Float
Gentle flow, small baits	Stick float/Wire-stemmed Stick
All-round trotting in streamy water	Wire-stemmed Avon
Streamy water with large baits	Loafer or Crystal Avon
Fast, shallow runs through weed, large baits	Double-rubber Balsa
Short-range laying on, stillwaters or very gentle flow	Peacock Waggler
Short- to medium-range laying on, stillwaters	Insert Crystal Waggler
Long-range laying on, calm conditions	Crystal Missile
Medium- to long-range laying on, windy conditions	Driftbeater
Pike fishing, free-ranging livebait	Crystal Piker
Pike fishing, deadbait	E.T. Dumpy Slider
Pike fishing, driftbait	E.T. Drifter

LEFT TO RIGHT: **Two loaded carp crystal floats, a stick float, a wire-stemmed stick float, a loafer and an inset crystal float.**

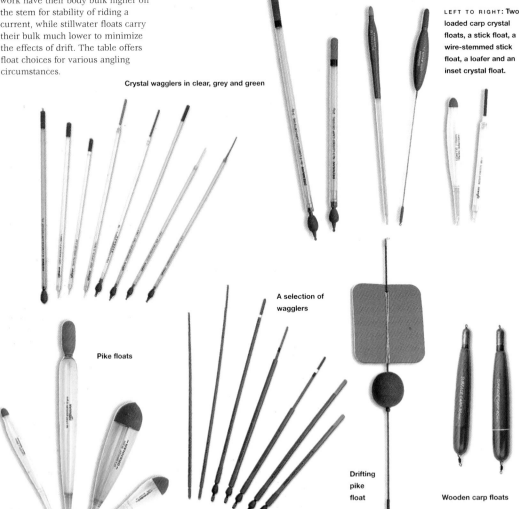

Crystal wagglers in clear, grey and green

A selection of wagglers

Pike floats

Drifting pike float

Wooden carp floats

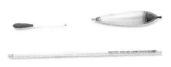

Missile float in pieces

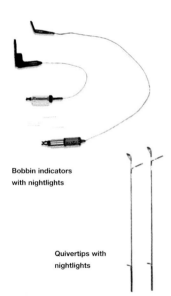

Bobbin indicators with nightlights

Quivertips with nightlights

Bobbins

The earliest form of legering incorporated a ball of dough hung on the line between the reel and the first rod ring to form an angle. A bite was signalled by the line tightening and the "dough bobbin" rising. This term now includes any free-hanging bite indicator, which may be the top of a washing-up liquid bottle or sophisticated commercially made bobbins incorporating beta lights for night fishing.

Most anglers equip their bobbins with a retaining cord, tied to the rod rest, to prevent them being lost on a hard strike. The cord can be loaded with lead wire to make the bobbin heavier and counteract drift.

Butt Indicators

Butt indicators are pivoted arms set at the front rod rest, with the head of the indicator placed on the line a short distance in front of the reel. There are several types available.

The arm designed by Bob Henderson features a cleverly designed angled slot in the head, so that the indicator automatically falls away from the line when it reaches the horizontal. Many butt indicators have a problem of resistance to the line when they are pulled out of their retaining device. With the Henderson, the line falls away sweetly, totally resistance free.

For deadbait fishing for predators, when the reel is often fished free spool, butt indicators can be mounted on the rear rod rest, so that they rise and then pull off the line when a run starts. Recommended for fishing this style, are the droparm indicators or, for longer sessions, the E.T. Backbiter, which works on the same principle but incorporates the facility for including beta lights and provides an adjustable audible alarm.

Swingtips

As the name implies, a swingtip is a stiff extension to the rod tip, hinged to a threaded base to fit a matching threaded tip ring on the rod. Once the bait has been cast out, the line is tightened until there is the required angle in the swingtip. A bite is signalled by the tip either rising or falling. Swingtips can be fitted with lead wire to counteract drift, and beta lights for night work. They are mainly used in stillwaters or very sluggish sections of rivers.

Quivertips

Separate quivertips are either supplied with rods, spigotted or overfitted to the rod top after removing the tip ring, or supplied with threaded adapters to fit threaded tip rings. Unlike a swingtip, the thread is not hinged to the body, which is tapered to accentuate a bite from a fish. They are supplied in a range of test curves, from 3 oz (85 gm) for strong fish such as barbel to only 1 oz (28 gm) or less to indicate the bite from the most delicately feeding fish.

Electronic Alarms

Most anglers will be equipped with electronic alarms of one kind or another, usually in combination with bobbins or butt indicators, in order to give both visual and audible bite warning. The line is placed in the slot in the alarm head and a bite is then indicated with a bleep and flashing LED display when the line moves. There are many very reliable alarms available on the market.

ABOVE: A rucksack is a convenient way to carry all the equipment you need when you are out on a short expedition. Waterproof rucksacks keep all your equipment dry.

Luggage

You will need a special rucksack or probably a carryall to transport your equipment easily and safely. Rucksacks are suitable for the normal range of equipment, and a carryall is good for baits and flavours, an insulated bait bag is very useful for frozen baits.

Rod Holdalls

There are four traditional holdalls available for carrying rods with reels attached. The Relum Logic Rod System takes up to five rod/reel assemblies on the outside, with an umbrella inside. External pockets accommodate rod rests, storm poles and landing nets. Separate sleeves can be purchased to accommodate up to 13 ft (3.96 m) two-piece rods, and the position of the reel pouches is adjustable.

Slings and Quivers

For the mobile angler, slings or quivers, in which one or two made-up rods are carried, together with a minimum of other bits and pieces, such as a landing net, rod rests and a lightweight umbrella are a boon. Some slings have a quick-fasten retaining strap on the outside to keep made-up rods under control when on the move.

Carryall/Unhooking Mat

A very useful item of luggage is the combined carryall/unhooking mat designed to carry a folding seat, plus items like buzzer bars, rod pods and bivvy; and when not in use, it opens out to make a good unhooking mat.

A large version has been made to accommodate the largest bedchair. For short fishing sessions, when you might just be carrying a rod and landing net, a large rucksack is not ideal, and in these circumstances a stalker bag may be preferable. This has four external and five internal pockets and sufficient room for the amount of gear and bait needed for a short session.

Ancillary Items

The list below is a general selection of useful items to include within your fishing equipment:

Range of leads from 0.25–3 oz (7–85 gm), container of split shot, range of floats.

Counterbalance and Flotsam, which are sinking and floating putty respectively.

Mini-night lights and screw-in beta light adapters.

Different strength screw in quivertips and swingtips.

Snap links, swivels and rig beads.

Hair rig needle and hair rig dumbbell stops.

Silicon tubing, for making semi-fixed bolt rigs and shrink tube.

Scissors, braid scissors, forceps and small screw-in scythe blade.

Polypops or cork balls, rig foam and superglue.

Line grease and a small bottle of washing-up liquid for degreasing.

Float and leger stops and float caps.

PVA string, tubes and bags.

Hook-sharpening stone plus small, sharp knife.

Rig, hooklink and licence wallets.

Headlamp torch, plus spare batteries and bulbs.

Camera, filters, spare films and batteries, cable release and air bulb for self portraits.

Insulating tape, rubber bands, Power Gum.

Bait droppers, catapults and Avon weighing scales.

Thermometer, notepad and pencil, small hand towel.

Syringe for air-injecting lobs.

First aid kit: including anti-allergy spray for insect bites and stings, headache tablets and suncream.

Mobile phone for emergencies.

BELOW: A special carryall designed to transport a number of rods and reels in safety.

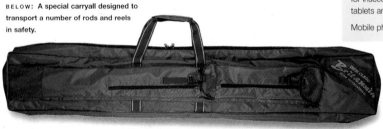

Ancillary Items

Silicone tubing

Carp boxes
with swivels,
beads, boilies
and small
leads

Ancillary items: baiting
needles, nut or boilie drill,
scalpel, hairstops, scissors,
forceps, baitfloss

Shot dispenser

Leads and weights

Streamline System
Sorcerer
HTPE Camouflaged
Braid
20mtrs 28lb
Richworth

Merlin
15lb 6.8KG

Super-Silk
20lb 9.7KG

Silkworm
15lb 6.8KG

Specialist CARP
DACRON
10lb 4·5kg

Super-Nova
ULTRA-BRAID

Specialist CARP
DACRON
12lb 5·4kg

Braid hooklength material and
braid scissors

Boilie punches for foam
inserts (pop-ups)

Lighter, candle,
lamp, torch and
waterproof
matches

Small catapult

71

Float Fishing

Float fishing is one of the most popular coarse fishing methods. Whether it be studying intently for the tiniest knock as the float trots downstream, searching for roach, watching for those tell-tale rings to appear around the float at dawn on a tench lake, or starting in excitement as a drifting pike float disappears in a dramatic vortex, there is something almost mystical about the connection between float, bait, fish and fisherman.

ABOVE: A drifting pike float. Drift floats catch the wind and take baits a long way out from the bank, often beyond casting range.

Choosing a Float

Float fishing takes many forms, but all demand one constant factor to achieve the most efficient fishing. Always take the trouble to ensure that your choice of float is as suitable for the job in hand as possible, and that it is shotted correctly for maximum sensitivity. One of the most common mistakes beginners make is in struggling with a float that is far too light, particularly when trotting in running water. Do not try to convince yourself you are fishing more sensitively with too light a model – you will suffer poor presentation as a result. It is far better to use a float that is a little on the heavy side, and shot properly for perfect control.

The choice of floats is vast, both in type and manufacture, and can be very confusing for the novice. The all-

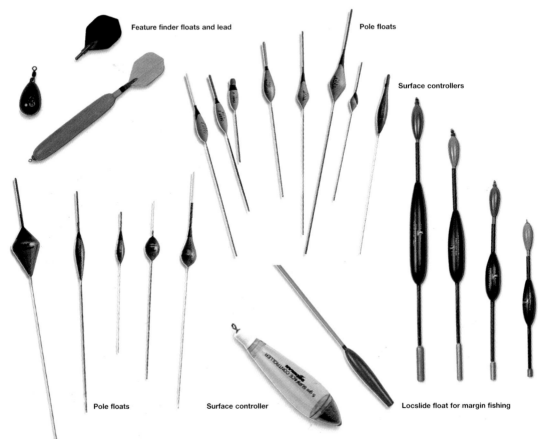

Feature finder floats and lead

Pole floats

Surface controllers

Pole floats

Surface controller

Locslide float for margin fishing

Trotting

ABOVE: A stick float on a correctly shotted line. A well-stocked shot dispenser is essential so extra shot can be added easily.

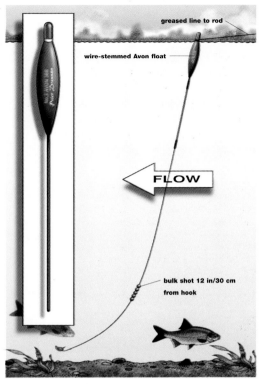

greased line to rod

wire-stemmed Avon float

FLOW

bulk shot 12 in/30 cm from hook

LEFT: A basic trotting rig for evenly paced water, presenting a bait near the bottom and showing the action of trotting a float downstream using an Avon float. The bait is lightly shotted, depending on the strength of the current, and drifts down naturally to the fish.

Check the depth of the swim and see that the float moves easily without any unnatural drag or disturbance.

rounder will require, however, floats of many types, and it is best to build up your collection slowly, getting to know how each one behaves and in what circumstances it is best used.

The most important thing, whatever type of float fishing you are doing, is that the float must be clearly visible. This sounds obvious, but light conditions can vary so much that one day you may need a red- or orange-tipped float, but on the next day you may require black. Extreme variations can also occur on the same day. For this reason, those floats available with a range of interchangeable sight tips of different colours are invaluable. Insert crystals, where you can not only change the float-tip colour in an instant, but also alter the tip for a night-light just as quickly when darkness falls, are recommended.

Trotting

Trotting simply means running a float down the current, taking the bait to the fish, and is most applicable to long, uniform, gravelly glides. Other good swims for trotting are runs under high banks or fringing overhanging foliage, or creases, where you can work the float along the junction of the two flows. Swims under steep vertical banks containing undercuts, in times of high water, are great for

trotting. In these conditions all species pack into these undercuts. Fish the float right along the edge of the bank, holding it back hard at short intervals, so that the bait swings upwards and inwards to search under the undercut.

Although it is possible to trot with a normal fixed-spool reel, a much more efficient presentation is achieved with a smooth running centrepin or, in difficult winds, a closed-face reel. To keep as close a contact with the float as possible, the longest rod you can practically handle is advisable, but it needs to be light and responsive. For general trotting work, a 14 ft (4.27 m) rod is ideal.

Most trotting is carried out with Avon or Stick floats of various sizes, depending on the depth and speed of flow, the bait, the presentation required and species sought. For the beginner, the wire-stemmed Avon float is suitable. Control does not have to be exact, and it is not easily pulled off course. Apart from steady loose feeding– a dozen maggots or a pinch of mashed bread before each trot –

one important aspect of a good trotting presentation is the avoidance of drag, created by a sinking line between float and rod top.

It is advisable to ensure that the line floats before fishing. A spray-on silicone line floatant is recommended.

It is simple to lift surplus floating line off the water, to compensate for wind or current deviation and to keep direct contact with the float without disturbance. If the line sinks, keeping a tight line to the float can pull it off course or check it unnaturally, causing a wake, both of which make fish suspicious. Gently checking the float occasionally, providing it is not pulled off course, is a good way of inducing bites, as it makes the hookbait swing upwards in the water with the current.

Most fish will rise quite a way off the bottom to intercept a bait, and so you should set the float to just clear the bottom at the shallowest point of the swim. This is easily achieved by running the float through a few times to see where it drags.

Stret Pegging

Bigger-than-average specimens can sometimes be caught by searching those areas where some loose feed has settled out of the main flow. This is particularly true when you are trotting a swim bordered by much slower water, such as a crease. Periodically, it pays to push up the float, cast to the normal position and then let the float drift round on a tight line to settle in this slacker water. This laying on in streamy water is known as stret pegging.

It is necessary to use a rod rest while stret pegging, as the float is less prone to swing around than if the rod is held by hand, and false bites are therefore eliminated. The float will normally be fishing at half-cock when fished on a tight line in flowing water, but if it continually goes under because of water pressure, keep deepening the float setting to reduce the line angle and eventually it will settle in one place. If you find it impossible to prevent the float submerging, you are almost certainly fishing in too fast a flow, in which no bait would have settled anyway. It is important not to fall into the trap of increasing the float size and loading to cope with the fast flow, as you will then lose all control. Use the same tackle you used for trotting. If that float can be stret pegged properly, then you are fishing the slacker water.

One important point with stret pegging is that you are float fishing on a tight line, in a similar way to tight-line legering. This means that you could experience savage bites, particularly if your river contains big barbel or chub. Therefore, although you should use a rest, keep your hand on the rod butt just in case. Rods can fly into a river in these circumstances.

Stret pegging need not be completely static. Having thoroughly searched one area, say 5 yds (4.6 m) down from your sitting position, let

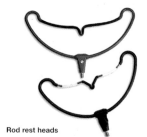

Rod rest heads

Stret Pegging

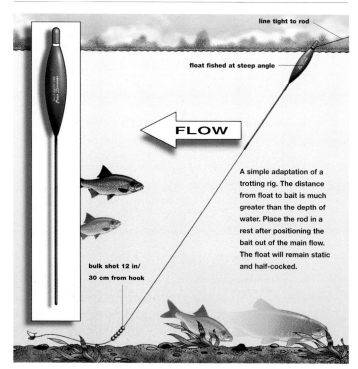

line tight to rod

float fished at steep angle

FLOW

A simple adaptation of a trotting rig. The distance from float to bait is much greater than the depth of water. Place the rod in a rest after positioning the bait out of the main flow. The float will remain static and half-cocked.

bulk shot 12 in/ 30 cm from hook

out some line and allow the float to trundle down a bit further. Close the bale arm and the float will resettle.

Try stret pegging at dusk. This is when the bigger fish move into the steadier water to feed, and you could well hook a bonus fish.

BELOW: Playing a good fish caught stret-pegging in the slacker water by the bush.

ABOVE: The diagram shows the effect of stret pegging, using the same tackle as for trotting (see page 73). Holding the float on a tight line pulls it half underwater, and the bait is held in one position. Fish move out of the streamy water and into the crease to feed. It is a good tactic to try in small streams like the one shown in the photograph below, and it is often surprising what large fish can be taken from relatively small waters.

Laying On: Short Range

Laying On: Long Range

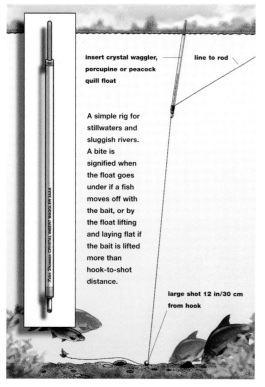

insert crystal waggler, porcupine or peacock quill float

line to rod

A simple rig for stillwaters and sluggish rivers. A bite is signified when the float goes under if a fish moves off with the bait, or by the float lifting and laying flat if the bait is lifted more than hook-to-shot distance.

large shot 12 in/30 cm from hook

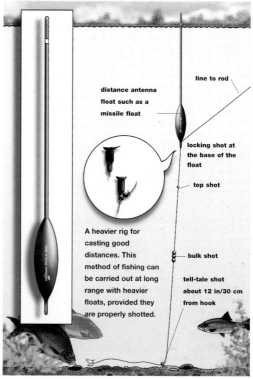

distance antenna float such as a missile float

line to rod

locking shot at the base of the float

top shot

A heavier rig for casting good distances. This method of fishing can be carried out at long range with heavier floats, provided they are properly shotted.

bulk shot

tell-tale shot about 12 in/30 cm from hook

Laying On

Laying on is similar in concept to stret pegging, except that where the latter is carried out in streamy water, laying on is used in stillwaters or very sluggish flows. There is another important difference. As stret pegging is a tight-line technique, it is best used with an Avon-type float fixed top and bottom. For laying on, you generally wish to prevent drift so the float to use is a waggler type, fished bottom end only, with the line between float and rod top sunken.

The simplest form of laying on is with a quill float such as a peacock, cocked by one large shot about 12 in (30 cm) from the hook. The depth is set so that the distance from float to shot is slightly overdepth, and obviously the float will lie flat on a slack line. By placing the rod on a rest and slowly drawing the line tight, thereby creating an angle in the line, the float cocks. The tighter the line can be drawn, the lower and straighter the float becomes. This is then an ultra-sensitive set-up, the

ABOVE LEFT: Laying on: short range. The diagram illustrates the principle of laying on in stillwaters. The float is a waggler type and attached bottom end only. The float is cocked by drawing the line tight and the single shot rests on the bottom.

attentions of a fish becoming immediately apparent when this delicate balance is disturbed. The light loading means that this particular laying on is only suitable for short range, and at longer ranges you will need to employ heavier floats.

However, the general principle is the same for all laying on, which is that there is always between 6–24 in (15–60 cm) of line on the bed, so that bottom-feeding fish can take the bait without feeling any initial resistance.

Although you would normally lay on with the intervening line sunken, there is one instance when you would lay on with that line greased, and that is when fishing a bottom bait amongst dense lily pads. The foliage itself prevents drift, while the greased line resists sinking down between the

ABOVE RIGHT: Laying on: long range. Traditional laying on is for tench and bream. The bulk of the float buoyancy is counter-balanced by top and bottom shots so that bite registration is still indicated by the float going under or lifting when the shot moves.

lilies, inviting snagging. This type of laying on is deadly for stillwater tench and small stream perch.

Possibly the most traditional laying on is for tench and bream in over-grown estate lakes at dawn. Most anglers of a few years' experience will have experienced the sheet of tench bubbles rising around the float, before it starts to dither and tilt to the attentions of the fish. This is one of the exciting moments in angling and it is important to let the float go away before striking. If you continually miss bites it is possible you are striking too soon, so increase the distance from hook to bottom shot. If you are not seeing bites, but there are obviously fish active, shorten that distance. Trial and error will arrive at the right combination for the day.

Laying On: Lift Method – Short Range

Laying On: Lift Method – Long Range

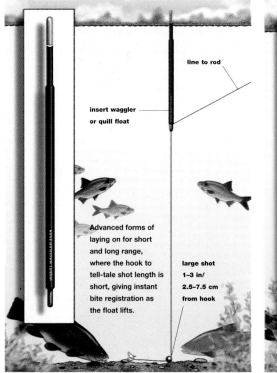

line to rod

insert waggler
or quill float

Advanced forms of
laying on for short
and long range,
where the hook to
tell-tale shot length is
short, giving instant
bite registration as
the float lifts.

large shot
1–3 in/
2.5–7.5 cm
from hook

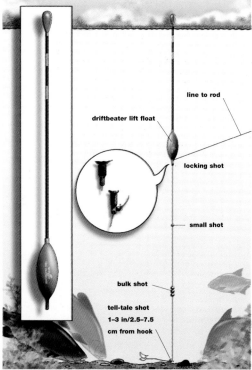

driftbeater lift float

line to rod

locking shot

small shot

bulk shot

tell-tale shot
1–3 in/2.5–7.5
cm from hook

Lift Method

The lift method is a very precise method of laying on and is great for stillwater float fishing. The general principle is similar to laying on, except that the bottom shot is generally fished much closer to the hook than in pure laying on: 2–3 in (5–7.5 cm) from the hook is normal. Once the line has been drawn tight, it can be seen that when a fish picks up the bait, it will almost immediately take the weight of the shot. Released from its loading, the float will now try and lie flat by shooting up in the water, or "lifting". The closer to the hook this bottom shot is, the more sensitive is the method.

While the single shot set-up gives the most dramatic lifts, any waggler float can be arranged to promote very obvious bites. Having carefully loaded the float until it sits at perfect depth, with the all-important bottom shot close to the hook, carefully plumb the depth. Initially, the bottom shot should just be resting on the lake bed. The float will then be riding too high,

ABOVE LEFT: The depth is accurately plumbed and the single shot rests on the bottom. Any bite will lift the shot and the float will automatically "lift" to indicate the bite. Even the most delicate of bites will register. Use any waggler float, although a light quill that can be cocked with a single shot gives the most dramatic and exciting lift. Ideal for shy biting fish such as crucian carp.

therefore you should place the rod on a rest and draw the line tight as before, so that the float is fishing at its correct setting. The most delicate of bites will lift that bottom shot, with the result that the float rises.

There is nothing that restricts this method to close range or specially delicate presentations. Provided the tackle is balanced, very heavy floats can be employed. Long-range missiles, for instance, taking many swan shot to cock, are just as sensitive as tiny quills. The difference is that, as they are designed for long range, and you must be able to see the lift, it is usually necessary to have the bottom shot bigger in order to give a

ABOVE RIGHT: Again the depth is accurately plumbed and the bottom shot rests on the bed. Even if you need to fish at long range, provided the tackle is properly balanced, even the most delicate of bites will still register. One of the most exciting forms of this method is fishing at night for crucians with a night-light. As the float lifts a dark band appears in the water.

more exaggerated lift. The same principle applies to driftbeater floats, where the sight bob is merely a visual aid in rough weather.

Lift float fishing at night for crucians using an insert waggler fitted with a night-light is exciting. If the rig is fished with one shot, say a BB, 1 in (2.5 cm) from the hook, and plumbed exactly so that it only just touches bottom, and the night-light is flush with the surface, the most delicate crucian bite is immediately detectable. Even the tiniest lift is seen as a dark band appearing in the middle of the shaft of brightness, which of course is twice as long as the light because of its own reflection (see page 80).

Slider Float

When you wish to fish with a float at any depth at which casting a fixed float the required distance is impossible, you have to resort to a slider. Any float can be converted to a slider by making it free running on the line and stopping it at the appropriate depth with a sliding stop knot and tiny bead.

Where a float has no bottom ring, an item of tackle called a swinger must be used. This was principally designed for very quick float changing to stop the need to break the tackle down completely, but is ideal also for use with the sliding float. The swinger is a fine length of silicon tubing force-fitted over a swivel, and the silicon itself adapts easily to a wide range of float stem thickness and then fits on to the bottom of the float.

To use the sliding float, shot the float as normal, with the float free running, and leave the stop knot only a short distance above the float so that you can check its setting. When you are satisfied, wrap a piece of counterbalance putty around the bottom shot. Cast to the required spot, and then keep adjusting the depth setting until the float tip just peeps above the water. You now know that the bottom shot is just touching the bottom. Then make a note of the position of your stop knot on the line for future reference, remove the counterbalance putty, and you're ready to start fishing.

Sliding floats are also useful for pike fishing with free-roving livebaits or when trolling free rovers behind a boat. This generally involves the use of slim, cigar-shaped pike floats with the line through the centre. The most effective way to fish them is as sliders, using stop knots and beads. One benefit of this approach is that it allows simple depth adjustments between each drift and presentation, thereby thoroughly searching the water at all depths to find the feeding fish.

To tie a stop knot, take a short length of monofilament of lower breaking strain than the main line, for instance 6 lb (2.72 kg) breaking strain when fishing with 12 lb (5.44 kg) breaking strain for pike, fold it in half and lay it along the main line. You will now have created a loop in the finer line. Hold one of the tails to the main line, while wrapping the other

Fishing with a Slider Float

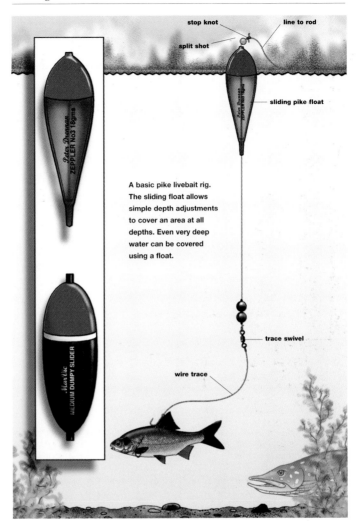

stop knot — line to rod

split shot

sliding pike float

A basic pike livebait rig. The sliding float allows simple depth adjustments to cover an area at all depths. Even very deep water can be covered using a float.

trace swivel

wire trace

ZEPPLER No3 18gms

MEDIUM DUMPY SLIDER

tail around the line four times and then passing it through the loop. Pull both tails tight, after first moistening the line to prevent excessive friction. Tighten until the knot slides only with difficulty, and you have it about right. Lastly, trim the tails to about $1/2$ in (1 cm,) and there you have your sliding stop knot. Many anglers recommend using power gum stop knots but ordinarily monofilament is quite sufficient.

Continual adjustment of power gum knots can eventually cut through the material so that it falls off the line, at which point you have to start all over again.

ABOVE: This diagram shows one example of a sliding float to present a free-roving livebait for pike. This method of presentation can be used from the bank or from a boat, although as most pike live close to the reed beds around the margins of lakes, bank fishing is most common.

When fishing from a boat, the boat is allowed to drift with the wind and the bait can be presented at various depths to search the water thoroughly for feeding fish.

The depth can be easily adjusted by moving the stop knot and bead up the line to increase the depth at which the bait is presented. The most normal presentation is as in laying on, when the bottom shot and bait are touching the bottom.

Float Legering

A specialized form of laying on is float legering, where the bottom shot is replaced by a standard leger weight. In this technique, the float is shotted so that it rides at its correct position, but is also anchored to the bottom to prevent drifting. The setting makes it very rare to get any bite indication other than a sudden disappearance of the float, as a fish takes line through the leger-weight swivel.

Float legering does not enjoy tremendous popularity now that very efficient butt indication systems are available, but it is worth considering in those circumstances where it still has great advantages.

The first is in medium- to long-range float fishing in very rough conditions where even a driftbeater lift float cannot cope with the undertow. These conditions are more easily tackled with conventional leger tactics, but if you gain more enjoyment from watching a float, then this is a situation that suits float leger tactics.

The second circumstance is if you need to fish over wide weed margins. A good approach is to grease the line from float to rod top to prevent it sinking into the foliage. This, though, can lead to severe drift problems with normal float fishing and the float leger is the ideal solution.

The third most common use is in predator fishing with legered deadbaits or paternostered livebaits off the bottom, especially from a boat. The paternoster is explained in the section on legering (page 93).

Pike and zander anglers wish to avoid one thing above all others: deep hooking. It can sometimes be difficult to know when to strike a pike run on leger tactics; in fact from a boat the motion of the waves can make bite detection difficult. The float leger solves that, as the only reason for the float to go under is the attentions of a pike. The float-paternostered livebait is also a good tactic for pike fishing in fast-flowing rivers, where a dragging paternoster link slows down the rate of progression of the bait downstream.

There are a handful of waters that actually have bans on straightforward legering; most of these waters have dense weed or lily-bed margins that have led to bad angling practices in the past, for example the use of excessively strong lines to drag fish through the undergrowth thereby causing damage. The famous tench water, Sywell reservoir, falls into this category and the float leger is now the standard tactic amongst Sywell angling regulars.

Float Leger: Wide Reed Margins

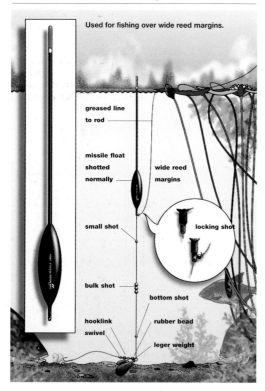

Used for fishing over wide reed margins.

greased line to rod

missile float shotted normally

wide reed margins

small shot

locking shot

bulk shot

bottom shot

hooklink swivel

rubber bead

leger weight

ABOVE: The float leger fished over wide reed margins. It is important to grease the line so that it does not sink as this would undoubtedly snag. The angler must ensure that the bottom lead is set at the correct depth and this may require trial and error to cope with the reed margin.

Float Leger: Deadbait Fishing for Pike

bead   stop knot

pike float fished as slider

TENPIN PIKE SLIDER No2

This rig is used as an alternative to simple freelining to give an early indication of a pike run. It is very appropriate when it is difficult to keep a tight line to the bait.

bulk shot to cock float normally

deadbait   wire trace   line of large shot   trace swivel

ABOVE: A traditional use for the float leger is when deadbait fishing for pike. The weight of the bait helps to anchor it to the bottom, preventing drift and the first indication the angler has of a bite is when the float disappears. This is a good rig when boat fishing.

Float Leger: Paternoster for Pike

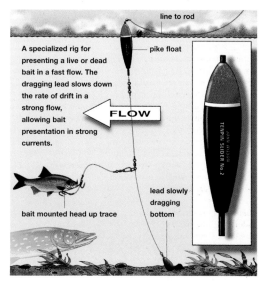

stop knot bead

pike float fished
as slider

A basic
paternoster rig
for presenting an
off-bottom bait.
This rig is for pike
but is also
effective for
zander.

swivel

snap link
trace swivel
wire trace

lead link of lower breaking
strain than
mainline
leger weight

Float Leger: Pike Paternoster for Rivers

line to rod

A specialized rig for
presenting a live or dead
bait in a fast flow. The
dragging lead slows down
the rate of drift in a
strong flow,
allowing bait
presentation in strong
currents.

pike float

FLOW

lead slowly
dragging
bottom

bait mounted head up trace

ABOVE: This is the same principle as the left diagram. The leger weight
slows down the progress of the livebait as it is carried downstream,
giving the pike more time to strike.

LEFT: Using this rig avoids the pike taking the bait right down and
prevents deep hooking as the angler can safely strike when the float
disappears. By substituting normal hooklink and normal baits, it can be
used to present static off-bottom bait for all coarse fish. The float is
used to keep the line taut.

Float Feeder

A natural progression from float
legering is float-feeder fishing, in
which the leger weight is replaced by
a swimfeeder, thereby ensuring
continual topping up of the loose feed
around the hookbait. The normal way
to feed when float fishing is to place
balls of groundbait around the float
periodically, or catapult quantities of
particles, or both. When fishing at
longer ranges, loose feeding with free
particles becomes impossible, and you
then have to rely on balls of
groundbait containing whatever
particles you are using.

The longer the range you fish, the
more problems you will have with
baiting accuracy, and in this
circumstance the float feeder is
appropriate. At least you can be
certain that there will always be feed
around the hook bait, whatever your
casting accuracy. You should still aim
to fish the same area consistently for
maximum angling efficiency, but
even the best anglers and finest

casters cannot hope to hit exactly the
same spot every time at 60 yds (55 m)
in a crosswind.

Why bother with a float in the first
place when it would be simpler to
revert to standard feeder tactics,
which in 99 per cent of cases would
be the most sensible course of action?
Many anglers do not enjoy their
fishing without a float to watch, and
this is a method that unites the
feeding benefits of the swimfeeder
with the aesthetic pleasure of
watching the float. The float feeder,
using very small feeders, is a popular
tactic at long range, especially on
bream waters where accurate baiting
of each cast is very important.

The most obvious use of the float
feeder, however, is in fishing over
wide weed or lily margins, in the
same way as for the float leger. Again,
straightforward feeder fishing may
create tremendous problems as the
weed inevitably wraps itself round
large lengths of sunken line. The float
feeder avoids this.

Float Feeder Rig

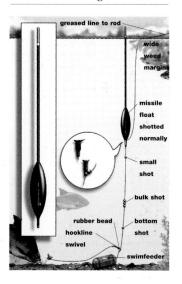

greased line to rod

wide
weed
margin

missile
float
shotted
normally

small
shot

bulk shot

rubber bead
hookline
swivel

bottom
shot

swimfeeder

ABOVE: An alternative to legering using a
swimfeeder that minimizes snagging.

Drift Float

On large stillwaters, normal methods of pike fishing limit the angler to about 80 yds (73 m) from the bank unless a boat is available, and considerably less if you are fishing with a livebait. To be able to fish beyond these limits demands the use of special drift floats designed both to catch the wind and to be visible at long range. The superb E.T. models fold flat during the retrieve, thereby presenting minimal water resistance, and are highly recommended.

As you can effectively fish the drift at ranges up to 200 yds (183 m) you need a large capacity fixed-spool reel loaded with a minimum of 12 lb (5.44 kg) line, which must be well greased. A long length of sunken line is going to present tremendous problems with drag. A useful piece of kit is an autogreaser, a rubber ring packed with grease that fits the butt ring. Fishing the drift float for pike demands great concentration at all times, because no other method of piking carries with it a greater risk of deep hooking. As soon as the float disappears, tighten down immediately, and set the hooks with a long sustained pull, walking backwards if possible. A normal strike is ineffective at such long range.

One of the real advantages of drift-float fishing is that it allows very thorough searching of a water at all ranges and depths. By progressively deepening the float setting between drifts, you can automatically locate hot spots such as gravel bars, as the float will stop drifting as it reaches the obstacle. As all predators love to hide behind such features, it is a good idea to search these areas thoroughly. The ideal weather conditions are a moderate to fresh breeze, which allows efficient drifting without the speed of drift being uncontrollable. Good drift floats will set lower in the water for more stability when there is a good wind and higher when you need to catch as much of a light breeze as possible.

The problem with drift-float fishing in very light winds is that having located a hot spot well offshore, it can be a frustratingly slow business getting another bait out there, especially if the wind changes direction quickly.

A livebait being retrieved long distances will quickly tire if it is attached to the trebles in the normal way – with the top treble attached below the dorsal and the lower treble in the top lip – as it will be retrieved against water pressure side on. If you are fishing with a drift float and a livebait, mount your livebaits head up the trace, as it is far easier on them during the retrieve.

Drift Float

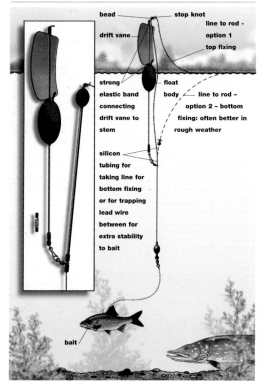

Night Float

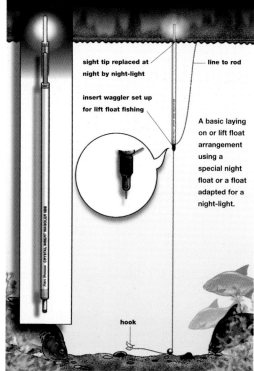

ABOVE: A specialized technique for taking pike at ultra-long range in large stillwaters. It demands constantly greased line to work effectively and the wind behind you.

ABOVE: An excellent rig for night fishing for crucian carp, bream, carp and roach. When a fish bites the float lifts and a dark band appears in the circle of light cast by the float.

Casting a Waggler Float

Fishing with a waggler float is a favourite method for many anglers and is commonly used on many stillwaters when fishing for roach, tench, carp and other species. The waggler is cast in an overhead manner, after which the line between the rod and the waggler is sunk beneath the surface of the water. This eliminates any drag on the float and enables it to hold its position. Once the float has settled in the water, the angler places the rod in the rod rest. When a fish bites and the float is drawn under, the angler picks up the rod and is into the fish. The tip of the waggler can be used as a marker at which to fire groundbait.

This photographic sequence shows the angler making the cast, after which the rod is placed in the rod rest and groundbaiting can begin.

1 The bale arm of the reel is opened to allow the line to run free. The line is trapped under a finger.

2 The rod is swept back over the head of the angler and then forward in one movement.

3 The float flies out towards the water and as it hits the water the angler slows down the line by cushioning the spool of the reel with his finger to act as a brake.

4 The bale arm of the reel is now engaged and the tip of the rod dipped under the surface. Two or three turns are wound on to the reel making the line sink under the water.

5 The rod is placed on the rod rest with the tip just under the surface. Should the angler have to react to a bite all he has to do is pick up the rod and connect with the fish.

6 Once the rod is safely in the rod rest the angler can start to catapult feed out towards the float. The tip of the float acts as a marker for the angler to aim at.

Casting and Striking with a Swimfeeder

Feeder fishing is a good way to catch bigger fish, especially bream, and uses a swimfeeder instead of a lead. The feeder is filled with groundbait and a few maggots and then cast to a mark in front of the angler. The feed inside will soon disperse, once the feeder has reached the bottom of the water. If the angler casts to the same spot each time eventually fish will be drawn to the swim. When the fish settle on the feed, the angler will start to catch them as they pick up the hookbait near the free offering of food.

This is a good method for bream. When hooked, play bream carefully as they are slow, dogged fighters, and if you are too hard on them they may throw the hook.

1 Fill the swimfeeder and then pick a mark on the far bank to aim at. Open the bale arm on the reel and face the front looking at the mark.

2 Swing the rod back and when the feeder is extended behind start the forward drive. Release the line so that it runs off the reel.

3 The rod is driven forward with the right hand and the left hand pulls the butt downwards to accelerate the progress of the cast.

4 As the swimfeeder and bait reach the water the angler cushions the spool with his forefinger to slow it down. The bale arm is still open.

5 When the feeder hits the bottom the rod tip falls back. Close the bale arm, bring the rod sideways and wind in until the rod has a slight curve.

ABOVE: A full moon rises on the water of a small lake. Fishing at night is full of surprises with strange noises and night creatures.

6 The angler places the rod in the rest and sits at a 45-degree angle as this will enable him to detect a bite from a fish. The soft-actioned rod tip will either be drawn forward or drop back slightly. The angler will strike if he sees either of these movements. Bigger bream tend to take the rod tip around in a slow, forward movement, giving plenty of time for the angler to connect with the bite.

7 When he sees a bite the angler raises the rod and strikes in a gentle manner. Smaller bream, called skimmers, will be lost if the strike is too hard. As the strike is made the angler watches the rod and feels the fish to gauge how large it is.

This fish is hooked and all that remains is for it to be brought to the net. Take care and do not be too hard on bream as they are easily lost.

Freelining

The simplest approach to angling is to have a hook and bait on the line and nothing else and where possible this is one of the most natural presentations you can make. Virtually every coarse fish can, at times, be pursued effectively using freelining tactics, from a single maggot on gossamer tackle trundling downstream towards a big dace over gravel shallows, or a chunk of liver fished in the margins for a giant catfish.

When to Use Freelining

True freelining is where the tackle is totally weightless, and therefore only certain conditions are suitable. For visual bite detection you have to rely on either watching the fish take the bait or seeing the line move, and if there is much wind the technique becomes difficult to apply and therefore ineffective.

Where you are freelining big baits for big fish in stillwaters, say large deadbaits for pike or catfish, you usually get decent runs, but even in these situations a good wind could force you to use some lead, so that you can tighten to the bait properly.

The most effective bite detection method for freelining in rivers is undoubtedly feeling the bites with your fingers, especially where there is a decent flow to tighten the line

naturally. Obviously, there will be a certain speed of flow where you will need to add lead, but where this can be avoided you can fish very delicately. Freelining slow-sinking flake over gravel shallows for chub, especially fishing upstream, allows the bait to bump back down towards you. Bouncing meat through a summer streamer bed for barbel is also an ideal freelining situation.

Stalking

Mobile stalking with natural baits is exciting fishing, especially on overgrown waters where your hunting instincts can come to the fore. Natural baits taken by fish include small fish, frogs, caterpillars, crayfish, and even young waterfowl. However, worms and slugs are the most common baits taken by fish and used by anglers.

The most important aspect of successful stalking is a stealthy approach. If you have managed to get within casting range of fish, say chub in a clearing in a rush bed or carp in dense lilies, without their being aware of your presence, and you are capable of a half-decent cast, there is no reason why the bait should not be taken instantly. All fish are opportunist feeders, and do not pass up the chance of a free meal if they have no reason to be alarmed.

Consider a large carp in the margins rooting around in the silt. This is a fish obviously feeding and searching for natural baits, an ideal situation for the presentation of free-lined lobworm or a bunch of redworms. If you have not spooked the fish on the cast, be prepared for what happens next, because it is very common for the carp to engulf the bait at top speed. You must be prepared for this potentially violent reaction by not having the line too tight, as this will result in a devastating smash and a badly spooked fish. Always allow a little slack to give the carp some time to turn with the bait before striking.

Sometimes, even if fish are not obviously perturbed by the bait's sudden appearance, they appear to treat it with indifference, and in these circumstances they need inducement to take your bait. This is particularly true of a chub. It can lie looking at the bait, totally disinterested, but suddenly pull it away and he pounces on it. Like a kitten with a ball of wool, it is an instinctive reaction.

A favourite example of stalking is fishing gravel shallows at dawn for big perch, using minnows or bleak. At this time of day, perch are voracious and very catchable from shallow water if you can keep quiet. Even though you may pinch a swan shot on the line when fishing minnow, it is still essentially freelining, and the bait is cast to the upstream end of the shallows and allowed to bump down with the flow. Takes can be savage, and you must stay alert and be prepared to give a little slack before striking. You may only retrieve the head of the minnow if you have the line too tight.

LEFT: An angler at his ease sits and lets the bait drop downstream in a fast-running weir pool. This is an excellent place to try freelining tactics.

Dense Baits

In high summer, many fish will be found lying in tiny gaps in foliage, and most of these swims will demand the use of totally static baits to prevent constant snagging. Natural baits such as slugs are nowhere near as effective here, as they are better fished on the move. For true static ambush baits in dense foliage, a heavy snag-resistant bait that hits the bottom quickly is ideal, and offerings such as cheese paste, luncheon meat or boilies can be more effective than naturals.

The swims that most require the use of dense-bait freelining are streamer weed beds, where the clear areas between the tresses are so narrow you need to be sure the bait sinks where it is cast. At first glance, a stretch of summer river apparently choked with ranunculus looks daunting, if not impossible, but 40 yds (36.6 m) of streamer weed can contain dozens of little clear runs, and each one can harbour fish, particularly chub, barbel and roach. Accurate casting is essential for successful freelining in streamer weed. The bait has to land in the clear water and sink naturally. If it alights on top of the weed itself and drags, you have blown your chances in that swim. Casting accuracy is easier with a heavier bait, and if chub or barbel are the quarry a good lump of cheese paste or luncheon meat is ideal. Fish lying under streamer weed take baits with great confidence as long as they arrive in a natural fashion, and large catches of summer fish are possible.

Apart from streamer beds, any densely overgrown area can often only be fished freelining heavy baits, and it is an undeniable fact that big fish of many species and dense snags go together. In such areas, rarely will you have the luxury of playing fish in the accepted sense of the word. The only option is one of hook and hold, for which adequate tackle is essential. You are well advised to step up your normal gear in these situations. For instance, a standard main line for carp fishing would be 12 lb (5.44 kg), but for short range stalking in snags 18 lb (8.16 kg) may be necessary. Strong hooks that will not pull out under extreme pressure are a must.

Deadbait

For really big pike, one of the most reliable methods is freelining large static deadbaits such as half a mackerel, herrings, or an eel section. These baits are dense enough to cast a fair distance without lead, but casting distance will be enhanced by using frozen baits. For a half mackerel, trim the tail fin and section the body at an angle, thus maximizing casting range. It goes without saying that you should freeze your baits individually and make sure they are straight. It is no fun on a freezing winter morning trying to unravel a whole block of frozen fish, and it's impossible to cast a herring shaped like a banana far .

You must utilize efficient bite registration when freelining for pike, in order to avoid a deeply hooked fish. It is therefore important to take in all the slack before attaching a drop-off pike indicator so you get instant warning of a pick-up. Make sure your indicator has enough weight to show drop-back bites. Very light arms may stay in place as the line is falling slack while a pike comes towards the bank with the bait. If wind or drift makes it difficult to tighten properly then you should use a little lead or a float. That bite must be seen immediately.

When freelining large deadbaits, a 20 lb (9.07 kg) wire trace at least 2 ft (60 cm) long carrying two treble hooks, in sizes 6 or 8, are suitable. The point of the upper treble is inserted firmly in the tail root while the lower treble is nicked as lightly as possible along the bait's flank.

For really tough-skinned baits, especially eel section, you can have problems pulling out of the bait and into the pike. You can either pare away a section of skin where the treble point is to go and then lightly hook into the flesh itself or, for long casting, nick the skin as lightly as possible and hold the trace in place for the cast by a tie of PVA string. It is a matter of personal preference whether you use barbless trebles or not; some anglers swear by them, while others have lost too many pike for their liking using them.

Whatever hooks you use, strike pike runs immediately and be properly equipped to unhook the pike quickly and without damage. Use wire cutters to snip off the barbs.

Making a Deadbait Trace for Pike

1 You will need: 20 lb (9.7 kg) seven strand wire; size 6 semi-barbless hooks; forceps; a twizzle stick; wire cutters; swivel; bomb weight with a large size 12 swivel; crimps; a pair of pliers; bore-run ring; an oval or rubber bead and bait.

5 Now thread on the second treble hook and move it down the trace until it is within 7 in (18 cm) of the bottom treble.

9 Thread the crimp on to the trace followed by the swivel. Now take the end of the wire back down through the crimp, trapping the swivel in the process. Pull the crimp tight to the eye of the swivel and crimp it in position using a pair of pliers.

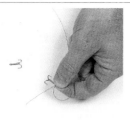

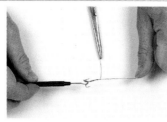

2 Cut a 20 in (50 cm) length of wire and thread a treble hook on to it at one end. Take the wire back through the eye of the hook, so the treble is now caught in a loop of wire.

3 Pull the tag end of the wire tight, trapping the hook. Then take the tag end in the forceps. Holding the hook in the twizzle stick, spin the forceps around the main wire trace.

4 Make sure the wire is twisted tightly in place and the hook is secure. Trim any remaining tag with wire cutters. This will not need crimping as twisting is sufficient.

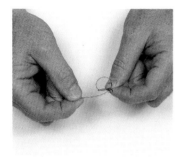

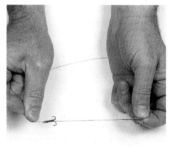

6 Bring the loose end of the trace around and under the treble hook so the wire is caught between the joint of the points on the treble. Pull the wire tight.

7 Start to wind the loose end of the wire back around the shank of the treble. At the top of the shank, take the wire up through the eye of the hook and pull it tight.

8 The second hook should now be held tightly in place by the wire trace. All that remains to be done is to crimp into position a size 12 swivel at the other end of the trace.

10 With the trace complete it is time to connect it to the mainline. Take the mainline from the rod tip and thread on a swivel bomb fitted with a large bore run-ring. The run-ring allows line to pass through it with minimal resistance when a pike picks up the bait. Thread on a bead; this acts as a shock stop for the lead. Take the mainline and tie it to the swivel with a five-turn blood knot.

11 With the rig tied up and ready to fish, all you need to do is add a bait. A whole mackerel can be used to good effect as a deadbait when seeking out pike. Take the top treble and push one of the hook points into the stem bone of the tail. The second treble is inserted into the flank of the mackerel. The bait is then cast out and the wait for a take begins.

Surface Fishing

Most species of coarse fish at some time or another will take baits off the surface, and this provides some of the most exciting visual angling there is. The surface-feeding behaviour of fish such as chub, rudd and carp is well known, but not so well known is that predators like pike, perch, catfish, eels and zander will take baits off the top. Even those bottom-feeding stalwarts, tench and barbel, occasionally behave in this manner, although this is rare.

Both stillwaters and rivers vary as to whether they are good surface-fishing venues or not, sometimes for no apparent reason. A general rule of thumb in rivers is depth; the shallower, more intimate venues are more prone to surface-feeding behaviour than deep, powerfully flowing stretches. This is no great mystery as fish in shallow waters are more likely to come into contact with surface food items on a regular basis.

Chub will be used to moths under trees, and roach and dace to small

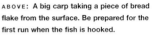

BELOW: Carp cruising on the surface on an estate lake. Good carp can very often be caught on a floating bait.

ABOVE: A big carp taking a piece of bread flake from the surface. Be prepared for the first run when the fish is hooked.

flies on the shallows. Narrow rivers are more likely to be overhung with foliage, especially in summer, and this leads to all manner of bugs, beetles and berries falling in to enhance the piscine larder beneath.

Although small intimate stillwaters often exhibit reliable surface feeding for similar reasons, there is no doubt that some waters are just not worth fishing off the top, while in others it is a deadly method. A famous example of this is the Redmire Pool, near Ross-on-Wye in Herefordshire. Although no one can deny that this is small,

overgrown and intimate, in fact it has always been a very poor surface water. Of all fish, carp are one of the happiest taking surface baits, but the Redmire carp are very reticent.

With all varieties of surface fishing except anchored techniques, the most important thing is to make sure the line between bait and rod top floats, otherwise long lengths of sunken line make any attempt at a natural presentation virtually impossible. Bear in mind the alternatives of line grease or silicone spray floatant, available in aerosol cans.

Running Water

There are certain river swims where floating baits are particularly effective. These are usually shallow, gravelly runs with a lively current, especially where the current starts to slow as the depth increases. These shallows often hold large numbers of fish in summer, as they are naturally high in oxygen.

The most reliable surface feeder in rivers is the chub, and the most basic bait is bread crust. Although allowing a chunk of crust to drift naturally with the flow is simple in concept, there are important considerations to avoid becoming frustrated with the technique. Natural bait presentation is vital. The crust must be free to follow all current variations, without moving unnaturally across the flow or, worse still, dragging and causing a wake. It requires practice to learn how much line to let out as the crust progresses downstream. Too little, too slowly, will result in drag, while too much will see loops of line on the surface drifting everywhere, possibly even pulling the crust off course, particularly on a windy day.

Other surface baits are often more effective for chub, especially when they have become spooked on crust after one or two have been taken on it. Items like dog biscuits, floating cereals or feed pellets can be used in

Pet-food mixer

Carp hook
and pellets

Surface controllers

A string of floating boilies

sufficient quantities to initiate preoccupied surface feeding, and this largely overcomes the chub's natural caution. Floating boilies also make superb chub baits.

Pet-food mixers and trout pellets are also very effective chub baits. They are the right size, visible at range, and remain buoyant for a long time. If you cannot obtain bait bands, trout pellets and pet-food mixers can be superglued to the back of the hook shank. For surface fishing, the floating putty, known as flotsam is good. A small rough piece attached to the line resembles a piece of bark and floats like cork. Attach flotsam approximately 18 in (45 cm) from the hook and it will serve both as an extra flotation aid and a sight bob, the latter being more important with small baits like trout or koi pellets, which can become extremely difficult to see at long range.

BELOW: A fast-running shallow on an overgrown stream. This type of water is ideal for surface fishing.

Calm and Stillwaters:
Fishing at Close Range

On quiet, overgrown river stretches, where a more orthodox approach is impossible, dapping is a method of fishing for chub in which you arrange for a natural bait to rest just on the surface film, with no surplus line to cause alarm. It is a particularly good method to use under overhanging trees, where the chub become used to insects of all types falling in the water. You can use deadbaits such as moths and caterpillars and impart life to them by gently twitching the line.

A similar process is fishing the margins of stillwaters for carp with crust. There the angler sits well back from the water's edge so that the rod just protrudes from the bankside cover. Slowly lower the baited hook so that it just breaks the surface film, and then stay alert, with slack line in your hand. Takes can be sudden and violent and these forms of close-range surface fishing are very exciting indeed. As this fishing will usually be close to snags, it pays to step up the gear, but this is not detrimental as no line will be on the surface anyway, the bait being all the fish sees.

Away from the margins of stillwaters, unfettered surface baits are still viable, but the further out you wish to fish the more casting weight you will require and the more troublesome any wind will become. An exception to this may be among dense lily pads, where the pads themselves both act as a brake again wind action and help to disguise the line. Good casting weight is provided by high-protein floaters, which despite being buoyant are quite dense. A terrific presentation is to hold a chunk of floater or crust hard against a lily pad with the line over it, which then looks completely natural.

Totally unfettered baits can also be used at greater range in stillwaters, taking advantage of any offshore breeze by drifting baits down the wind lanes. As with fishing rivers with trout pellets for chub, the longer you spend prebaiting these wind lanes with free offerings, say for carp or rudd, the greater will be the chances of success when they are followed by a hook bait. One ploy to use when surface fishing for carp in this way, when a good breeze is blowing across a bay and the windward bank has dense

rushy margins, is drifting freebies down wind. These will then pile up against the rushes, leading eventually to a good number of carp feeding there furiously.

In exactly the same way as river fishing, this drifting of freebies demands the use of greased line to fish properly. Carp will not tolerate any unnatural movement of the bait.

Drifting Stillwaters

If you want to fish a stillwater at long range with small, lightweight baits such as cereals, dog biscuits and trout pellets, extra casting weight is required to make the tackle controllable and some form of visual bite indication is needed. The simplest addition is a small self-cocking float, and this is the choice if you are simply drifting baits down wind lanes. Where much more casting weight is required, say for reaching a group of carp basking alongside lilies 50 yds (46 m) away, or a shoal of rudd priming well offshore, you will need to substitute the relatively light float for a floating carp bomb or controller. In essence this is a floating leger weight. With a controller, it is possible

to fish just as effectively on the surface as it is legering at the same distance, although obviously it is more difficult to maintain as direct a contact. Keep the controller about 30 in (76 cm) from the bait, and keep the line well greased.

One of the main problems with the method is false bites, or coming short, caused by fish spooking at the sight or feel of the hooklink. This can be tremendously frustrating when fishing for big carp, especially if a couple of fish have already been taken using this method.

An ingenious way round the problem is to use what is known as a suspender rig, designed to keep all but the bait off the water, even at long range. To make a suspender, take about 18 in (45 cm) of thin rigid rig tubing, and then glue a large polyball about a third from one end. Closer to the same end of the tubing, wrap lead wire until when testing in a bath of water it floats tilted at about 45 degrees. For fishing the suspender, run the line through the weighted end first and attach hook and bait. At this point you need to take care that the rig is exactly the right distance from

Controller Used for Floating Bait

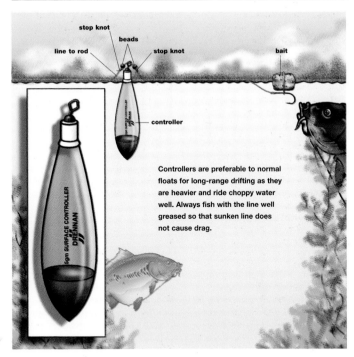

stop knot

beads

line to rod

stop knot

bait

controller

Controllers are preferable to normal floats for long-range drifting as they are heavier and ride choppy water well. Always fish with the line well greased so that sunken line does not cause drag.

Suspender Rig for Stillwater Drifting

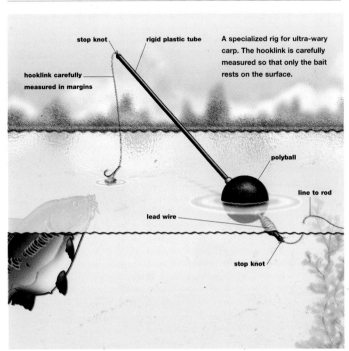

stop knot

rigid plastic tube

hooklink carefully measured in margins

A specialized rig for ultra-wary carp. The hooklink is carefully measured so that only the bait rests on the surface.

polyball

line to rod

lead wire

stop knot

the hook, as you want the bait to just rest on the surface; experiment in the margins to get this exactly right. When it is correct, place power gum stop knots at each end of the rig in order to keep it fixed. Hook-to-rig distance must be measured very accurately. If it is too long, line could lie round the bait in coils, destroying the whole purpose of the rig. If it is too short, a very light bait could actually hang clear of the water. When fishing the suspender, bites are very obvious and often very savage. The tilted tubing is highly visible, and really slaps down in the water when you get a take.

TOP: A floating bait with a controller. This enables the angler to present a floating bait to fish a considerable distance away in stillwater. The line needs to be well greased.

LEFT: A suspender rig is an ingenious device designed to keep everything off the water except the bait. It can be difficult to achieve the correct distance between hook and rig.

OPPOSITE: Surface fishing for carp feeding close-in on a still stretch of river. This can be one of the most exciting forms of angling.

Anchored Baits

When you wish to present a surface bait to carp or rudd out of normal casting range and there is so much wind or drift that you find it impossible to keep the bait where it is required, the anchored floater rig provides the solution. It is fished with a heavy lead of at least 2 oz (57 g), connected to a large diameter plastic ring, or floater loop, by a length of line that is lighter than the main line.

Having cast into position, leave the pick-up open to allow the bait to rise to the surface, which it does easily through the low-friction floater loop. Close the pick-up, take in the slack and wait for the bite. You will find that floating baits like chunks of crust or high-protein floater rise easily, whereas for items like pet-food mixers even the small amount of friction and line drag can hold the bait down below the surface. For these baits, it is advisable to doctor the hook with a little rig foam to increase its buoyancy. For bite detection, as it is essentially a tight line-legering technique, normal butt indication systems are ideal.

One of the major problems with all surface fishing, particularly with baits such as bread crust, is the attention of birds, both of water and air. This is where anchored methods have a slight edge. By taking in 1 ft (30 cm) of extra line, the bait can actually be fished just below the surface. This is still perfectly acceptable to the fish but not quite as obvious to passing feathered traffic, especially if there is a nice ripple. Obviously, birds will eventually find it, but the delay gives the fish you are seeking that much longer to get in first.

The deeper the water, and the weedier the bottom, the more difficult it becomes to fish the rig properly, and you need to use the longest bomb link possible, say with a free-running balsa float body to keep it up, so that the hooklink has the minimum distance to travel before breaking the surface. As it is obviously difficult to cast out with a 15 ft (4.6 m) lead link in place, you need to coil it carefully and tie it in place with PVA ties. As the PVA dissolves in water after the cast, the balsa takes the link to its full extension. The major problem with this set-up comes when playing a fish, as you now have a 15 ft (4.6 m) lead link swinging around, which is

The Anchored Floating Bait

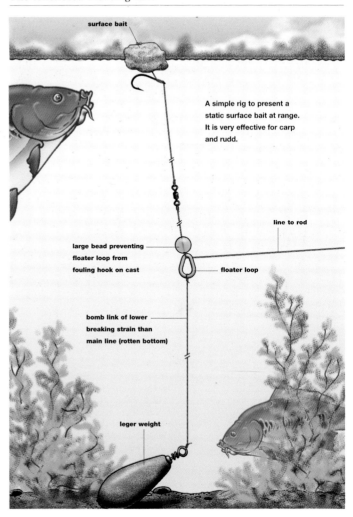

A simple rig to present a static surface bait at range. It is very effective for carp and rudd.

surface bait

line to rod

large bead preventing floater loop from fouling hook on cast

floater loop

bomb link of lower breaking strain than main line (rotten bottom)

leger weight

ABOVE: The principle of the anchored floating bait is simple in concept but it can be quite difficult to use in practice. It is really only needed when fish are moving on the surface, but there is a strong wind that blows the bait away from them. The best baits are chunks of bread crust or high-protein floaters that rise easily.

obviously a snagged line waiting to happen. It is always best, therefore, for the last 2 ft (60 cm) of the lead link to be of very weak mono, about 3 lb (1.36 kg), so that the lead breaks away easily if it does become hung up when you are playing a fish. If you do try this technique, do not use your best leads.

A variety of leads

Fly Fishing

At one time or another, most coarse fish can be taken fly fishing. The species most susceptible to this approach in rivers are chub, rudd, dace and grayling, and all these can be taken on either dry or wet fly depending on the day and the insects that are hatching. Chub are very appreciative of large patterns offering a substantial mouthful, and mayfly imitations in season, as well as large white moth and sedge patterns at dusk. They are also suckers for Pheasant Tail nymphs. Roach and dace will take any small dry fly pattern over streamy shallows. Grayling are very receptive to the dry fly, or standard wet fly such as Mallard and Claret, and also nymphs such as the Montana or Pheasant Tail.

Most fly-caught coarse fish will obviously be accidental captures taken when fishing trout reservoirs, but some of these are eye openers. Fly fishing with lures has proved one of the deadliest methods of taking perch. The most famous lure of all time for perch fishing was developed by the famous fisherman Richard Walker at

Hanningfield reservoir in Essex, called, not surprisingly, the Hanningfield lure. It was designed to imitate fry with two hooks in tandem, and is fished fairly deep in the water. Since then, most of the big trout waters have produced large perch that have fallen to lures fished on fast-sinking lines, three of the best patterns being Jack Frost, Sweeney Todd and Polystickle.

Lures and nymphs have also taken their share of roach and bream from trout reservoirs, while more and more anglers are targeting pike on large lures, drawn across reed beds presumably to imitate the flapping of young ducklings. Fishing for pike like this obviously requires a wire trace and it is better to use a trace of around 30 lb (13.6 kg). Lighter traces can be used but they are prone to kinking because of the continual casting required.

On intimate stillwaters, carp and rudd, when present, are frequently caught by anglers fly fishing – especially rudd, which are more tolerant of the heavy fly line than many other species.

TOP: A north country river that holds good chub, dace and grayling. Wet fly is the favoured form of presentation and the angler is here casting across under the trees.

ABOVE: Many good perch are caught in trout reservoirs usually on lures fished deep which they take for fry. Perch are a fine sporting fish and this is a good specimen.

Legering

Although basic freelining is an effective technique in ideal circumstances, it has inherent weaknesses. The casting range is obviously limited and will be dictated by the size of bait. Even with a large bait it will never be more than a modest distance, with the exception of freelined deadbaits for pike or catfish. Secondly, with a slack line out, it is sometimes impossible to tighten properly to the bait, and bite detection can be very hit and miss. This can lead to the unsatisfactory situation of the bait being moved a short distance before any indication is seen at the rod. This is unsafe as it has the potential for deep hooking. Bite-offs, when the fish sever the hooklink with their throat teeth can occur all too easily and all anglers know how easily perch, for instance, gorge baits.

ABOVE: Waiting for a bite. The contemplative angler sits beside the river as the water flows gently past him. Could any day be spent in more pleasant surroundings?

Using Leads

These problems are largely minimized by legering, which simply means using lead on the terminal tackle. This increases casting range and makes early bite indication more likely as the lead allows the slack in the line to be tightened up.

In its simplest forms, legering can be subdivided into fixed or running leads. A simple fixed-lead leger could be pinching two swan shot on the line 4 in (10 cm) from the hook – still an effective presentation for winter chub – while the simplest running leger could be using a standard Arlesey bomb leger weight, with the line free to run through the swivel. This is stopped by a bead above the swivel of the hooklink. This simple running

lead overcomes the problems of missed bites at range, the principle being that, as line is taken by a fish, it pulls through the swivel of the lead, giving early bite warning in whichever direction the fish is moving. The heavier the lead you use the more this will be true, because of its increased inertia.

There are many permutations and refinements of these basic legering principles to meet differing water conditions, such as heavy bottom weed. Each one is designed to allow easily adjusted bait presentation and to encourage timidly biting fish to give good bite indications. In the following pages are basic legering techniques that cover 99 per cent of the angling situations you are likely to encounter.

Sliding Link

The sliding link leger is a natural progression from the running bomb, and entails the weight being mounted on a separate link rather than on the main line itself. The simplest link leger of all is to pinch swan shot on to a doubled length of nylon, leaving a small loop in the nylon through which the main line runs. This is stopped from sliding to the hook by either a leger stop or a small shot.

The advantages of this arrangement over the lead being on the main line are twofold. Firstly, if you wish to change the amount of lead, there is no need to break down the terminal rig, you simply add or subtract the amount of shot. Secondly, in the event of snagging, the shots

Making a Simple Sliding Link

1 To make a simple sliding link you just need split shot, nylon monofilament and a hook.

2 Cut off a short length of nylon, fold it in half and pinch on the shot as shown, leaving a small loop.

3 Slide the link on to the main line and tie on the hook. Place a stop shot on the main line where required.

Making a Sliding Link with Swivels

1 You will need snap-link swivels, a suitable leger weight, nylon, hook and a rubber bead.

2 Tie the hooklink to the swivel. Place snap-link swivel and bead up the main line; tie in the second swivel.

3 Attach the hooklink to the bottom snap link. Clip the leger weight to the sliding snap link.

will pull off the nylon link, very often allowing recovery of the hook.

When you need to use lead more substantial than a few shot, the nylon loop is substituted for a snap-link swivel on the main line, which allows different leger weights to be clipped and unclipped in seconds. The extra mass means that it is rarely satisfactory to stop them above the hook by simple leger stops or split shot as they continually slip.

It is far better to prepare separate hooklinks with their own swivels, with a rubber shock bead between the swivel and the sliding lead link to protect the knots. For even greater versatility, terminate the main line with a second swivel and snap link, to which the hooklink swivel attaches. With this arrangement, not only can you change leads in seconds, but you can also change hooklinks as quickly.

Another variation on this principle is to attach the lead to a short length of nylon and a swivel before attaching it to the main line snap link. This is always used with the nylon link of low breaking strain, known as a "rotten bottom", the idea being that if the lead becomes trapped in a snag it will break away but leave the main terminal rig in place. Use this arrangement if adding a lead link for freelining for pike.

A further extension is to make the nylon link much longer – up to several feet – if you are trying to cope with deep bottom weed or silt in a still water, and combine that with a hookbait of neutral buoyancy so that it comes to rest gently on the weed or

silt, while the lead link sinks through it to the lake bottom, anchoring the rig in place. Again, this would usually incorporate a link of lower breaking strain than the main line. If you want to get really fancy, you can also place a balsa float body free-running on the lead link, ensuring that the main line is kept up in the water away from the bottom debris.

Fixed Paternoster

What differentiates the paternoster from link legers is that, whereas link legers have the lead on the main line above the hook, the paternoster is the opposite. They are weight-forward arrangements, with the hooklink above the lead. An example from modern carp fishing is the helicopter rig, designed for ultra-long casting with heavy leads. In this case, the distance from hooklink swivel to lead is usually shorter than the hooklink, but as it is a weight-forward arrangement it can be classed as belonging to the paternoster family.

When you have the problem of deep bottom weed or silt, the paternoster is a better solution, and far easier to cast than the sliding link. This will be incorporated with a free-running or semi-fixed hooklink several feet above the lead link, which again will be of lighter line than the main line in order to give the "rotten bottom" effect if necessary.

A semi-fixed hooklink can be created by connecting it to a run bead and plugging that to the lead swivel with silicon tubing, or by tying a stop knot and bead above the hooklink,

effectively jamming it. A fish pulling hard enough can move the hooklink in both cases, hence the "semi-fixed" label. Semi-fixed links often give more positive bite indication.

As the paternoster is a more aerodynamic rig than the standard link arrangement, it is the one to choose when long casting is required, and as long-range fishing often carries with it extra difficulty in seeing and hooking bites efficiently, the rig usually incorporates fairly short fixed hooklinks of only a few inches, which encourage positive bites. The fixed short hooklink paternoster has become a standard approach for still-water bream and tench anglers. This would normally include a heavy lead of at least 2 oz (50 g), pulling the line as tight as possible and using a heavy butt indicator. For stillwater bream especially, hooking on this arrangement is 100 per cent successful, most bites being sudden drops back of the indicator as a fish lifting the bait relaxes the tension in the tackle. The fixed hooklinks would normally be tied into the main line using water knots.

Bolt Rig

Where educated or nervous fish are giving tentative bites on normal legering tactics, often referred to as "twitch" bites, you have to find a way of accentuating the bites you are getting by encouraging the fish to move off with the bait in a more positive manner. The short hooklink paternoster encourages positive bites when used with a heavy lead and in

Making a Fixed Paternoster Rig

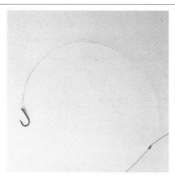

1 To make a fixed paternoster you will just require a leger weight or feeder, nylon monofilament and hook.

2 Tie the hooklink the required distance from the main line, using a water knot.

3 Attach the leger weight, or feeder if you are using one, to the end of the main line.

4 Feeders can be used in a paternoster instead of a leger.

5 The completed rig, as step 3, with a feeder instead of a weight.

fact this could be considered to be a type of bolt rig, as indeed can the carp angler's helicopter rig. The name originated because the purpose of the rigs is to make the fish bolt with the baits in their mouths, thereby giving unmistakable indications.

Pure bolt rigs, however, take that general principle one stage further in that they will normally feature the bait mounted on a hair rig with the hook itself being bare, so that the hook point pricking the fish further encourages it to bolt.

The standard bolt rig is very similar to the earliest leger arrangement of a running or semi-fixed lead on the main line above the hooklink, although the bolt features a much heavier lead than is actually needed for the cast, coupled with a very short hooklink of about 6 in (15 cm). It is fair to say that such rigs are mainly used by carp anglers, although they are becoming more in

vogue with barbel anglers fishing statically for bigger-than-average fish.

One adaptation, which is now the most often used rig by carp anglers, is to swap the normal bomb leger weight for an in-line, drilled streamlined lead, which is very resistant to snagging. These leads are used with stiff tubing through the centre, through which the main line passes, this tubing being connected by silicon tubing to the hooklink swivel to make the lead semi-fixed.

Most anglers using bolt rigs will do so in combination with braided or dacron hooklinks, and if long casting is involved a substantial problem exists as the limp hooklink materials will tangle around the main line. To overcome this, these rigs usually incorporate a length of rig tubing longer than the hooklink above the lead. During flight, the heavy lead obviously flies in advance, with the hooklink trailing behind. It is at this

stage that the anti-tangle tube prevents the link curling around the main line. If you want to avoid tubing but still use braids, another solution is to use a setting gel that quickly dissolves in water. Some gels stiffen the link for casting, but revert to normal after a few minutes immersion in the water.

Feeder Bolt Rig

There are three variations of the feeder bolt rig for use in stillwaters, the most commonly used being in essence identical to the short hooklink paternoster, with a heavy swimfeeder replacing the lead. This is the rig that has become a standard for stillwater roach anglers, and has solved the infuriating problem of missed bites. It normally features a light hooklink about 18 in (45 cm) above a 2 oz (50 g) blockend feeder, baited with maggots or casters. After casting, the line is drawn tight, a heavy butt indicator attached, and most bites are indicated by a dramatic drop back.

The second version has an in-line swimfeeder on the main line 18 in (45 cm) above the hooklink, with a 2 oz (50 g) bomb on the end of the line, as in a normal paternoster. When the cast has been made, the action of drawing the tackle tight invariably pulls the terminal rig a little way towards the bank. In the first arrangement, this will pull the hookbait away from the maggots escaping from the swimfeeder whereas in this case, it pulls the hook towards the free offerings. This is a small point that could make all the difference on a hard day.

1 The components required are hook-link material, leger weight or feeder, swivels, snap links, silicon tubing, a bolt bead snap link and a hook.

2 Tie the hooklink to the hook and swivel. Slide the bolt-bead snap link up the main line, then the silicon tubing. Attach second snap-link swivel.

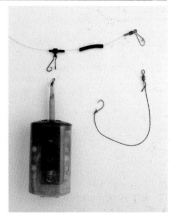

3 Make sure that the hooklink is the correct length and then attach the leger weight or swimfeeder to the top link.

4 The completed bolt rig using a swimfeeder.

5 The completed bolt rig using a leger weight.

6 The completed bolt rig with a lead and a hair loop at the hook.

When roach fishing in either of these styles, which could see only 2 lb (0.91 kg) hooklinks and size 16 hooks, it is fatal to strike as such, as it is easy to crack off on a tight line. It is sufficient to simply lift the rod and start playing the fish. It is also one of those occasions to backwind rather than use a clutch.

Casting heavy feeders requires a main line of at least 6 lb (2.72 kg) breaking strain, and it is impossible to set a clutch to suit a 2 lb (0.91 kg) hooklink in these circumstances. To protect the light hooklinks during the playing of a big roach, or anything else that takes the bait for that matter, many anglers insert a short length of power gum or pole elastic above the hooklink as a shock absorber.

The third bolt-feeder arrangement is very much in vogue these days, especially on commercial small carp fisheries, and it is called the method feeder rig. A ball of groundbait and mixed feed particles is moulded round a special method feeder and the hookbait, invariably mounted on a very short hooklink, is pushed into the side of the feed. The idea is that the fish start rooting around in the bait, breaking it down, and the hookbait is taken quite naturally as it falls free of the whole. It is a devastating presentation and has led to many large catches.

7 The bolt rig ready to fish with a boilie mounted on the hair rig.

The Knotless Knot

The knotless knot or 'no knot' is widely used by carp and specimen hunters when presenting baits like boilies on a hair rig. It is so called because no knot is actually tied and the whole tying relies on tension and whipping to keep it in place. It allows the angler to incorporate the use of a hair rig on to the hook without the need to tie off a separate knot for the hook, and then a separate knot for the hair. The knotless knot provides both in the same tying sequence. To make the best of this knot it is advised that the hair loop is tied into a length of hooklength material and that the bait is actually mounted on to the hair, before the hook is tied in, as shown in this sequence. Doing this allows the angler to measure out an exact distance for the hair in relation to the size of the bait and the hook used.

Once the bait has been mounted on to the hair, the free end of the hooklength is passed through the eye of the hook and the baited hair is lined up with the back of the shank on the hook. When it is in the correct position the 'no knot' can be tied. With the bait in the correct position the angler would be well advised to whip the hooklength line around the hook shank, trapping the hair, in a manner that takes the hooklength line away from any join in the eye of the hook. This stops the hooklength line biting into a groove and doing any damage to the hooklength material.

Once the line has been whipped around the shank six to eight times the end of the hooklength is passed back down through the eye of the hook. When pulled tight, the tension holds in place both the hook and the hair rig. For added security a dab of strong glue can be used on the finished whipping. It is important that the hooklength is passed back through the eye in a downward fashion. Doing this ensures that the hook is held at an offset angle, and this allows a better hooking presentation. This knot can only be used with eyed hooks, as it is the eye of the hook that provides the anchorage hold for the hooklength.

ABOVE: You will need: scissors, hooklink material, boilie stops, boilie needle, swivel and a hook.

Presenting a Pop-up Boilie with a Knotless Knot

1 A completed knotless knot tied with a pop-up boilie. This knot is easy to tie and reliable.

2 Here a small silicone sleeve has been threaded on to the hooklink and over the shoulder of the hook.

3 The sleeve holds the hair rig in place. The hair rig is attached to the lead and the rig is now ready to cast.

4 The cast has been made and the boilie rises "popped-up" from the bottom.

Tying the Knotless Knot

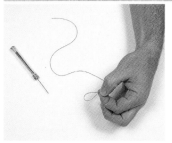

1 Form a loop in the end of the hooklink. Hold it in place between thumb and forefinger.

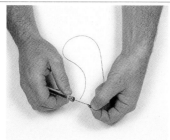

2 Pass this loop around the line to form a second loop. Pull first loop through and catch it with the needle.

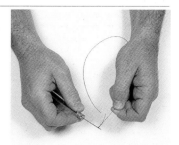

3 Pull the first loop tight making a tight loop in the hooklink and trim off the spare end.

4 Select the boilie that you want to use and then push the boilie on to the needle.

5 Pass the boilie needle through hooklink loop so that the boilie can be threaded on to the hooklink.

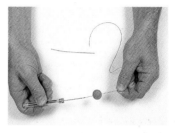

6 Pull the boilie over the loop so that it lies on the hooklink, ready for the next stage.

7 Push the boilie stop through the loop, and pull it tight to hold the boilie securely in place.

8 Thread the hooklink through the eye of the hook and position it the required distance from the boilie.

9 Tightly whip seven turns of line around the hook shank and hair rig. See the turns are even.

10 Pass the end of the hooklink back through the hook eye.

11 Pull tight and the knotless knot is now complete.

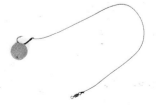

12 Attach swivel to the hooklink and the rig is now ready.

Touch Legering

Although the quivertip is certainly the most common form of bite detection when legering in flowing water, there is no method of bite detection that can match the sensitivity of touch legering, especially at night.

Touch legering requires some current to tension the line and requires practice to perfect, but once mastered you will find that no other method of bite detection gives such an instant warning. This applies equally upstream or down. For normal downstreaming, the urgent tightening of the line acts like an electric shock, while in the upstreaming situation, the sudden removal of tension from line that was as taut as a banjo string is equally unmistakable.

Initially, take a few trips to an easy river, one perhaps containing a good head of medium-sized chub. With bites plentiful, you will soon experience the range of bite variations. It is a good idea to touch leger without a quivertip in daylight to start with, as it is a good grounding for when you start fishing after dark and your fingers provide the only early-warning system.

There are two methods of touch legering, both equally efficient. The one you choose depends on personal preference. You can crook a little line

Ways of Touch Legering

1 Touch legering with the line held on the forefinger of the right hand holding the rod.

2 Touch legering with the line held in the left hand. The choice of method is entirely personal.

over the index finger of the hand holding the rod or you may prefer to take a loop of line in the other hand.

Bites on your fingers are generally unmistakable, an initial pluck being followed by a slow draw. Occasionally, however, you will experience a succession of small plucks and often these will be so delicate that no indication is seen on the rod top. These are sometimes caused by fish rolling the bait in the mouth and a strike can provide a bonus fish. More often, however, small bites take the form of fast jabs, particularly from suspicious fish in hard-fished stretches. There is a high percentage of missed bites when striking at these

indications. In these circumstances, a switch to upstreaming often works, as you are then waiting for the collapse of the line tension over your fingers, which is easier to detect.

For the most efficient touch legering, arrange for the rod top to be pointing at the bait as much as possible, although modern frictionless rod rings make this less vital than it used to be. The shallower the line angle, the more direct contact you have with your quarry. Touch legering, especially in the dark, is fascinating fishing.

BELOW: **Fishing the swimfeeder at long range on a stillwater.**

Swimfeeder Fishing

Although the feeder has wide application in stillwaters, the orthodox application of the swimfeeder is in streamy water, where its use is in ensuring a constant flow of bait down the current. A general rig arrangement is exactly the same as a sliding link with snap link swivels, the swimfeeder merely replacing the lead. In summer, feeder fishing in fast-running water is more effective the more often you cast and the more bait you use. This is particularly true when using maggots, and the minimum bait to use is 4 pints (2.28 litres). Cost is obviously a limiting factor, but this is one technique where you can buy your bait.

Streamer Beds

Streamer beds are particularly good feeder swims, as careful positioning of each cast between streamer tresses ensures that the loose feed continually follows the same narrow band. Accuracy of casting with a feeder, and then ensuring it remains put after settling, gives the most efficient presentation possible. To prevent rolling, oval blockends are good for streamer work and you may also want to carry a selection of clip-on leads to cope with brisker than normal flows. Use as long a tail as possible, up to 3 ft (90 cm), so that the maggot hookbait is free to follow the same undulating path as the streamer tresses. The density of the vegetation will be the limiting factor for how long that link can be before it becomes a handicap. Always fish the feeder free running. Fixed blockends do not travel easily through streamer roots.

Main Species

The species of interest to the summer river feeder angler are roach, dace, bream, chub and barbel, and for all those species except barbel ready-tied super spades, in sizes 12 to 16, to 4.5 lb (2 kg) nylon are recommended. For barbel, a size 12 super spade is appropriate, but tie it to a minimum of 6 lb (2.72 kg) invisible line.

As well as maggots, feeder techniques are effective with all other baits, using open-ended feeders loaded with suitable loose feed. Obviously, open-ended work is best utilized in the streamier flows, where the current does the important bait distribution work. Of the larger baits, bread flake fished on a longish tail, in conjunction with a mixture of liquidized bread, grilled hemp and milk powder for visual attraction is a favourite. If you are using a flavoured bait, make sure that the feed is similarly flavoured.

Open-ended feeder work with particles is carried out in conjunction with "exploding" groundbait plugs, which blow the particles free of the feeder. This is achieved by the simple expedient of mixing the normal liquidized bread/additive combination with a quantity of dry sausage rusk. Only moments after the cast, the rusk absorbs water so quickly that it rapidly expands, causing an underwater bait explosion. The most used particles with the open-ended feeder are casters and sweetcorn.

Winter Fishing

Feeder applications for winter fishing will follow similar lines when water temperatures are good, although maggots are used far more in the winter than in summer, when other particles are favoured, as small fish are far less troublesome.

The obvious differences in winter are sparser weed growth, enhanced height and flow speeds, and lower water temperatures, factors which affect winter feed rates. Approach depends entirely on water temperature. If favourable, even more bait than normal is used, to offset the dispersal effect of the flow. For winter chub or barbel fishing, a gallon of maggots would not be too much when recasting every few minutes throughout the day. The other important detail is to ensure that your feeder consistently presents the stream of bait down the same line. The faster the current, the easier it is to get this vital ingredient of successful feeder fishing wrong. Do not be afraid to pile lead on the feeder to ensure that it stays put. Bait that is scattered all over the river because the feeder is too light, and rolling all over the place, is worse than useless. This is when flat-bottomed feeders come into their own.

Another feature of winter fishing with the feeder, when the weed is much sparser, is that you can use lighter hooklinks, and this can make all the difference in clear water.

When the water temperature is 40°F (5°C) or less, and the water is low and clear, maggots fished in conjunction with the feeder can be one of the most effective methods for chub, roach, dace and grayling, but the clarity of water demands the finest terminal rig you can safely use. A size 16 Super Spade to 18 in (45 cm) of 2.6 lb (1.18 kg) mono is typical.

The quantity of free feed should be cut right back, and you should use a far smaller feeder in winter so that there really is the most modest trickle of loose maggots becoming available at any one time. In very cold water, though, even the maggots become lethargic, and it pays to enlarge the holes in the feeder to facilitate the ease with which they can escape.

Making a Sliding Swimfeeder

1 You need: snap-link swivels, rubber bead, swimfeeder, nylon, a hook. First tie hooklink to swivel, then place the feeder up the main line.

2 Add the bead, then tie in the snap-link swivel to the end of the main line. Finally attach the hooklink to the bottom snap link.

Upstream Legering

It is true to say that 99 per cent of all legering on rivers is carried out downstream, with bites being signalled by the quivertip pulling round. Much of the time, however, an upstream presentation is superior, for example when dealing with jabs on the rod top which prove difficult or impossible to hit, the kind of indication common with roach at short range. The upstream presentation will see all resistance removed when the fish pulls the bait downstream, so it holds on to the bait for that vital few moments longer.

A second major advantage of upstream legering is that it can automatically locate a hot spot in a swim, by periodically shifting the lead so that it bumps down the flow. Natural obstructions such as rises in the gravel bed and weed roots will halt the progress of the lead.

When legering downstream, most anglers sit upstream of the swim and fish each area in turn by casting across and down to it, and this simple method catches fish consistently. However, there are weaknesses associated with a succession of down and across presentations. First, as you cast to each area in turn, there is the initially alarming effect of a lead

plummeting into the swim. Obviously, the fish soon recover their composure if they are feeding hard, but it is nevertheless a frightening effect you can do without. You may decide to cut down the amount of casting by rolling the bait into position rather than casting directly to the swim. You can do this by casting to the far bank, fishing that side for a while and then, by lifting the rod point, encourage the terminal rig to roll across river to search other areas. Although this minimizes disturbance, the tautness in the tackle means that, when the bait rolls into midstream and then into the near bank, it does so in an arc across the flow. This is highly unnatural and could be enough to dissuade a suspicious fish from intercepting the bait. Also, the bait will only ever fish on the line of each arc, and in a big swim this can mean a lot of water being unfished.

Upstreaming largely overcomes these objections. Sit at the furthest downstream extremity of the swim and cast two yards above the upstream point of the swim on the far bank. After the lead has settled, the intention is to work the bait progressively down the flow, allowing it to settle for perhaps five minutes and then repeating this at intervals

down the run or where a natural feature halts the lead's progress. To do this, the rod point is lifted, and a little line is drawn, which dislodges the lead so that it bumps downstream into the required position. That is the first difference to note. The lead bumps downstream in a straight line rather than moving in an arc because the upstream presentation has allowed the creation of slack line when the lead is disturbed.

The entire far bank run could be searched in this progressive manner, every inch of bottom having been covered perfectly naturally and without once having to cast directly at a feeding fish. The next move is to cover the midstream run and near bank run in the same way.

Using Different Leads

For efficient upstream legering, the standard snap-link leger gives the ability to change leads quickly. This is important as a single swim may require a different lead at different points along its length to attain the correct presentation. The lead must be such that it holds steadily against the flow, but only requires a gentle

BELOW: **A barbel swim on the River Thames, best fished upstream.**

pull to be dislodged. Once disturbed, it should quickly settle again and not wash downstream too easily. Generally speaking, if the lead moves a couple of feet downstream and then re-settles, you have it about right.

The quivertip is essential for efficient upstreaming. Work on the principle that you need a 4 in (10 cm) upstream deflection in the tip to be maintainable before the lead yields to the pressure and bumps downstream.

Bites are normally a bump on the tip followed by a kickback due to relaxation of tension.

Certain static situations demand the upstream leger. These include slacks behind rush beds or rafts, or fishing the downstream areas of a line of bushes or trees. Often, the only efficient approach is from downstream of the swim. Reliable winter swims are a "V" of quiet water created by mid-river rush beds.

ABOVE: A lively weir pool much loved by both fish and fishermen. This type of water is ideal for presenting a bait on an upstream leger – use a weight of lead that holds against the flow, but is easily dislodged by a pull.

This area can be tiny, so aim for the bait to fish at the point of the "V" in normal flow, or tighter behind the obstruction at higher levels.

You do not want the bait to move once it is in position, and it pays to use a little more lead in these places when fishing a steady glide. The reason is that although the bait is fishing an area of quieter water, often an intervening faster flow has to be taken into account.

Upstreaming is vulnerable to false bites if there is much flotsam in the river. It takes very little drifting weed to dislodge a critically balanced terminal rig. If this is a problem, and it is quite likely to be so in a flood, put more lead on than normal, and try to ignore the rubbish hitting the line. A bite from a big fish will still be obvious. These conditions are ideal for barbel, and you won't mistake bites from those.

LEFT: Using an upstream leger in winter, searching out chub behind a weed raft.

Pole Fishing

A pole is simply a rod without a reel, with the line attached directly to the end of the pole and spare sections added to the butt section to present a bait delicately or to give extra cushioning effect to any bigger fish you might hook. Long poles are available so you can easily fish the far bank of a fairly wide river. When a fish is hooked, if it requires netting, it is brought close enough by dismantling the butt of the pole section by section.

When to Use a Pole

Despite the fact that quite big fish can be landed on the pole, it is essentially a technique best suited for small- to medium-sized fish and is not suitable for specimen hunting. Match fishing, where speed fishing for small fish is vitally important, is where the pole comes into its own.

Its advantage is in the accuracy and delicacy of bait presentation it allows. It is possible, for example, to place a bait right under the foliage of the far bank of a canal. As there is very little line in the water between float and pole top, problems with wind or drift are largely eliminated, allowing you to keep your bait tight to your loose feed at all times. Tackle can be very fine indeed, and because of the close control, floats need only have whisker-fine tips, shotted down so that the merest flicker from a small fish is registered.

There are three types of pole assembly: put in, put over and telescopic. The first two are relevant to long poles, the put-over joints being the better arrangement. In this, the smaller section near the tip fits over the thinner section of the next section down and so on. This arrangement gives a uniform taper. The put over has two advantages. First, if the joint starts to wear, the thinner section, being on the lower joint, merely inserts slightly deeper and is still a good fit.

In the "put in" arrangement, the top sections fit in to the lower sections and not over. Joint wear could see the entire thinner section sliding into the one below it, making an expensive pole unusable. The other disadvantage of "put in" is that, like a normal rod spigot, the thinner section has a parallel taper on the joint section for a snug fit, but this makes unshipping butt sections very difficult when the pole is flexed with a bigger than average fish.

Telescopic poles are much shorter, to a maximum of around 23 ft (7m) and are known as whips.

Poles and Whips

There are a tremendous number of poles available and as with all things in life, you get what you pay for.

Poles

Pay as much as you can afford. As cheaper poles can be either too heavy, too fragile or too floppy, they can be difficult and inefficient to use. As a general principle, the lighter and stiffer the pole is, the more relaxing it will be. Always give consideration to the type of fishing you will be doing before buying. A match angler might opt for a very stiff and light pole, which he can hold effortlessly for the duration of the contest, whereas the pleasure angler targeting carp needs a little more flexibility in the tip. The latter would be the choice for the all rounder, but the pole must come with a "spare top three" kit.

This means that you have the option of using the spare three top joints fitted with stronger elastic (see pages 104–5). In a situation where you are fishing with, say, a number 3 elastic for small bream and decent tench move into the swim, you might need a heavier grade elastic, say number 8. Rather than breaking down the rig, it is far quicker and easier to replace it with spare top sections, which are already rigged with heavier grade. The top match anglers will carry several spare "top threes"

ABOVE: **Pole fishing on the river Shannon, Ireland.**

rigged with different elastics, in order to save valuable fishing time.

The elastic used in pole fishing is the shock absorber, as you cannot give line as you can with rod and reel. With fine elastics 1 and 2 for small fish, you need only rig the tip section. Elastics 3 to 6 are preferably set inside the top two sections, while the top three sections should be rigged with the heavier elastic grades when bigger fish are expected.

Whips

With telescopic whips, it is impossible to remove sections once you are fishing. The bottom sections can only be removed by sliding them over the top, and you therefore set the length before fishing commences. You could, for instance, fish a 13 ft (4 m) whip using the top four sections of a 23 ft (7 m) assembly. Match anglers would again carry several different length whips. Elastics are not used as top sections, known as "flick tips", are ultra fine. The line is fitted directly to the flick tip by first passing it through two lengths of fine silicon tubing. The first length is slid over the tip, trapping the end of the line, which is then wound round the tip several times before the second length of tubing is slid halfway over the end.

Tackle

Pole fishing requires a good deal of specialist tackle.

Bungs, Bushes and Connectors

Elastic is anchored at the base of the appropriate pole section with a bung. In the case of the "put over" pole, the bung must be sited far enough inside the pole section so that it does not interfere with the fitting of the next section. It is fitted with a strong length of nylon for removing it. At the pole tip, the elastic runs through a PTFE (Teflon) bush, which must fit the tip snugly. As tips are usually uncut, trim it a fraction at a time until the bush will barely fit the hole. It should have the smallest practical bore for the elastic. Finish with fine wet-and-dry sandpaper. Where the elastic emerges from the pole tip, it must be secured in a Stonflo tip connector, a little device attaching the elastic to the terminal rig nylon.

Elastics

Elastics come in ten grades, numbered 1–6, plus 8, 10, 12 and 14, ranging from 2.5 lb (1.13 kg) breaking strain to 16 lb (7.26 kg) for number 14. It is very important to keep pole bushes as clean as possible, and apply a little pole-elastic lubricant before each fishing session.

Pole Floats

In general terms, pole float design follows the rules for ordinary floats. For stillwaters you would generally opt for a body-down design with a longish tip for stability; for canals with a little drift or very slow rivers the classic shallow oval or stick float is appropriate; while for faster flowing rivers you need the body-up design of the Avon float. Obviously, pole floats are far smaller, and extensive ranges are available. Most pole anglers have their various rigs, plus spares, made up on winders for quick changing.

Although the top match anglers will use pole floats with very fine wire or bristle tips for ultimate sensitivity, they are extremely difficult to shot correctly and the pleasure angler is better off selecting a float with a more substantial tip. Also, pole stem material can be important. For fishing hard on the bottom, a wire-stemmed float gives more stability, whereas a carbon-stemmed design gives a slower terminal rig descent for fishing "on the drop".

Most anglers use three lengths of silicon tubing to secure the float to the main line to prevent float slippage when playing a fish. The bottom piece normally overlaps the float base to eliminate tangles.

Pole Weights

These will be either small split shot, styl weights or olivettes. Styls are sausage-shaped and need to be put on the rig with special pliers. Olivettes are pear-shaped with a centre bore and are usually used as bulk shot with tiny split shot at the business end. They are available non-bored with bristle ends, so that they can be fitted to the line with two bits of fine silicon tubing for quick weight adjustment.

Pole Hooks

Hook sizes rarely exceed size 16 for pole fishing, although anglers that are pole fishing carp fisheries with pastes may go as big as size 8. In the smaller sizes, from 16–22 eyed hooks are too bulky and a more delicate presentation is achieved with spade-end patterns. For casters, maggots and hemp, the normal choice is sizes 18–22 fine wire hooks, with hemp mounted on a wide-gape pattern. Bread and paste baits would normally be fished using a longer shank hook with an in-curved point.

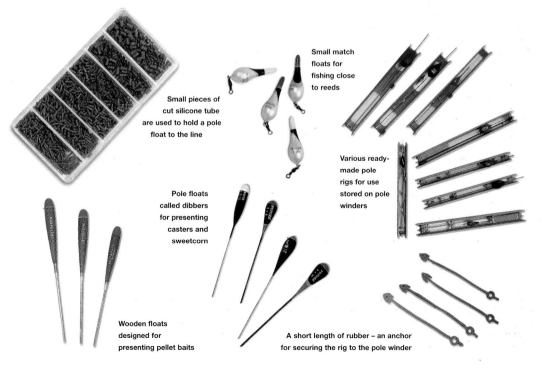

Small pieces of cut silicone tube are used to hold a pole float to the line

Small match floats for fishing close to reeds

Various ready-made pole rigs for use stored on pole winders

Pole floats called dibbers for presenting casters and sweetcorn

Wooden floats designed for presenting pellet baits

A short length of rubber – an anchor for securing the rig to the pole winder

Lines

Main lines and hook lengths should be balanced to the pole elastic when they are in use. For instance if you were using a very fine number 2 elastic, you would want no thicker than 0.08 mm Pro Micron, whereas you could double that diameter if fishing a size 14 elastic.

Pole Rollers

When fishing the longer poles, you will need a roller behind you to take the weight. The technique with a roller is to first find the balance point of the pole when sitting on your box. Then place the roller at the end of the pole. This means that when pushing the pole backwards the weight is supported at all times, and when pulling it forwards to put a bait out the pole will be balanced when it comes off the roller, which avoids jerking as you take the weight.

Pole Cups

For accurate loose feeding, a clip-on pole cup is invaluable. Place the selected feed in the cup, clip it to the pole, and deposit it at exactly the right place. Nothing could be simpler.

Catapults

For constant drip feeding of bait samples, a fine latex catapult is invaluable. A catapult with a mini or micro pouch is perfect for delivering a few maggots or casters at one time.

Pole Elastic

When playing a fish while using a pole all the shock of the fish fighting the hook is absorbed through an internal elastic. The type used will depend on the size of the species the pole angler is fishing for. Small, silver fish, such as roach and small bream, skimmers, need a size 3 or 4 elastic. When it comes to tench or carp, a heavy elastic with a rating of 8, 10 or even 12 would be the right choice.

To elasticate the pole you will need the following equipment: the elastic of the number you require; a bung to go at the base of the pole section; a PTFE (hard plastic) bush to fit the tip of the pole; a connector to join the elastic to the end tackle; a fine wire elastic threader used to thread the elastic through the pole

How to Elasticate a Pole

1 Here a number eight elastic has been selected as the pole is to be elasticated for small carp. Alongside the elastic are a bung, bung retractor, PTFE tip and a connector.

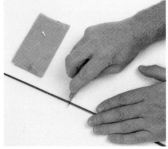

2 As the pole is to be fitted with a heavy-grade elastic, the tip should be cut back to accommodate this. If the tip were left at its full length, there is a possibility that it might snap if a bigger carp was hooked.

3 Score the outer wall of the pole tip. Once the whole circumference of the pole tip has been scored, it can be snapped. The cut-back tip section should then be cleaned with a small piece of fine sandpaper.

4 The PTFE bush tip is then inserted into the end of the tip. You may find trial and error is the only way you are going to get an exact fit. If this is the case, cut away a small bit of the tip section at a time, until you arrive at the right fit for the PTFE tip.

5 Thread the wire elastic threader through the tip section and out at the base of the second or third section of the pole. The end of the threader has a diamond eye. This will grip the elastic while it is being drawn up through the inside of the pole.

6 Once the elastic has been drawn through the inner walls of the pole sections, the bung can be fitted. A simple overhand knot should be used to form a loop, which can be fitted to the bung.

sections; a modelling knife, and wet-and-dry sandpaper that is used to clean off any rough edges. A special bung retractor can also be used with certain bungs so that they can be removed easily at a later stage.

ABOVE: Equipment you will need.

RIGHT: Netting a good bream while pole fishing. A long-handled net is essential.

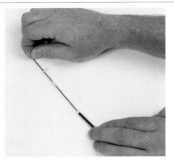

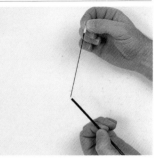

7 Some bungs come complete with a bung remover. As this pole is of a put-over type, the bung is inserted up inside the wall of the pole. At some stage the bung will have to be retrieved to change the elastic.

8 Take the end of the elastic at the tip end, draw it taut until a small amount of tension is placed on it. For this size of elastic, the connector needs to be fitted so that the elastic is just placed under tension.

9 Thread on the connector sleeve on and then the elastic through the hole in the connector. Secure the elastic to the connector using a granny knot. Make sure the knot does not slip.

ABOVE: Olivettes are very good for fishing in deep water or to get the bait to the bottom very quickly. There are several different sizes of olivette available to the pole angler. The choice of weight will be governed by the depth of water and the size of the pole float being used.

10 With the knot secured, slide the sleeve down over the connector to protect the knot. Now test the elastic for a smooth, bump-free exit from the pole tip.

11 To join a pole rig to the connector, simply slide back the sleeve and fit the loop at the top end of the rig on to the hook. Once in place, close the sleeve to trap the line.

Holding a Pole and Landing a Fish

1 The pole being used is 13.5 m (44 ft) long. The pole is supported in both hands with the left hand under the butt. The angler's back is straight, and the right leg is used as a support.

2 The back view shows how the right leg serves as a platform for the pole to rest on. The angler's body is slightly turned to the right for comfort. The tip of the pole is just above the water.

3 Contact has been made with a fish and the angler starts to ship the pole back on to the bank behind. The internal elastic of the pole takes the shock of the fish.

4 Shipping back the pole is done slowly and carefully. The angler must aim to keep the pole moving backwards continuously, maintaining contact with the fish.

5 On the bank behind the angler the butt section of the rod is fed back over a special pole roller. Once the pole reaches the roller, the pole can be pulled in more smoothly.

6 The angler then breaks down the pole by removing the back sections. This is usually at the depth of the rig being used. Small fish can then be swung into the hand and unhooked.

7 LEFT: Larger fish should be netted, Competition anglers always net their fish in case they drop off the hook when they are swung out of the water. Once the fish has been unhooked the rig can be rebaited and the pole re-assembled and shipped back out to the swim.

Stillwater Techniques

You can use either a long pole or a whip on stillwaters. The long pole is best suited to reservoirs and lakes while the whip comes into its own fishing a canal.

Long Pole

Before fishing, make sure you are comfortable with the box at the correct height and the roller positioned correctly. If you are fishing on the bottom, plumb accurately and then mark the line with a marker pen at the bottom of the float stem. That way, if you come up in the water later you can re-set the depth easily. Next introduce a little free feed with the pole cup, but do not overdo it at this stage. You can always put more in but it is impossible to take it out.

When you get your bite, strike firmly upwards to set the hook, remembering that you have to overcome the cushioning effect of the elastic. If it is a small fish, then ship it towards you by removing pole sections until you can swing in or net the fish. However, if a slightly bigger fish pulls elastic from the pole tip, get it under control as soon as possible, pulling it away from the swim to avoid scaring the shoal.

In a situation where you are fishing mid-range with the top few sections of a pole, always keep the butt sections handy, ready to ship out if necessary, if a big fish heads directly away from you. If you get line bites, the fish may have moved up in the water. You can then change to an "on the drop" presentation, with strung out tiny shot. Keep the bait on the move. Once it has settled, bring it to the top and let it drop again.

Whip

Whip fishing in stillwaters is probably most applicable to canals, where 23 ft (7 m) covers most situations. Casting with a whip is normally a case of a simple overhead flick, and landing the fish on these shorter poles is as straightforward as with rod and line. Thirteen feet (4 m) of line at hand means that a small fish can easily be swung to hand for unhooking. It is sometimes difficult to see the advantage of a 13 ft (4 m) whip over a 13 ft (4 m) rod and line, but it must be remembered that a whip is far lighter with an ultra-fine tip, and generally presents an extremely delicate terminal rig.

Even the lightest traditional rod may not have the tip sensitivity to set the hook into quick-biting small fish, or the flexibility to prevent them being bumped off the barbless hooks often used in speed fishing. Also, casting a very light rig with rod and line is far more inaccurate, while the overhead flick cast leads to tangles. Pole cups cannot be used with whips, but regular feeding by hand or a catapult is perfectly accurate at the short ranges involved.

ABOVE: The angler lands a good bream caught on a pole. Note the long terminal rig.

River Techniques

The secrets of successful pole fishing on rivers are the same as for trotting: keeping a steady trickle of feed going in on the right line, ensuring the correct amount and consistency of groundbait, and making sure that the float follows the current without jerking or being pulled off line. In trotting, the overriding principle is to keep contact with the float by having as little line between float and rod top as possible. When "trotting" with the pole you simply follow the float with the pole tip. The restriction is that you cannot fish past the extent of your reach. Another parallel with trotting is that at the end of a trot, a bonus fish often results from holding the float back and making the bait rise in the water. Exactly the same applies to pole work, and by delaying slightly at the end of the run through, as the pole float lifts, the bait will rise, often inducing that bonus bite.

On small to medium rivers, especially those with rush margins, good fish of many species feed tight against the marginal vegetation, and a pole in these circumstances allows presentation that would be impossible with rod and line, no matter how accurate your casting. By consistently running through only inches from the far bank rushes, keeping up a steady feed line at the same time, good catches of fish can be accumulated. Not only is the placement of each bait deadly accurate, it is also disturbance free, two critical factors in efficient angling of any kind. If you are fishing this close to far bank rushes, or even under far bank branches, step up the elastic strength from that which you would normally use. This will give you extra stopping power when the unexpected big chub takes the bait.

Before you start fishing, run your rig through the swim a few times with a bare hook to see if the float buries consistently at one spot, indicating a snag or a rise in the river bed. If you are on a pleasure session, you could move fractionally upstream so that the feature is at the end of the run through. This will mean the float swinging up at the critical point as you hold it back. Also, fish could congregate at the feature as food items become trapped against it. In other words, the bare hook trick could have located a hot spot for you.

With all pole fishing, avoid fishing under power lines. There have already been too many deaths by electrocution. Always take the trouble to warn others.

Groundbait Feeding

Pole fishing is a major part of coarse angling. It is a method used by competition anglers all over the world, and it is also becoming increasingly popular among the ranks of pleasure anglers. It does enable any angler to catch a lot of fish quickly and gives unparalleled control over float and bait placement.

There are many different poles available made in super-light materials up to 53 ft (16 m) in length and their main disadvantage is that they can be difficult to control when there is a strong wind. Correct holding of the pole is vital at all times, when fishing, feeding groundbait, feeding loosefeed or playing a fish. The sequences shown here and on the previous pages show how to do this.

1 Feeding groundbait is as easy as loosefeeding and all it requires is a little practice to become perfect. The groundbait needs to be in position close to the angler so that it can be reached by hand.

2 The pole is moved to the forward position and the butt section is clamped between the knees and supported on the underside with the left hand. Should a fish take, the angler will strike with his left hand.

3 The right hand moves to the groundbait bowl and moulds a small nugget of groundbait into a ball. The groundbait needs to be formed just tight enough so that it will hold together when it is thrown.

4 The angler measures the distance the groundbait has to be thrown and as the float is usually fished just off the tip of the pole, the end of the pole acts as a marker. With practice great accuracy can be achieved.

5 To make sure of reaching the correct distance the angler takes up a standing position. The small nugget of groundbait is held in the palm of the right hand and is to be thrown forward underarm.

6 Once the angler is ready the groundbait is thrown upwards and outwards towards the pole tip. The tip of the pole may be slightly submerged when the throw is taking place, to help the angler to hold it. However, all the time that this action has been occurring, any movement of the float can still be struck with the left hand by flicking the pole upwards.

1 The angler wedges the bait catapult under his leg and fills it from the bowl with his left hand. The right hand controls the pole.

2 Lift the catapult with the left hand and guide it over to meet the right hand. Grasp the tag of the catapult with the right hand.

3 The pole is supported on the angler's leg by pressure of the arm and three fingers of the right hand. Thumb and forefinger hold the tag.

4 The catapult is extended with the left hand, and the loosefeed is aimed at the tip of the pole. When the angler lets go with his right hand the catapult shoots the feed forward. Although this may look a bit difficult to accomplish, with a little practice the angler can get the feed accurately over the tip of the pole every time. If at any time while feeding the float is drawn under, the angler can always react instantly by pushing the pole up with his right hand to set the hook.

BELOW: Pole fishing beside a lock. Canal traffic may slow sport at times, but boats have as much right to be on these waterways.

Lure Fishing

At one time or another all predatory fish can be taken on lures, and occasionally fish that are not normally predatory can also be taken. There are well-documented instances of carp, bream and barbel being caught on lures, and hooked in the mouth. Generally speaking, however, the coarse angler will be targeting pike and perch on lure fishing methods, and less frequently zander and chub. The idea of a lure is to imitate the prey of a predatory fish, not necessarily in visual appearance but more in behaviour. Most predators react strongly to sudden movement and vibration, and these are the factors behind lure design and use.

ABOVE: The equipment required for lure fishing for pike gathered on the bank.

Types of Lure Fishing

Modern lure fishing had its origins in a method that appears very neglected today: that of wobbling dead fish on special flights. Using freshly killed coarse fish with their swim bladders intact, simply attached by two trebles and mounted so the tail is kinked, wobbled deadbaits are buoyant and lethally effective when drawn over shallows with heavy weed growth. The more disturbance they make the better and the parallel with fishing a floating plug is obvious. You can mimic the diving plug by adding lead to the head of the fish. In fact, a method to try when deadbaiting for

pike in rivers is to insert a short length of steel bar into the throat of the bait. This is then fished sink-and-draw style and the action is tremendous, especially against a current. As the fish is drawn towards you, it appears to swim quite normally, but slacken off and the bait dives. This is irresistible to pike.

Deadbait spinning was the forerunner of spinning with artificials, with the bait attached to special mounts equipped with vanes at the bait's head to make it revolve rapidly when drawn through the water. Fishing with lures can be exciting, especially in the warmer months

when the method is at its most productive. In particular, fishing with surface lures can be heart-stopping stuff, and it is an unforgettable sight to see a big pike launch itself from the depths and clear the water in an explosion of spray with your plug clamped firmly in its jaws.

Sub-surface lure fishing relies more on feel for timing the strike, but is no less exciting. When a spoon comes to a sudden juddering halt, to be followed by the vicious head shake as a pike turns away, or a light spinning rod buckles to the attentions of a big perch as it grabs a spinner, the experiences are not quickly forgotten.

ABOVE: A floating plug being drawn across the surface. As you always see the fish take when fishing a floating lure, you must let the fish turn with the lure before striking.

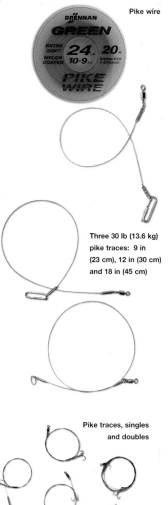

Pike wire

Three 30 lb (13.6 kg) pike traces: 9 in (23 cm), 12 in (30 cm) and 18 in (45 cm)

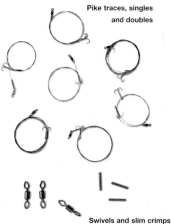

Pike traces, singles and doubles

Swivels and slim crimps

Tackle

You will not require a great deal of extra equipment for lure fishing. It depends on how much you plan to do.

Rods

If you are only intending to go on the occasional lure fishing trip, then you can certainly get away with the normal rods you would use for bait fishing. A light feeder rod will certainly be adequate for perch spinning, while a medium 10–11 ft (3–3.35 m) carp rod will handle any pike that swims. However, if you intend lure fishing to be a major part of your angling, it will reward you to invest in the right equipment. If you are going to be doing a lot of boat fishing, single-handed bait casting rods of around 9 ft (2.74 m) are ideal. The 9 ft (2.74 m) Spinflex, which can take main lines from 5–12 lb (2.27–5.44 kg), is a very versatile tool for the lure angler.

Reels

Regular lure casting and retrieval places great strain on reels, by wearing gears, loosening handles and weakening bail arm springs. For

OPPOSITE: Netting a pike. It helps to have a companion if you have to land a large fish.

efficient lure fishing, you also need very smooth line lay and long cast facilities, as well as a totally reliable clutch for when you eventually hook that monster. Aero GT reels have everything the lure angler needs. They are strong, light (most important when holding the rod constantly), and very smooth in operation with no bail arm backlash to create tangles. Most importantly, the better reels are vibration free, as continually retrieving a lure with a reel that is constantly wobbling is a tremendous irritation. Also important is the fighting drag system, an important safeguard when a very big fish intercepts your lure.

Lines and Trace Wires

Trace wire for lure fishing should be no less than 15 lb (6.8 kg), but this should be stepped up if you intend some big pike fishing at some of the large trout reservoirs. Where the pike are known to run to 40 lb (18.14 kg) you want traces of at least 25 lb (11.34 kg). Stainless seven strand trace wire, as well as being of very consistent quality, is thin and supple. This is important as it has minimum impact on lure action. As far as main lines are concerned, 12 lb (5.44 kg) is about right on most fisheries, but if

you are fishing very light spinners for perch you need to go lighter as you will find the action of the lure impaired. The frequent casting demands good abrasion resistance, and one of the best lines for this purpose is Sufix synergy.

Lure Fishing for Pike

Lure fishing for pike can be a thrilling experience, especially if you are fishing in clear water. If you wear a pair of polarized sunglasses you will be able to see the lure as it weaves its way back to the rod tip. A pike can often be seen following the lure and will strike it at the last possible moment, usually as the lure is being lifted to the surface of the water at the end of the retrieve. As the pike follows the lure, the excitement mounts and the angler's heartbeat races; when the pike strikes and is hooked, the speed and strength of the fight is frightening. In this sequence the angler is fishing fairly shallow water by a sluice with a floating plug. This type of water is a well-known haunt for pike and every part of the water is covered systematically: the photographs tell the tale.

1 This angler is fishing with a floating plug. Although the plug is buoyant and floats, it is fitted with a vane under its chin, which will make it dive under the surface as it is being retrieved. The faster the angler retrieves the plug, the deeper it dives. The skilled angler can make the plug go up and down in the water to attract the interest of the pike.

2 Having picked a target area to cast towards, the cast is made. When fishing with any form of lure, it is common practice to search out all of the water you have in front of you. Start fishing to your left and then slowly fish around in an arc, covering every part of the water.

3 Once the plug hits the water in the centre of the swim, the bale arm on the reel is closed. The retrieve can now begin, and you should vary the speed. Slow, jerky movements will catch the eye of a roaming pike and it will quickly move in to investigate.

4 Keep watching the water for signs of a following pike, and keep a tight hold on the rod as a pike could strike the lure at any point of the retrieve. By wearing polarized glasses you will be able to see right down into the depths of the water and watch for the lure as it approaches.

5 As the lure approaches the rod tip, slow the retrieve down. If a pike has followed the lure this is usually the time it will strike as they like a slow-moving target. Very often the take will occur just as you are lifting the lure from the water.

6 A pike has taken the lure and the fight between the angler and pike is in full swing. The angler kneels on the bank to bring the pike under better control. This pike took the lure just as it was being lifted from the water at the end of the retrieve.

7 The pike is tiring and has been brought under control by the angler. This fish has not been deeply hooked and the treble of the floating plug can clearly be seen in the side of the pike's mouth.

8 The pike is landed safely and the angler shows the correct way to hold the fish with his fingers in the "V" shape under the pike's jaw. The thumb is then clamped against the outer jaw to hold the pike firmly. Pike can be landed in this way even if you have no net. But take great care not to get your fingers in the pike's mouth.

9 Use a mat while removing the hooks. Turn the pike on its back and use a pair of long-nosed forceps. Hold the jaws open by inserting two fingers under the gill cover on the underside of the jaw. The thumb is pressed on the lower jaw to force the jaws open. No damage can come to the fish and it can be returned to the water safely.

Fishing with Plugs

Plugs are wooden, plastic or metal lures designed to imitate the prey of predatory fish. There are now four basic types of plugs: floating divers, floaters, slow sinkers and suspenders. It is important to match the lure to the quarry and take note of the conditions, too.

Floating Diver Plugs

An old, established and well-known example of a floating diver plug is the Big S, which comes in a wide range of sizes. These lures carry a diving vane on the front, creating the dive effect when they are wound in: the faster the retrieve the deeper the dive. By altering the vane angle, the steepness of dive can be controlled. A small, steeply angled lip on the plug indicates that it is a shallow diver and a deep-running bait will have a quite, shallow-angled lip. A useful feature of this type of plug is that once you have submerged it with a sharp pull, say to 2 ft (60 cm) below the surface, a steady, constant retrieve will keep it at that depth, which is very useful for searching shallow, weedy areas.

Plugs with the ability to run at a set level at a controlled speed are the ones to select when you are searching a large water by trolling – towing the lure behind a slow-moving boat. Many plugs are now made in hollow plastic, and the body cavity filled with multi-reflective surfaces to mimic silver fish

scales. They are also filled with ball bearings so that they rattle, increasing the sound attraction. A further refinement in the floating diver category is jointed plugs, which have two body sections that can move independently, increasing even further the action and disturbance as they are brought through the water.

The Rapala is one of a family known as minnow plugs, which are all successful lures. Drifting a floating minnow plug downstream can help you fish at a further distance than you could probably cast with a light lure. Probably the best known is the Devon minnow, which is a finned revolving variant well loved by salmon anglers.

Floating Plugs

All kinds of weird and wonderful designs are available, to imitate almost every animal, insect or reptile. Some of these are ideal for chub fishing as well as for pike. With these surface lures, a very erratic retrieve – stopping and starting in a jerky fashion to make them pop on to the water – can produce spectacular takes.

Another exciting surface presentation that produces vicious attacks is possible with an adaptation of the standard surface plug, which includes a small propeller at the front end, so that it actually buzzes when pulled at a high speed through the surface film. These are appropriately enough called propbaits. It is better to

tie these lures directly on to the line or trace with an open-looped knot without using snaps or swivels. When fishing with these, and in fact all surface lures, always keep your striking arm in check for a vital second or two. It is very easy to strike instantly in the excitement of the moment and pull the lure straight out of the fish's mouth. Just like the take of a chub on floating crust, let the pike turn with the bait before setting the hooks. Bear in mind that many lures have hook points that are far too blunt and it will pay to spend time sharpening them before fishing, especially when piking.

Diving Plugs

These are probably the least used, and reserved for those occasions when fishing a water of very variable depth with some deep holes to explore. They can be sub-divided into slow divers, like the Kwikfish, and fast divers like the Hi-Lo, which actually has an adjustable diving vane to vary its rate of descent. With divers, the technique is to count a set number of seconds after the plug hits the water before starting a steady retrieve, altering the delay periodically to vary the retrieve depth. Once at the required depth, increasing retrieve speed will send the lure deeper.

Suspending Plugs

These are interesting to use, the general idea being that they are of neutral buoyancy, and just hang "suspended" in the water when you stop retrieving for a moment. Restarting the retrieve makes them dive. This stop-and-go retrieve technique is effective for all species but is apparently the most efficient way of lure fishing for zander, which are ultra-suspicious predators. When fishing for zander in this way, some of the takes to suspender plugs are vicious in the extreme and at high speed, so do not have your clutch setting too tight.

As fish see surface lures in silhouette, they often miss at the first attempt because of light refraction. Give them a chance to catch up with the lure and have another go. Anglers often mistakenly feel that the pike has deliberately "come short" at the lure when in fact it has genuinely missed its target and ends up just as frustrated as the angler.

A selection of popper lures

Plugs for salmon

A selection of deep floating diver plugs, shallow diving plugs and a jointed floating diver plug

Black-and-silver minnow plug

Fishing with Spinners and Spoons

The secret of successful spinning is speed and variation of retrieve. The perfect presentation is a nice, slow, controlled retrieve, occasionally flipping the lure to one side to cause additional vibration. Spinners are so called because at least part of the lure revolves. They attract fish by visual stimulus and create vibrations that act on the fish's lateral lines; if used correctly, they are sure to appeal to most predatory fish.

Many spinners are a little too heavy to allow a slow enough retrieve, especially in shallow water, and although a fast-moving lure will occasionally work, it is usually better to elect a lightweight spinner with an aluminium revolving blade. One of the best all round spinners is the Rublex Ondex, available in various sizes and weights, closely followed by the Mepps Black Fury. Choose the Mepps in the deeper waters as, being slightly heavier than the Ondex, it requires a slightly faster retrieve in shallow water.

Swivel spinners

Spinning for Pike

When starting a spinning session for pike, always search first of all those areas where the pike are most likely to be, close to cover or ambush points. Reedy margins, lily beds and drop-offs at the edges of gravel bars. In rivers, the same rules apply, but, like stalking chub, always work upstream if spinning. Another tip is to start operations with the smallest spinner you have. Even big pike have been put down by big heavy lures, particularly in intimate little areas.

Spinning for Perch

This is one of the most effective methods of taking perch, especially in the large stillwaters, and if you know there are only jack pike present you can safely drop the trace strength to around 8 lb (3.63 kg) to achieve a

better presentation. Perch rely more on visual stimulus to attack lures than pike, which react to sound vibrations, and flashing spinner blades imitate shoals of small fish turning in the water. This also explains why tasselled spinners are so effective. A red tassel imitates the tail of a roach or rudd.

In coloured water, in which perch feed avidly, more flashy lures will be needed, and it then pays to increase the size of the lure to make it more visible. In these conditions, choose one that gives good colour contrast.

Lures for pike and perch

Spinners should be retrieved as slowly as possible when fishing for perch, with occasional short bursts of speed to vary the presentation. In the event of the fish coming short, or hitting the lure without taking it, baiting the hooks with lobworms often makes a difference.

If you wish to spin very deep waters, heavier lures are among the best. These are designed to be bounced along close to the bottom, so should not be your choice in heavily snagged waters as it could prove expensive on tackle.

Spinning for Other Species

As well as pike and perch, spinning can also be a very effective method for taking chub. The same applies to zander in coloured water where these lightweight spinners are best fished very slowly. Also effective for zander are fish-shaped spoons.

Chub can also be tackled with fly spinners, which are tiny spinners with the hook dressed as an artificial fly. This provides the very effective combination of the insect imitation with the flash of the spinning blade. Similar are fly spoons, which are tiny spoons with a dressed hook attached. The lightest lures of this family are designed to float or fish just below the surface, where, in combination with

Brightly coloured spinners

their mini blades or spoons, they make very effective hybrid lures.

These little lures are good for fishing over very snaggy areas and can be fished "dapping" by lowering them on to the water under trees, leaving them to float for a minute or two and then giving them a quick buzz across the water surface.

It is a common misconception that the only lures that can be used on the surface are plugs, when in fact lightweight spinners and spoons, as well as the more specialized spinner baits and hybrid lures, can all be fished on top very effectively. A spinner bait is a combination of a spinning blade and a skirted jig bait, which looks a bit weird but is a very effective lure in the upper layers of water. A hybrid lure could be a spinner-spoon, which is similar to the spinner bait but with a spoon blade replacing the jig bait. The effectiveness of all these lures on top is the splash they create on touch down and then the wake they leave behind them, which provokes some dramatic responses from pike.

Generally, the shape and thickness of the blade affects the action of the lure. A broad blade is ideal for stillwaters and slow streams, but it will rise to the surface. Thin blades have less resistance and can be fished in fast water without skating on the water surface.

Jerk bait

Reading the Water

Before you can catch fish you must fish where they are, but most anglers still select river swims with their own comfort in mind, rather than giving thought as to whether the swim actually contains the fish they are seeking. For consistent success in all aspects of river angling, you must develop ways of reliably locating your quarry.

The Summer River

Even if you only fish rivers in the winter, time spent investigating the river in summer is never wasted. When the water is low and clear, and the weed beds and bankside vegetation are at their height, river features are at their most obvious. Logging their position now is invaluable later in the season when the banks are barer and the river high and murky. Also, of course, the various species of fish are more easily seen in summer, and their feeding areas will always be a good starting point in winter.

Features to look for include smooth gravelly shallows, lily beds, undercut banks, positions of all rush beds, depressions in the river bed, underwater snags, deep runs under overgrown banks and so on. All these features will be attractive to one or more species of fish. Dace, roach and grayling will colonize the fast gravel, as will barbel, particularly at night. Big perch have an affinity for undercut banks and sedate, deep

marginal flows. Chub, barbel and big roach will often be found in depressions, while river bream and tench like nothing better than browsing through lily beds. Marginal rushes are favourite ambush points for pike, while the angler seeking specimen barbel and chub need look no further than the underwater snag.

Any area of smooth flow overhung by trees will be a banker in winter for many species, especially if the river rises sufficiently to form rafts of flotsam around the lower branches. Many of these features will be obvious by eye, but, if the river is shallow enough, you can wade through it. This is the fastest way to discover the variations in the bottom contours. If you are not comfortable doing that, or the river is too deep, take the trouble to plumb all the areas where the bottom is not visible, and make a careful note of the results.

There are many anglers who only fish rivers in the winter months, when much of the fishing is undoubtedly at its peak, and they base

ABOVE: The margins of lakes around the shores and reed beds are always likely spots to try for many species.

their fish location on previous experience of the river plus their ability to read the water. Only stretches of river with character and variation in flow can be read accurately, and these will generally be of small to medium size. Straight, evenly flowing stretches, possibly wide and deep, present different location problems. In these, finding fish is often a painstaking process of elimination.

The Winter River

Swims that are good in summer will be equally reliable in winter, unless river conditions force the fish to move out. When higher, faster flows force them to move, they only move as far as they need to in order to find a comfortable station. This is where the ability to read the flow variations of a winter river is crucial to determining where the fish will relocate.

Examining the set of the various flows of a river at winter level soon confirms that what at first glance may appear unvarying current speed and direction from bank to bank is actually anything but uniform. There are usually numerous variations in the current, with regular divisions between fast and slower water, some of which are very pronounced. Such divisions between fast and slower flows are known as creases, and they are among the most reliable of all winter swims for many species.

LEFT: In a small stream, clear, shallow water and sparkling gravel enable you to check the depths of the river without trouble. They are also ideal conditions for spotting fish.

The Water Surface

Whatever the speed of flow, the water surface itself gives us vital clues to the sub-surface contours and vegetation. Certain areas run smoothly, while others are constantly or intermittently turbulent. Whether it be a gentle ripple or a substantial boil, such surface disturbance is a reflection of underwater irregularities. A constant boil or vortex is caused either by the shelving up of the river bed or by a large obstruction, such as an old tree stump. A shelving river bed is often accompanied by a diversion of flow if the bottom gravel slopes across river, and such a feature is a natural food trap, attractive to all species. But this is only true where the surface flow is relatively smooth away from the actual feature. If the current is fierce enough to result in heavily broken, boiling water, fish will vacate the area.

Constantly boiling water, caused by large irregular bottom debris, is rarely worth a second look. The whirlpools caused by such obstructions make it very uncomfortable for fish to cope with the constantly changing currents. One exception might be an area of very localized boiling, created where a large boulder or something similar rests on otherwise smooth gravel. Such a feature often causes a depression on the downstream side hollowed out by the current, and that creates a food trap. Such swims are most effectively fished upstream.

It is important to differentiate between heavily broken water caused by large debris and the moderate constant ripple of shallows. The surface of shallow water will ripple even if the bottom is quite fine gravel containing small stones, and such areas only become unfishable when heavy flood water creates unacceptable levels of turbulence.

Depressions

These hollows in the river bed in extensive shallows are excellent holding areas, especially for chub, roach and barbel; look for smooth bits of surface amongst the ripple. Even a small depression is an important swim to locate, particularly if it is located in a long stretch of shallow water, when it may be the only natural holding spot in that section of river, particularly in high water. It is quite amazing how many big fish can pack into a tiny depression.

The Winter River – The Effect of Aquatic Vegetation

Intermittent undulations on the water surface betray the presence of sunken weed beds. Submerged rushes cause variable surface ripple, but of a different type from that over shallows, in that it is much more broken and, at normal height at least, the odd rush stem breaks the surface. An underwater rush bed also splits the flow, creating two types of swim. As the roots hold back the central water, a lee of slacker water forms downstream, before the two separated flows rejoin. Such slacks are very reliable swims, especially for chub, barbel and pike. Current diversion across river will create creases alongside the submerged rushes.

Ranunculus, or streamer weed, gives great variation of surface activity, as the long tresses undulate

TOP: Steady runs behind beds of rushes in mid river are likely to prove reliable swims for many species. Experience will teach you the likely places that are worth exploring.

ABOVE: Trees on the far bank are popular holding places. They are particularly loved by chub who feed on insects from the trees.

up and down in the flow. The water will run smoothly for a while, followed by a boil as the weed rises to just under the surface. This type of boil is short lived and subsides quickly.

Fishing in Streamer Weed

A deadly method of fishing in streamer weed is to place a bait right under the trailing fronds, by casting upstream and across from the boil, so that the bait alights on clean gravel beyond the root. The bait will then be settled naturally under the weed by

current action. The faster the flow, and the deeper the water, the further upstream of the boil you will need to cast to allow for the current speed. There is no doubt that interpreting the flows created by beds of streamer weed, particularly in high water, gives anglers the greatest difficulty.

However, as some of our finest fisheries have long stretches adorned with ranunculus, it is vitally important to know how to go about it. Initially, spend a few minutes just looking and making mental notes of the various surface characteristics. You will see many places where the water boils and then flattens, as the tresses wash up and down in the flow. But most important are those narrow areas of surface which run smoothly, without any boils or vortices. These indicate smooth gravel runs between streamer beds. A correctly presented bait on this gravel will slowly roll

round and settle under the adjacent streamer fronds. If there is a fish there this nearly always produces a take.

The Winter River – Crease Swims
Excellent swims are where the main current suddenly diverts across river. Shelving gravel banks create such swims, and where the current is steady this makes a hot spot. Food items drifting downstream are diverted across river by the shelf in a fairly narrow band, and fish are quick to take advantage of the easy pickings. The secondary consequence of this diversion is that it creates quite a sharp demarcation between the fast main current and the more sedate water that does not deviate across river. In higher, faster water, when fish are unwilling to fight the main flow, they will shift position on to the crease, or move to the slower water away from the demarcation line.

ABOVE: Barbel fishing during a winter flood. High, coloured water in winter is a good time for barbel, and also other species, such as roach. Success in these conditions, especially if the day is relatively mild, is almost guaranteed.

All junctions between fast and slow water can be considered crease swims, and their causes are many. A section of protruding bank, an old tree stump, a feeder stream ingress, a bend in the river, and a marginal weed bed can all lead to a diversion of the main flow and therefore a crease swim. Under normal conditions, the junction between the two flows is the most reliable area to fish.

If there is one rule of thumb with winter river angling, it is to locate an area of evenly paced flow and oily, smooth surface, of whatever depth. There is an excellent chance you will have located fish of many species.

The Winter River – Assessing More Featureless Stretches

Even on rivers that are mainly fast and shallow, with lots of character, there will be stretches which are deeper than average, sluggish, dead straight and virtually featureless. Although much less interesting, such sections can harbour some of the biggest fish on the river. The lower beats of many of our rivers are also more difficult to read the slower and wider they become. The lower reaches of the Severn and the Great Ouse are cases in point.

Where there is a distinct lack of features, it is even more important to locate those that are present, as they could attract very high concentrations of fish. On the Severn, for instance, sunken snags are magnets for barbel.

Any feature on a largely featureless stretch could be extremely significant and is well worth investigating. For example, an insignificant trickle from a rivulet or land drain will often attract roach, and a tangle of fallen branches may be colonized by big perch. Marginal bushes are important, even when they do not actually overhang the water. This is because the foliage ensures less bankside disturbance at that point, and bush root systems, especially hawthorn and blackthorn, often lead to undercutting the bank. Undercuts provide quiet refuges for fish on all stretches, but on a stretch with a lack of other features, they assume much greater significance.

Before starting to fish a uniform stretch, it is worth spending some time plumbing, to see whether

underwater irregularities, such as depressions, exist. Also, unsuspected snags or sunken weed beds may manifest themselves. Even a small dip in the river bed could create a hot spot, as could an area of gravel in an otherwise muddy bottom.

Although it is sensible to devote time to any feature that is present, much of the fishing in fairly bland stretches of river will be a matter of painstaking elimination, or trusting to luck. Obviously, the latter is not an option if consistent success is your objective. If you are faced with a perfectly uniform stretch with no discernible variations of any type, there is no way of knowing exactly where the fish will be. You have to find them either by trial and error or by creating artificial hot spots and hoping the fish will come to you.

BELOW: A good chub taken in midwinter with snow on the ground. This fish was taken from a depression in midstream.

Stillwaters

Stillwaters present more of a problem than rivers. They all have distinctive taking places but often these are less apparent. Small stillwaters can be learned fairly quickly; vast trout lakes and reservoirs take much longer.

Understanding Estate Lakes

Estate lakes usually have bottom compositions of mud or silt and are frequently very weedy indeed. Bulrushes, reeds and water lilies are particularly common and these are favoured feeding sites of most species, and excellent ambush points for predators. The winter pike angler should make careful note of water lily beds. In the winter, roach love to feed among the dead roots which provide perfect camouflage for a hungry pike.

The essential difference between an estate lake and a gravel pit is that most such waters have much more even bottom contours. There will, however, be interesting features on most waters, generally caused by natural land undulations. The even bottom contours and rich feeding sites make many species much less nomadic than they are in gravel pits. Roach and bream shoals, for instance, can take up permanent residence in certain areas and their feeding times in these swims can be very predictable. Bream often travel around on well-defined patrol routes.

Many estate lakes, particularly the more naturally occurring or heavily wooded pond types, exhibit deep marginal areas, possibly as a result of land faults having created the water in the first place. Such marginal deeps, often overhung with foliage and possibly containing bottom debris of fallen timber, are a haven for pike and perch, as they attract hordes of fry. Carp also are fond of them.

One last general observation about estate lakes is that because they are very often fairly small and enclosed, the effects of wind on where the fish are is less significant than on larger, more open waters. The only possible exception are carp, which are probably more affected by wind than other species. Even on smaller lakes, there is evidence that carp migrate to the windward bank in a steady wind.

An obvious location aid is seeing the fish themselves, and here estate lake fish are very obliging. Shallow water roach in rich lakes have the helpful habit of rolling regularly at dawn and dusk, as well as through the dark hours, and rudd regularly prime at the surface. Rudd are one of the more nomadic fish and on a large water binoculars are a boon to follow their dorsal fins breaking the surface.

Carp also show themselves readily, by rolling, head and tailing or swirling at the surface. They also betray their presence by bow waving – where a wake follows a carp swimming close under the surface; tenting – where a mound appears by magic in surface weed as the carp's back pushes upwards; and smoke screening – where large clouds of disturbed silt colour localized areas. Another common phenomenon is the sight of a faint "V", as the merest tip of the carp's dorsal cuts the surface film as it swims. To find estate lake tench, look no further than the margins. Hard against marginal rushes or lilies is a reliable swim, but the most reliable way of finding tench is to be there at dawn and watch for the characteristic frothy patches of "needle bubbles".

Location of pike in estate lakes, as in all waters, is obviously governed by the location of the prey fish, and they will therefore be found in the vicinity of any feature. Edges of rush beds or where rushes protrude out into the lake are good. Such rush headlands are popular ambush points.

Bays and inlets are used by perch shoals as traps in which to herd fry. Of all estate lakes, the one that seems to have the greatest affinity for big perch is the small but deep farm pond – the kind of water that appears to contain shoals of stunted rudd and crucians, but little else. When fishing these deep ponds for big perch, any area of underwater snags will be favoured, as will bankside root formations and overhanging foliage.

Mapping Gravel Pits

The important features to locate on pits are the bars, gullies, gravel plateaux, sudden drop-offs and weedbeds. You need to know the bottom composition and the nature of bottom weed, especially if there are areas which are weed free amongst otherwise densely weeded areas. These are important for the bream or pike angler. Bream, for instance, like to feed over areas that are naturally weed-free, while tench will happily browse amongst dense weed.

Some of these features can be indicated by visual evidence taken from the surrounding land. For instance, a gently sloping marginal area will indicate a similar gradient running out into the pit, while a steep shelf may indicate a deep marginal trench. Perhaps the most important evidence is a prominent point, or a spit of land protruding into the pit. This usually indicates the presence of an underwater gravel bar, a feature attractive to all gravel pit species.

Other visual evidence can be gleaned from the activities of water birds, particularly swans, coots and grebes. Swans can only feed on bottom weed that they can reach,

while coots are great feeders on bottom weed, but do not like to feed too deeply. If coots are continually diving in one spot, you may have discovered an important gravel plateau. The pike or perch angler can do a lot worse than study the activities of great crested grebes, as they will continually dive where hordes of fry are to be found.

Finding the sub-surface features of a pit can be a long and laborious process, and mapping is far simpler if you have access to a boat, especially if it is coupled with an echo sounder. If you have no boat, mapping a gravel pit with standard plumbing methods is very efficient if you know what you

are doing. Set up a large, easily visible sliding pike float with a 2 oz (50 g) lead. Set the float shallow, say about 4 ft (1.22 m), and cast it out to maximum fishing range to the left-hand extremity of the swim, aiming at an easily identifiable point on the horizon. If the float lands in water deeper than this, it will obviously sink like a stone. Then begin a slow retrieve, reeling in about 6 ft (1.83 m) of line at a time before allowing out a little slack to let the sliding float work properly. If the lead has moved on to a feature shallower than 4 ft (1.22 m), the float will pop up to the surface. By covering the swim this way, at progressively greater depth settings, you can soon discover the location and extent of all features in the water in front of you.

On the day of fishing you may need a permanent marker, and this is simple to achieve. Having identified the feature, cut the line about 12 in (30 cm) above the sliding float stop knot. Form a loop in the line and form another loop in the reel line. Tie both loops tightly together with PVA and cast out to the required spot. After a few minutes, retrieve the main line, leaving the marker in place with no trailing line that might foul the line when you are fishing. At the end of the day, use a grapple lead with treble hook attached to retrieve these markers from the water.

OPPOSITE: Water lilies growing at the edge of a small lake. Carp and tench find them particularly attractive.

RIGHT: The feeder stream of a large reservoir in a very dry summer. A gully like this will always hold good fish when filled.

Understanding Reservoirs

Reservoirs fall into two types: those created by damming natural valleys, so that their feeder streams backfill the valley to the limits dictated by the dam and the land contours, and those more artificially formed by creating huge bowls supported by earthworks.

Some of our best stillwater coarse fishing is to be found on water supply reservoirs and it is essential to devote time to determining the underwater contours if you are going to get the best out of them. Bowl-type reservoirs are usually of fairly consistent depth, although they will normally get shallower towards one end. Any sudden depth variation in a reservoir of this type will be rare, and if one exists it will always be worth concentrating on.

Naturally flooded valleys provide far more interesting fishing. The original stream or streams that drain into the valley are the most important features to locate, as they will be deeper, with hard gravel beds, while the surrounding land could be mud. They will have a natural current, against which fish like to swim, and will be the first areas to show the ingress of coloured water when it rains and high water swells the feeder streams. A simple way to pinpoint the route of a stream bed is to visit the reservoir the day after heavy rain, particularly if you can gain a high vantage point. You will often see coloured water snaking along the path of the stream bed. It needs, however, to be calm. If there is a wind and the

water is rough, rapid mixing occurs and the browner fresh water quickly becomes general.

The land surrounding a reservoir gives accurate clues as to the marginal bottom contours. A section of steep bank, therefore, will indicate similarly steeply increasing marginal water depth. Conversely, long fingers of water are likely to be shallow and gently shelving, and these are places where the angler can expect to find shoal fish, such as perch and roach when they are present.

Having made note of all the visual clues you must then fill in the gaps with the more painstaking manual mapping, although there will usually be less dramatic depth variations in reservoirs than in natural lakes.

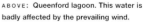

ABOVE: Queenford lagoon. This water is badly affected by the prevailing wind.

The Effects of Wind and Weather on Stillwaters

Carp, rudd and bream are the first fish to be influenced by strong winds, usually migrating to the windward shores. On reservoirs and lakes, a favourable wind is one off the dam and pushing towards the shallows. These fish love to feed along the windward slopes of gravel bars in pits and similarly, they love to browse on the rising ground towards lake shallows. Tench also feed avidly on shallows in rough conditions, but it is the rough conditions that stimulate their feeding rather than their following of the wind.

Roach also respond to strong wind, although it is the secondary effects of the wind that are important, such as the sub-currents that are created in stream-fed reservoirs. If these streams are swollen with rain, the increased flows, combined with the effects of wind, create all manner of complex sub-flows, known as undertows. Find a good undertow, at or near a stream bed, in coloured water, and roach will not be far away. For the predatory species, the prevailing weather and water conditions will affect their location only in as much as it affects the movements of the prey fish.

LEFT: A man-made reservoir. The land around slopes gently down to the water and the margins are relatively shallow. The prevailing wind blows across the water to the north-east shore.

Fishing in Europe

Many of our coarse fish, principally roach, tench, bream, barbel and zander, are found in many parts of Europe, particularly France, Germany, Holland and Belgium, but it is fair to say that the main interest of British anglers travelling abroad for coarse fish will be in pursuing big catfish, carp or pike.

ABOVE: **A giant catfish caught in France.**

Catfish

Closest to home is France, and the rivers Saône and Loire have both produced catfish in excess of 100 lb (45.4 kg). On the River Saône the best fishing is the 100 miles (161 km) or so stretching from Lyon to Chalon. The Loire is productive between Decize and Gien. As well as these two rivers, one or two lakes in France hold big catfish, notably Lake Cassien which produced a monstrous fish estimated at well over 100 lb (45.4 kg) a few years ago.

Another European river holding huge cats to over 300 lb (136 kg) is the River Danube, which runs through Germany, Austria, Czechoslovakia, Romania and Hungary. In all those countries the river has been fished successfully by British cat hunters. As far as stillwaters are concerned, most of the large Hungarian, Austrian and Swiss lakes hold big catfish, and one

of the most famous fisheries in Yugoslavia for catfish is the huge Vransko lake.

The two countries most of interest to British anglers who want organized catfishing are Germany and Spain. Most of the lakes in southern Germany hold cats, the most famous day-ticket fishery being Schnackensee, near Nuremburg. In Spain, it is the mighty River Ebro that has produced dozens of enormous cats, some weighing well over 100 lb (45.4 kg) for visiting anglers.

For those seeking that real leviathan however, eastern Europe now holds the allure, and the Rivers Desna and Volga of Russia regularly produce cats over a staggering 400 lb (181 kg). Before you go abroad on a catfish expedition make sure you obtain the correct, up-to-the-minute information, especially if you intend visits to politically sensitive regions.

ABOVE: **A beautifully streamlined carp caught in France.**

Carp

By far the greatest numbers of British anglers travelling abroad are going in search of the very big carp that are available. Probably the most famous venues are in France, with Lake Cassien leading the way. Other famous waters include Salagou and St Quoix. Most stillwaters in France contain carp, as do many of the rivers, the River Seine having produced some very big fish indeed.

As well as France, big carp are to be found over a good part of the globe. There are big fish to be found in the lakes of most countries of Europe, as well as in Canada, the United States, the Canary Islands, the Far East, Africa and Australia. Very reliable, too, are the canal drainage systems of the Netherlands, which are known to hold a good head of carp to large sizes.

The casual angler who wishes to fish for carp abroad and be looked after has good opportunities. The Carp Society should be contacted as it owns overseas carp waters where its members can fish.

Pike

Some of the biggest pike in Europe are found in the Scottish lochs, Irish loughs and the huge trout reservoirs of Wales and England. For this reason, few anglers seem to travel abroad in search of big pike. However, some of the big waters of Holland still offer excellent potential, while there are undoubtedly huge fish in other European countries. The problem is that in many European countries people eat their catch, and in Germany all fish are killed. As pike are one of the slower-growing fish, and react badly to pressure, they have suffered as a consequence. Around Great Britain we still have excellent pike fishing. Sweden, also has some huge pike – some weighing nearly 50 lb (22.7 kg) – have been taken from estuaries in the Baltic Sea. Swedish pike fishing is tightly controlled.

ABOVE: **A trio of huge Swedish pike.**

Sea Angling

Sea angling is a continually progressive sport. Many sea anglers start fishing when they are very young. They may be fortunate and live by the sea, or they may go to the seaside each year for the family's holiday. The first steps are often fishing off a pier wall, lowering a baited hook into the water and waiting for the fish to take; or when the young angler becomes more experienced, walking to a good coastal mark and fishing with a brightly coloured float cast out on to the shimmering green waves, sitting patiently waiting for the fish to bite, which they sometimes do.

As time progresses and the young angler learns new techniques from experienced anglers, he or she will target different species from piers, beaches and rocky shores. The final step is to progress to boat fishing over wrecks and noted marks offshore.

As in all angling there is much to learn, and so the fascination for each angler lies in developing his or her knowledge, learning and practising new techniques and realising that this knowledge is resulting in catching more and better fish.

Introduction

Sea angling, both from the shore and boat fishing, offers great variety and excitement, whether you want to challenge the sporting qualities of bass or partake in a night-time fight with a rough ground conger eel. The successful angler will have to learn and master the techniques of distance casting, experiment to find the best baits and tackle, and will, no doubt, fish through many nights on beaches hoping for a catch. But for many sea anglers, big fish are the main target, and plenty of conger eels, ling and pollack can be caught from all manner of wrecks and reefs offshore.

ABOVE: A fishing expedition puts out to sea from a crowded harbour in south England. Sea fishing is a big tourist attraction in many coastal resorts.

Where to Fish

Sea fishing can be divided into two parts: boat fishing and fishing from the shore. Shore fishing itself can be divided into fishing from marks, harbours and piers, and fishing from the beach. This division may be somewhat artificial as many of the techniques are the same but there can be differences in the species targeted.

The first thing the sea angler has to learn is the type of fish that lives in each habitat. Fishing from a pier or harbour can produce a number of species, but dogfish, garfish, mackerel and mullet can all be caught from harbours, and the beginner has to learn to target each of these species. If you have a rocky coastline available to you then you may well be able to spin for bass and catch pollack, pouting, wrasse, whiting, and bream, even the occasional conger eel, while if you live near sandy beaches or on an estuary your quarry will be flounders, dabs and plaice, with codling the target in the winter months. Fish change their habitats during the season, and if you are lucky enough to be able to enjoy access to the sea all the year round then you can fish for different species at different times of the year.

The other things the sea angler has to learn are the technicalities of the

BELOW: The sun slips away as two anglers spin for bass from the shore. Late evening is one of the best times for fish to take.

ABOVE: Sea fishing from a boat on a blissfully calm day in midsummer. A good cod is being brought to the net while the other rod waits for a bite.

craft: what baits to use for each species and how these are best collected; what rods and reels are most effective and what rods suit your purpose. All this takes time.

The sea angler who has access to a boat or belongs to a club that organizes sea-fishing trips has many opportunities. At the top end of the scale many anglers try for shark in the warmer waters of the coasts of Cornwall and Devon in the south-west. If you are a trophy hunter then you may well try and catch a giant thornback ray, now alas only present in any quantity in the seas off the west coast of the Scottish Highlands. Otherwise children and beginners can have their first chance of success trailing a trace of feathers for mackerel or plumbing the depths to tempt cod or flatfish. As you become more experienced, so you will learn what rigs to use and what baits are most effective, and later you will learn how to reach the wrecks and marks on the sea bed and how these should be fished to most effect.

Sea angling is a fascinating sport. It is limitless in the variety that it offers, both in the number of species that can be caught and the methods that can be used. It is about understanding the way of the tides and species that swim beneath its waters. It is also an endless learning curve, as each day something will change. No two trips, either on shore or in a boat far out to sea, are ever the same, and that above all makes it continuously challenging.

RIGHT: Fishing from a harbour wall in high summer. Many youngsters get their first taste of sea fishing on holidays by the sea.

Species

Garfish *(Belone belone)*

Like a relic from the prehistoric age the garfish, or "green bone" as it is sometimes called, is a real sporting fighter. It is a distant relative of the tropical flying-fish and displays an acrobatic skill of tail walking when hooked. It has the characteristics of a scaled-down swordfish with its protruding, tooth-lined bill, but rarely exceeds 1.5 lb (0.68 kg) in weight.

Long and slim with a blue-green back and silvery underside, the garfish is often caught in mackerel shoals. Very common around the south-west shores of Britain during the summer months, the garfish likes to feed high up in the water, just below the surface. It will often leap clear from the water when hooked and tail walk across the water in an effort to lose the hook.

To the beginner, the garfish can provide an easy quarry and can be caught from a pier using light float tackle. It is also referred to as the mackerel guard or mackerel guide due to the fact that where there are garfish present, mackerel are always close by.

Current Records
Shore **3 lb 4 oz 12 drm (1.477 kg)**
Boat **3 lb 9 oz 8 drm (1.63 kg)**

Season
April through to October.

Distribution
Widespread but mainly found in the warmer waters of the south-west coast of Britain.

Natural Diet
They are mainly surface feeders, feeding on small fry such as whitebait.

Top Spots
Every pier and breakwater along the south, south-east and south-west coast.

Top Tip
Fish with a light line of 6 lb (2.72 kg) and use a small float with a thin strip of mackerel as bait. This will provide you with a sporting fight as the hooked garfish displays its acrobatic skills.

Conger Eel *(Conger conger)*

Current Records
Shore **68 lb 8 oz (31.072 kg)**
Boat **133 lb 4 oz (60.442 kg) USA**

Season
Can be caught all through the year but June to October is the peak time.

Distribution
All around the British coast, but especially off the southern coastline. Also present in the Atlantic Ocean and North Sea.

Natural Diet
Small species of fish such as pouting and bream, common lobsters, squids and small octopus.

Top Spots
Wrecks off the south and south-west coast.

Top Tip
A freshly caught mackerel head-and-guts bait is one of the most successful known.

Despite its enormous size the conger is a shy, timid creature and retreats from the slightest sign of danger. However, it is an inquisitive fish and will readily swim out of its lair to search out food. It is a powerful fighting fish and once hooked has the ability to latch on to an obstacle on the bottom if allowed to do so.

Body colourings vary depending on the depth of water in which the conger is caught. Most conger eels are of a dark, smoke-grey colouring along the back with a pale silvery-yellow belly. The dorsal fin of the conger living in deeper water is tipped with a harsh black rim. Their teeth are set in the depths of powerful jaws and are rarely seen. The conger prefers to grip its prey in the clasp of its jaws before taking it into the mouth to be chewed up. When on the move it tends to travel at mid-water depths and when hunting it stays close to the bottom, feeding on smaller fish. Most of the bigger species are caught by boat anglers fishing over deep-water wrecks and reefs. The conger only spawns once in its lifetime, this taking place far away from our shores in deep water near Madeira. A spawning conger will lay up to 15 million eggs which are carried on the slow-moving currents of the North Atlantic Drift towards the Continental Shelf.

As the larger species are found on wrecks and rough ground, commercial fishing has little effect on the stocks. Big congers in excess of 100 lb (45.36 kg) can therefore thrive in comparative safety. Conger eels caught from the shore tend to be smaller and are mainly caught at night over rough ground and rock-gully marks. At night they move inshore into the shallower water to feed on the abundance of food that these areas attract.

Pouting *(Gadus luscus)*

Sometimes called a bib, the pouting is another member of the cod family and is regarded as a nuisance fish by many sea anglers. This is due to its bait-robbing habits when small. Widespread around British shores, small pouting can be caught in vast numbers when fishing from the beach at night. They don't grow to huge sizes, and the average shore-caught pouting is likely to be under 1 lb (0.45 kg) in weight. Boat anglers are more likely to catch a bigger specimen, and a 3 lb (1.36 kg) pouting is a good fish.

As with the cod the pouting also has a barbule positioned under the chin. However, it is thinner than that of the cod. It has a sheen of pink in its colouring which extends from behind the head to the tail, over a coppery-brown back. The underside is pale cream and a black spot can be found at the base of the pectoral fin. Once taken from the water, the pink sheen melts away and the skin turns a dreary copper colour. Pouting spawn in the late winter or early spring, the eggs taking around two weeks to hatch out. Smaller pouting will inhabit areas of shore line offering firm sandy beaches and rocky foreshores, even entering estuaries in search of food, while big pouting live in deeper water over rough ground and wrecks. When caught, pouting scales can be difficult to remove from the angler's hands and clothing.

The fish makes an excellent bait for bigger species such as cod, conger and bass. Each year many thousands of pouting are caught commercially and used to make fishmeal feeds and fertilizers.

Current Records
Shore **4 lb 9 oz (2.07 kg)**
Boat **5 lb 8 oz (2.495 kg)**

Season
All year round.

Distribution
Widely distributed around the British coast, they are most abundant along the south coast.

Natural Diet
Shrimps, swimming crabs, worms, shellfish and squid.

Top Spots
Down the side of pier and breakwater walls, notably Dover Breakwater.

Top Tip
Use short hook snoods when fishing for pouting as they have a habit of spinning in the tide. which often results in a tangled trace.

Cod *(Gadus morrhua)*

The cod is widespread around the coast of Britain, but is particularly found off the coast of Scotland where it comes in from the Icelandic breeding grounds to feed.

Furnished with a large mouth, the cod has a reputation as an eater of all that comes its way. With its pot belly and cylindrical body shape, the cod is not rated highly as a fighting fish. Cod may vary considerably in colour but are usually greeny-brown or olive grey. They will often have a light marbling pattern or spots on the flanks and back. The upper jaw exceeds the lower, which results in a receding chin, upon the underside of which a large barbule is located. Cod are primarily bottom feeders, favouring deep water marks.

Shore anglers in the north can catch cod all year round, but in the south, smaller cod, or codling as they are known, are more of a winter species. The coasts of Kent and Sussex are popular venues for the shore angler in search of prime winter cod fishing. Bigger cod can be caught from the Needles area off the Isle of Wight. Inshore they will search out their food over the rough grounds of rock and pebble beaches at high water, while from a boat they can be located in deep water over wrecks. Being scavengers they feed on almost anything that comes their way, such as lugworms, prawns, small flatfish, crabs, squid and cuttlefish. Big cod are often caught on artificial eels, pirks or other types of artificial lure.

Current Records
Shore **44 lb 8 oz (20.185 kg)**
Boat **58 lb 6 oz (25.572 kg)**
World **98 lb 12 oz (44.79 kg) USA**

Season
January to December in the north, October to February in the south.

Distribution
In northern waters cod are present throughout the year, especially in Scottish waters. During the winter months in the south, venues such as the north coast of Devon can produce good cod fishing.

Natural Diet
Lugworms, cuttlefish, squids, prawns, crabs and small flatfish such as plaice.

Top Spots
Estuary marks such as the Thames and Bristol Channel produce good numbers of smaller cod each year. Bigger specimens are to be found from such marks as the Needles and wrecks off the south-west and eastern coasts.

Top Tip
The use of modern braided lines makes cod fishing from a boat much easier. The lack of stretch in the line means that bites are more positive and can be felt by holding the line. This gives the angler an early bite indication.

Tope *(Galeorhinus galeus)*

A member of the shark family, the tope has a reputation as a dogged fighter. Unlike the shark, the tope is a bottom feeder and spends its time searching out food over smooth, sandy, shell-grit bottoms. Sometimes confused with the smoothhound, it is easy to identify by the lack of white dots along its back. It also has serrated, razor-sharp teeth, which the smoothhound lacks. The tope is of a similar shape and build to a shark but is much smaller in size. The body is sleek with a brownish-grey back and flanks, while the underside is a bright, polished white colour. Positioned behind the head and on the edge of the pectoral fins on each side are five gill slits. Males and females can be distinguished by looking closely at the fins. The male fish have fleshy appendages, known as claspers, alongside the anal fin, which are not present on the female. The female tope gives birth to live young, usually up to 20 at a time and sometimes as many as 50. The eye is specially adapted, with what is known as a third eyelid: a separate membrane that can be drawn across the eye to clean the eyeball and protect it as it lashes out at its prey.

The average boat-caught tope weighs around 40 lb (18.14 kg). However they do grow in excess of 70 lb (31.75 kg) and are a hard-fighting species once hooked. Tope fishing from the shore tends to result in smaller fish, of around the 20 lb (9.07 kg) mark, that have come into shallower water to feed on small flatfish. The bigger specimens have a tendency to keep to sandy or patchy rough ground found in deeper waters. Highly regarded for their sporting quality, it has become good practice by many sea anglers to return tope to the sea after capture.

Current Records
Shore **58 lb 2 oz (26.366 kg)**
Boat **82 lb 8 oz (37.422 kg)**
World **98 lb 8 oz (44.67 kg) USA**

Season
May through to October, with June and July the most productive months.

Distribution
Spread around the British coast with strongholds off the west coast and the Thames Estuary.

Natural Diet
Tope feed on various bottom-dwelling creatures including starfish and lobsters. The mainstays of their diet are small cod, whiting, flatfish and pouting.

Top Spots
The Thames Estuary, Poole in Dorset, Rhyl in Wales and off Hayling, Sussex.

Top Tip
Mackerel or a fresh eel section make very good tope baits.

Bass *(Dicentrarchus labrax)*

The bass is a member of the perch family and is sometimes referred to as the sea perch. It is coated in small, firm, silvery-blue scales, which give it a striking appearance. Being a predator, the body is muscular and streamlined as it often swims at high speeds when chasing prey. Smaller bass vary in colour and bear a slight resemblance to the mullet. However, they are easily identified by the spikes on their dorsal fin and boney gill covers.

Small school bass, as they are known, can often be caught in estuaries and will make their way right up into the brackish water, and even freshwater, on a rising tide. Once the tide starts to ebb, they follow the flow back towards the sea and feed in earnest on food caught in the tide's fall. Over the past ten years the bass population has suffered severely due to overfishing by commercial fishermen, and nowadays few big bass are caught from the shore. During the spring and summer months, small bass move inshore to feed in the warmer waters and can be found in good numbers on the south and west coasts of Britain. In the far west country, bass have been known to be caught all year round if the weather stays mild. From time to time bigger species do get caught from shore marks, but as a rule the angler seeking a specimen bass is better advised to fish from a boat. Larger bass tend to be lone fish but will, during stormy weather, move inshore to feed over rocky gullies and around storm beaches. The rough weather and pounding surf will have the bass searching for razor fish and crabs flushed out of their homes by the rough sea.

Current Records
Shore **19 lb (8.618 kg)**
Boat **19 lb 9 oz 2 drm (8.877 kg)**
World **20 lb 11 oz (9.4 kg) France**

Season
May through to October (later if warm).

Distribution
More common around the south-east and west coasts of Britain and Ireland.

Natural Diet
Crustaceans, small shrimps and sandeels. Larger bass are predators and will feed on sprats, squid, crab, mackerel and occasionally sea trout.

Top Spots
The Thames Estuary and Bristol Channel consistently produce double-figure bass.

Top Tip
Try fishing with a live sandeel using minimum weight like a split shot or drilled bullet lead. This will give the sandeel a natural appearance and will not hinder its ability to swim.

Ballan Wrasse *(Labrus bergylta)*

Ballan wrasse are the largest and most common fish of the wrasse family. The ballan has a deep, solid body and a large, long dorsal fin running from behind the head down to the wrist of the tail. The dorsal fin has 20 sharp spiny rays near the top of the back and requires careful handling. The jaws are very powerful, and the rubbery lips and sharp teeth are designed for tearing shellfish from rock faces. The peg-like front teeth are bright white in colour and are only used for tearing. The wrasse grinds its food down with a set of pharyngeal teeth located further back in the mouth. Its colour depends on where it is caught.

The newcomer to sea angling often makes the mistake of wrong identification, because of variations in colouration. In general, the ballan wrasse is of a greenish-brown colour with the addition of a reddish, fire-orange belly dotted with white spots.

The average size for the ballan wrasse is around 2–3 lb (0.91–1.36 kg); a bigger fish of 7 lb (3.18 kg) is a once-in-a-lifetime catch. Larger fish are commonly found in deeper water, near rocky overhangs and gullies. In the cover of thick kelp weed they can feed at leisure on small crustaceans, such as crabs and lobsters. Smaller ballan wrasse are often caught from breakwater walls and piers and can offer endless sport for the beginner to sea angling as they are relatively easy to catch.

Current Records
Shore **9 lb 1 oz (4.110 kg)**
Boat **9 lb 7 oz 12 drm (4.302 kg)**
World **9 lb 9 oz (4.35 kg) Ireland**

Season
April through to October.

Distribution
Widespread in the British Isles. Bigger specimens are found on the west coast of Britain around the Scillies and Channel Islands. South Cornwall and the south-western coast of Ireland also offer specimen-sized ballans.

Natural Diet
Limpets, common mussels, velvet-swimming crabs, other crustaceans and molluscs.

Top Spot
Alderney in the Channel Islands is famous for producing big wrasse.

Top Tip
Try float fishing or legering a small, hard-backed shore crab for instant results. Look under the rocks and weed near to where you are fishing for crabs about 1 in (2.5 cm) across.

Whiting *(Merlangius merlangus)*

A member of the cod family, the whiting is the most common of sea species to be caught off the British coast. From the shore it is mostly caught throughout the winter months and does not grow to a great size. One look inside the mouth will reveal that the whiting is a predator. It has a protruding upper jaw and an array of small teeth which it uses to feed on smaller fish close to the sea bed. Colouring on the whiting sometimes leads to confusion for the novice angler, and it is often wrongly identified as a pouting. The whiting has a pinkish-brown sheen across its back and the silver flanks lead to a whitish belly. Some fish have small black dots across the back, but this is not common in all whiting. The whiting spawns between the months of March and June and larger females can lay many thousands of eggs. Growth in the young fish is prolific and it can double its size in two years, reaching 15–18 in (38–45 cm) by the fourth year.

Whiting are more at home in shallower water and are caught from the shore in greater numbers than from a boat. However, boat-caught species tend to be bigger and may reach weights of 3 lb (1.36 kg) and upwards. Towards the end of August the whiting start to move inshore to feed for the winter, and the best sport can be had during late evenings on a high tide from the beach or a pier. Shallow, sandy storm beaches and bays are good places for whiting in the winter.

Current Records
Shore **4 lb 7 drm (1.827 kg)**
Boat **6 lb 12 oz (3.062 kg)**
World **6 lb 13 oz (3.11 kg) Norway**

Season
August through to January.

Distribution
All through the coastal waters of Britain. They are also found in Norway, the North Sea and the English Channel.

Natural diet
The whiting feeds on practically any small fish but especially on sprats.

Top Spot
Both the Norfolk and Suffolk coasts produce good catches, especially around Aldeburgh. Whiting to 4 lb (1.814 kg) can be caught from boats in the English Channel.

Top Tip
Mackerel strip-baited feathers are excellent from a boat, while lugworms tipped with either squid or mackerel strip work best from the shore.

Coalfish *(Pollachius virens)*

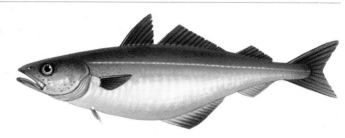

Current Records
Shore **37 lb 5 oz (16.925 kg)**
Boat **24 lb 11 oz 12 drm (11.22 kg)**

Season
September through to March.

Distribution
They are widely distributed around the British coastline, but are more common to the northern waters of Scotland.

Natural Diet
Small fish, herring fry and whitebait.

Top Spot
Big coalfish are often caught over the Plymouth wrecks by anglers targeting pollack.

Top Tip
Artificial eels such as the Eddystone and Redgill patterns work very well, both from the shore and while boat fishing.

Known in Scottish waters as the saithe, the coalfish is a member of the cod family and is often mistaken for, and bears a resemblance to, its cousin the pollack. The obvious difference between the two is that the lower jaw of the pollack protrudes the upper jaw and it has a barbule under the chin. The lateral line of the coalfish is different to that of the pollack as it is of light appearance on a dark background. Like other sea fishes the coalfish will often vary in colour depending on what depth of water it is caught from. Shore-caught coalfish from relatively shallow water will appear very bright and silvery. They are often burnished with a tint of golden green and have a cream or white belly. Deep-water coalfish are more of a greeny-grey with pale, white bellies. They are very active hunters and form large shoals as they plunder small food fish. They will travel long distances in search of rich food supplies such as herring fry and whitebait and have been known to take small salmon smolts entering the sea in May.

Boat anglers tend to catch the bigger specimens over deep water wrecks on a variety of baits. The smaller specimens come close into the shore and are more commonly caught from rocky shores during the hours of darkness.

Ling *(Molva molva)*

The largest and most prolific member of the cod family, the ling can reach a weight of 80 lb (36.3 kg) but is normally caught between 10–50 lb (4.54–22.68 kg). It is primarily a deep-water species living amongst the deep-water wrecks and reefs off the coast of Britain. Similar to an eel in shape it can often extend to 6 ft (1.83 m) in length. Being a predator it is well-equipped to eat most smaller species and items of bait with its well-toothed mouth. As with the cod, the ling has a barbule hanging from the underside of the chin. Its long body is coated in slime secreted from the skin to form a protective covering against disease.

Colouration is normally of a greyish-brown marbled back with a creamy-white underside.

The ling is well distributed around the British coastline and favoured grounds lie off the south-west coast of Cornwall. Ling are mostly caught by boat anglers but there are a few rocky, deep-water shore marks where ling to 20 lb (9.07 kg) have been caught by anglers fishing at night. They feed extensively on smaller species and among the best baits are pouting and codling. For the novice angler out on a boat trip, ling can provide a good day's sport as they are relatively easy to catch. A large baited pirk is a good method to use for this species.

Current Records
Shore **21 lb 10 oz (9.809 kg)**
Boat **59 lb 8 oz (26.989 kg)**
World **82 lb (37.2 kg) Norway**

Season
All year round.

Distribution
Well distributed around the British coast but particularly off Cornwall. They are also common to the Orkneys, Shetland Isles and the west coast of Ireland. They can be found in the waters of the Arctic Circle, the coast of Iceland and Norway as well.

Natural Diet
Mostly small fish such as herring, flatfish, codling and pouting.

Top Spots
Wrecks off the north-east, south-west and Irish coasts. Ports such as Brixham in Devon and Bridlington in Yorkshire, are recognized for producing big ling hauls.

Top Tip
Try fishing over a wreck with a large baited pirk.

Flounder *(Platichthys flesus)*

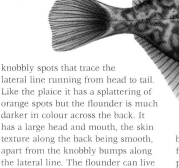

Current Records
Shore **5 lb 7 oz (2.466 kg)**
Boat **5 lb 11 oz 8 drm (2.594 kg)**

Season
All year round, but particularly in the winter.

Distribution
Common throughout the British Isles in creeks and estuaries.

Natural Diet
Crustaceans, worms, cockles and small crabs.

Top Spots
Rivers Teign, Plym, Yealm and Exe in South Devon, but also the River Tyne.

Top Tip
The addition of a flounder spoon about 6 in (15 cm) up the trace from the hook will help attract the flounder to your bait.

The flounder is a very popular species and is caught mainly from creeks or muddy estuaries. It is a member of the flatfish family and can be identified by the row of hard knobbly spots that trace the lateral line running from head to tail. Like the plaice it has a splattering of orange spots but the flounder is much darker in colour across the back. It has a large head and mouth, the skin texture along the back being smooth, apart from the knobbly bumps along the lateral line. The flounder can live quite happily in very brackish water and is often caught right at the top of the estuary where freshwater meets salt.

Not overlarge in size and mainly caught at between 2–3 lb (0.91–1.36 kg), the flounder can provide good sport on light tackle and is relatively easy to catch. It has a maximum size of around 6 lb (2.72 kg) and a 4 lb (1.81 kg) flounder is considered a specimen fish. It can be caught all year round, but the better sport is to be had in the winter. They will often feed when all other species will not, particularly when the weather is really cold. During the summer months they leave the estuaries in order to return to the sea to spawn. They are very much at home over a muddy, sandy bottom and can be located in the many gullies or troughs ploughed out by the ebbing tide in estuaries and creeks around the coast. A good bait for flounder fishing is without doubt the peeler crab. Some big flounders have been caught from the storm beaches of Ireland on peeler crab intended for bass.

Dab *(Pleuronectes limanda)*

Current Records
Shore **2 lb 9 oz 8 drm (1.177 kg)**
Boat **2 lb 12 oz 4 drm (1.248 kg)**

Season
March through to August.

Distribution
Present around the south-west coast of Britain in good numbers. Also spread widely along the European coastline.

Natural diet
Crabs, worms, fish fry, molluscs and several types of seaweed.

Top Spots
The Norfolk and Suffolk coastlines offer superb dab sport.

Top Tip
Due to the small mouth it is advisable to fish with small baits on small hooks. Many sea anglers use a short-shank, size 6 freshwater carp hook.

The smallest member of the flatfish family, the dab rarely exceeds 12 in (30 cm) in length. Sandy brown in colour with a white creamy underside, it's very often mistaken for a small plaice by the beginner to sea angling. One quick way to spot the difference is to look at the lateral line on the top side of the dab. Trace the lateral line from behind the head at the opening to the gill cover, and you will see that it curves away slightly before becoming straight again. On the plaice it is straight, from the gill cover to the tail. Another way of telling the difference is to run your finger from tail to head on the back. You will find the skin is of a rough texture, while the same test on a plaice will reveal a smooth skin. At birth the dab is actually a round fish, and during growth the left eye moves around the head to take up position slightly forward of the right. The dab will then lie on its left side on the bottom of the sea bed with no impediment to its sight. When fishing sandy open beaches, you are likely to encounter the dab. It is mainly found in shallow waters all around our coast and is also present in large numbers in inshore waters along the European coast all the way to Iceland.

Plaice *(Pleuronectes platessa)*

Current Records
Shore **8 lb 6 oz 14 drm (3.824 kg)**
Boat **10 lb 3 oz 8 drm (4.635 kg)**

Season
February through to end of September.

Distribution
All round the British coastline, they are very common in the deeper waters of the North Sea. They are also distributed as far north as Iceland and as far south as the Mediterranean.

Natural Diet
Mostly shellfish, such as razorfish, mussels and cockles. The strong mouth of the plaice is able to crush and grind away the shell to get to the inner meat. They also feed on most marine worms.

Top Spots
The Shambles Bank off Weymouth in Dorset is a well-known hot spot. Also Skerries Banks, Devon.

Top Tip
The addition of half a dozen or so brightly coloured beads or sequins above the hook attracts plaice. Like other flatfish, they are very inquisitive.

The plaice is probably the most commonly known member of the flatfish family, due to its easy identification. Colour will vary depending on the location and depth of water. However, it is usually marked with a dark-brown back, with a series of orange or scarlet spots scattered at random over the skin. The eyes on the plaice, as with other flatfish, are positioned on the top side of the fish, allowing it to have a wide scope of vision while lying flat on the sea bed. The female plaice is capable of producing 250,000 eggs when spawning takes place early in the year in January or February.

Plaice do not grow to huge sizes and a fish of 5 lb (2.27 kg) is considered a worthy specimen. Areas of the sea bed offering a sandy or shingle grit bottom are the ideal location for fishing. The most famous marks of all for plaice fishing are the Skerries Banks, a series of sand banks off the coast of Dartmouth in Devon. Plaice will frequent areas of the sea bed where small mussels have established themselves in good numbers as the mussel makes up a high percentage of their dietary requirement. Many bigger plaice are caught by boat anglers fishing over deep water sand banks, but plaice will venture close into the shore, especially during the winter. Storm beaches with a steep shelf dropping away into the water are a good place to try. They respond well to all manner of baits and a ragworm and squid cocktail is a firm favourite.

Pollack *(Pollachius pollachius)*

Pollack are well-documented as great sport-fish when hooked on light tackle. They have the ability to fight hard and often tear off on a heart-stopping run when first hooked. A member of the cod family, pollack are often confused with their close relative the coalfish. However, they can be easily recognized by the distinct protruding lower jaw. The jaw provides the fish with a means to disable its prey when attacking from below. Colouring is another form of identification when confusion arises between the two. The pollack is greenish brown with a very dark lateral line, while the coalfish is more blue-black. The tail of the pollack is of a square appearance, whereas the coalfish has a defined fork in the centre of the tail fin. It is built with power and speed in mind, as being a predator

it has to move fast to ambush smaller species. The pollack can be located over rocky ground, but in the colder months bigger specimens stay well out in deeper water. Once the warmer weather arrives smaller pollack venture into the shallower water to feed, especially after the hours of darkness. They spawn early in the year, from March to the end of April.

Most shore-caught species rarely exceed 3 lb (1.36 kg) and to catch a bigger specimen you will have to hunt them out over deep-water wrecks. Pollack between 12–16 lb (5.44–7.26 kg) are plentiful from this type of area and can be caught on baited hooks or lures such as artificial eels. For the beginner, the smaller pollack can offer great sport when fishing the night tide from a pier or harbour wall using float tackle.

Current Records
Shore **18 lb 4 oz (8.278 kg)**
Boat **29 lb 4 oz (13.268 kg)**

Season
Can be caught all year round.particularly in the south west.

Distribution
Spread all around the coast of Britain especially off the south-west coast. Also present off the coast of Ireland and the Atlantic shores of Iceland.

Natural Diet
Small crabs, wrasse, sandeels, rocklings and prawns.

Top Spot
The Eddystone reef in Plymouth, Devon is a prolific mark, as most of the offshore wrecks along the south coast.

Top Tip
Using an artificial eel on light tackle over a wreck is the most exiting method for catching pollack. Drop the eel on a 15 ft (4.6 m) trace to the sea bed and wind up at a steady rate. If you feel the fish plucking at the eel don't stop, just keep on winding until it hooks itself.

Blue Shark *(Prionace glauca)*

Current Records
Shore **40 lb (18.14 kg)**
Boat **218 lb (98.88 kg)**
World **454 lb (205.93 kg) USA**

Season
May through to October.

Distribution
All around the British coastline and especially south-west Cornwall. They are also present around the southern and western shores of Ireland.

Natural Diet
Most smaller species of fish. The mackerel and herring are two prime examples.

Top Spot
South-west Cornish coast during the warmer months of the year.

Top Tip
When sharking, don't stop other activities such as mackerel fishing. The activity in the water will draw sharks closer to the boat.

A member of the shark family, the blue shark is one of the two most common around UK coastlines, the other being the porbeagle. Blue sharks can be found in the warmer waters of the southern coast of Britain, especially around the Cornish coastline. It takes its name from its distinctive dark-blue back and light-blue flanks. However, once removed from the sea and killed, its blue coat fades away to a dreary grey colour. The blue shark is a voracious predator and has been known to attack swimmers off beaches.

It can grow to over 12 ft (3.66 m) in length and blue sharks over 200 lb (90.72 kg) have been caught in British waters. Evidence suggests they can grow much larger, but smaller fish in the 60–70 lb (21–31.75 kg) class are more commonly caught. A fish of this size can be a very testing target for the novice fisherman.

Like other species of shark, the blue has what is known as a spiracle or an opening behind the eye. This is connected to the gill system, which controls respiration. They have no swim bladder and regulate their buoyancy by controlling the amount of water within the body cavity.

The blue shark is a roving species and can be found in deep-water areas off rocky, cliff-lined shores. Where there is a good supply of smaller prey fish the blue shark will not be far away. In the warmer weather they will venture close to the shore in pursuit of food.

Thornback Ray *(Raja clavata)*

Probably the most widely caught member of the ray family, thornbacks are so named due to the array of thorny spines that adorn the tail and wings. The mouth is positioned on the underside, allowing it to move over the sea bed and cover its selected food item before passing it through a set of grinding teeth, which are powerful enough to crush shells and molluscs. The eyes are set on the top side and it is thought that eyesight is very poor; instead the thornback relies on an internal radar system thought to be triggered by a form of electromagnetism and vibration. Directly behind the eyes are two holes which are breathing vents, or spiracles. Colouration of the body varies depending on the type of bottom the ray is living over. The adult thornback is usually a pale brownish-yellow and is coated in patchy black speckles. Towards the rear of the body and

extending down the tail there will often be a brownish-red pigment to the skin. Thornback rays are not commonly found in very deep water, preferring the inshore clean grounds of sand and mud. They are a popular target for both dinghy and shore anglers who are advised to take time when striking at a thornback bite, in order for the ray to work the bait well into its mouth. They are not caught in huge sizes and are the second smallest species in the ray family. A specimen of 15 lb (6.8 kg) is a good catch, and thornbacks above this weight tend to be females. They are often found close to estuaries and even travel up into the estuary to feed on sandeels.

Current Records
Shore **21 lb 12 oz (9.866 kg)**
Boat **31 lb 7 oz (14.26 kg)**

Season
March through to the end of October.

Distribution
Throughout the British Isles, Ireland, North Sea, Baltic Sea and the Mediterranean Sea.

Natural Diet
Being a predator it thrives on small fish such as young flatfish, sandeels, herrings, sprats and crustaceans.

Top Spots
The Thames Estuary and Bristol Channel are famous for their thornback ray fishing.

Top Tip
Early on in the season the top bait is a chunk of fresh herring. As the summer approaches, fresh peeler crabs take over as the number one bait. On the east coast, hermit crabs are another favoured bait.

Common Skate (Raja batis)

Current Records
Shore **169 lb 6 oz (76.828 kg)**
Boat **227 lb (102.967 kg)**

Season
May through to October, with September offering the best fishing.

Distribution
Mainly the waters of the Scottish Islands and off the coast of south-west Ireland.

Natural Diet
Dogfish and small ray are a major part of the diet, but they also eat small flatfish, edible crab and starfish.

Top Spot
The Sound of Mull, Western Scotland.

Top Tip
Use a very large bait such as three whole mackerel or a 4 lb (1.8 kg) pollack.

The common skate belongs to the skate family, three of whose members are of importance to the sea angler: the white skate, the long-nosed skate and the common skate.

The common skate is sometimes referred to as the blue or grey skate, due to its greyish-blue colouration when first taken from the sea. They are usually a dark, greenish-brown colour across the top side, with a whitish-grey underside littered with dark-rimmed pores, and will often have golden-coloured spots and pinkish stripes on the back. The body is shaped like a diamond, while the front end resembles the head of a shovel. Like other skates and rays they have two large holes, spiracles, just behind the eyes. Skates breathe through these for if, like other species, they had to take water in through their mouths, they would not survive, as each breath would mean a mouthful of mud.

Once common around the whole coast of Britain, these giants of the sea are mainly sought after off the Western Isles of Scotland. They grow to a huge size, up to 8 ft (2.44 m) in length, live in waters of up to 600 ft (183 m) deep and have been caught weighing 150 lb (68 kg) or more. Many anglers who fish for the skate return their quarry to the sea after capture in a bid to preserve this wonderful creature. The larger common skate can be found over sand and mud bottoms and spends much of its time half-buried in the sea bed. This gives it the cover to seize its prey. Smaller common skate are often found in shallower water.

Thick-Lipped Mullet (Chelon labrosus)

Current Records
Shore **14 lb 2 oz 12 drm (6.428 kg)**
Boat **10 lb 1 oz (4.564 kg)**

Season
April through to October.

Distribution
They are present throughout the shallower waters of the British coast, the Channel Islands and north-west Europe.

Natural Diet
Mainly plant life, small crustaceans and algae.

Top Spot
Dover's Admiralty Pier is just one of the man-made structures around which mullet love to live.

Top Tip
Filling an onion sack with mashed bread and lowering it over the side of a pier or breakwater often attracts mullet to the surface. Fish with light tackle and use bread flake on the hook as bait.

There are three species of grey mullet that the angler is likely to observe while out fishing: the golden grey, the thin-lipped and the most common, the thick-lipped. When small they are often confused with the bass, but there are a few differences that help to identify them correctly. Mullet are covered in large scales all over the body, even over their gill covers, unlike the bass. It is possible to tell the age of a good-sized mullet from the scales by counting the number of rings present. The thick-lipped mullet is coloured in a shade of grey across the back and has a white belly. As the name suggests it has a pair of thick lips and contrary to belief can be hooked and caught by the angler. Mullet have long been surrounded by a myth that they are uncatchable, and if hooked by the angler they are easily lost, due to the soft lips. However, although they are a shy, clever fish and often seem to ignore anglers' baits, they can be caught, and the lips of the mullet are actually quite tough.

Thick-lipped mullet move in shoals and feed close to the surface on small crustaceans and vegetable matter. They have poor teeth, so food is swallowed and broken down in the stomach. They can be located close to the shore and in the summer are present in many harbours and estuaries. Visit any harbour in the warmer months and you will see the mullet cruising around just under the surface, searching out scraps of food and sucking items of waste from the underside of fishing boats. As they are able to tolerate brackish water, they are very often caught in the lower reaches and estuaries of many river systems.

Mackerel *(Scomber scombrus)*

The mackerel is one of the hardest fighting sea species. Similar in looks to its relative the tuna fish, mackerel are built for speed and power. The head is pointed and the sleek, slim body resembles a torpedo, finishing off with a large, forked tail. It has a very distinctive colouration with a metallic, marine blue back, shaded over with black bars. When the fish is removed from water the colour soon fades away to a dull grey. The white flanks and underside of the species are covered with a film of silver, pink, gold and blue which shines like a rainbow.

The mackerel spends its time in search of fry and sandeels. They will charge headlong into a shoal of fry, twisting and turning at speed with mouths open until they catch their prey.

Mackerel are often caught on feathers or while float fishing. Being a shoal fish mackerel can be caught in great numbers. It is thought that the mackerel never stops swimming and as they are always on the move, more water passes through the gills, helping them to breathe more easily while maintaining fast, active movement. Spawning in the months of January through to June, they are a slow-growing species and it is thought that a mackerel of 1 lb (0.45 kg) in weight could be as old as eight years. During the winter they head for the deeper, warmer waters of the Irish Sea, while in the spring they move back into the shallow waters. Huge shoals can often be seen breaking the surface as they chase brit or sandeels in summer.

Current Records
Shore **5 lb 11 oz 14 drm (2.605 kg)**
Boat **6 lb 2 oz 7 drm (2.791 kg)**

Season
April to October, with the peak season for the shore angler in June and July.

Distribution
Present in large numbers around the coastline of Cornwall. Other hot spots include the North Yorkshire coastline, the south of Ireland and west Scotland.

Natural Diet
Plankton, squid, brit, whitebait, sandeels and any small fry.

Top Spots
Most piers and breakwater walls around the UK. Rock marks such as Hope's Nose and Berry Head in Devon are well-known mackerel marks.

Top Tip
When fishing with float tackle, fish the bait very shallow, set at a depth of 4 ft (1.22 m) or even less. Mackerel spend a lot of time near the surface chasing smaller fry.

Turbot *(Scophthalmus maximus)*

The turbot is one of the most prized members of the flatfish family and makes an excellent meal for the angler's table. It is very similar to the brill, both in looks and habits. Identification in comparison to the brill can be made from the shape of the body, as turbot are round. Another form of identification is the number of rays featured on the anal fin. The turbot has around 46 while the brill is blessed with some 60, housed on a longer fin. Turbot are coloured to blend in with their surroundings and are usually of a light-brown or sandy appearance on the top with a spattering of fine bony tubercles.

They bear a resemblance to a polished marble surface and are masters of disguise when half-buried in the sandy bottom of the sea bed. The large mouth can accommodate a whole small fish when the jaws are fully extended. It is fitted with very fine teeth running up each side to grip the food. Turbot spawn in the months of March to June and a female is capable of laying ten million eggs, each one being 1 mm in size.

Turbot can be found in good numbers around the coast of Britain and enjoy the rich hunting grounds of sandy bays and the sides of shallow, sloping sandbanks. They are also caught close to estuary marks which have muddy bottoms and many of the deep-water wrecks. Capable of growing upwards of 30 lb (13.61 kg) in weight they can give the sea angler a good spirited fight if they are hooked on light tackle. They can often be caught by drifting a moving bottom bait over the slopes of a sandbank once the tide starts to run. The turbot will follow a moving bait for some distance before moving in and attacking the bait.

Current Records
Shore **28 lb 8 oz (12.927 kg)**
Boat **33 lb 12 oz (15.3 kg)**

Season
From May through to the end of October.

Distribution
Widespread around the coast of Britain, but more so in the south-west.

Natural Diet
Shrimps, sandeels, sprats, whiting and small flatfish.

Top Spots
Around the offshore wrecks off the north-east coast and the Shambles Bank off Weymouth, Dorset.

Top Tip
Use a long trace of around 8–12 ft (2.44–3.66 m), baited with sandeel or mackerel strip.

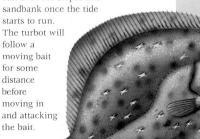

Lesser-spotted Dogfish *(Scyllium canicula)*

The lesser-spotted dogfish is the most common of the dogfish to be found along the British coast. It is a member of the shark family, and although it bears a similarity in looks, it is considerably smaller. Often called the roughhound due to its sandpaper-textured skin, it can be easily identified by the newcomer to sea angling by the vast array of spots peppered over its back and sides. Its orange-brown back and pale cream belly distinguish the lesser-spotted dogfish from its close cousin the greater-spotted dogfish. The greater spotted has larger spots, and the two have different positioning of the nose flaps. On the greater-spotted dogfish the nose flap does not join and is positioned above the mouth, while with the lesser-spotted variety the nose flap is continuous and almost joins the mouth. Their eyesight is poor and the dogfish relies on its keen sense of smell to hunt down prey. Its small sharp teeth are used to bite and tear at food.

Caught from both boat and shore, the lesser-spotted dogfish can be located over sandy, muddy or gravel bottom areas. When caught, the angler may experience difficulty in holding the fish still, and the dogfish may inflict a nasty graze with its rough skin. Holding the dogfish behind the head and bringing the tail up to meet it is the correct way to immobilize the fish. It has a skeleton of cartilage rather than hard bone and held in this way you will do no harm to the fish.

Current Records
Shore **4 lb 15 oz 3 drm (2.245 kg)**
Boat **4 lb 6 oz 8 drm (1.998 kg)**

Season
April through to November.

Distribution
Widespread throughout the British Isles, North Sea and Mediterranean Sea.

Natural Diet
Crabs, lobsters, shrimps, prawns, sandeels and small flatfish.

Top Spot
The Welsh coast offers some superb dogfish sport, both from shore and boat. Pick a sandy beach fringed by rocks.

Top Tip
A three-hook paternoster rig with size 2/0 sea hooks baited with either mackerel or sandeel is the top method for catching good dogfish.

Dover Sole *(Solea solea)*

A member of the flatfish family, the name Dover derives from the days when the sole was transported from the Kent coast to the London restaurants for the gentry to eat. Sometimes called slips or tongues due to their small size and resemblance to an animal's tongue, the Dover sole is of a pale-brown colour with darker patches and widespread speckling across its top side. It does not grow to a large size, and a sole of 2 lb (0.91 kg) is regarded as a fine specimen. Like others in the flatfish family, the eyes are mounted close together on the right or upper side of the body. The underside or belly is pure white, although on some occasions colouring does occur over the belly on freak fish. For quick identification there is a dark spot located on the tip of the right pectoral fin. It has a very small mouth, which explains why not that many are caught by anglers who normally use big baits. The entire body, with the exception of the underside of the head, is coated in tiny scales, giving the Dover sole a rough texture to its skin while its cousin the lemon sole is smooth to touch and has bigger blotches on the back. When caught commercially and presented at the table the skin is removed by peeling it from the body in one continuous strip.

Spawning usually takes place between the months of March and May over inshore marks in warmer water. When the colder weather arrives the sole moves back out to deeper water and in extremely low temperatures becomes almost comatose. Dover sole like gravel and sandy sea beds, burying themselves under the surface of the sand to make themselves less conspicuous to predators. Anglers in search of the Dover sole should fish with small hooks and very small pieces of ragworm or lugworm bait.

Current Records
Shore **6 lb 8 oz 10 drm (2.966 kg)**
Boat **4 lb 1 oz 12 drm (1.864 kg)**

Season
April through to the end of September.

Distribution
Spread throughout the English Channel, west coast of Ireland and the Irish Sea, scarcer in the north of Scotland.

Natural Diet
Crustaceans, molluscs, sandeels, worms and small fishes.

Top Spot
The town beach at Aldeburgh in Suffolk is a well-known sole hot spot.

Top Tip
Let bites develop: sole have small mouths, and it takes time for them to reach the hook, even with small bait.

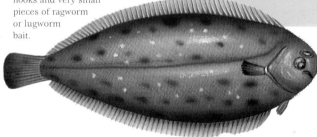

Black Bream *(Spondyliosoma cantharus)*

Current Records
Shore **5 lb 2 drm (2.272 kg)**
Boat **6 lb 14 oz 4 drm (3.126 kg)**

Season
May through to September.

Distribution
Found in coastal waters all around the British Isles and Channel Islands.

Natural Diet
Small blennies, crustaceans, marine worms, plankton and seaweed.

Top Spots
The south coast ports; Littlehampton, Hayling, Lymington and Poole.

Top Tip
A ragworm tipped with a strip of squid.

The black bream shares many of the characteristics of the marine fish family Sparidae. Its colouring and shape give a clue to its name, as its deep-bodied shape is similar to that of the freshwater bream. Colouring on the black bream may vary slightly depending on the area and the depth of water from which it is caught. The flanks are normally grey or silver, with the back dark grey with a blue sheen, shading into black around the top of the back.

This fully scaled species has a long dorsal fin with sharp spines and a shorter anal fin fitted with three further spines. It has a small head in comparison to the body and the upper jaw is fitted with a front row of sharp white teeth. Sitting behind these are an additional set of curved, needle-like teeth. The black bream spawns in April or May and differs from other sea bream as it makes a nest on the bottom of the sea bed to lay its spawn in.

In recent years the black bream has not been caught in the large numbers previously seen. This has been attributed to overfishing. However, stocks are said to be on the increase off the south coast of Britain.

Black bream do not grow to a great size and a bream of 3 lb (1.36 kg) can be considered a fine specimen of a fish. They are more commonly caught by boat anglers fishing over areas of broken rocky ground and reefs. Some of the smaller fish do get caught from the shore, but this tends to be from marks in deeper water. A broken reef with a wreck located on it is the ideal hunting ground for the black bream. Here it can feed in the safety of deep water on small crustaceans, plankton and seaweed. Black bream are renowned as a sporty, hard fighter on appropriate tackle.

Spurdog *(Squalus acanthias)*

A member of the shark family, the spurdog is easily distinguished from other dogfish. There are two main features which determine the species, one of which is the two extremely sharp spines present on the back, at the front of each of the two dorsal fins. To the unwary angler these spines can inflict a nasty cut that may require medical attention. When handling, the spurdog should be held by the neck of the tail with one hand and supported by the underside of the throat with the other. This will stop the spurdog from twisting its tail around the arm or wrist of the angler. The other aid to identification is the absence of the anal fin present on other members of the dogfish group. Looking very much like a small shark, it lacks the third eyelid or membrane, used to cover or clean the eyeball, present in the shark family group. Spurdogs are also sometimes mistaken

for tope by the novice angler. The spurdog has a dreary, pale, greyish back and sides, with a pale-white underside. The long and slender body is built for speed and it travels in packs when hunting prey, usually at a mid-water depth. The mouth contains a set of sharp teeth built for ripping and shredding prey fish.

It is more likely to be caught from the boat by the angler fishing for other species. This is due to the fact that the spurdog prefers the deeper water marks of clean sandy bottoms. However, a few are caught from the shore, and the bulk of these have been identified as females, probably because the female of the species moves into shallower waters to expel its young during the months of August and October.

Current Records
Shore **16 lb 12 oz 8 drm ((7.612 kg)**
Boat **21 lb 3 oz 7 drm (9.623 kg)**

Season
May through to November, sometimes late December.

Distribution
Present throughout the British Isles, they are caught in larger numbers from the western coastline.

Natural Diet
Any small fish, including soles, sprats, sardines, squids and sandeels.

Top Spots
Boats out of Swansea and Rhyl, Wales, catch lots of spurdogs. Scottish sea lochs are also renowned for their spurdog sport.

Top Tip
Herring are one of the top spurdog baits. In some areas a large chunk of garfish flesh is favoured.

Sea Angling Baits

The sea angler has a wealth of baits at his or her disposal and is blessed with many free offerings from the sea shore. From ragworm to razorfish, a good angler will never be short of the right bait for the species sought. Modern-day tackle shops offer a wide variety of commercially produced blast-frozen baits, which will be totally fresh. The bigger shops, in particular, will have a good weekly trade in freshly dug live worms and regular supplies of the much-prized peeler crab. You can also buy fresh sea baits straight from the fish markets as the daily catch is landed. Even the local fishmonger's shop might have what you are looking for. Bait often plays second fiddle to quality tackle but a fresh bait in educated hands will out-fish an expensive fishing rod and poor-quality bait. There is no excuse for presenting a poor-quality bait, especially if you are able to collect or dig your own. If you are lucky enough to be in a position to do this, and you can combine quality bait with good angling skills, the rewards can be high.

Peeler Crab

This is probably the most popular bait used by the sea angler and is used up and down the coast as it attracts a variety of different species. It gets its name from the fact that it sheds or peels its skin at several stages throughout its life.

When the crab is in a state of peeling it is a much sought-after bait. Due to the sheer demand, the price of peeler crabs in tackle shops can soar in the winter months, when they are very much in short supply. If you are lucky enough to live near an estuary where peelers are present, you may be in a position to collect them yourself at low tide. Many anglers have established areas of the sea shore where they have placed special peeler traps. These usually consist of a length of broken pipe or a semi-circular roof tile which the crab will hide under while peeling its shell. The trap is inserted into the mud or shingle at an angle allowing the

peeler to crawl under it to shed its shell. When the tide drops the crab will be found sheltering deep in the back end of the trap. It's hard work collecting peelers and in some areas you may only find five crabs in 100 traps per tide. However, if you are fishing in competitions in the winter, it's well worth the effort for this is without doubt a superior bait.

Peeler crabs are widely used for flounder and cod fishing and are easy to prepare for the hook. If you look at the shell on the back of the crab you will see a split forming around the base of the shell near to the legs. With your thumb and forefinger gently prise the shell upwards and it will come off. This will reveal a soft skin and once exposed it is a deadly bait.

To make the bait go further the crab can be cut into two sections. Simply take a knife and cut down through the centre of the body. Don't discard the legs as they are a good bait in their own right. The legs, once peeled, can either be used to hold the body of the crab on the hook, or can be used by themselves as a bait. By picking away the shell at the end of the legs you will soon be able to peel away the rest of the protective coating to reveal the soft flesh.

The best way to store peelers is to collect them and keep them alive in a bucket, covering them with damp seaweed. If you are going to keep

TOP: Peeler crabs are regarded by many anglers as the top bait for a large variety of species.

LEFT: Search around the sea shore as the tide drops away and a wealth of free bait becomes available.

them for a few days you will need to replace the seaweed as it will dry out. It is advisable to remove any dead or dying peelers from the bucket and freeze them, but peel them first before freezing. They should be frozen individually and wrapped in clear film to protect them from freezer burn. A good tip when freezing is to remove the gills which can be found at the side of the crab under the eyes. This will help to keep them fresher if they are to be frozen for long periods.

Hooking Peeler Crab

To get the best from your bait it is advisable to peel the body completely and remove the gills and legs. The legs should also be fully peeled. Lay the peeled crab on its back and cut the body in half long-ways, down through the centre with a knife. Take half the body and thread the point of the hook through the leg sockets, starting at one end and working up through the sockets to the other. The crab should be quite secure on the hook at this stage.

To enhance the bait and help to keep the body on the hook if casting a fair distance, the legs can be impaled on the hook below the body. Using the legs in this manner will give the impression of the bait being a whole, live crab. If you like to fish at a long distance and place a considerable force on the bait when casting, use an elastic cotton thread to bind the bait into position on the hook for added security.

RIGHT: Quite often anglers will use crab mixed with another type of bait to form a cocktail. Here it is being used with lugworm.

Mounting a Peeler Crab

1 Peeler crab has long been regarded as a top all-round sea-angling bait. It is widely used in competitions and is attractive to all manner of species.

2 Fresh crabs should be used when they are ready to shed their shells and are completely peeled as shown, including the legs.

3 Take a sharp knife and cut the body of the crab almost in half. Leave a hinge in the flesh at the lower end of the crab, like this.

4 Start to thread the crab on to the hook. For shore fishing this should be a size 1/0 or 2/0. Thread the hook in and out of the leg sockets, to hold the crab in position on the hook.

5 Once the crab is mounted, if you wish to use a cotton thread, hold the cotton thread by binding the crab into position around the body as shown.

6 To complement the body part of the crab, the legs should now be added to the hook. This is called "tipping a bait" and gives the appearance of a whole, live crab.

Mackerel

Mackerel is widely available to the angler and is a top sea bait for a variety of species. They can be caught on feathers, purchased from the tackle shop frozen, or bought fresh from the fishmonger's shop.

There are many ways of presenting mackerel on the hook, as it can be used in its whole form or cut into small strips. Most shore anglers cut fillets, one from each side, and then cut these into small strips. To cut the fillets away from the bone, simply hold the mackerel down on a cutting board by the head and insert a sharp knife into the flesh behind the gills. Cut so that the knife blade reaches the central bone. Then turn the knife away from the head, cutting all the way down the body to the tail. By keeping the knife blade flat and following the top of the central bone, the knife will exit at the wrist of the tail. The cut fillet should lift away from the main body in one piece.

If you then require a number of smaller strips of mackerel flesh it is simply a case of cutting uniform strips from one of the fillets. When your are shore fishing with float tackle for mackerel and garfish it is advisable to cut small strips.

Boat anglers fishing for conger eels, tope or sharks will use what is known as a flapper. This is a whole mackerel with the backbone cut away to leave the head and side fillets intact. When presented on the hook the fillets flap around in the tide giving the impression the bait is on the move. If you catch a few mackerel next time you are out fishing, why not gut and freeze them to use later on in the year. If you are freezing mackerel it is a good idea to wrap them individually in clear film (plastic wrap) after cleaning them, as this will protect the flesh from freezer burn.

Hooking Mackerel

For boat fishing, anglers will usually use a whole or half-mackerel bait, depending on the species they are fishing for. For larger species such as conger a whole mackerel is the standard approach. The mackerel is mounted up whole on a large hook in a fashion known as a "flapper bait". This consists of a whole mackerel that has had the backbone removed giving the appearance of a moving target for the conger to grab at. This also helps

Mounting a Flapper and Strips of Mackerel Bait

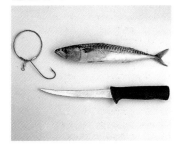

1 Whole mackerel are a good bottom fishing bait for conger eels. They can be prepared for the hook as follows and should be fished on a large hook and a wire trace.

2 Take a sharp knife and cut the mackerel in half from the gill cover near the head to the tail end, keeping the knife flat against the central backbone.

3 Turn the mackerel over and repeat the process until you have two cut wings as shown. Now remove the backbone so you have just the head of the mackerel and the two side fillets.

to release a very strong scent trail for the fish to home in on. The seahook which should be a size 6/0 or 8/0, is passed through the head with the point left clear.

When fishing for bass or cod a simple whole side fillet can be mounted on the hook by passing the hook through the bait at the top of the fillet twice. This will ensure the bait stays firmly on the hook, but it allows the tail end of the fillet to move freely in the tide, imitating a small fish.

The shore angler will be using smaller baits for species like garfish, cod, dogfish, whiting and even mackerel themselves. The most common way of preparing a shore bait when using mackerel is to cut it into long strips. Each strip is then used as an individual bait on a small seahook, such as a 1/0. When cutting the strips it is a good idea to make the cuts at an angle across the body so the bottom of the strip tapers down to a point. The hook is inserted through the top end of the strip once only. Once presented in the water the strip of mackerel will give the appearance of a small fish or fry; this is perfect for any larger fish on the lookout for a free meal.

4 These are the two methods of presenting a mackerel "flapper bait". Use a large hook and wire trace with both: this is because, when fished on the bottom, a large fish such as a conger eel is expected to take the bait.

5 The most common way of preparing mackerel for shore fishing is to cut it into strips. Cut at an angle with the strips tapering downwards. This is a good bait for cod, dogfish and whiting.

RIGHT: Buy fillets of mackerel for shore fishing. Let them thaw and then prepare them as shown above.

OPPOSITE: Fresh mackerel can be caught on feathers, either cooked to eat or used as a bait.

ABOVE: Frozen mackerel can be bought from your local tackle shop in packs of two or more. It is a good idea to buy whole mackerel if you are fishing for large species such as congers, dogfish or cod, or if you are boat fishing and cannot catch fresh mackerel bait. Make sure the mackerel is straight as it will be easier to prepare.

Lugworms

The yellowtail lugworm is highly favoured by sea anglers as it is a natural bait. The name yellowtail derives from the fact that once handled, the worm emits a yellow iodine liquid that will stain the angler's hand. The black lugworm is so named because of its black colouring caused by the black mud it passes through its body when digging its burrow. It can be dug from muddy shore lines as the tide recedes. Some of the best yellowtail lug comes from the shore around Kent. It can be purchased from tackle shops or the angler can dig his own. To dig your own you will need a fork or a device known as a bait pump. You will also need a collection bucket or a container to keep the worms in while digging for others. Digging with a fork can be hard work and may take a considerable amount of time to collect a hundred or so worms.

A bait pump is a type of pump-action tube inserted into the mud over what is known as the worm cast. The worm is sucked into the chamber of the pump when suction is applied by lifting the handle. To operate the pump you will first need to find a worm cast, which is a mark left by the worm where it has come to the surface and begun to burrow back down again.

Place the pump over the cast and push it slightly into the ground. When you have the pump set in the ground, pull up the handle and this will create a vacuum which traps the mud and worm in the cylinder of the pump. Once the pump has been withdrawn the handle is pushed down, spewing the contents out on to the floor. You then pick up any worms caught in the pump and place them in your bucket.

There are also specialist lugworm spades available from good tackle shops. These are a worthwhile investment if the worms you seek are in deep burrows, sometimes as deep as 2 ft (60 cm) below the surface. To store the lugworms it is preferable to use a shallow tray with a small amount of sea water in the bottom. The tray should be kept in the bottom of a fridge to keep it at an even, cool temperature, and the sea water should be changed each day. Any dead or dying worms should be removed. You can freeze lugworms by first squeezing out their innards, and then

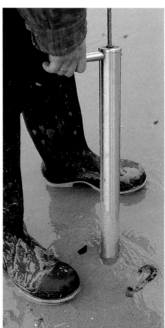

TOP: Black lugworms are widely used for cod fishing and should be threaded on the hook like this.

ABOVE CENTRE: Common or blow lugworms can be dug from the beach.

ABOVE: Lugworms can be dug with a fork, or a special bait pump can be used.

wrapping them individually in newspaper. Frozen in this manner they will keep for long periods. When defrosted, this tough, rubbery worm is a good bait for winter cod fishing.

Common Lugworm

Common lugworms, or blow lugworms as they are often called, are more usually found in a sandy environment. They can be dug from many beaches around the coastline. They can also be found in estuaries and make an excellent bait for many different species, including cod and whiting. As with the yellowtail lugworm, their burrow holes can be identified by the cast they leave on the surface of the sand. Unlike the yellowtail, the common lug favours a U-shaped tunnel or burrow, which rarely exceeds 15 in (38 cm). When spotting the cast on the surface it is advisable to look for the blow hole, which will be a short way behind the cast. This will give you a rough idea of where the worm will be lying before you attempt to dig down to it.

For collection purposes a bucket and garden fork will be needed. During the warmer months the worms can be dug out of the sand or mud with a fork quite easily. However, in colder weather they will burrow slightly deeper and will be harder to find. To store them, simply collect them in a bucket filled with a small amount of sea water. If you are going to keep them for a couple of days, store them in a fridge in a shallow tray with a shallow covering of sea water. Using this method it is possible to keep them alive for a considerable amount of time. Common lugworms do not make good baits for freezing, the problem being that the content of the common lugworm is mainly water.

Hooking Lugworms

When fishing for cod and casting lugworms any distance it is advisable to get as many as five or six worms on the same hook. It will help if the hook is of the long shank variety. To hook them, simply enter the hook point into the centre of the head and thread the hook right down through the centre of the body. Once on the hook the worm should be worked up the long shank and over the eye. Keep doing this until you have enough worms on the hook. It's usually the

Hooking Sandeels

When fishing for bass in a tidal run it is better to present the eel on a long trace with minimal or no weight. A single split shot can be used to force the eel down in the water, leaving it to swim freely. If you need more weight due to the pull of the tide, a small drilled ball weight can be used free-running on the line. When hooking sandeels for this method it is important that they are only lightly hooked so they can swim unhindered. A size 1 or even size 2 Aberdeen-style hook should be inserted into the flesh under the jaw once only. To fish a frozen eel in the same manner as described above it is advisable to pass the hook through the mouth and exit it just behind the gills. The hook will act as a means of support in keeping the eel upright and will let the tail sway in the flow in a natural manner. For other species like rays the hook is passed all the way through the eel's body. The point of the hook is then left pointing out from the side of the eel near the tail. This is done because a ray will often take a moment or two to take the bait well into its mouth. Approaching the eel from behind, the hook is therefore in the right position to enable a good hook hold should the ray try and eject the bait. Sandeels can be cut in half when used fresh or frozen, and fished under a float for pollack, mackerel and garfish.

case that the tail of the last worm is left hanging from the hook in an enticing manner. It's important to fill the hook completely if you are casting any distance, because live lugworms are a very soft bait and the impact on the worms when casting may result in some being lost while the tackle is in flight. When hooking frozen black lugworm you can be assured it will stay on the hook due to its thick, rubbery skin. A tip that many sea anglers use is to inject the skin with a flavour or oil before casting. This replaces the innards removed prior to freezing.

Sandeels

Sandeels are a terrific all-round sea bait and can be used alive or frozen. If you live in the south-west of Britain you may have seen them caught in large seine nets from the local beaches. It is best to get live sandeels, and species such as bass, pollack and rays are suckers for them. Once purchased or caught they can be stored for long periods in a floating wooden box known as a courge. The courge can be kept in sea water and tied to a mooring buoy until you need the eels. The sides of the box have very small holes to allow a constant flow of sea water to enter and leave, thus keeping the sandeels alive. If fishing from boat or shore you will need a bucket with an aerator pump to keep the eels in tip-top condition. Used alive, the sandeel is rated highly as a bass bait.

A small hook is used so as not to damage the eel or unbalance it. The hook is pushed through the skin under the jaw, and the eel is left to

swim freely. It is advisable to use little or no weight on the line, and many bass specialists use a single split shot weight to take the eel down in the tide. If you can't get hold of live sandeels then the next best thing is a packet of good-quality frozen ones. Many bait companies use a blast-freezing process which keeps the sandeel as fresh as the day it was caught. Frozen sandeels can be presented whole, cut into halves or used in strips. In the summer they can often be dug from the sand right on the tide line as the water drops. You will need a fork to do this and a quick eye to spot the eels as they try to burrow away in the soft sand.

TOP: **Lugworm being threaded on to a Pennell rig. This is a good bait to use in a cocktail with crab or squid.**

RIGHT: **Sandeels can usually be bought from the local tackle dealer and are available live and frozen. Live sandeels are best if you can get them.**

BELOW: **The best form of presentation using a live sandeel is to mount it on a single hook. The sandeel then moves naturally in the water. They are a good bait for bass.**

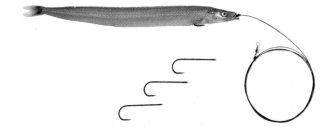

Razorfish

The razorfish is an excellent bait and is widely used for bass, cod and flatfish. It takes its name from the razor-shaped shell that surrounds the body. There are four species of razorfish found in British waters and the most common is the Pod razor which is usually about 3–5 in (7.62–12.7 cm) in length.

Razors can be gathered from the beach after a storm and are usually found right on the tide line buried beneath the sand. Anglers who have collected razors will be aware of a neat little trick you can employ to get the razor up to the surface of the sand. Using a bag of household salt, sprinkle it down the keyhole-shaped depressions in the sand, which are the razor's burrows. After a short time they will come up to the surface and investigate the irritating salt, thus giving their presence away. When spotted they should be held tightly until they relinquish their grip. Try and keep movement and sound to a bare minimum as once the razorfish are aware of your presence, they will bury deeper into the sand. You may need to employ the use of a fork to dig them out and this is hard work as they move down through the sand very quickly. To prize the meat out, insert a knife carefully into the hinge of the shell. Don't force the shell apart as all this will do is tear the meat inside. The main attraction as a bait is

ABOVE: Razors come in all shapes and sizes and can be frozen. Fresh razor fish can be dug from the sand on a storm beach and should be kept stored in sea water. The orange-and-cream meat inside the razor is a particularly good bass bait.

BELOW: Many anglers buy frozen calamari squid in bulk packs like this.

the meaty foot, which, when placed on a hook, will support the rest of the body. Razors are best used fresh when the meat is tough. After freezing, the meat tends to go soft and it becomes difficult to keep on the hook. If you have enough razors and wish to freeze them it is advisable to blanch them in the shell with boiling water prior to freezing. This will help to make the skin tougher. However, as with many other baits, there is no substitute for a fresh razor, which is a great bait for bass and cod in the winter.

Hooking Razorfish

For best results small razors can be hooked in a similar fashion to worm baits. This will involve taking the whole razor from the shell and threading the hook down through the centre of the flesh. As they are only 3 in (7.5 cm) long it is advisable to present two on the hook. Bigger razors can be used as a single bait and are threaded on in the same manner. The tough fleshy skin of the foot can be used to keep the bait on the hook once the main body has been threaded on. Razors cut into smaller bits are good for tipping lugworm baits when cod fishing. The tough texture of the skin helps keep the softer worm on the hook.

Squid

Squid is a widely used sea fishing bait and is probably more readily available than any other bait in Britain. Both the large common squid caught by commercial fishermen in the North Sea, and the calamari squid which is smaller in size and imported, are available to the angler in most tackle shops or fishmongers. Commercially caught squid is bigger and is cream in skin colour with yellowy white flesh. Calamari is smaller, 6–7 in (15–20 cm) long, but has a similar colouring. Squid is a very versatile sea bait and can be used on its own or mixed with other baits on the hook to provide a cocktail bait. Frozen squid bought from the tackle shop is usually of the calamari type and when defrosted can be used in two ways. When boat fishing for bass, cod, or congers over deep-water marks the squid can be used as a whole bait. As the bait bounces across the bottom it almost looks alive and is eagerly taken by bigger species. Shore anglers tend to remove the plastic-type backbone found in the squid and cut them into long strips. These strips can be threaded up the hook to the eye and are long enough to leave a trailing tail, so simulating a worm bait. This is a great method for black and red bream.

ABOVE: The most popular type of squid is the calamari which is approximately 6 in (15 cm) in length. Whole calamari squid is a good bait for larger fish such as bass and cod.

Hooking Squid

For bigger species such as bass and cod a whole calamari squid mounted up on a double-hook Pennell rig is the best method. The squid can be mounted in such a way that it seems alive. If using a single hook with a whole calamari, then it is advisable to bind the body section to the line above the eye of the hook. This will stop it slipping down on to the shank of the hook. Bigger common squid can be cleaned and gutted. In the centre

Preparing Squid

of a squid you will find the ink bag used for squirting its enemies, while running up the back you will find a transparent, plastic-type quill. This is removed, and the skin is peeled off to reveal the white flesh. The squid's body is then slit open using a sharp knife. Once opened out it can be cut into whatever size strips of flesh you require. For bigger species use bigger strips and for smaller species such as bream and whiting use the squid in small, fine strips.

1 Spread the squid on a board and allow it to thaw. Squid can either be used whole for large fish or cut into strips for smaller species.

2 If you plan to use the squid in strips the first thing to do is to remove the head. Do this with a sharp knife as shown.

3 Once the head has been removed, cut open the body and remove the plastic-type backbone, the ink sack and all the innards.

4 The cape or body can then be cut into small strips and used for smaller species, or the squid can be mounted whole as shown.

Cockles

Easy to collect from the sea shore the cockle is a great bait for catching dabs and other flatfish. Cockles can be gathered in their hundreds on the sea shore at low tide, and shingle banks and estuaries are popular places to look for them. To collect them you will need a garden rake and a sack to put them in. By raking back the surface of the shore, cockles can be found lying in abundance.

ABOVE: Cockles can be gathered from the sea shore and are a good bait for all forms of flatfish.

BELOW: Being a small bait, cockles are used two or three at a time to make sure the hook is covered.

Cockles are best prepared by immersing in boiling water for a few seconds and prizing open the shell using a pointed instrument such as a knife. If you want to keep a good supply on the go, tie a sack to a mooring buoy, leaving the cockles in sea water until you need them.

Cockles make good hookbaits when fishing for species like dabs or whiting. When fishing for dabs use a small hook, such as a freshwater size 6. The angler can thread three or four cockles on to the hook and present a reasonable-sized bait.

Although cockles are a good bait by themselves, they are more widely used to tip the hook when using other baits such as lugworms or ragworms, which appeal to a much wider variety of fish.

Hooking Cockles

As they are a very small bait it is necessary to use several cockles on the hook at once to have any impact at all.

Simply prize the shell open and remove the contents. Thread the cockle on to the hook and push it up to the eye of the hook. Repeat the process until you have completely filled the hook. The last cockle should be put on to allow the hook to be pushed into the small orange foot. This is a much tougher part of the flesh and will help to keep the bait on the hook.

Ragworm

There are four members of the ragworm family that the sea angler uses for bait: the king ragworm, the white ragworm, the harbour rag or maddy, and the red ragworm. Harbour rags or maddies are the smallest of the ragworms and tend to be used when mullet or flounders are the main quarry. Red ragworm are the most commonly found of the four and are an excellent summer bait for both bass and flatfish.

The two most popular types of ragworm the sea angler is likely to use are the king rag and white ragworm. The king ragworm is the most widely used and can be bought from tackle shops or dug by the angler from the sea shore. It is possible to dig king ragworm that have grown to some 2 ft (60 cm) in length. However, the average size is around 14 in (35.6 cm), and the angler should take care when handling the king ragworm, as it has a pair of sharp pincers located within the mouth. These pincers are thrust out and retracted at random and can inflict a painful bite. Anglers digging their own worms are advised to seek out an area of sea shore close to the low water mark for digging. A garden fork and a bucket to keep the worms in will be needed. Estuaries can provide good numbers of king ragworm from a short period of digging in the shingle-type mud at low water. When walking over an area looking for signs of the ragworm, watch the surface of the mud for small jets of water spouting upward as the burrow is compressed under foot.

Some ragworms bury themselves deep and it may be necessary to dig down2 ft (60 cm) or more. For long-term storage, ragworms may be kept in a shallow tank of sea water fitted with an air pump. Ensure you remove any damaged or dying worms, or the whole stock of worms will be ruined. If you are going to use them the next day, store them in newspaper in a fridge. It is advisable to change the newspaper after a few hours to ensure the worms are dry. This toughens up the skin and helps keep them on the hook longer. Ragworms are no good for freezing and should be used alive.

The white ragworm is much smaller in size than the king ragworm and, as the name suggests, it is a creamy white or pale brown in colour. Much prized by the shore match angler it can be gathered in the same manner as the king ragworm. They are more likely to be found living in softer sand or light shingle, usually in sheltered bays or similar areas. They seldom exceed 8 in (20 cm) in length and are easier to dig as they lie just under the surface. When collected they can be kept in a plastic container in a shallow covering of sea water. The white ragworm is a very delicate worm and care should be taken when threading it on to the hook. As with the king ragworm it is no good for freezing and should be used alive.

Hooking Ragworm

Large king ragworms should be threaded up the shank of the hook by passing the point of the hook through the centre of the ragworm. The head of the worm is pushed up over the eye of the hook and up on to the line above it. The lower body is held in place on the shank of the hook, and the tail is left hanging from the bend. Fine wire hooks are a good pattern to use when hooking any ragworm, as they allow an easy passage through the body. Smaller ragworms like the harbour rag can be hooked in bunches of four or five in the same manner until the hook is full. These make a good summer bait for mullet.

TOP: Ragworms and lugworms can be dug from the shore line or purchased from the tackle shop. They should be stored wrapped in newspaper in a cool place. If you are not going to use them straight away, examine them carefully; any dead or dying worms should be removed.

ABOVE LEFT: When hooking ragworms the hook should be worked right through the centre of the worm, and the head should be worked up over the eye of the hook. A piece of squid can be used to tip the hook and hold the worm in place as shown. This is a very good bait for plaice and other flatfish.

ABOVE RIGHT: For flatfish such as plaice or flounders, a cocktail of ragworm and peeler crab is often a deadly bait. They should be mounted on the hook together as shown.

RIGHT: Bigger ragworm like the king rag can be used whole on the hook and should be threaded up the hook like this. To hook the worm, thread the hook through the centre of the worm, starting at the head end, and work the hook through the body, pushing the worm up the line. Leave the tail dangling.

Limpets

Limpets can be found in great numbers clinging to the rocks once the tide has dropped. This free bait is often overlooked by the sea angler, but during a storm, or directly after, they can be a top fish catcher. This is because many of them will have been washed from the rocks and will be rolling free in the surf. Species such as bass and flatfish will be among the first to pick up this free meal.

There are two types of limpet to be found along the British shore line. One is the common limpet and the other the slipper limpet. The common limpet is the smaller of the two, reaching a size of 2 in (5 cm) across the shell. It can be found among great colonies, stuck to the rocky shores. The shell is dome-shaped, and the meat within is fitted with a suction pad at the base for clamping the limpet on to rocks.

The slipper, or American limpet, is not native to Britain. It appeared along the shores of Britain by accident and is thought to have arrived here among gravel imported from the United States. Slipper limpets can be found buried in shale and shingle, often near to white ragworm beds. They are larger in size than the common limpet and resemble a large mussel. They are a good bait for flounders and dabs. To collect limpets for bait, you will need a sharp knife and a bucket to store them in. When you have found a patch of limpets, insert the knife carefully under the side of the domed shell, twisting it to one side. This will allow air to enter the underside of the shell and force the limpet to retract, resulting in loss of suction. Limpets are best used fresh from the shell, but if you find you have taken more than you need for a day's fishing, they can be salted and frozen. Adding salt to them before freezing helps to preserve them and toughens up the flesh.

Hooking Limpets

Of the two types the slipper limpet is the more favoured for a hookbait. It is slightly softer in the flesh than the common, and brighter in colour. Once removed from the shell, insert the hook twice into the flesh above the tough, fleshy foot. Once you have done this, take the point of the hook into the foot. Hooking in this manner will ensure the limpet stays on the

ABOVE: Limpets can be found clinging to rocks on and around the beach and make an excellent bait for flatfish. Once scooped out of the shell they can be put on to the hook two or three at a time.

hook. For small species such as dabs you will only need to use one limpet on a small hook, probably a size 6. When fishing for bass or wrasse it is advisable to fill a larger seahook like a 1/0 or 2/0 with at least half a dozen.

Limpets are a good bait to use when tipping the hook. Indeed, one of the best combinations to use for catching cod and dabs is a lugworm and limpet cocktail.

Mussels

Another shellfish bait that can be easily gathered from the sea shore is the mussel. They can be gathered by the angler from the rocks as the tide drops away to reveal them. The mussel is easily identified by the blue-black elongated shell and is found in great clusters around jetty piles and on rocks. There are eight different varieties of mussel found around the British coast. The angler is most likely to use just two of them: the common mussel and the horse mussel. Once the meat is removed from the shell the hook should be passed through the tougher flesh several times to ensure it stays on. This is a good bait to use when inshore boat fishing as the very soft bait can be lowered into the water instead of being cast. If cast from the beach the mussel may slip the hook due to its softness, unless it is bound with shearing elastic. Due to the soft nature of the flesh many sea anglers now freeze the mussel bait on the rig they are going to use. Doing this provides the angler with a solid bait that can be cast a fair distance. Once in the water and in position on the sea bed the mussel bait will slowly defrost, but will remain intact on the hook. This is an excellent method for

BELOW: Mussels are a popular shellfish bait, easy to gather from the shore, and provide the angler with a good, all-round cheap bait.

catching winter cod and codling when distance casting is a requirement.

To store mussels keep them in the bottom of a fridge at a cool temperature. It is advisable to wrap them in a cloth soaked in sea water, keeping the cloth damp at all times. If this is done properly, they can be kept like this for a week or more. To open them without damaging the flesh a knife with a ground edge will be necessary. It is not advisable to use a sharp, pointed blade as this could slip off the shell and cut the angler's hand.

Other Baits

There are a number of other baits available for the sea angler to use. Every sea angler must experiment to find the bait that he or she prefers and also those that are readily available. Cost enters into it as it does to everything, but often the baits you can find around the sea shore or those that can be purchased cheaply are just as good as the more expensive offerings bought from tackle shops.

Hermit Crabs

Hermit crabs make excellent baits and can often be found in rocks around the shore. They are particularly good for bass and should be used whole.

Herring

Herring is another bait that is generally readily available from the fishmonger and is most effective for both conger eels and ling. The herring is a very oily fish and gives off a powerful odour that is attractive to predators and scavengers.

A short blade with a rounded edge can be inserted into the groove where the two halves of the shell meet. Once in, the blade is twisted around, forcing the shell apart. Take time in doing this, for if a shell is forced too hard the mussel inside will be damaged, leaving a handful of mushy gunge that will be useless as a bait.

Hooking Mussels

As they are a soft bait it is necessary to get a good hook hold by threading the mussel well up the shank. It should be hooked as many times as

Preparing Hermit Crabs

1 Hermit crabs live under stones and rocks and live ones make a good bass bait. Once extracted from the shell the crab should be used whole. Gently ease the hermit crab out of its shell in one piece, and it is then ready to be used as a bait.

2 Mount the hermit crab on a large single hook. They can also be used in conjunction with ragworm as a bait for cod and flatfish.

possible in the tougher skin, working the hook through and through until a good hold is achieved. If using fresh from the shell it is a good idea to bind the bait to the hook using elasticized cotton. This will hold it on the hook while it is being cast.

Two or three mussels on a hook make a good bait for cod and pollack especially when fishing from a boat. As with other shellfish the mussel makes an excellent tipping bait. Fished in conjunction with a ragworm or squid it is also one of the top baits for plaice.

Preparing Herring

1 Herrings make a good cheap bait, and the flesh is very oily. Cut a whole herring into chunks like this.

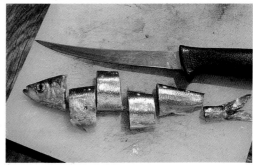

2 Use the chunks as a single bait or try two or three chunks on a larger hook for conger eels and ling.

Artificial Baits

Artificial baits are often a good alternative to fresh bait, especially for the boat angler. Due to the way in which the tidal flow moves, an artificial bait such as a Redgill sandeel can be made to look very much like the real thing. Many shore anglers derive endless hours of sport from the use of spinners or plugs. For the inshore dinghy angler a baited spoon for flounder fishing is a top method when drifting in a running tide. There are a host of different artificials available to the sea angler for both shore and boat fishing, and they can be placed in several different categories. The categories are: spinners, spoons, feathers, plugs (both sinking and floating), rubber eels, pirks (for wreck fishing), jelly worms and even rubber squid, called muppets. With so much choice there is often difficulty in deciding which is best. All the above artificial lures are used by both the boat and shore angler. Some of the more specialist items such as plugs are the tools of the specialist bass angler. Whichever you choose to try they all have their place in sea angling.

ABOVE: A traditional spinner used mainly for mackerel but which has taken other species. Spinners, which revolve rapidly on their own axis, have reflective panels that shine as they are retrieved through the water, and mimic the action of smaller fish.

ABOVE: Pollack and coalfish are prime targets of the artificial bait angler. Specimens like this can be caught using pirks and rubber eels.

Spinners

Spinners come in many shapes and sizes and are usually made from metal. They are more commonly used by shore anglers fishing for pollack and mackerel. The weight of the spinner aids casting and will sink the spinner down into the depths of the sea. Once cast, the angler can count the spinner down to the bottom to determine the depth. On or near the bottom, the spinner is retrieved by winding it back on a slow or fast wind of the reel. The slower the retrieve, the deeper the spinner will fish. To fish the upper layers of the water a faster retrieve will be needed to keep the spinner from sinking too deep. The angler should also try to vary the speed of retrieve. This will make the spinner behave in an erratic way and resemble a small fish in distress. Using this method is usually the key to enticing a passing fish to strike at it.

Spinners are available in a wide variety of sizes and colours. Among the more popular designs is the range including the famous Toby and Krill designs, well used by thousands of shore anglers up and down the coast. Smaller round-bladed spinners are usually used for tempting species such as thin-lipped mullet. When using a small-bladed spinner it is a good idea to tip the hook with a fresh bait like ragworm. This adds to the spinner's attraction and will tempt several species. Bigger bar-shaped spinners can be used for pollack or bass. Probably the most popular type for the shore angler is the small- to medium-weight elongated variety used for mackerel.

Spinners are usually silver, gold or bronze in colour and will often have a reflective panel on each side. This reflective surface shines when it is caught by the light rays penetrating the sea's surface as the spinner is being retrieved. At the front end of the spinner, where it is tied to the

line, is a split ring, to which a swivel is fitted. The swivel allows the spinner to rotate freely and move with ease as it is retrieved through the water, and prevents line twist. The back end of the spinner is also fitted with a split ring, to which a treble hook is attached. A treble hook is used to ensure a good hook hold, as the attacking fish will be taking the spinner while it is on the move. The use of a single hook would be impractical, as it could be missed by the fish as it attacks the spinner.

Plain spinners can be decorated with a stick-on metallic strip called Flectolite. This is often a good way of improving an otherwise dull-looking lure. Spinners can be used from the boat, especially when fishing in the mouth of an estuary over sand banks. Species like mackerel and bass will provide good sport for the boat angler using a balanced, light-line approach with a proven pattern of spinner.

When to Use

If the mackerel are shoaling on or near the surface they will probably be chasing fry. This is a good opportunity to use a small- to medium-weight silver spinner.

Top Tip

Counting the spinner down through the water at a rate of 12 in (30.5 cm) per second, and varying the depths at which you start the retrieve, will give you an indication of the depth the fish are swimming at when you get a take.

Silver and gold spoons

Spoons

Spoons are rather a specialist item of tackle and tend to be used by the sea angler when fishing for flatfish. As the name suggests, the shape is that of a spoon, and some sea anglers make their own from old metal spoons. They are available from tackle shops in two varieties: metal and plastic, in sizes from 2–4 in (5–10 cm) in length.

ABOVE: Spoons are often used with the addition of a baited hook. As the spoon flutters over the sand and silt the movement imitates a small crab scurrying for cover.

The plastic variety is produced in a number of different colours, including orange, yellow and white, while metal spoons can be made more attractive by tipping the edges with a red or white paint. However, a custom-built, home-made version with a string of attractor beads may well out-fish a shop-bought spoon. It is the boat angler who will benefit most from using spoons, as they are easier to work in the tide from a boat and will require little or no weight.

Species such as flounder, plaice and turbot can all be tricked by the fluttering movement of a spoon as it rotates in the tidal flow. Like the spinner, some spoons have a split ring fitted at each end. A small swivel is fitted to each split ring, allowing the spoon to rotate as it is retrieved. One

RIGHT: Dabs, plaice and flounder are all prime candidates for the spoon angler.

ARTIFICIAL BAITS

of the swivels is tied to the main line, and a short length of 10 lb (4.54 kg) line some 6 in (15 cm) long is tied to the other line. To the end of this a hook is attached, usually a long shank, fine wire, size 1 or similar. The addition of a few coloured beads on the hook length gives the spoon that vital bit of added attraction.

Another version of the spoon rig is where the spoon is threaded on to a central axis at the narrow end only. A weight is fitted below and the hook is attached further down. This method of attachment allows the spoon to rotate around the axis, disturbing the sand and mud with the larger end of the blade. This imitates small flatfish trying to escape and is a good presentation for turbot.

With either method the hook is baited with ragworm, lugworm or crab bait. As the spoon moves across the bottom with the tide, it sends up small clouds of sand and mud. This suggests to any nearby flatfish that a small crab or prawn is scurrying over the sand. Once spotted, the hungry flatfish moves in for the kill and is hooked in the process. Another reason for the spoon's great catching ability is said to be that bigger flatfish look upon the spoon as a small flatfish, trying to run off with a piece of bait. In an effort to stop this supposed smaller fish, the spoon is often hit quite hard by a larger specimen.

An important note to bear in mind when using a spoon is to fish it with the tidal flow. This is due to the fact that flounder, in particular, feed and swim with the flow. Spoons can also be used from the shore, but it will be necessary to add weight to the spoon if it is to be cast any distance. If weight is added this should be done in the form of a barrel lead or series of small ball weights that can be fitted on to the central axis.

When to Use

Spoons are, in the right hands, more effective than a static bait and should be used at every opportunity, especially if flounder are the quarry.

Top Tip

If making your own spoons or buying shop-bought patterns, it's good practice to add plenty of colourful beads to the trace below the spoon. These beads will give the spoon an extra attraction.

Plugs

Over the past few years plugs have become the main method of attack for many a specialist bass angler, but they can be used for pollack, coalfish and mackerel as well. Plugs come in two different forms: sinking and floating. They are machine-made from plastic or hand-crafted from wood and are constructed either as a single or as a jointed body version. Many are coloured in a wide variety of different designs. Some have eyes painted on, while others have stick-on bubble eyes with a moving eyeball. When selecting your plugs be careful not to get caught yourself, as many are designed to catch anglers and not fish.

The jointed-body versions give extra movement and wobble violently when retrieved through the water. They are designed to mimic smaller species and have the ability to deceive fish into taking them if fished properly. As the plug is on the move, the hunting fish has only a split second as it passes across its line of vision to decide whether to take it or not. When the take occurs, it is usually quite savage, as the hunting fish will hit the target to kill.

Of the two types in use, the bass angler is likely to place more faith in the floating patterns. Floating plugs float on the surface when cast, but when retrieved at speed will dive under the surface as they are worked back to the rod. The front of the plug is usually fitted with a plastic vane or lip, which when hit by water pressure forces the plug down or up, depending on the angle at which the vane or lip is set. A floating plug is a good choice over rocky or weedy ground, as it is not so easy to lose on snags or rocks.

Sinking plugs are built in a similar fashion, but as the name suggests, they sink. This is due to extra weight in the body, plus additional weight such as a metal insert or heavy lip positioned at the head of the plug. Sinking and floating plugs will catch bass, mackerel and even pollack, and some great sport can be had fishing with them on light tackle.

One of the top plugs in use for bass fishing is the Rapala Silver. Many bass anglers favour the jointed version, which is a very good imitation of a large sandeel. The Silver is coloured with a blue back and a silvery-white underside.

When fishing with both types it is important to make the plug work for you. This is achieved by varying the speed of retrieve and working the rod tip from side to side as you wind in the line. Although more effective from the shore, plugs do have their place on the boat. They can be effective for larger pollack and coalfish when wreck fishing.

When to Use

If in search of big bass, try a floating plug fished at the mouth of an estuary. Bass will wait here for the tide to turn so they can ambush any smaller fish leaving the river.

Top Tip

Many plugs come fitted with small, inferior treble hooks. It's a good idea to remove these and replace them with a larger, stronger pattern.

Pirks

Pirks are used by boat anglers for catching cod, pollack and ling when fishing over wrecks or rough ground. A pirk is basically a cylindrical metal tube of varying length. It is heavy enough to sink down to the bottom under its own weight, so no additional lead on the line is required.

Many boat anglers make their own pirks from lengths of chrome tubing. A quantity of lead is poured into the centre of the tubing giving weight to the finished pirk. This enables the angler to get the pirk down to the wreck faster, especially in a strong tide. At each end of the pirk a large split ring is fitted by drilling a hole so the ring can be threaded on to the main body. A large treble hook is fitted to one end, a swivel to the other. The swivel is used to tie the pirk to the main line. The pirk can then be decorated by using a stick-on metallic strip, called Flectolite. This will add a touch of sparkle to the pirk as it is being worked over a wreck.

Although pirks can be bought in tackle shops, they tend to be on the expensive side considering their simple construction. Many of the commercially produced pirks have the added attraction of a muppet or plastic skirt fitted to the hook. When

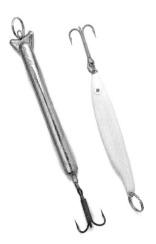

ABOVE: These large, heavy pirks are for fishing off deep-water wrecks. They can be used as they are, or additional bait can be tipped on to the hook.

LEFT: This brightly coloured wrasse has fallen for the charms of a plug that was intended for bass.

ABOVE: A pirk can be used to provide the weight when using muppet lures.

used over a deep-water mark, big fish will be attracted to the silver flash as the pirk is worked up and down in the tide. They will home in on its movement thinking it is a smaller fish. Some anglers use a pirk in place of a weight when fishing with a team of feathers. This increases their chances even further as a larger specimen may take the pirk in preference to the feathers. Pirks can be made or bought in various sizes. The bigger ones, weighing upward of 1 lb (0.45 kg), are used for deep water and strong tides. Some of the smaller models are bent or kinked in the centre to make them wobble as they are brought back towards the surface. Small pirks with a kink in them are often used in shallower water where bass may be present.

When to Use
Every boat angler who is fishing over a wreck should have a pirk in his tackle box. There are days when big cod will look at nothing else.

Top Tip
Big ling are often caught on a pirk baited with squid or mackerel.

Feathers
Feathers come in many different colours and sizes, from mixed red, yellow and blue, to plain white and even silver foil. The most common type available are the sets of multi-coloured feathers. These are usually fished in sets of three, four, six or twelve. From the boat or off the shore, feathers are a primary lure when mackerel fishing.

The idea behind a set of feathers is to create a simulated shoal of small fry that mackerel and pollack in

particular will pursue. When shore fishing, the feathers are cast out as far as you can get them. They are then wound back to the rod in a jerking fashion to draw attention.

Mackerel feathers can be bought ready-tied from a tackle shop. They will consist of different colours and be tied to a smallish seahook, usually a 1/0. At each end of the trace there will be a loop. The two loops are for joining a weight at one end and a swivel at the other. To join the weight or swivel, pass the loop through the eye of the swivel or loop of the weight and then take the swivel or weight back through the loop. When fishing from a boat for mackerel it is better to use a set of six feathers. Using any more may result in a tangle when you hook a full house.

Using a six-hook trace for mackerel can soon result in plenty of fresh bait for other species when out on the

boat. Larger white feathers in sets of three or six are used by cod, ling and bass anglers. For some reason cod in particular seem to have a preference for white. Cod feathers are tied on bigger hooks, usually a size 4/0 to 6/0. If needed, the hooks can be tipped with a piece of fresh mackerel to give them an added attraction.

When to Use
It's always worth trying a set of feathers from a boat, especially when catching mackerel for bait. If cod are the target make sure you have a trace of big white feathers available.

Top Tip
Many commercially made feathers are too long with too many feathers whipped to the hook. This can result in short takes. Take a pair of scissors and trim down the feathers so that the hook shows clearly.

TOP: Feathers can be used six or twelve at a time for catching large numbers of mackerel from a boat.

ABOVE: A new generation of feather imitations has been introduced on to the market. These imitation feathers are made from soft plastics and are very bright and work particularly well.

LEFT: This pirk is being used in conjunction with a muppet skirt and bait.

Artificial Eels

As the name suggests, these imitation sandeels are constructed to mimic the real thing. Artificial eels are killer lures for such species as pollack, bass and coalfish, and are catchers of large species when fished over a wreck from a boat. Made from materials such as latex or rubber, these deadly imitations are fitted with a hook that is tied on to a trace running through the centre of the body.

The two main attractions of artificial eels are the colour and the incredibly lifelike tail. On most models the tail is made of a flimsy thin rubber, which incorporates a small but sensitive rudder at the tip. When retrieved through the water the rudder is forced from side to side, making the tail wobble in the tide. It is this movement that brings the artificial to life.

Artificial eels are effective from both shore and boat. However, it's the bigger patterns that tend to be used when boat fishing over a wreck and the smaller ones for rock, pier and jetty work. Eels as large as 15 in (38 cm) in length are standard wreck tackle for the boat angler. These are fished on a flying collar rig. This involves the use of a long 15 lb (6.8 kg) trace, 15–20 ft (4.57–6.1 m) in length. One end of the trace is tied to a boom, which stands out of the main line. The other end of the trace is

ABOVE: A good selection of rubber eels will be needed when fishing over a wreck.

threaded through the nose of the eel and out through the underside at the beginning of the tail. A hook is then tied to the trace, and the trace and hook are pulled back into position inside the eel's body. The lead, which may be as heavy as 8 oz (227 g), is tied on a weak link of line directly under the bottom of the boom. The weak link of line should be of a breaking strain lower than 6 lb (2.72 kg). This is so the lead can break away from the rig, leaving the eel

ABOVE: An artificial eel accounted for this fine pollack, caught over a wreck.

intact if the angler gets caught up on the wreck.

When sent down to the wreck in a running tide, the artificial eel sits out away from the boom in the tidal flow. The tidal flow works the eel's tail, making it look natural. From the shore, the smaller types are good lures to use for bass and pollack when fishing at night.

These work really well if the sea is calm. This is because species like bass are able to pick up on the vibration caused by the tail as the eel is wound in. Colours for both boat and shore are a matter of personal choice. However, over the years a few colours have gained great popularity. Boat anglers in particular favour black, orange or red. There are many different makes of artificial eel available, but two designs in particular have probably

ABOVE: The line runs through the centre of the eel and is tied to a hook that sits inside the body of the eel. Once on the move, the rubber tail sways in the flow and looks just like the real thing.

accounted for more captures of specimen fish than any other makes. These are the Redgill and the Eddystone eels. Both are constructed from rubber and have a flexible tail which moves when worked in the tide's flow. They are available in different colours and in sizes from 3–18 in (7.5–45 cm).

When to Use

From the shore a small black artificial fished at dusk around rocky ground will attract bass. From a boat, the bigger patterns are regarded as standard wreck fare.

Top Tip

When buying artificial eels some of the patterns have too heavy a gauge hook fitted. Remove this and replace it with a fine wire pattern. This will ensure that the eel acts as naturally as possible.

Muppets

Muppets are another example of a rubber lure that catch their fair share of sea species. They are sold in packs of three or six, loose or ready-tied to a trace. There are three sizes to choose from: small, medium and large. Like other artificials the muppet is also available in a multitude of colours. Among the most popular are the fluorescent green, red and black patterns favoured by boat anglers for pollack and cod. In the smaller sizes, which are around 3 in (7.5 cm) in length, they can be used on a trace of three, with the lead fixed beneath them. The medium size, approximately 6 in (15 cm) in length, is a good pattern to try added to the hook of a pirk. Red is a top catching colour when using this method; cod in particular seem to home in on this combination. Medium-sized muppets are also good for fishing as a trio when the hooks are tipped with mackerel strip. The largest size of muppet is around 12 in (30 cm) in length and is used as a single lure.

There are two main ways of attaching a muppet to the hook. The first is correct when using a small or medium-sized muppet with a single hook. The point of the single hook is simply inserted into the dome at the tip of the head, pushed through the rubber, and the point brought round and under the skirt of tentacles. When ready to fish, the point of the hook needs to be exposed from one side of the muppet to ensure a good hook hold when the fish takes.

When using on a pirk which has a treble hook fitted, a small hole will have to be cut in the tip of the head of the muppet. The hook should then be

ABOVE: Muppets are available in all sizes and colours. Some of the more popular makes have a glitter effect on the body. This acts as an attractor when caught in the light.

removed from the pirk and the eye of the treble hook worked back through the hole. The three points of the hook should sit under the muppet skirt with the points protruding. The hook is then clipped back on to the pirk and the deadly combination is ready for fishing. Muppets can be fished in two different ways.

The first is to let the tide do the work for you if you are fishing from a boat in a tidal run. It's simply a case of lowering the muppets down near the bottom and letting them wave about in the tide.

The second requires a little bit of work from the angler. With little or no tide movement it is important to keep muppets on the move and it is necessary to work the muppets up and down to draw attention. This is done by lifting and lowering the rod tip as the muppets are retrieved.

Muppets of all sizes can account for some bumper hauls of pollack and cod when fishing over wrecks or rough ground. They can be used from the shore just as effectively and the smaller sizes, fished in a team of three, can account for some action from pollack and bass.

When to Fish
No wreck angler worth his salt should contemplate a fishing trip without an assortment of muppets in his tackle box. Try jigging a team of three up from the bottom when pollack or cod are the target species.

Top Tip
When the tide runs slow, jig the rod tip up and down and this will make the muppets work as they are brought up from the depths. When sport is slow it can often pay to bait the muppets with squid strips. This tactic often produces a fish and is a particularly deadly combination for big ling.

RIGHT AND BELOW: Muppets are available in a range of colours from purple, orange and blue to pink.

RIGHT: This trace of three muppets is decorated with luminous paint. When fished in deep, dark water, the heads will glow.

Jellies and Twisters

Jellies and twister lures have become a big part of sea angling over the past few years. Imported from the United States, this new breed of soft rubber lure is at home on the boat or from the shore. There are hundreds of different designs and patterns to choose from. Jelly lures have a worm-shaped body and are usually impregnated with a colourful glitter pattern and fish-catching smell. The worm is very soft and flexible and will often have a built-in tail action to tantalize and tease fish into striking at it. As a rule they tend to be unweighted, and it is merely a case of inserting a sharp seahook, such as a 1/0 or 2/0.

When hooking, they should be treated in a similar manner as a live worm, with the hook threaded down through the centre of the worm's head and exiting at the side, a short distance from the entry point. From the shore they can be fished for bass, pollack and mackerel. Lighter colours tend to work better from the shore during the day as they resemble sandeels, a favourite food of these species. After dark, the colour is not that important, as the predator relies on vibration and shape to find its target. The smaller variety can be fished on a three-hook trace from the boat and it is extremely effective for species such as pollack and coalfish.

Leadheads or twister lures are a weighted lure. As the name suggests the twister lure works on the principle of a twisting tail in order to attract the predator fish.

These are made from soft rubber and have a double tail fin that twists on the retrieve. Shore anglers and boat anglers catch many different species using this type of lure. Being weighted they are a good choice for the shore angler: there will be no need to add any additional lead to the line for casting.

With a separate leadhead section the angler is free to choose any colour tail he or she wishes to use, and can vary it at will during the day. A real bonus with this system is that the tail can be changed easily, and the angler does not have to break down the complete rig to do so.

LEFT: This large leadhead lure is ready to be dropped into the depths. Species like bass, pollack, coalfish and cod will all take such a lure.

ABOVE: Red gill eels also have a twister tail action when retrieved.

BELOW: A selection of leadhead lures showing the different sizes available.

Many of the original leadhead twister lures are designed to fish with the hook positioned upside down. This is a good point to watch out for when buying them as this pattern will rarely snag on the bottom over rocky ground. If you browse through the pages of any sea-angling magazine you will see companies in America advertising every kind of rubber twister lure available.

When to Use

The original Mr Twister lures with the leadhead are a must for the shore angler in search of pollack and bass. Fish them over rocks and rough ground on the high tide or just as the tide starts to drop. Leadhead lures also account for some huge catches of ling over the wrecks in the Irish Sea.

Top Tip

If you keep getting hit on a jelly worm but can't hook the fish, cut 1 in (2.5 cm) from the head and re-hook the worm. It could be that the worm is too long for the species chasing it.

Shore Fishing

For a great number of sea anglers, fishing from the shore is where it all begins. Many start as young children on holiday who have been taken mackerel fishing on the local pier. Armed with borrowed tackle, a string of brightly coloured feathers and the promise of a fresh mackerel for dinner, that first day out by the sea is a treasured one that will be remembered forever. Once that first fish is hooked, so too, is the angler – invariably for life.

Various Coastlines

The coastlines of Britain and other countries are full of opportunities for the shore angler to explore. From beach to rock fishing, piers, breakwater walls and the countless numbers of estuaries, there is a whole host of venues to choose from.

The species of fish the angler wishes to pursue will often determine the location he is likely to choose. Wide, sandy beaches are a top spot for summer ray fishing. Piers and jetties attract shoals of mullet and mackerel. Rocky headlands provide sport from bass, wrasse and dogfish.

Breakwater walls often give deep water and can offer the chance of a large conger eel if you are prepared to fish at night. The estuary angler will find rich pickings when the winter flounder fishing is in full swing, or casting from the beach for codling.

This section deals with everything from the most appropriate choice of rod and reel, right down to that all-important hook and how to present it. It offers advice on the various locations and how to choose suitable tackle and methods for the species you are fishing, with plenty of tips and tactics.

Whichever venue you choose and whatever species you fish for, ensure a future for your sport by unhooking undersized fish carefully and returning them to the sea.

ABOVE: A successful day's fishing for the shore angler.

BELOW: The sun slips away as two beach anglers wait for action.

Equipment

With so many different makes of rods, reels and lines in the tackle shops, it's often a daunting task for the shore angler, especially the beginner, to make the correct choice.

Rods

Rods for shore fishing will vary in length depending on the type of fishing they are going to be used for. Spinning rods can be anything from 6–10 ft (1.83–3.05 m) in length; pier rods are usually around 10 ft (3.05 m) and can be used for leger and float work, and beachcasters are almost always 12 ft (3.66 m), or in some cases 13 ft (3.96 m) long. Other types of rod that can be used are freshwater rods, such as light carp or float rods. These models play key roles in specialist bass and mullet fishing. However, in general, most sea anglers choose a 12 ft (3.66 m) beach rod that can be used from a beach, a pier, an

RIGHT: This rod is for use with a multiplier reel. It also has an extension butt so that the reel can be positioned further down the handle.

estuary or from rocks for many different applications, including legering and even float fishing.

A beachcaster is usually made up of two 6 ft (1.83 m) pieces, a tip section and butt section. The butt section is the lower end of the rod which houses the reel. It is important to use a rod of at least 12 ft (3.66 m) as this will increase the casting ability. There are several factors to take into account when purchasing a beachcaster. First, there is the type of reel you are going to use with it; second there is cost; and third there is the type of fishing you are going to use it for and what material the rod is made of.

The reel you intend to use will have great bearing on the selection of the rod. There are two types of reels in common use among sea anglers: fixed-spool and multiplier reels. When buying a rod to match up with a fixed-spool reel, you will find the design differs from a rod used in conjunction with a multiplier reel.

The rings on a rod for fixed-spool reels will be larger in size and will number four or five in total, including the tip ring. It is common to find all the guides only on the tip section of the rod with nothing on the butt section apart from the reel seating. The four or five guides should be large in circumference around the inner ring, decreasing in size towards the tip ring. This is because when casting with a fixed-spool reel, the guides on the rod need to allow a clear passage of non-friction to the line as it leaves the reel. Since the line is coiled as it leaves the reel, fewer rings on the rod allows for a smooth, unhindered cast. On a beach rod to be matched with a multiplier reel the opposite applies.

There can be as many as nine guides of a much smaller size and inner-ring circumference. There is usually one guide on the butt section of the rod with the other seven or eight, including the tip ring, whipped on to the tip section. Once again, the guides are dictated by the way in which the line leaves the reel.

In the case of the multiplier reel, the line leaves in a free motion from a revolving spool. Due to the speed it releases from the spool, the small guides are needed to pull the line down quickly towards the rod blank, keeping it in-line with the action of

ABOVE: Pictured are a pair of distance casting rods complete with multiplier reels.

the rod. On the cast, as the line travels down the guides, each one gets smaller towards the tip, pulling the line down quickly to the blank. This gives better control and reduces stress on the line.

For the beginner, the better choice for a first rod would be a model suited to a fixed-spool reel. For the more experienced angler who has mastered casting, a rod with rings for a multiplier is usually the choice. Both types of beach rod will have different actions, and this is an important factor when choosing a rod for the type of fishing you are going to do.

Shore anglers who need to cast a bait a fair distance to reach the fish will need to look at models that are stiffer in the butt and middle, but have a softer tip. This type of rod has what is called a fast taper, and will very much aid distance casting. The stiffer lower and middle sections will transmit power through the rod during the cast. The softer tip will allow good bite detection when fishing.

If distance is not required then a through-action rod is more suitable. This type of rod bends progressively from the top of the butt to the tip. With regard to cost and materials used to manufacture rods, the best advice would be to save for a decent carbon rod capable of doing what is required. There are a lot of cheaper rods around made from fibreglass and composite (glass and low-grade carbon mixed). They break very easily if pushed beyond their casting limits, leaving the angler to pay out for another rod.

Many of the more expensive rods are made from high grades of carbon. However, they do cost much more. Nevertheless, there are many examples of good-quality carbon beach rods from starting at reasonable prices that will do all they proclaim and are long-lasting.

There are a couple of things you should do when purchasing a rod. Look at the butt of the rod you are thinking of buying as it should have a maximum casting weight printed on it. This will help you with your choice as it will tell you about the casting ability of the rod. It may also pay to take your reel along to the shop. Try this fitted on to the rod and see if it feels comfortable and balanced. Only when you are satisfied you have the correct rod for the job should you make your purchase.

Fixed-spool Reels

As with rods, there is a vast array of reels for the shore angler to choose from. The two main reels in use are the fixed-spool and the multiplier. The fixed-spool is the easier to use, and a sensible choice for the beginner. For shore fishing from the beach, pier or rocks the fixed-spool reel needs to be large enough to hold a good capacity of line, and robust enough to deal with casting heavy weights.

The reel is fixed to the rod by inserting it into the reel seat on the butt of the rod. For the fixed-spool reel this is on the underside of the rod. The line is loaded on to a cone-shaped spool and when cast, leaves the reel in coil form travelling up through the rod guides. You should be able to load at least 150 yds (137 m) of 20 lb (9.07 kg) line on to the reel. Most shore anglers use 15–18 lb (6.8–8.16 kg) main line and fill with line to just below the lip of the spool.

ABOVE: The fixed-spool beach reel, a good reel to learn to cast with.

When filling the spool make sure the line is evenly distributed, as this will help to prevent tangles when casting. It is crucial not to underfill or overfill the spool, as both will hinder smooth casting.

There is a mechanism called a bale arm on the outer edge of the reel. This traps the line and winds it around the spool when it is engaged and the reel handle is turned. When the bale arm is opened, the line is free to run from the spool. The bale arm on most models is automatically shut when the handle is turned after the cast has been made. Some anglers cut the bail arm right down to a bare minimum for tournament casting purposes. They do this to avoid the bail arm accidentally shutting and trapping the line during a long cast. Many models of fixed-spool reel offer an adaptable handle that can be

ABOVE: Many beginners to sea angling will start off using a fixed-spool reel as these are easier to use.

switched to the left- or right-hand side of the reel, depending on the angler. At the front of the reel there should be a tensioning nut at the head of the spool. This is called a drag system and determines how tight or slack the spool is set. If set in a slack position, line is able to be pulled from the spool in a free movement, usually by a large fish when the angler is playing it. If set tight, no line will be allowed to run free. It's always advisable to pre-set the drag to suit the species you are likely to encounter. At the rear of the reel there is usually an anti-reverse switch. This is so the angler can switch from forward to backward wind allowing him to yield line if not using the drag system.

Expect to pay anything from £39.99 up to £150 depending on the make

and model of reel you choose. For specialist fishing where a light-line approach can be used, smaller models are more suited. Many sea anglers are turning to freshwater, fixed-spool carp reels when float fishing for mullet or plug fishing for bass.

Multipliers

Mention multipliers and a vast majority of shore anglers will tell you they are the ultimate reel for distance casting. Several of the country's top casters use a multiplier when competing on the tournament casting circuit. Modern multipliers are now so light and small it's no wonder they are favoured by the distance caster over the heavier, fixed-spool reel.

Multiplier reels are very different in design to the fixed-spool reel. For a start the spool, instead of being cone-shaped, is a drum shape. This revolves on a central axis within the reel's casing. The multiplier is mounted on the top-side of the rod with the guides facing upward. It is either placed into a fixed reel seat, or in a few cases where extreme distance is required, it is fitted well down towards the end of the butt with special reel clips called coasters. With the reel positioned in the low butt position the angler is able to exert greater leverage through the rod as the cast is made.

One big problem the newcomer faces when using a multiplier reel is the overrunning of the spool during the cast. This can cause a terrible mess in the line, called a bird's nest. Overruns are caused by lack of braking control on the rotating spool as the lead touches down at the end of the cast. At this point of the cast, if your reel has no braking system, you will need to apply slight pressure with your thumb to prevent an overrun. Many modern multipliers have a built-in braking system in the form of either magnetic brakes or centrifugal brakes, which is a great help.

Magnetic brakes work on the principle of a magnet fixed opposite the spool end. This draws the side plate of the spool closer to slow it down. Alternatively, the magnet can be set further away to allow more freedom of movement. Centrifugal brakes are two small brake blocks fitted to a pin at the end of the spool. These blocks are forced to the end of the pin when the spool is in motion.

ABOVE: There are several different models of multiplier reels available. Make sure you make the right choice.

Once at the end they come into contact with a small metal loop in the side plate, causing friction. This in turn slows the spool down.

Several makes of multiplier have what is called a level-wind fitted to a bar running across the face of the reel. This little gadget ensures the line is retrieved back on to the reel evenly. It works when the handle is turned, moving from side to side across the reel, laying the line evenly for the next cast. Once the angler's casting has progressed, the level-wind can be removed to increase the distance of the cast. Looking down on the reel from above, a double handle is usually located at the right-hand side of the reel. Most of the models on the market today have the handles fitted on the right.

One point to consider when purchasing a multiplier is to buy one suited to the fishing you are likely to do. You may need to purchase two models, one for beach work and one for rough ground. The models vary in their design, and a small multiplier used for casting from a beach will be no good for heavy rough-ground work. Prices for multipliers have evened out over the past years, and there are many good examples on sale. However, if you want the latest model, then be prepared to pay a little more.

Whatever model of reel you use, always rinse it under a tap when returning from a fishing trip, then place it somewhere warm, such as an airing cupboard, to dry. Saltwater is

ABOVE: When you visit any tackle shop, you will be met with a vast array of rods and reels to choose from. Ask your tackle dealer for advice when buying equipment for the first time.

extremely corrosive, and reels not washed in freshwater after fishing in the sea will quickly deteriorate.

Lines

There are several different brands of line on the market. Many make all sorts of claims to being the best available, being the most abrasive-resistant and having the lowest diameter for breaking strain. Take care, when making a purchase, that the line you have bought will be suited to the type of fishing you are going to do. It's pointless trying to fish over extremely rough ground for conger eels with a line of 15 lb (6.8 kg) breaking strain. If you don't snap the line on a snag the first conger you hook will snap it for you. Look carefully at all the hazards you are likely to encounter before buying your line. When you have made your choice of breaking strain, select a well-known brand that has stood the test of time with other anglers. There are some very good lines on the market, and there are also some very bad ones. Go to a reputable dealer and tell him what you are looking for in a line. If he values your custom he will advise you correctly. Among some of the more popular brands are the tried and tested Sylcast line, Drennan Sea line and Daiwa Sea line. All are of good quality, are available in bulk spools and are reasonably priced.

Lines for shore fishing will vary in breaking strain in accordance with the species you are fishing for and the type of sea bed you are fishing over.

ABOVE: There is a wide variety of line available to the sea angler. The market place is extremely competitive with hundreds of different brands, colours and breaking strains.

As a rule, from the open beach the angler will usually use 15–18 lb (6.8–8.16 kg) breaking strain main line with a 50–60 lb (22.68–27.22 kg) shock leader. An angler fishing over rough ground will increase the strength of the main line to 35 lb (15.88 kg) to combat the rough seabed or rock he or she is fishing over. When in pursuit of bass and fishing with plugs or spinners, it is better to use a lighter line. A line with a breaking strain of 8–10 lb (3.63–4.54 kg) will allow the bait to behave more naturally and will allow smoother, longer casting, which is important.

It is important that shock leaders are used when punching heavy leads out at distance. A shock leader is a length of heavier line which is attached to the end of the main line. As the leader is heavier, the line is able to cope with the strain, and this avoids any unnecessary break-offs on the lighter main line. Shock leaders are usually coloured fluorescent yellow or orange. This helps the angler to see the line when fishing at night or in rough conditions when winding the lead back to the rod.

Line can be bought in bulk spools.

ABOVE: Line is available in a wide range of colours. Many anglers now prefer to use a fluorescent line as it is easier to see, particularly at night.

Loading a Leader for Casting

When using the pendulum cast to achieve maximum distance it is advisable to incorporate the use of a leader. The leader is a stronger breaking-strain line which acts as a shock absorber when the rod is fully compressed.

This leader line is usually a minimum of 50 lb (22.68 kg) breaking strain and approximately 18 ft (5.5 m) in length. When ready to cast, the leader will be hanging from the end of the rod with three or four turns on the reel. As the cast is made and the rod begins to compress, the strain is transmitted to this part of the line and prevents the main line breaking unnecessarily.

1 To load the leader on to the reel before casting, first make sure the line on the spool is lying in a flat even manner across the drum of the reel.

2 Wind on the leader, making sure that the leader joint knot is wound on at one end of the spool. Here it is on the right-hand side of the spool.

ABOVE: A long-distance caster needs a well serviced reel and good-quality shock leader material.

3 This avoids the knot catching on your thumb as the line leaves the spool. As the knot is tapered at one end it will be drawn up through the rod rings easily. Make sure the leader is wound on evenly.

4 This is how the line should be trapped before casting. Grip the rod tightly with one hand around the blank by the reel. Press your thumb firmly down on the leader to trap it until the release is made.

Terminal Tackle and Equipment Hooks

The shore angler will need several items of terminal tackle if he is to be successful in the pursuit of different species of sea fish. One key component is the hook. When choosing a hook it's important to think about the species and the bait. The hook needs to be strong enough to cope with the species, but it must

RIGHT: Hooks come in all shapes and sizes.

also be balanced to suit the bait. A basic rule is the bigger the bait the bigger the hook. There are many patterns to choose from and the shore angler will need to arm himself with a wide variety to meet different situations. Most hooks are available in packets of ten or boxes of 50. It is a good idea to have a selection of sizes, from a size 4/0 through to a 6/0, of different patterns. These patterns and sizes should cover most shore situations the angler is likely to encounter.

The three main patterns used for shore angling are Aberdeen,

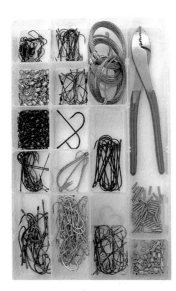

ABOVE: This box contains a good selection of hooks to cover every situation.

ABOVE: Long-shanked fine wire O'Shaughnessy and Aberdeen hooks in varying sizes.

O'Shaughnessy and Limerick hooks. Aberdeens are made in fine and thick wire gauges. This pattern is probably the most commonly used. For bigger fish, such as cod or conger eels, and when presenting a bigger bait, the O'Shaughnessy represents a good strong hook and should be used.

ABOVE: A sharpening stone is a useful tool to take on a fishing trip.

For delicate baits such as live sandeels it is advisable to use a long shank, fine-wire Aberdeen hook. For species like mullet, dabs and sole, a small hook is the order of the day. The shore angler may be better turning to the freshwater angler's tackle box where sizes 6 and 8 short shank hooks are a good choice. Small baits like bread flake for mullet and cockles for dabs can be used to completely conceal the hook for these small-mouthed species. Limerick hooks are used for presenting larger bulky baits and are a good choice for the shore angler when fishing crab. The Limerick hook has a wider gape than the other two patterns, and this prevents the point of the hook being masked by the bait. When storing hooks, the shore angler should keep them in a watertight container as fine-

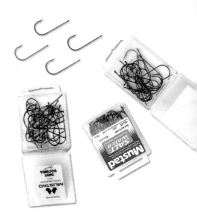

ABOVE: Hooks are available in packets or as shown here in boxes. The label will tell you what size and make the hook is.

wire hooks in particular will deteriorate when damp. Carry a sharpening stone in your tackle box, and remember to check your hooks for damage when fishing over rough ground.

Weights

The weight you fix to the end of your trace will very much depend on how far you want to cast or how strong the tide is. There are many designs of lead and each has its own special use. Some of the more common types are as follows: standard swivel bombs, available in sizes 2–6 oz (57–170 g), generally used from a pier when legering; torpedo leads, available in sizes 3–8 oz (85–227 g), also used from the pier or beach; fixed-wire leads, available in sizes 4–8 oz (113–227 g). These are used to hold the tackle still on the bottom in a strong tide. Breakaway leads, available in sizes

RIGHT: These weights are specifically designed for beach fishing and uptiding. The wires fitted to the side of the lead act as an anchor for the bait when the tide is running. When pressure is applied to the lead, the wires fold back, enabling the lead to break free from the bottom either because a fish has been hooked or because the angler must cast again.

3–8 oz (85–227 g), are widely used from beach, pier and rough ground. The wire grips are set in place before casting so the bait is held still on the bottom. Once the angler pulls the lead the grips break free and the lead is wound in.

When fishing over extremely rough ground it's a good idea to incorporate the use of a lead lift. This is a flight which is fitted above the lead and brings the lead up off the bottom as the line is being retrieved. Small ball leads and a tub of mixed split shot are a good addition to the shore angler's tackle box for mullet, mackerel, garfish and bass fishing. The ball leads can be used for float fishing and the shot for weighing down a live sandeel.

General Terminal Tackle

Other items the shore angler will need to carry are a selection of beads and sequins for trace-making. Beads or sequins can be added to the trace above the hook, and these will attract flatfish in particular. A good selection of swivels will be needed for joining traces to the mainline. Clip swivels are also needed for linking traces and leads. Split rings, round and oval, are both useful additions for linking traces to leads.

For running leger fishing, small sliding booms called zip sliders are handy to have in the tackle box. A selection of longer, fixed booms will be needed for paternoster traces. A sharp knife is essential for preparing bait and should be kept in a sheath for protection when not in use. This can also be used to cut line. It is a good idea to carry a pair of sharp nail clippers for cleaning off the ends of knot tails. A head torch is a good investment for night fishing as it can be worn around the head leaving the hands free. However, for the more serious angler, purchasing a gas or liquid-fuel burning lamp will give much better lighting to work under. For the shore angler fishing with two rods, a rod stand or beach tripod will be needed. There are many modern stands on the market for the beach angler. The best are constructed from lightweight aluminium and are extremely light to carry, but very stable. They have a double head rest and double cup units to hold two rods securely. Most models are fitted with lamp and trace-holding hooks.

To carry all your terminal tackle, a good strong tackle box will be needed. Of the many available the seat-box style seems to be the most popular. Not only will it provide waterproof protection and storage room for tackle, it will also double up as a seat for the angler. During the winter months when the weather is often at its worst, investing in a brolly or a specialist beach-buddy shelter unit will keep you dry and comfortable, especially if you are contemplating an all-night session.

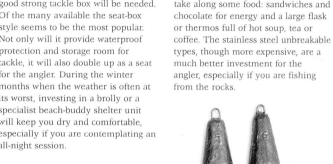

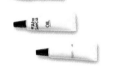

ABOVE: The basic tools of the long-distance caster: a well-serviced reel with special spanners for maintaining it in good condition, and high-quality shock leader material that will stand the strain of the weight when the cast is made.

For long sessions it is advisable to take along some food: sandwiches and chocolate for energy and a large flask or thermos full of hot soup, tea or coffee. The stainless steel unbreakable types, though more expensive, are a much better investment for the angler, especially if you are fishing from the rocks.

ABOVE: These pear-shaped leads are used for fishing a light rig over clean ground.

BELOW: Shown here is a selection of trace components. Each of the pieces shown can be used to make your own trace.

ABOVE: Small beads and swivels are essential for trace making.

LEFT: Ready-made rigs can be bought from the tackle shop. However, the beginner is advised to seek some advice to ensure the correct rig is purchased.

Beachcasting

When fishing from the beach it may be necessary to cast the bait some distance to get in touch with the fish. Distances will vary but quite often this could be 100 yds (91 m) or more. To achieve these distances the angler will need suitable tackle and plenty of practice at casting. Many anglers opt for the use of a multiplier reel in preference to a fixed-spool reel for distance casting. The choice is a personal one and is down to the individual. Both types of reel are capable of giving the required distance once a casting method has been perfected.

The rod that the angler uses to achieve the cast is of great importance. It must be able to react to the amount of pressure forced through the blank during the cast. It is no good using a stiff poker-type rod, since there will be no flexibility in the rod as the cast is made. On the other hand, it isn't any good using a rod that is soft and pliable, because it will not stand up to the amount of pressure placed on it and will probably end up breaking during the first hard cast. The right type of rod to use should have a softish tip, progressing down to a stiffer middle and butt section. The soft tip will allow for better bite detection, while the stiffer lower section will greatly improve casting ability.

There are three main ways of casting: the overhead cast, the off-the-ground cast and the pendulum cast. The latter is the most difficult to master but is recognized as the ultimate distance gainer. Many sea anglers fishing from the beach will opt for the off-the-ground cast as this will,

ABOVE: The fixed-spool reel is easier to use than a multiplier and is still capable of casting a bait 100 yds (91 m) or more.

The Off-the-Ground Cast

1 Stand with your body facing side on to the sea and swing the lead out behind you on to the beach. Make sure there is a tight line between the tip of the rod and the lead.

2 Now face forward and look toward the target area, out to sea. The weight of your body should be resting on the right leg and you should have a good grip on the rod.

Pendulum Casting

1 Lift and then tilt the rod downwards to enable the lead to start swinging in a pendulum fashion. This starts the lead travelling towards and then away from the caster. Let the lead reach the forward horizontal position. When it reaches this position dip the rod tip.

2 This absorbs any sharp kick and the lead will now drop back towards the caster. When it reaches the bottom of the drop, raise the rod tip slightly to push the lead upward and away on the back swing. The caster's weight is on the right leg.

given practice, punch the bait out upwards of 100 yds (91 m). The overhead cast is used when there is limited space, and providing the angler is able to load the rod, a decent distance is obtainable.

Loading the rod occurs when backward pressure is placed on the tip. When overhead casting, a gentle swing of the bait out behind the angler will be enough to draw the tip of the rod downward, thus loading the blank. As the rod is pushed forward into the cast the load is released, and the lead and bait are punched skyward towards the horizon. This method of casting is really another version of the more popular off-the-ground cast.

Off-the-ground casting originated in South Africa and is now widely practised on the beach when fishing, or at special casting events held for anglers. In the off-the-ground cast the angler starts the cast with the lead laid on the ground behind him: with the rod held in casting position, which is with one hand down the butt and the other covering the reel, the lead is swung back and laid on the ground. There is usually 5–6 ft (1.52–1.83 m) of line between the lead and rod tip.

At this stage the upper body is facing the lead and the feet are slightly apart and facing side on to the sea. All the weight of the body is pushed on to the back leg and foot, the front foot acting as a stabilizer.

3 Transfer the weight of your body on to your left leg and draw the tip of the rod upward. This will cause the rod to load as it is being pulled back by the lead and forward by the angler.

4 Push forward with your right arm and pull down with your left to put power into the cast. As the rod passes your right eye, release the line. The lead rockets upward and outward.

5 Guide the tip of the rod down as the lead approaches the sea and slow the line by cushioning the spool with your finger. Once the lead has landed, shut the bale arm on the reel.

3 When the lead reaches the vertical on the back swing, start to swing the body to the forward position. The body weight is transferred from the right leg to the left leg and the rod blank is loaded and takes up the tension of the lead.

4 As the rod is brought around the body the right-hand thumb trapping the line is released, and the lead rockets up and outwards. Push the rod out with the right arm and pull down with the left to increase the drive through the cast.

5 As the lead approaches the sea the thumb of the right hand is used to act as a brake on the revolving spool. When the lead reaches the sea the rod tip can be lowered, and when the lead hits the bottom the gearing on the reel can be engaged by turning the handle.

To set the cast in motion the angler turns the upper body forward as he lifts the rod and places strain on the tip. As the rod is lifted the tip is pulled back by the lead, causing the rod to load. With the cast in motion, the angler pulls the rod in an upward arc, and the lead begins to travel, placing more pressure on the tip and increasing the loading of the rod. Aiming high into the air, the lead is released once it starts to move into forward motion above the angler's head. The body weight of the angler is transferred on to the front leg and foot. At this stage the loading of the rod and the power in the cast propels the lead upward and forward at the same time.

Mastering this is a step towards progressing to the pendulum cast. The key to this cast is timing and applying the power at the precise moment. It is a hard art to master, and it's advisable to seek the help of a professional casting instructor if you wish to learn. The cast is made with the lead in motion. It is swung from one side of the body to the other in a pendulum fashion to compress and load the rod. At a precise moment and with the rod in full compression, the lead is forced upward and outward towards the sea.

It's a good idea to practise your casting in an open field using just a lead on the line. Casts of 150 yds (137 m) will be possible in a short time if you get it right. However, don't

expect a baited hook to go so far when fishing from the beach. The shape and bulk of the baited hook, plus a wind blowing inland will reduce distance.

Casting Safety
A word of warning! When casting from the beach using any of the above styles for maximizing your distance, always use a shock leader on the line. Most beach-fishing reels will be loaded with lines of 15–18 lb (6.8–8.16 kg) breaking strain line. Putting a line of this strength under the pressure needed to cast any distance, will result in a break-off and possibly an accident. A shock leader of 50 lb or more (22.7 kg) breaking strain will stop break-offs, and result in safe fishing.

Beach Fishing

The open beach with its pounding surf and golden sand is a most inviting place for the angler to fish. There are many famous beach marks up and down the coast but probably the most famous is Chesil beach, in Dorset. The beach is more shingle than sand and as it enters the sea, its steep shingle banks drop away quickly into deep water. Many different species can be caught here, and this superb venue provides excellent sport for the sea angler all year round.

All beaches will have certain species that visit them during different times of the year. Flatfish of all kinds will move inshore and feed avidly on marine worms and crustaceans hiding in the sandy sea bed during the summer and autumn. They can be caught by the angler fishing with crab or worm bait on a running leger rig. Plaice and flounders are two species the angler can target at this time of year. Mackerel can also be caught in great numbers from the beach during the summer months, on brightly coloured traces of feathers. Summer evenings will draw rays into shallow water to hunt down sandeels and crabs over the sand. Often a whole fresh sandeel presented on a long-shanked hook will score with this species.

In the winter, cod is the prominent species to be caught from many of the beach marks along the coastline, particularly along the north coast. Fishing at night from the beach will often result in bigger cod being caught. A favourite method for the bigger cod is to fish with a lugworm and squid cocktail on the hook. Hooks need to be large and strong to accommodate a large bait and ensure a good hold once the cod is hooked.

In the autumn, after a storm, bass will be patrolling the surf in search of a free meal. This is a prime time to catch a specimen fish. The beaches of Dawlish and Teignmouth in south Devon regularly give up double-figure bass under these conditions. Fishing with a whole soft crab or using a large hook baited with razorfish are two successful methods to try. Don't cast too far though, as many of the bigger bass are just beyond the white foaming surf at a range of 30 yds (27 m) or less from the shore. Whiting and pouting figure highly in catches at night from the beach and they can be caught easily by fishing at short range. A lot of anglers fish with a two- or three-hook trace baited with lugworm or squid to tempt these smaller fish.

TOP LEFT: This angler is using a beach tripod to keep the rods secure and steady.

ABOVE: An angler tails a smoothhound hooked while fishing at distance from rocky ground. This is a species that can often be caught fishing from the shore.

Many of the country's fishing clubs hold beach competitions at night as the catches are often better than fishing in daylight. Whichever species you choose to pursue and whatever time of year you do it, beach fishing is well worth a go.

Species to Catch from the Beach

Plaice, rays, bass, mackerel, whiting, dabs, cod, flounders, dogfish, soles and eels.

BELOW: A beach is an exposed and cold place in rough weather. It is wise to be properly dressed and equipped.

Pier Fishing

Piers are probably the first place most sea anglers get their grounding. High tide will bring many different species within casting range of the angler. In the summer months, mackerel will be the main target during the day. They can be caught very easily on light float tackle using mackerel strips or sandeel as a bait. Garfish will also be present throughout the months of May to September. Again, fishing with light float tackle baited with mackerel strip, with the float set at a shallow depth, will ensure good sport.

Piers are also a much-favoured night-fishing spot, and many species of sea fish will venture closer to the stone or wooden structure of a pier once the light begins to fade. Pollack and small pouting are prime candidates for a spot of fishing by lamplight, and it is said that a lamp hung from a pier shining out over the water will attract such species. Legering with ragworm close into the structure of the pier is the perfect tactic for pollack, coalfish and pouting. If there is enough light shining across the water from nearby street lamps or the promenade, a float can be used to good effect. Many of the modern-day sea floats actually have a fitting to accommodate a small chemical night light, known as a

starlight. Once the small tube of chemicals is slightly bent the liquids inside are triggered, and mix together to create a bright light. The light can last for up to six hours and is a good way of detecting bites when float fishing at night. If legering at night, a starlight can also be fitted to the tip of the rod. When a bite occurs, the tip will bounce forward quickly, alerting the angler to the bite.

Another night-feeding species that can be caught close to the shore is the dogfish, especially in the late summer and early autumn. A nice fresh strip of mackerel on a running leger will sort out the bigger species. The occasional large bass is not out of the question, especially if fishing with mackerel or a whole soft crab bait after a storm. Larger bass are often alone and will follow prey fish in close to the shore at night. The pier is just the place for the bass to target an easy meal. Other species you may encounter are dabs and plaice if the pier is erected out over a sandy sea bed. A leger rig with a two-hook paternoster baited with cockles or squid is a method well worth trying.

Species to Catch from the Pier
Mackerel, dogfish, garfish, pollack, pouting, dabs, coalfish, whiting, bass, mullet, flounders, cod, plaice and eels.

ABOVE: Pier fishing is one of the sights of a British summer. Piers can provide the angler with some great fishing, and this angler has caught a small flatfish.

BELOW: Grey skies, gales and cold weather are bad for the holidaymaker, but a combination of rough weather and high tides will bring many species close to the shore.

Rock and Rough Ground

Many of the bigger species of sea fish are to be found over rock or rough ground, as it is these marks that are usually associated with deeper water. When the tide is low the angler has a great opportunity to explore the terrain he will be fishing over when the tide turns.

Rock and rough-ground marks are natural larders and the weedy gullies hold rich supplies of food for the bigger species. Fish such as bass, bull huss and the lesser-spotted dogfish will all visit these areas in the search for a meal at high tide. Walking the

ABOVE: These anglers are fishing for bass and dogfish from a rock mark. Bass in particular will often venture into the rock gullies as the tide rises.

BELOW: This angler is casting his bait from a rock plateau.

area at low tide will reveal every gully and trough created by the wash of the tide. It will also give the angler a valuable opportunity to pinpoint key marks such as deep gullies or clear areas on the rough ground.

Big cod and conger eels are two favourite species of the rough ground angler. These can be pursued by day or night with the latter being the more popular. From certain rough-ground marks these species can be caught at both low and high tides. With the tide high, fish will venture in closer and spend time delving through the weed and rock gullies. As the tide drops away they move back out into a secondary position, waiting for the tide to rise again. Find these secondary lairs, which are revealed on a low spring tide, and you can reap the rewards.

One of the main problems the sea angler faces when fishing over rough or rocky ground is loss of terminal tackle. This is usually caused by the hook or lead getting caught up on the rough sea bed. The tackle used must be strong enough to cope with these situations. A good strong rod of 12 ft (3.66 m) in length, matched with a robust reel and a line of 30 lb (13.6 kg) breaking strain is standard rough-ground fare. To keep losses to a minimum, expensive shop-bought leads can be replaced with a used spark plug from a car. These can easily be tied to the bottom of a trace and if lost, little cost is involved. Strong hooks and big baits are the key to catching and landing the bigger species likely to inhabit rough ground.

Conger eels are a prime target and can be tempted from their lairs with a nice, freshly cut mackerel flapper. This should be mounted up on a size 3/0 or 4/0 O'Shaughnessy hook on a trace of no less than 50 lb (22.68 kg). The lead or spark plug can be attached on what is called a rotten bottom. This is a length of low-breaking strain line, which will snap if the lead becomes caught. This is positioned above the bait on a running link. If, for any reason, the lead should become stuck on the bottom, the angler can pull for a break. This will jettison the lead leaving the hooked conger still intact.

Species to Catch from Rock and Rough Ground

Bass, conger eels, bull huss, dogfish, cod, wrasse.

Estuary Fishing

Estuaries can provide some excellent opportunities for the shore angler, and for the flatfish enthusiast in particular they are a key feature. Many species of fish will venture into the shelter of the estuary in search of food as the tide begins to flood. Mullet and flounder are probably the best-known species associated with estuary fishing. Mullet can often be spotted entering the fresh water right at the top of the estuary. Stalking them with a light float rod and bread baits or even using a small spinner baited with ragworm can provide some entertaining sport. On the south coast of Britain many bass are caught from estuary marks as they pursue the large shoals of sandeels that move into the estuary with the rising tide. In the lower reaches of the estuary, mackerel and pollack will spend time swimming around piers and jetties chasing shoals of brit. Both these species can be caught using float tactics, with a strip of mackerel or a sandeel as bait.

However, there is one species which is probably targeted more in the estuary than from any other venue. This species is the flounder, which will feed freely on each tide. More associated with winter fishing, many estuaries offer flounder fishing for nearly all of the year. But in the months from October to February, flounder are in their peak condition, and the chances of a specimen fish are far greater. The Teign estuary in

South Devon is a very good example of a prime winter flounder venue. Many of the big winter competitions are held here in December each year. It also holds the current British record for the species, with a fish weighing 5 lb 7 oz (2.66 kg). The Teign regularly produces flounder of 3 lb (1.36 kg) and over to the visiting shore angler.

To target flounder or any other species in the estuary, a 12 ft (3.66 m) beach rod with a medium action, matched with a reel holding 15 lb (6.8 kg) mainline is suitable. As the bottom of the estuary is usually soft mud and generally free of snags, a light hooklength of 10–12 lb (4.54–5.44 kg) can be used.

Flounder in particular can't resist a nice piece of fresh peeler crab used as bait. Present the crab bait on a size 1 or 1/0 fine-wire Aberdeen hook.

ABOVE: Take a close look at the estuary at low tide, and you will be able to pick out the channels. Casting to these marks on a high tide will put you on the fish.

If you go for some time without a bite it often pays to move the baited rig a short distance along the bottom.

Quite often a bite will materialize as the bait re-settles. The flounder may have been watching and waiting for the bait to move and the movement tricks it into thinking the bait is escaping. A good point for the shore angler to consider is that estuaries are a larder for fresh bait. It's well worth getting there as the tide is about to turn and flood again. Bait can be dug or collected and the angler can fish at the same time whilst the tide rises. The best times to fish in the estuary are usually one hour before the high tide and two hours after.

Species to Catch in the Estuary
Flounders, bass, mullet, mackerel, garfish and eels.

Making a Flatfish Rig

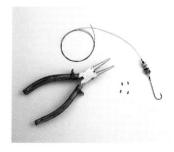

1 Beginner or experienced angler, you may prefer to make your own traces rather than buy them ready made. One of the easiest to make is an attractor rig for flatfish.

2 A 20 in (50 cm) length of memory-free line is used for the hooklength. A size 1/0 fine-wire Aberdeen hook is tied on securely to one end.

3 A few bright beads or sequins are threaded on to the line above the hook. These act as attractors and the bottom bead acts as a guard to stop the bait travelling up the hook.

4 A very small crimp is now threaded on to the trace behind the array of beads and sequins. This is crimped in place with the aid of a pair of bottle-nosed pliers.

5 Once the crimp holding the beads is tightly in place, all that remains to do is to tie on a size 10 swivel at the other end of the hooklength and the flatfish rig is ready.

ABOVE: As well as making hooklengths for flatfish, with the right materials the sea angler can make many different variations of rigs. Here are just a few home-made rigs, made with Gemini components, that save the angler a good deal of money.

Spinning

When the sun is shining and its rays are penetrating the sea, a bright shiny spinner retrieved through the clear blue water can be a very effective way of catching fish. Mackerel, bass and pollack can all be fooled into mistaking the spinner for a sandeel or fry. Spinning is a method mainly used during the summer months by the sea angler fishing from the shore. Fishing with a bright shiny spinner can account for big catches of mackerel from piers and jetties and is an equally effective method for catching school bass from the rocks.

There are many different patterns of spinners available and a wide variety of colours to choose from. To spin successfully the rod and reel must be light and well balanced. A spinning rod is usually of a soft to medium action, and is around 10 ft (3.05 m)in length. It is matched with a fixed-spool reel of medium size, loaded with 8–10 lb (3.63–4.54 kg) breaking strain line. The soft to medium action in the rod allows small spinners to be cast a great distance. It also helps to absorb some of the shock when a fish is hooked and is making its first dive.

Many of the popular patterns of spinners are heavy enough to cast by themselves and need no additional weight on the line. At the head of the spinner will be a small swivel which is tied directly to the main line from the rod. A good overhead cast will have the spinner zooming through the air and into the sea some 50 yds (46 m) out. Let the spinner sink down for a few seconds and then start to wind the reel handle to retrieve it. Some days a straightforward slow retrieve will be all that is needed to trigger a reaction from a passing fish. When the fishing is harder, try retrieving the spinner at different speeds and work the rod from side to side as you retrieve. This will cause the spinner to slow and quicken as it is darting from side to side. Working it in this manner will give the appearance of a distressed fish, and therefore an easy target.

Spinning for bass from the rocks can be good sport, especially if they are present in any numbers. Bass caught on a spinner tend to be on the small side and are known as schoolies. Silver-coloured spinners are good patterns to use. Remember

though, small bass are now a protected species, and it is illegal to take them from the sea at a length of 14 in (35 cm) or less.

Patterns of Spinners to Try

Toby and Krill for bass. Use standard mackerel spinners for mackerel and pollack.

ABOVE: A large and well conditioned bass caught by fishing with a plug. Next to it lie a variety of plugs available on the market, including one that resembles a mackerel.

BELOW: These anglers are spinning for bass at dawn from a rocky shore.

Plug Fishing for Bass

Plug fishing for big bass has become a very select method of catching specimen-sized fish. If you have access to a rock-strewn coastline then the chances of latching into a double-figure bass are high, especially if you target bass with a plug. The beauty of plug fishing is that you seldom have to cast out too far, and many of the bigger bass are caught very close to the shore. Most rocky sea shores will be littered with gullies and crevices, which at high water are flooded by the tide. Many of these gullies are only 20–30 yds (18–27 m) from the shore. These are prime target areas for the plug angler in search of bigger bass. Big bass will follow the tide in and wait at the entrances of these gullies to ambush the small prey fish as they leave with the dropping tide. Once the small fish begin to move back to the open sea the bass moves in for the kill. Timing is the key to success, and the tide will dictate this. For the best results, target these areas one hour before high tide and an hour after. Once the tide has dropped away, the bass will be long gone.

There are two types of plug the bass angler can use: floating and sinking. Taking into account the rough terrain, it is advisable to use the floating pattern as there will be less chance of it snagging on the rocks or weed. Popular patterns include plugs that resemble a sandeel or small mackerel. Many anglers make their own plugs from balsa wood and colour them to imitate the fish.

You can buy plugs from the tackle shop but they can be rather expensive. The Rapala make of plugs is world famous and catches a lot of the bigger bass. Some of the top patterns of plugs that are successful for bass fishing are from the range. Two of these are the Silver, which imitates a large sandeel, and the J13B. When fishing a gully, the plug should be cast to just beyond the gully entrance and worked just under the surface back to the rod. Work the plug as slowly as you can without it floating to the surface. This will give the bass time to see it and just enough time to decide whether to strike at it.

The most exciting thing about plug fishing is the take. When a large bass hits a plug, its sole intention is to kill. Once it realizes it's hooked it will tear off on a powerful run. Bass can also be caught from the beach with a plug. Many are taken from the surf 30 yds (27 m) from the shore. A floating plug is again the best choice for a bass as the water will be shallow.

For maximum sport, a freshwater carp rod of 11 ft (3.35 m) in length, matched with a small multiplier or fixed-spool reel loaded with 8–10 lb (3.63–4.54 kg) line should be used. When fishing from rocks a landing net is a useful item to carry with you to land your bass safely. Please remember to return any bass under 14 in (35 cm) in length to the sea.

BELOW: If you are lucky and choose the right pattern, you could catch a specimen bass like this one below.

BOTTOM: Rocks, pounding waves and rocky gullies are good conditions to try for bass. This is one of the most exciting of all forms of sea angling.

Float Fishing for Mullet

Float fishing can be a very effective way of catching sea fish throughout the year and is a method mainly used by the shore angler. Watching a bright orange-topped float bobbing in the sea can be a most relaxing way of spending a day's fishing. When float fishing, the bait is fished up off the bottom and for species like mackerel and garfish the bait is fished very near to the surface. A variety of species can be tempted on the float, and among the more popular are mackerel, garfish, pollack, wrasse and mullet.

Float fishing for mullet demands a specialist approach. Light lines and smaller floats are the order of the day for this shy, cautious species. Many anglers are led to believe the mullet is uncatchable, but this is far from true. The right approach from the thinking angler can produce good results. Mullet are to be found in most harbours or cruising close to piers and jetty walls. They are also found in estuaries, sometimes right in the top reaches in brackish water. Where there is one, others will be close by, as they move in shoals. A light rod (a freshwater float rod is the ideal tool), and a fixed-spool reel loaded with 5 lb (2.27 kg) line, will give the sea angler a good chance of deceiving the mullet. A small float like a freshwater waggler or a quill float should be used. It should be fixed to the line, top and bottom, and set at a shallow depth. Under the float a small amount of weight in the form of split shot is positioned to cock the float in the water, and then the hook is tied on. The hook size is critical as mullet have small mouths and the tissue surrounding the lips is quite soft.

Freshwater hooks in sizes 10 and 12 are ideal as they will complement the bait size.

Small baits are the key to catching mullet, and among the best are harbour ragworm, bread and fish flesh. Once the angler has located a shoal of mullet it is a good idea to introduce some form of mashed-up groundbait to work as an attractor. This will stimulate the mullet into feeding and hold them in one area for a longer period. Mashed bread treated with pilchard oil is a good mix to try.

ABOVE: Prebaiting with mashed fish and bran, a form of rubby dubby often used for shark fishing, will often keep mullet feeding in the area for quite a while.

BELOW LEFT: Even though the mullet is small and has very soft lip tissue, the mouth is large and therefore large baits, bread flake, worms and strips of fish flesh are all taken with ease.

When mashed and mixed with the oil, the mix can be placed into an old onion sack and hung in the water from a wall. As the water soaks into the mix it will break up, sending small clouds of feed through the water. Baiting the hook with a small piece of bread flake can be the downfall of half a dozen mullet from the shoal before they move off with the tide. It is a good idea to carry a landing net with you if mullet fishing, as it will come in handy when landing the fish on such a light line.

Top Tip

Try groundbaiting with mashed fish and bread mixed together. This will pre-occupy the mullet and hold the shoal for longer periods.

General Float Fishing

Mackerel and garfish are two favourite targets for the float angler, especially during the summer. A pier rod, or better still a freshwater carp rod, can be used in conjunction with a small fixed-spool reel holding 8–10 lb (3.63–4.54 kg) line. Fishing with light, balanced tackle like this will maximize sport from the powerful fighting mackerel and the acrobatic garfish. Setting a medium-sized float at a shallow depth of say 4ft (1.22 m) is a well-practised method for mackerel. The float is fixed to the line by first threading the line through a stop bead. The stop bead will slide up to a stop knot of power gum or an elastic band set at the depth required. A float is then put on the line, by passing the line up through the centre of the float. Another bead is placed under the float and under this a ball lead heavy enough to cock the float is positioned. Another bead is placed under the weight and then a swivel is tied on to the line. To this swivel a 12 in (30 cm) length of line is tied and a size 1 Aberdeen hook is tied at the bottom end. Bait the hook with a strip of sandeel or even mackerel and you should catch a good quantity of these fish should there be any in the immediate area.

Where there are mackerel the sea angler is also likely to encounter garfish. The garfish tends to feed on, or very near the surface, and it often pays to fish one bait below the float and one bait above it. Using the same set-up described for the mackerel, simply add a separate snood above the float. The baited hook on this snood will sink just below the surface and will sit in prime position for the shallow-feeding garfish. For other species like pollack and wrasse the float is usually a bit larger, and only one hook is used. The only difference is that it is fished at a deeper depth and different baits are used. When fishing for wrasse from the rocks or pier, try baiting up the hook with a whole soft-back crab. The smaller the crab the better as it will allow better hooking. For pollack or coalfish a ragworm bait is preferred, especially if you are fishing at night from the pier.

Species to Catch when Float Fishing

Bass, pollack, wrasse, coalfish, mackerel, garfish, mullet.

ABOVE: During the summer months mullet can be caught close to rocks, piers and jetties. Stalking this shy fish with a light floating line can be a very pleasant way of spending a summer's afternoon.

RIGHT: Float Rig for Mackerel Fishing
This is a basic rig set up that can be used for many different situations when float fishing.

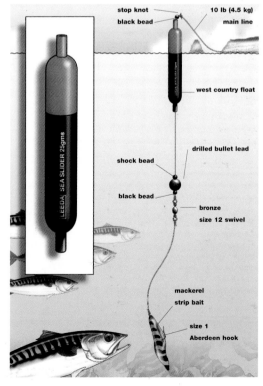

stop knot
black bead
10 lb (4.5 kg) main line

west country float

shock bead

drilled bullet lead

black bead

bronze size 12 swivel

mackerel strip bait

size 1 Aberdeen hook

Shore Angling Rigs

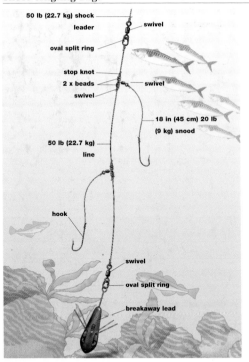

50 lb (22.7 kg) shock leader
swivel
oval split ring
stop knot
2 x beads
swivel
swivel
18 in (45 cm) 20 lb (9 kg) snood
50 lb (22.7 kg) line
hook
swivel
oval split ring
breakaway lead

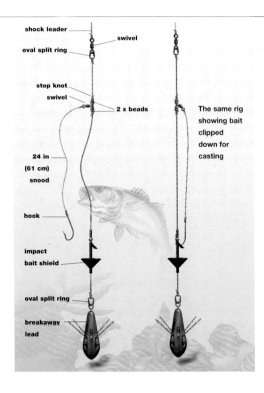

shock leader
swivel
oval split ring
stop knot
swivel
2 x beads
The same rig showing bait clipped down for casting
24 in (61 cm) snood
hook
impact bait shield
oval split ring
breakaway lead

Two Hook Paternoster (above)

The two hook paternoster is a popular rig to use from the shore when beach or pier fishing. Having two hooks set on the rig at a short distance apart, gives the angler a chance to try two different types of bait at the same time. If one of the baits proves to be more popular than the other it is a simple matter of changing the one that has failed. This rig is widely used when fishing for shoal fish such as whiting.

One Hook Distance Rig (above right)

This rig is often used by the distance caster in search of cod and smoothhounds. The one hook rig can be clipped down so it is able to be cast a considerable distance. Used in a strong tide the baited hook will sway in the tide attracting the fish. A bait shield is fitted to protect the bait on the cast.

Wishbone Rig (right)

The wishbone rig is a firm favourite of the cod angler who is fishing at distance from the shore in a strong tide. The two hook rig is able to run free, through a swivel and provides a 'bolt hooking' effect when either of the hooks is taken by a large fish. The addition of a bait shield will allow delicate baits like lugworm to be cast great distances with minimal damage to the bait.

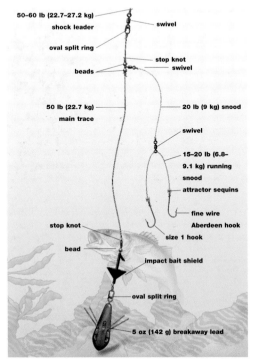

50–60 lb (22.7–27.2 kg) shock leader
swivel
oval split ring
stop knot
swivel
beads
50 lb (22.7 kg) main trace
20 lb (9 kg) snood
swivel
15–20 lb (6.8–9.1 kg) running snood
attractor sequins
fine wire Aberdeen hook
size 1 hook
stop knot
bead
impact bait shield
oval split ring
5 oz (142 g) breakaway lead

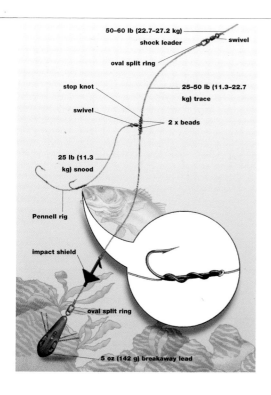

50–60 lb (22.7–27.2 kg)
shock leader
swivel
oval split ring
stop knot
25–50 lb (11.3–22.7 kg) trace
swivel
2 x beads
25 lb (11.3 kg) snood
Pennell rig
impact shield
oval split ring
5 oz (142 g) breakaway lead

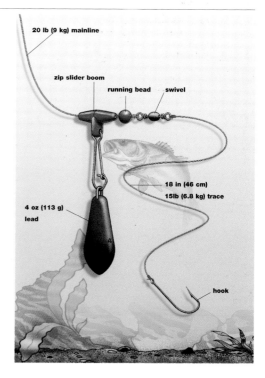

20 lb (9 kg) mainline
zip slider boom
running bead
swivel
18 in (46 cm)
15lb (6.8 kg) trace
4 oz (113 g) lead
hook

The Pennell Rig *(above)*

This is a well-used rig when fishing for bigger species like bass, dogfish, cod and smoothhounds. The addition of the second hook on the snood allows the use of a bigger bait. Whole calamari squid can be mounted up to imitate a live bait when bass fishing. For dogfish, a side of mackerel can be mounted on both hooks, offering a large treat to tempt a take.

Running Leger Rig *(above right)*

This rig is used when fishing over light shingle or sand. It is popular among sea anglers who are targeting flatfish, such as plaice or flounder. Using a small sliding boom with a quick-release clip on it, enables the weight to be changed very quickly without having to break down the tackle. The small rubber bead on the trace below the boom acts as a shock absorber.

Rough-ground Rig *(right)*

This rig is used when fishing over rough and rocky ground. It is widely used when fishing for conger, tope, rays and dogfish. A spark plug can be used as a weight to keep losses of tackle down to a minimum. Also a rotten bottom link is used at the lead to enable the angler to jettison the lead and break free from a snag without losing a hooked fish.

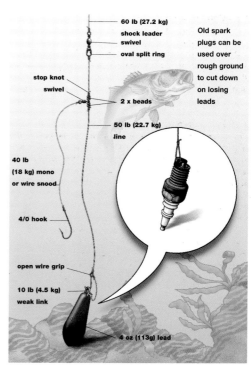

60 lb (27.2 kg)
shock leader
swivel
oval split ring
stop knot
swivel
2 x beads
50 lb (22.7 kg) line
40 lb (18 kg) mono or wire snood
4/0 hook
open wire grip
10 lb (4.5 kg) weak link
4 oz (113g) lead

Old spark plugs can be used over rough ground to cut down on losing leads

Boat Fishing

The sea angler can improve his or her chances of catching bigger, and often more fish, by fishing from a boat. There are a host of different methods that open new gateways into the sport that in practical terms can only be employed from a boat. Fishing over sunken wrecks is a prime example, allowing the angler to present baits or lures directly over a fish-holding feature on the sea bed, something which is not possible when fishing from the shore.

Fishing Afloat

The beauty of fishing afloat is that the marks and methods available are infinite, whereas fishing from the shore, pier or rocks is limited to how far you can cast and the make-up of the sea bed.

Of course, fishing afloat does have its drawbacks: you need a completely new set of tackle, including rods, reels and terminal gear such as hooks, swivels and leads. There is also the problem of sea sickness, being stuck out at sea on a boat that is rocking and rolling, and feeling or being sick is not the most pleasant of situations.

Safety at sea is also an important issue, and under current laws every charter boat must conform to strict safety codes. These include having enough quality life jackets and life rafts on board, as well as a spare ship-to-shore radio, a comprehensive first aid kit and sufficient emergency flares. Remember if you do take to the open sea in a boat, always ensure you are wearing a life jacket. No amount of big fish is worth risking your life for. If you do not own your own boat it is possible to select a trip aboard a boat owned by a professional skipper.

Cost is an important factor as many of the deep-sea wrecking trips are more expensive than a charter hire. This is due to the amount of time and fuel the skipper will need to use to get you and other anglers out to the deeper water marks and on to the fish. An average price for chartering a good boat, including bait, is around £35 for a day's fishing. This may sound expensive, but when you come home completely exhausted with enough fish to fill up your freezer, it all seems worthwhile. It pays to shop around and ask for advice at your local tackle shop. Several sea angling clubs arrange their own trips, and it is good to be a member of an active club as there will always be the chance of a good day out at sea in the company of friends.

The last and most influential factor when boat fishing is the weather. Unlike shore angling, fishing from a boat is governed by the wind. A force six wind is considered to be the strongest that can be fished in for safety and comfort. In some areas the wind direction also plays a vital part, and a force four easterly may be totally unfishable at one mark, whereas a force six northerly is fishable.

Boat Rods

There are numerous rods available for boat fishing, but there are really only three or four types you will need to be a successful all-round boat fisherman.

A good general-purpose boat rod for downtiding and wrecking is a 30 lb (13.6 kg) class model. These usually measure between 6-7 ft (1.83-2.13 m) and are excellent for fishing in deep water or strong tides for species such as cod, rays, turbot and other medium-sized fish. Many anglers who choose to use one rod for everything tend to pick the 30 lb (13.6 kg) class model. For the heavier species such as conger eels, skate and sharks it is recommended that you use either a 50 lb (22.68 kg) or 80 lb (36.39 kg) class boat rod, usually between 6-8 ft (1.83-2.44 m) in length. There are many available that have twin power ratings such as 30-80 lb (13.6-36.29 kg) or 50-80 lb (22.68-36.29 kg) class, and these are usually the shorter, American-style stand-up rods. The term stand-up means to stand up and fight your fish. Last, but by no means least, for the sporting angler, a good 12-20 lb (5.44-9.07 kg) class rod is ideal for a number of boat angling situations. These include drifting for cod and pollack over wrecks when using artificial eels and drifting for bass, plaice, turbot and brill over sand banks. Most of the modern rods on the market today are made from carbon fibre. The amount of carbon present in the rod will be depicted by the price tag. Some of the early models of boat rod are still available, and these are constructed from fibre glass. Many boat anglers still prefer to use the fibre glass models as they are often stronger than a budget-priced

LEFT: Take a mobile phone with you: you never know when you might need it.

OPPOSITE: Even when big fish are the quarry, a light, well-balanced boat outfit can give maximum sport.

carbon rod. Whichever you choose to use make sure it can stand up to the work you expect it to accomplish. There is nothing worse than being miles out at sea with the wrong kind of equipment. If you are going boat fishing for the first time, many boat skippers will often supply tackle for the beginner. This is a good option to take before you invest in your own tackle. It will give you a better idea which rod and reel suit the style of boat fishing you are going to be doing.

Since most rods are designed to be used in conjunction with a multiplier reel, the rings on the rod will be in the upward facing position when you are fishing. Therefore, it is important to make sure the rod has enough rings and that they are correctly spaced along the blank. This can be done by attaching the reel and threading the line through the rings. You can then tie the end of the line to a heavy object and put the rod under pressure. The rings should prevent your line from touching the rod blank; if they do not, then the rod either has too few rings or they are incorrectly spaced.

Boat Reels

Most boat anglers use multiplier reels because there are few, if any, fixed-spool reels that can stand the pressure and load that boat angling puts them under. There are three main multipliers that every good boat angler should own. First there is the 7000-sized multiplier, which can be used for general uptiding, drifting and downtiding. The second is the 6500-sized multiplier, which is perfect for light uptiding and all light-line fishing.

The last reel is a large 6/0-sized multiplier, capable of holding 300-500 yds (274-460 m) of 30 lb (13.6 kg) line. This is used for deep-water wreck fishing or downtiding and can also be used for conger eels and sharks.

There are two key points to look for when choosing a multiplier for boat angling. First of all it must hold enough line for the type of fishing you intend to do. Second, and most important of the two, the reel must have a smooth, powerful drag system that can be easily adjusted.

There are two types of drag: a star drag – a star-shaped disk found underneath the handle – or a lever drag usually found on the end plate of the reel. Most experienced boat anglers will go for a star-drag

ABOVE: A reel with a level-wind is a good idea for novices.

ABOVE: This reel is better suited to big fish and deep water.

RIGHT: Make sure you match the correct reel to your rod.

ABOVE: This 7000-sized reel is ideal for uptiding.

multiplier for their general downtide and uptide reels, choosing a lever drag for bigger reels that are intended for playing big fish. The star drag is adjusted by turning the star either clockwise to apply more drag, or anti-clockwise to reduce it. A lever-drag works by pushing the lever up for more drag or down for less. It is easier to adjust a lever drag when playing a big fish than a star drag. Whatever reel you choose, make sure it is matched to your rod to provide you with a balanced outfit.

Boat Terminal Tackle and Sundries

The average boat angler is likely to encounter many different species and marks, and will need a wider variety of tackle than that of the shore angler.

For instance, depending on where he wishes to fish regularly, a good selection of leads, including both plain and grip leads from 2 oz (57 gm) right up to 2 lb (0.91 kg), are needed. Sizes and patterns of hooks will also have to be varied from the smallest size 2 Aberdeen-style for catching dabs,

ABOVE: Boat fishing line needs to be reliable and strong. It can be purchased on spools containing hundreds of yards (metres) of line.

black bream and soles right up to huge size 8/0 or 10/0 forged O'Shaughnessy hooks for conger eels, skate and sharks. Rods and reels have to be matched to the particular species or conditions, too, and this means carrying at least two or three different rods, plus the same number of reels loaded with different breaking strains of line. Line breaking strain will depend on the species sought.

As a rule the angler will need two reels, one of which will be loaded with 30 lb (13.6 kg) class line and the other with 50 lb (22.68 kg) or even 80 lb (36.29 kg) breaking-strain line. If you eventually drift into light-line lure fishing then a reel loaded with 12–15 lb (5.44–6.8 kg) breaking-strain line will allow some excellent sport for

ABOVE: A variety of weights will be needed to cover different methods.

species such as pollack and coalfish. Remember to go prepared, because there is nothing more frustrating than losing the fish of a lifetime through the line breaking. It is also a good idea to carry three or four spools of trace line for constructing the hooklength or trace. For instance, when fishing for rays, cod and smoothhounds a trace of around 40 lb (18.14 kg) breaking strain is needed, but for species such as pollack and bass the angler can use lighter lines between 12–20 lb (5.44–9.07 kg).

It is also advisable to arm yourself with a few ready-made conger traces fitted with large hooks. These can be purchased ready-tied to steel wire in most tackle shops. More experienced boat anglers often carry a selection of ready-made traces in a rig wallet.

ABOVE: Swivels of all sizes are used for tying traces and joining lines.

Unlike shore fishing, boat angling offers a wide diversity of methods, and to become a good boat angler you need to be aware of what these are and make sure you have the gear to practise them effectively. The main types of boat angling are uptiding, downtiding, sharking, wrecking, drifting and light line angling, each of which requires a completely different set-up.

Until you actually start thinking about becoming a serious boat angler, it is hard to imagine the diversity of tackle and tactics used. For the average boat angler a selection of leads from 2 oz (57 gm) to 2 lb (0.91 kg) should be sufficient. When you book your trip you will often find that many charter boat skippers will have a stock of bigger leads on board if they are needed.

Other items to consider are hooks. The size and pattern of hook will depend very much on the species of fish you are after. Carry a wide

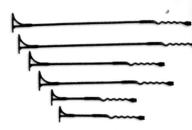

ABOVE: Booms come in all manner of lengths, and the longer types are usually used when fishing an artificial eel bait.

selection of sizes in different patterns; as time goes on you will get to use them. Swivels of various sizes and breaking strains along with a selection of beads will also be needed. Booms are widely used when fishing over deep water, and there are many different varieties available. Two of the most essential are the standard zip slider boom and the new revolutionary Ziplock running booms. This boom is available in different lengths and will cope with all manner of rig presentations. It will also allow the angler to adjust the length of the trace without having to break down the terminal tackle.

Lures play a large part in boat angling, especially wreck fishing and drifting, so a good selection of pirks, artificial eels and jellyworms is essential. Probably the widest practised form of lure fishing is the use of an artificial eel for pollack and cod when fishing over a wreck.

ABOVE: Small hooks and large hooks all play their role in boat fishing.

No boat angler should leave the dock without a handful of rubber eels. The bigger the species you are after, the bigger the artificial eel you will need. These are fished on a long boom to hold a long flowing trace away from the mainline and are very effective. When buying artificial eels it sometimes pays to change the hook for a bigger, stronger pattern.

Another form of lure that will take its fair share of the catch is the pirk. A pirk is a chrome tube fitted with a large treble hook, and it resembles a

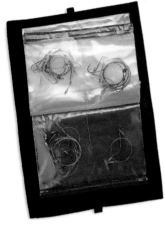

ABOVE: A rig wallet like this will protect your terminal tackle and traces.

smaller prey fish. Cod in particular fall foul to the pirk, and when baited with strips of mackerel or squid it is a deadly method for ling. Pirks can be made at home or bought in different weights from the tackle shop.

With all the bits of terminal tackle you are likely to take with you on a trip it is a good idea to invest in a tackle box for storing your kit. Some of the smaller items like hooks, swivels and beads, should be stored in a rig wallet. Bigger items like leads and other sundries can be stored in a tackle box or small seat box, which should also be waterproof and airtight. A good filleting knife for cutting bait and cleaning the catch is recommended, and if you are out at sea for long periods then a flask, preferably an unbreakable stainless steel one, is essential.

When playing out a big fish over a wreck a butt pad can be a good investment. This allows the angler to balance the strain on the rod.

Clothing

For the shore angler clothing will be dictated by the weather. If the sun is shining and the air is warm a T-shirt, shorts and training shoes will be adequate. However, if you choose to fish in the colder months from beach or rock marks, it is important to wear suitable clothing to protect yourself from the elements and to keep yourself both warm and dry. A smock worn over a warm jumper will keep the warmth in on an autumn evening, but for the night angler it is advisable to wear a waterproof suit with a hood. If fishing from rocks or rough ground, investing in a flotation suit as worn by boat anglers is a sensible option. You can never predict the way of the sea, and it is better to be safe than sorry.

Footwear for the beach and rock angler needs to be waterproof and comfortable. Waders are fine for the short beach session and a strong pair of walking boots will support your ankles when rock hopping. Neoprene waders and chest waders are becoming more popular for the beach and rock angler as they are light, waterproof and will keep you warm. Head wear in the form of a woolly hat and a pair of neoprene gloves for your hands will stop any heat escaping from the body.

Every licensed charter boat must have enough life jackets and life rafts for the number of passengers it is registered to carry. However, most boat anglers protect themselves by means of a flotation suit. Not only do flotation suits keep you warm during the colder weather, they also keep you dry. Each suit has enough buoyancy to keep even the heaviest angler afloat should he fall overboard. They come in a wide range of sizes, but most are either bright red or yellow in colour. Some manufacturers also incorporate special reflective material

RIGHT: A flotation suit with a built-in buoyancy aid should always be worn when out boat fishing.

to help the rescue services spot you at night, and most include a whistle of some sort in one of the pockets, so you can attract attention to yourself should you fall over and get swept away by the current.

You can buy a good flotation suit for as little as £75, which seems a worthwhile investment to guarantee your safety. Most makes are available as either one-piece or two-piece suits, which come as a jacket and separate salopette trousers. There have been so many developments in recent years with regard to fabrics, that you can now be both safe and warm without losing much of your mobility.

Other very useful items of boat fishing attire include fingerless neoprene gloves, woolly hats, thermal underwear, thick socks and Wellington boots, all of which help to keep you warm when the cold weather threatens. It's no fun being stuck out at sea when you are freezing cold, so make sure you prepare yourself well if you want to enjoy your boat fishing.

During the summer months it is important to wear some sort of hat, usually a baseball cap, and a decent pair of sunglasses. It is also important to wear high-level sun protection on exposed areas of skin – when out on the sea you catch double the amount of sunshine because it reflects off the surface of the water. Also the wind dries your skin and increases the effects of exposure.

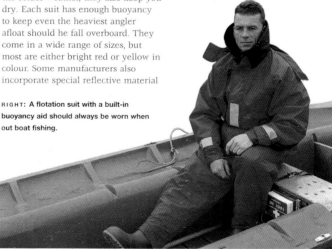

Charter Boat Fishing

Sea angling on board charter boats is by far the most popular form of boat angling in this country. Most coastal ports have their own charter boat fleet, and there are literally thousands to choose from.

All you have to do is book the boat for the day you require, which simply takes a telephone call. Most skippers will ask you for a small deposit. All you do then is telephone the skipper the night before your trip to make sure the weather is okay and will not keep you in port, and off you go.

Nearly all of the boats available are fully licensed and insured for having up to 12 anglers on board, but for comfort reasons it is better to fish with only eight or ten.

Charter boats can offer a wide range of trips from three hours of mackerel fishing right up to twenty-four-hour wrecking trips. However, the location of the port obviously has an effect on the fishing any charter boat can provide. The charter boat trip is often the first taste of boat fishing for many would-be boat anglers. This is a good way to get to know about the local inshore marks before contemplating a deep-water trip that could last for twenty-four hours. Take note of what the skipper or his deck-hand is telling you. They will be well-educated in the methods used – after all, it is their job.

ABOVE: A party of anglers boarding a charter boat for a day's fishing.

ABOVE: The stern of the boat can often be the hot spot for catching fish over a wreck.

Any charter boat can get a 3 mile (4.83 km) licence from its local authority, which allows it to fish within these boundaries. All charter boats that wish to fish further than three miles offshore have to be DOT approved. If the boat conforms to certain safety and technical standards, it will be issued with a licence that allows the crew to fish 20, 40 or 60 miles (32, 64, or 96 km) offshore. Check that the skipper of your chosen boat has this licence if you are planning a long-distance fishing trip.

Most skippers are, or have been fishermen themselves, and are only too pleased to take novices and show them the ropes. However, the best way to start boat fishing is to join a local sea angling club. Here you can meet and make friends who will take you fishing with them and pass on their knowledge and experience in a practical manner.

Wreck Fishing

Fishing over a wreck is considered by many to be one of the most productive methods of sea angling. Often tons of fish can be hauled up from the depths by fishing over a deep-water wreck mark, using both baited hooks and lures.

The main species encountered when wreck fishing are cod, pollack, coalfish, bass, ling and conger eels. Methods vary from coast to coast, but the two main variations are either drifting with lures or baited feathers, or anchoring uptide of the wreck and dropping baited traces downtide towards and into it.

As far as tackle is concerned, the species you are targeting will govern the type of gear you use and weight of line and lure.

When fishing for conger eels, which is usually done while at anchor, a 50 lb (22.68 kg) class boat rod and suitable multiplier reel loaded with 50 lb (22.68 kg) mainline is required. Conger eels can grow in excess of 200 lb (90.72 kg), so sturdy tackle is a necessity. A whole mackerel bait with the backbone removed as shown on pages 142–3, is mounted on a large hook that is crimped to a wire trace.

Due to the fact that the backbone of the mackerel has been removed, the two side fillets will flap around in the tidal flow. This presentation is known as a flapper bait, and is extremely effective for catching conger eels.

When drifting over a wreck for cod, pollack or bass it is advisable to use a 20 lb (9.07 kg) or 30 lb (13.6 kg) class set-up. The lighter you go, the more sport you will have, but be careful not to under-gun yourself. Fishing on the drift is a method that allows the boat to move freely in the tidal flow. The skipper will position the boat in an uptide position and then cut the engine. The boat is then allowed to drift downtide, allowing the anglers on board to fish their lures or baits while the boat is on the move. This is a good way of catching pollack and bass when using artificial eels as a lure. The eel is presented on a long flowing trace attached to a boom. The longer the trace the more natural the eel will look and many anglers use a trace of anything up to 25 ft (7.62 m). As the boat moves downtide the rhythm of the tide works the eel, making it look like the real thing. It is slowly retrieved to give added attraction, which often makes the fish attack it vigorously.

The method of pirking or jigging is well-recognised as a good method for catching cod over wrecks. This is where a metal lure is worked over the wreck while the boat is drifting. The pirk is jigged up and down in the tide run and the cod sees the pirk as a prey fish and attacks it. It often pays to tip the hooks of the pirk with squid

strips or mackerel fillet; this will give it added attraction. Another good method for catching cod and pollack is to use jellyworms on a long flowing trace, again while the boat is drifting (see page 158). This is one of the

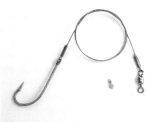

LEFT: The world-famous Eddystone eels are used all over the world for wreck and reef fishing. They are mainly taken by pollack and bass.

more exciting methods because you can usually feel the fish tapping away at the lure before it finally takes it. Jellyworms are a new breed of latex and rubber worm-like lures from the United States. Generally they are smaller in size than the big artificial eels but are just as productive and are fished in a similar manner.

Superbraids

The use of modern superbraids as a mainline has revolutionized the way sea anglers fish over wrecks. Its lack of stretch allows the use of lighter leads and puts the angler in direct contact with the bait or lure so that they can feel a bite instantly. When using a braided line it is important not to strike at the fish too quickly. This can result in tearing the bait or lure from the fish's mouth. Owing to the lack of stretch in braid the angler will be able to feel every little tap and pull as the fish mouths the bait. However, you should wait a second or two before you set the hook. Having fished with monofilament lines you will find the change to braid different to start off with. Once mastered, and with a little time and a bit of patience, the technique is not difficult: the use of braid can add a few extra fish to your catch.

How to Make a Conger Eel Trace

1 When fishing for conger eels, a steel trace and large hook are used. A steel trace can easily be made with little effort. You need 60 lb (27.3 kg) wire, size 6 or 8/0 hooks, some wire crimps and a pair of crimping pliers.

2 Cut a length of wire and thread on a crimp, followed by the hook. Then thread the wire back through the crimp, trapping the hook on the wire. Pull the crimp down tight to the eye of the hook.

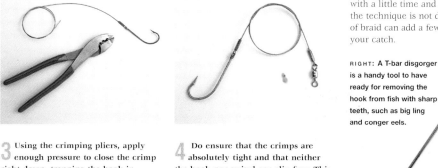

3 Using the crimping pliers, apply enough pressure to close the crimp right down, trapping the hook in position. Trim away any waste wire. At the other end of the trace a large swivel is crimped in place in the same manner and the wire trimmed as before. The trace is now complete.

4 Do ensure that the crimps are absolutely tight and that neither the hook nor swivel can slip free. This tackle is designed for big fish and you do not want to lose the largest fish you have ever hooked through badly made or faulty tackle. Store the completed trace in your rig wallet.

RIGHT: A T-bar disgorger is a handy tool to have ready for removing the hook from fish with sharp teeth, such as big ling and conger eels.

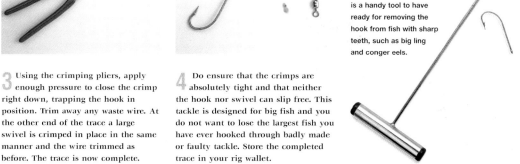

Shark Fishing

Fishing for sharks is one of the more specialized branches of boat angling. Many boat anglers are not prepared to spend the time or money needed on a charter boat to target sharks successfully. In the United Kingdom there are three main species of shark caught on rod and line: porbeagle, thresher and blue sharks. Other species are available, but they are few and far between. Of the three sharks that inhabit our waters the blue is the most common. It can grow up to 200 lb (90.72 kg), but the average size is between 70–100 lb (31.75–45.36 kg).

Both the porbeagle and thresher sharks grow bigger, some may weigh as much as 500 lb (227 kg), but again the average size is much smaller at around 100–200 lb (45.36–90.72 kg).

Strong tackle is a must when targeting big sharks. A good quality 50–80 lb (22.68–36.23 kg) class rod is needed, as is a suitable multiplier reel capable of holding several hundred yards (metres) of 50 lb (22.68 kg) mainline – a big shark can strip 200 yds (183 m) of line from a reel on its initial run in the blink of an eye.

Perhaps the most important item is the trace. A typical shark trace consists of around 6 ft (1.83 m) of 300–400 lb (136–181 kg) breaking-strain wire joined to a further 10–15 ft (3.05–4.57 m) of 150–200lb (68–90.72 kg) wire via a quality barrel swivel. On the end there is usually a very strong hook, something like a size 10/0 or 12/0 O'Shaughnessy.

The Bait

Quite often a whole mackerel is suspended below the surface with the aid of a party balloon, which acts as a float. The usual set up for a day's shark fishing involves no more than four anglers fishing at any one time. The four (or less) baits are suspended at different depths, usually from 50–60 ft (15.2–18.3 m) up to 10 ft (3.05 m) under the surface. Even though the trace may be 20 ft (6.1 m) long, the action of a drifting boat dragging the baits behind it sets the lines at an angle, so the bait ends up higher in the water. The drag is set on the reel, so that line can be taken easily, and the ratchet is engaged – a loud audible click that helps deter-mine a run. There is nothing more exciting than hearing a ratchet scream as a shark picks up the bait and runs off with it.

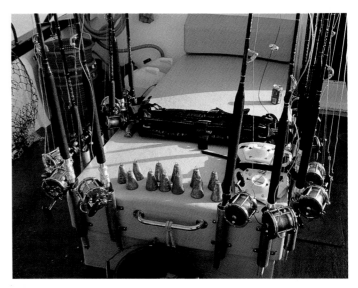

At this point the angler should pick up the rod and disengage the ratchet. It is wise to let the fish run for 20 seconds or so before striking, and many experienced shark anglers will let the shark run until it stops, then strike when the shark starts its second run. Fishing for sharks is not for the faint-hearted as the fight can last for hours. For the bigger species the angler is usually strapped into a fighting chair, and the rod is attached to a harness to aid with leverage on the fish. Shark fishing takes time as the shark seizes line and then the angler gets it back, only to have the shark run again. Due to the sheer size of the shark, once under control and alongside the boat, normally the trace is cut and it is allowed to swim free. There is no point in killing such a wonderful creature that provides so much sport.

ABOVE: **A charter boat fully equipped for a day's shark fishing.**

ABOVE: **The successful and delighted angler boats a shark before release.**

BELOW: **A beaten shark is brought alongside the boat when the trace will be cut.**

Uptiding

The method of uptiding has proven to be one of the most successful ways of bait fishing over ground other than wrecks and reefs, such as sand or mud banks and rough ground. For many years boat anglers were limited to dropping their baits over the side of the boat, commonly known as downtiding. This method is still the most popular today, but having the knowledge to be able to fish uptide has its advantages. It all started in the 1970s when Bob Cox and John Rawle were experimenting in the River Thames. They discovered that by using a lead with wires protruding from the base they were able to anchor their baits uptide of the boat. This method of casting a baited rig uptide and away from the boat allows the angler to get outside the so-called "scare area", an area created by the disturbance of the anchor and waves slapping the hull of the boat.

Not only does it enable the angler to fish in an area away from the boat, it also often results in a much higher hook-up rate, because the fish often hook themselves.

The basic method involves casting a baited rig uptide and allowing it to hit the sea bed. The angler then pays off a few extra yards of line from the reel which creates a bow of line in the tide. This ensures that even though the bait is anchored uptide, the angler's line still points downtide. When a fish picks up the bait, the resistance of the bow of line and the anchoring qualities of the lead drive the hook home into its mouth. A medium-sized fish often pulls the lead out of the sea bed when it gets hooked and a tell-tale bite is given as the fish, lead and trace trundle downtide. However, uptiding does have its limitations and is only suitable for marks in less than 100 ft (30.5 m) of water and those places that do not have strong tides. Standard uptide tackle usually consists of a 10 ft (3.05 m) rod with a fairly sensitive tip and a powerful middle and butt section. The length of the rod is required to be able to cast the bait away from the boat. The main reason why a sensitive tip is needed is so that the action of the waves on the boat doesn't "bounce" the lead out of the sea bed. Another reason why the tip needs to be sensitive is so the angler can spot bites quickly.

ABOVE: This angler connects with his quarry while fishing uptide off a boat.

A multiplier reel suitable for casting such as a 6500 or 7000 size loaded with a minimum of 250 yds (229 m) of line is required. If you prefer to use a light line approach of say 12–15 lb (5.44–6.8 kg) class line then a shock leader will be required to take the initial shock of the cast. Even with lines up to 20 lb (9.07 kg) it is recommended a leader of 30–35 lb (13.6–15.9 kg) be used. The strength of the tide will dictate the size of the lead you will need to use. In general, a breakaway lead or grip lead of 5–8 oz (142–227 gm) will do the job. The most simple rig for uptiding is a running leger, where the lead is

mounted on to the mainline so it is able to run freely. This is usually done by means of a sliding boom, and there are a number of booms available specifically for use when uptiding in this way. After the boom has been placed on to the mainline it is followed by a small bead. A swivel is then tied on to the mainline to stop the lead running on to the hooklength. A hooklength made up of around 3 ft (0.9 m) of 30–40 lb (13.61–18.14 kg) breaking-strain line is tied to the other end of this swivel.

The choice of style and size of hooks varies depending on the species the angler is targeting. In general an Aberdeen or Viking pattern between size 3/0 to 6/0 is used.

Another popular rig is a sliding paternoster. This is made in exactly the same way, but the lead is attached to a length of line that is shorter than the hooklength, and instead of a boom, another swivel is used. When casting the rig, the angler needs to make sure the lead is outside the boat and that no other angler is in the way. The cast is then made away from the boat and uptide. As the flow of the tide increases, the angler may need to cast closer towards the anchor chain to reduce the amount of pressure that the force of the tide puts on the mainline, otherwise the lead will break free from the bottom.

As there is casting involved, soft baits such as peeler crabs and

ABOVE: The successful angler with a good cod weighing 7 lb (3.17 kg).

sandeels may need to be whipped to the hook with fine bait elastic prior to casting to hold them in place.

When a bite is detected, the angler simply picks up the rod and starts to reel in quickly. There is no need to strike because the fish should already be hooked. At first it may seem that the bite has been missed, but this is not so. The trace, lead and fish move back towards the angler with the tide. By the time the angler has taken up the slack line the whole lot should be much nearer the boat. The angler will often only connect with the fish once all the slack line has been retrieved and a direct line and contact with the fish has been properly established.

It is important to wind in as quickly as possible until the weight of the fish is felt, to prevent the fish travelling too far downtide, or even shaking the hook free. This is particularly so in fast-flowing tides.

Six Boat Rigs

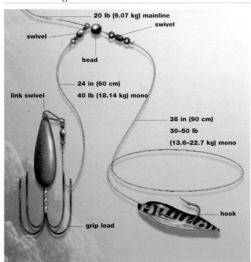
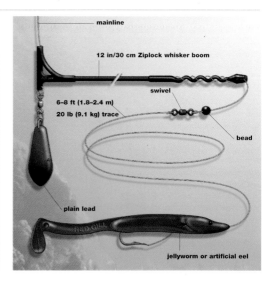

Uptide Rig (above)

The uptide rig is employed by the boat angler who is targeting tope and cod. With the use of a grip lead this rig can be anchored against the flow of the tide, allowing the bait to flap around in the current. Bigger species like tope are drawn to the life-like bait. Big hooks and big baits are the key to catching those bigger species.

Artificial Eel Rig (above right)

This is a popular presentation for catching large numbers of pollack and cod when fishing over a wreck. The skipper of the boat will use the tide to position the boat over the wreck. As the wreck appears on the screen of the fish finder, the angler will lower the eel down over the wreck. A long, flowing trace is used as long as 25 ft (7.6 m) in length to gain perfect presentation, allowing the rubber eel to behave in a life-like fashion. The use of a Ziplock boom will ensure a tangle-free presentation, and a special retention clip allows the lead to slide down the line when a fish has been hooked. This means the angler can play the fish out on a short trace.

Pirking Rig (opposite)

Often referred to as the 'Killer' rig, this combination of pirk and artificial muppets is a dead cert when fishing for cod or pollack. The pirk, which is made from chrome piping, acts not only as an attractor but also as the weight needed to get the rig down deep, quickly. There is a large treble hook on the end of the pirk and two further hooks on the muppets that are fished on traces above the pirk. Fish attracted to the silver glint of the pirk will often be caught on the muppets.

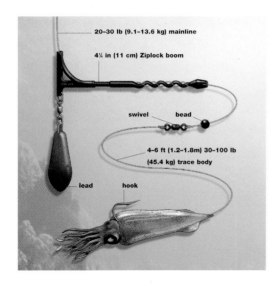

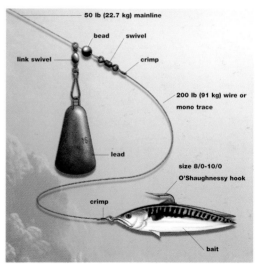

Downtide Rig *(above)*

The downtide rig is used when fishing in the tidal current downtide of the boat. It is a good all-round rig for a variety of species. Pollack, coalfish, cod and bass can all be targeted with this rig. Hook and bait size will depend on the species being targeted. The use of a Ziplock boom ensures the bait is held well away from the mainline and lead as the rig is allowed to drift downtide, eliminating any tangles.

Conger Rig *(above)*

This plain but efficient rig is used to target the large conger eels that inhabit many wrecks and rough ground marks. A large hook and heavy lead ensure the bait is fished on the bottom, and strong line is used to cope with the powerful fight of a large eel. The hook snood will often be constructed of wire or very heavy gauge line as the conger has razor sharp teeth. Use of a lighter line will result in a lost eel.

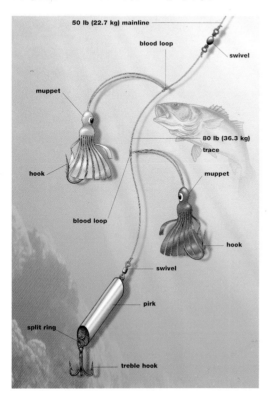

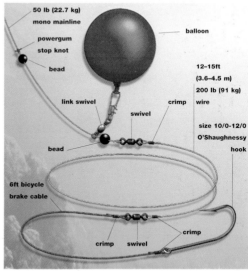

Shark Rig *(above)*

When fishing for sharks it is common to present a drifting bait. This is done with the aid of a highly visible balloon. The balloon acts as a visual indicator and also as a carrying aid for the bait. It is picked up in the tidal current and drifts the bait away from the boat. When a shark picks up the bait, the balloon will pull free from the line. Strong tackle in the form of wire traces and large hooks are the order of the day for the shark angler.

Game Fishing

In fishing parlance, game fishing means fishing for members of the salmonidae family: salmon, sea trout, brown trout, rainbow trout and grayling, and it is difficult to say precisely why these fish have such a fascination for anglers. Other fish, notably the big sea fish such as sharks and tope, fight harder. Some coarse fish are more difficult to outwit and capture, and a number of coarse fish such as carp and barbel, are renowned for their strength and guile when they have been hooked.

It is true that game fish, particularly salmon and sea trout, make a notable contribution to the table, but many would prefer to eat Dover sole or fresh turbot, and some trout caught in reservoirs can taste rather indifferent. Nevertheless, game fishing retains its hold on many anglers and can provide the pinnacle of an angler's career.

Introduction

The reason for the fascination of game fishing is probably a combination of factors. First of all there is the challenge of outwitting the quarry: shy trout in chalk streams are easily scared and can be infuriatingly choosy when they are feeding on one particular natural fly. If the angler is to be successful, he or she must identify and imitate that fly to stand any chance of success. The capture of a large chalk-stream trout is something to be celebrated.

The Right Conditions

Trout in lakes and reservoirs can feed on many different creatures at many different depths in the water, and the angler has to solve a number of problems successfully. Salmon and sea trout will only take freely when conditions are favourable, which they seldom are, and even then they may not take when conditions seem absolutely right. Salmon, sea trout and many rainbows also fight with great strength and determination and all game fish can be extremely choosy about the type of baits or flies they will accept.

Probably the main reason why game fishing holds such a fascination is the rivers, lakes and lochs where it takes place. Salmon rivers and Highland lochs, particularly, are

BELOW: The River Test at Kimbridge, Hampshire. The Test is the most famous of all the chalk streams of southern England and can provide a great challenge for the angler.

places of supreme beauty and the fisherman is conscious of being surrounded by and being close to nature. The primitive hunting instinct that exists in all anglers thrives in beautiful locations. The game fish described in this book are five in number although many anglers place the grayling as a coarse fish for it breeds in the spring and has the same season as coarse fish. However both the grayling and brown trout are to be found in unpolluted clear streams and the grayling is particularly sensitive to the quality of the water.

Brown trout are found all over the country in both rivers and stillwaters and nowadays are frequently stocked in reservoirs and lakes. The finest trout fishing is on the chalk streams of southern England, where the water is crystal clear, and the fishing exacting in the extreme. Trout fishing, generally, is a local pursuit and many anglers fish for trout near where they live, although with the advent of

stocked waters populated by enormous fish, bred for their size, more and more anglers are visiting far waters in search of these monsters.

Rainbow trout, too, have become very popular for they generally fight better than brown trout and they are easy to stock in all waters, not just reservoirs and lakes, for they tolerate higher water temperatures and poorer water quality than the native brown trout. They grow quicker and commercially offer a better return.

Species Under Threat

The game fish that have had to struggle to survive are the two migratory species where humankind is unable to give a helping hand and the environment changes have worked against them. Sea trout in particular have suffered, firstly from UDN (ulcerative dermal necrosis) disease in the 1960s that virtually wiped out the population on many rivers, and latterly with offshore pollution caused by the salmon farms in the estuaries, particularly around the west coast of Scotland. Sea trout have also suffered because the sandeel, their main diet in the sea, has been badly overfished by commercial fishermen for use as fertilizer and to make fish pellets. Some rivers in Wales still support a good number of sea trout but in many places their survival is in doubt.

The plight of the salmon is well-documented and many rivers are now taking drastic steps to preserve their stock by banning all methods of fishing except the fly and insisting on fish being returned to the river unharmed so that they have a chance

of spawning and reproducing the species. These matters are the concern of every angler and it is important to all that the salmon and sea trout continue to run and spawn in the 21st century.

It is the capture of these species that is the summit of the angler's ambition. There is no doubt that the hooking, playing and landing of a salmon is one of the great moments in an angler's life. Sea trout, too, hooked in the dark on a river when they take with a great jolt on the line, or coming to the dap on a Highland loch with a heart-stopping splash are a quarry fit for all.

BELOW: Fishing the sedge rise as the sun sets on Rutland Water.

Tackle

Modern tackle has made game fishing a great deal easier. Rods are lighter and more powerful; modern technology has led to the development of many different types of line that make casting easier; and various lines can be purchased that will sink through the water at different rates or float on the surface. Nylon leaders are stronger and thinner and modern nylon can be virtually invisible in water. Flies and lures also are now made from modern materials that are better than many old-fashioned ones and the design of salmon flies, in particular, has improved drastically.

BOTTOM LEFT: A variety of duns and spinners in a dry-fly fisher's fly box.

ABOVE LEFT: Fishing the evening rise on the River Wharfe, Yorkshire, in a fall of spinners.

ABOVE: Netting a good rainbow trout in spring on a north of England reservoir.

Also game fishing is now available to everyone. Whereas years ago most of the best game fishing was in private hands and reserved, nowadays much of the best trout fishing is on modern reservoirs where anyone can buy a day ticket, and even if the best salmon beats are still prohibitively expensive there are tickets available on a number of local waters in Scotland with the chance of a fish.

BELOW: Changing the fly on a successful day fishing a loch in the Orkneys.

Species

Atlantic Salmon *(Salmo salar)*

Current Records
British **64 lb (29.029 kg)**
World **79 lb (35.9 kg) Norway**

Season
January to November, depending on the river.

Distribution
Widespread in Scotland, northern England and the west coast of Ireland.

Natural Diet
Does not feed in freshwater.

Top Spots
Rivers Tweed, Tay, Spey and Aberdeenshire Dee.

Top Tip
Fish in good water with a gently-falling river.

Recognition

For many freshwater game anglers the Atlantic salmon, *Salmo salar*, is the greatest prize of all. Fresh in from the tide it is a magnificent fish. Bright silver flanks, occasionally flushed with a tinge of purple, are contrasted by a dark steely back. The body is muscular and streamlined, the tail pointed. Often the fish has sea lice still attached and, as these soon fall off once the fish has left the sea, they are a good indication as to how fresh it is. Its perfection slowly diminishes the longer the salmon remains in freshwater. Silver flanks dull and become coloured, the fish lose condition, and the males develop reddish brown spots, red diagonal squares and a large hooked jaw, known as a kype. Fish like this are coming into spawning condition and if caught should always be returned. Although salmon spawn during October to December, they enter the river at any month of the year so one may have spent a full year in freshwater, living off its accumulated fat.

Habitat and Location

Atlantic salmon occur from the east coast of the United States and Canada, across northern Europe and Scandinavia and into Russia. They are also found as far south as northern Spain and Portugal. In the UK they are found throughout the river systems of Scotland, Wales, northern England, the West Country and the west coast of Ireland.

Behaviour and Feeding Habits

Salmon are anadromous, living and feeding at sea but returning to freshwater to reproduce. Once a male and female salmon have paired off, a depression or redd is cut in the gravel, the female lays her eggs and the male fertilizes them with his milt. The fertilized eggs take approximately a hundred days to hatch after which the tiny alevins stay buried in the gravel for several weeks. Once the yolk sac has been absorbed the baby salmon, now called fry, leave the redd and begin to feed. As the fry grow they develop into parr and then eventually into silver-flanked smolts, a process which can take from two to four years. The young salmon are now ready to migrate downstream to the sea, which they do in May.

After leaving the river of their birth most salmon feed in the ocean around Greenland and the Faroe Islands, returning to spawn one, two or three years later. Salmon that spend only one winter at sea are known as grilse, and return to their rivers during mid summer. They weigh from 4–8 lb (1.81–3.63 kg).

LEFT: Fly fishing for salmon in summer. The Castle Connel water, River Shannon. In the summer most anglers fish with floating lines and small flies.

ABOVE: A spring salmon caught fishing from a boat in the lower beat of the River Beauly.

The fish that return to their rivers after more than one winter at sea normally weigh from 6–20 lb (2.72–9.07 kg). Atlantic salmon can reach 70 lb (32 kg) or more, but fish this size are extremely rare and very few fish over 30 lb (13.6 kg) are caught by anglers.

Salmon can be caught in both rivers and lakes. They are reliant on rain to trigger their migration into the river, and in smaller rivers in summer when the water is low, large numbers build up in the estuary. When the rain comes and the river rises and colours they pour upstream, resting every now and then behind rocks – in fact

anywhere that provides protection from the powerful current. This urge to run is very strong, and salmon leap falls and other major obstructions such as weirs on their way to reach their spawning grounds.

In the UK salmon rivers fall into two main types. The larger east coast Scottish rivers, the Tweed, Spey and Tay, do require reasonable amounts of water for the salmon to run, but even in normal summer conditions fish will continue to enter them in limited numbers. The smaller spate rivers on the other hand are more dependent on rain for them to contain salmon. Many are fast flowing and rocky; the rain soon runs off, and the peak times to fish can be only a few hours after the river level starts to fall, let alone days. As salmon do not feed in freshwater the angler has to try and stimulate the old feeding response in the fish, and good water conditions are very important for this.

Spring and autumn are the best times of the year to catch a larger fish and each year some salmon over 30 lb (13.6 kg) are caught both on fly and spinner. Unfortunately these runs of big fish, especially the "springers", have become increasingly rare, largely because of netting on the high seas,

and on many rivers anglers now return these fish in an effort to maintain stocks. Fish are also held in hatcheries and stripped at spawning time and the fry returned to the rivers to increase the stock.

Apart from when the river is in flood, salmon can be caught on the fly right through the season, although techniques need to be altered to suit the conditions. When the river is still high and cold during spring, fishing a deep sunk line and a large fly is the most effective tactic. On smaller rivers and even on larger ones when the water is low it is quite possible to catch salmon on trout tackle. Indeed during very low water conditions a size 10 or 12 fly fished on a 7 weight rod can actually be more effective than standard salmon tackle.

Salmon can also be caught in lochs, particularly in Scotland and Ireland. The usual method is to troll from a boat around rocky headlands and other well-known holding areas. When fly fishing the boat is allowed to drift side-on to the wind in classic loch style. A floating line and a team of three wet flies are used – patterns such as the Black Pennell, Peter Ross and Kate MacLaren are effective. Due to the size and power of the fish, leader strength should be 8–10 lb (3.63–4.54 kg).

Occasionally there is some confusion as to whether the fish caught is a salmon or sea trout, especially when it is fresh and bright silver. There are a few pointers to help identification. For example in salmon the tail is forked and the wrist at the tail base wide enough to be gripped easily, whereas in the sea trout the tail is square or convex and the wrist too thin to be gripped securely. Also when the mouth is closed the rear edge of the salmon's upper lip is level with the rear of its eye while in the sea trout it reaches beyond it. Additionally the salmon's spots are X-shaped rather than round as in the sea trout.

LEFT: Spinning for salmon in early spring on the Dalguise water, River Tay. Fish enter the Tay system from December the previous year, and fishing on Loch Tay traditionally starts the season on 1st January each year.

RIGHT: A fresh-run summer salmon in the peak of condition caught on the fly. Most rivers have a run of smaller summer fish.

Sea Trout *(Salmo trutta)*

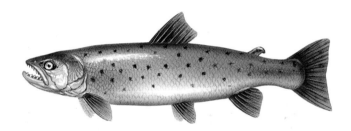

Current Record
British **22 lb 8 oz (10.205 kg)**

Season
April to September.

Distribution
Found in all salmon rivers especially the West Country, Wales and western Scotland.

Natural Diet
Sandeels, invertebrates and small fish.

Top Spots
Lochs and lakes close to the sea, Loch Hope and Loch Maree in Scotland.

Top Tip
Fish at night in rivers, dap on sea trout lochs.

Recognition

Sea trout are the sea-run form of the brown trout and, like salmon, are anadromous, running from the sea to freshwater to spawn, although unlike salmon, sea trout will feed spasmodically when in fresh water. When they first enter the river, adult sea trout are bright silver with hardly any spots, but the longer they are in freshwater the darker they become, and towards the end of the season many are almost black. When they reach this stage they are nearly ready to spawn and if caught should be returned carefully.

Habitat and Location

Sea trout are found in much of the coastal water surrounding Ireland and the UK, along with much of northern Europe and Scandinavia. Like salmon they have been under a great deal of pressure in recent years, and in some

areas, most notably the west coast of Ireland, populations appear to have collapsed and many fisheries are experiencing very limited runs. Much of the blame has been placed on salmon farms, where great net cages containing thousands of salmon have sprung up in many coastal regions – just the areas where the sea trout live. What has caused the problem is not the salmon themselves but the sea lice which parasitize them. Although the farmers treat the salmon to kill this pest, the vast numbers of fish make easy hosts and mean that sea lice numbers have rocketed, infesting the wild sea trout which rapidly lose condition and die. Inshore and estuary netting also take their toll, considerably reducing the numbers of fish able to return to spawn, while the commercial fishing of sandeels to create the pellets for feeding the farmed salmon also reduces the sea trout's food supply.

However, it is not all bad news. Many waters such as those in Wales and the West Country, where salmon farming is not such an issue, still have good runs of sea trout including some very large fish well into double figures. Welsh rivers in particular, including the Dovey, Towy and Rheidol, have produced some wonderful sea trout fishing over the last few years.

Behaviour and Feeding Habits

When the sea trout comes into spawning condition it is far less reliant than the salmon on a large spate to induce it to run. While extra water will bring sea trout in to the

LEFT: Landing a good sea trout at night. Night fishing can be most exciting if the fish are taking well.

ABOVE: A fine sea trout caught at night in Wales. Note the square tail.

river system, they are quite capable of working their way upstream even in low summer levels. Although in exceptional circumstances sea trout will enter a river as early as March and as late as October, the main runs take place during the summer months from June through to September, with July and August being the peak months. Actual spawning takes place from October through to January. Like the salmon the sea trout goes through stages from egg through to parr and eventually smolt before heading for the sea.

Sea trout can be caught both in freshwater and saltwater. Traditionally they have been taken from lakes and rivers, but increasing numbers of anglers are finding areas where they can be caught from the sea shore. The west of Ireland, Scotland and Wales are the most productive coastlines, along with island groups such as the Orkneys and Shetlands. Tackle is quite

simple, either light spinning gear or medium-weight fly tackle similar to that used for reservoir lure fishing. Fly patterns are also similar, the most effective being large streamer patterns that imitate small fish.

While catching sea trout from saltwater is growing in popularity the majority of fish are still taken when they return to freshwater. In rivers they may be caught on bait, spinner or fly. Worm fishing is very effective, particularly when the water is high and coloured, while spinning with a small Mepps spinner or a light Quill Minnow is deadly when the river is clearing. The Quill Minnow can be particularly effective even in low water – and is often fished upstream rather than down.

When the river is low, typically at summer level, fly fishing comes into its own. Although sea trout can be caught on the fly during daylight if the water is still carrying a little colour, clear low water, under the cover of darkness is when they take best. Night fishing for sea trout is an exciting experience although not without its problems. Casting and

wading are the most obvious two and, if you are fishing a river for the first time, it is essential to observe the pools first in daylight to learn their characteristics before night falls.

When it is dark the shoals of sea trout, which during the day remain concealed under banks and in the deeper pools, move into the shallower water and are keen to take a fly. When the river is low small trout patterns such as the Butcher or the Peter Ross tied on a size 10 hook work well, but for normal conditions a larger fly such as the Blackie or the Medicine Fly is more effective. These may be fished on either a floating or slow-sinking line working the fly across and downstream.

On lakes and lochs sea trout may be caught on standard wet-fly tackle almost identical to that used for loch-style trout fishing. They are also caught dapping, where a large bushy fly is allowed to blow out in front of the boat on a floss line and bounced on the top of the water. They may also be caught on spinners, either cast and retrieved or trolled from a boat under power.

ABOVE: Fishing for sea trout on South Uist, Outer Hebrides, with a wet fly.

BELOW: A 3½ lb (1.59 kg) sea trout caught on a wet fly on Loch Hope in the far north of Scotland.

Brown Trout *(Salmo trutta)*

Recognition

Brown trout are the indigenous
species of trout throughout Britain
and large parts of northern Europe.
They grow large, well in excess of 20
lb (9.01 kg), but the average is nearer
the 1 lb (0.45 kg) mark. They are
extremely variable in colouration,
which is largely dictated by the
individual fish's habitat. Where the
water is dark or peat-stained the fish
themselves are often very dark with
many large black spots. Conversely,
where the trout are living over a light
sandy bottom they are much lighter
with either pale or silver flanks and
much smaller and less profuse spots.

Most brown trout have a brownish-
coloured back and pale, liberally
spotted flanks. Normally there are no
spots on the tail, which is a useful
guide to distinguishing them from
rainbow trout. Usually these flank
spots are large and black, but
occasionally, in trout living in small
brooks, they can be mixed with a few
red ones. Some populations also have
bright-yellow bellies, giving them an
extremely colourful appearance, yet
in others the spots are almost absent,
the flanks being bright silver and
making the trout look very similar to
its sea-run form, the sea trout.

Habitat and Location

Brown trout can be caught on a wide
range of methods including bait,
spinner and fly although in the UK,
due mainly to fishery rules, most are
taken on the latter. Although the
brown trout is the natural species in
the UK and Europe, fishing pressure
and fluctuating water conditions
mean that many are actually stocked
in the same way as rainbow trout.
However, due to the fact that the
brown trout is less tolerant of high
water temperatures and is slower
growing than the rainbow, it is more
expensive to produce and, as a result,
stocked far less extensively. However,
this still means that brown trout can
be caught in many waters that would
not normally contain them, most
noticeably small put-and-take fisheries
and large lowland reservoirs.

Some of the smaller waters, most
famously Dever Springs in Hampshire
and Felindre in South Wales, stock
farmed brown trout of unnaturally
huge proportions. Here fish of 10 lb
(4.54 kg) or more are caught regularly
and the cultivated record now stands
at over 26 lb (11.8 kg). On reservoirs

LEFT: **Netting a wild trout on the River
Wharfe in Yorkshire.**

TOP: **Returning a trout caught on the River
Itchen, one of the famous chalk streams of
southern England.**

ABOVE: **Three fine brown trout caught on a
wet fly in Ireland.**

where the brown trout is stocked but
must attain the bulk of its weight in
the reservoir, a specimen brown trout
would be classed as anything over 5 lb
(2.27 kg). Even here there are very big
grown-on fish, and each year venues
such as Rutland Water and Grafham
Water produce brown trout into
double figures. In a river a trout over
4 lb (1.81 kg) is a prize specimen.

Most small lakes and reservoirs have to be stocked, but even some rivers which already contain indigenous populations of brown trout have their numbers supplemented with stock fish. While this makes the fishing initially better, it does raise the issue, should stock and wild fish interbreed, leading to the destruction of the wild fish's genetic integrity? To counteract this trend some enlightened fishery owners are now looking to habitat conservation and catch-and-release fishing to maintain viable, natural populations.

Almost all trout are caught on a fly, although spinning with minnows and fishing with a worm in small burns in Scotland and Wales is a good method for the young. The most sophisticated fishing is with a dry fly or nymph in a clear chalk stream, although wet flies are the normal method in stillwaters.

Brown trout in lakes provide the best wild brown trout fishing in the UK and Ireland. Because they are so large and less susceptible to over-fishing and loss of water through abstraction, many of our big natural lakes, particularly those in Scotland, northern England, Wales and the west coast of Ireland still contain substantial populations of brown trout. These fisheries have a long tradition of trout fishing, and the usual technique is loch style, casting a team of wet flies from a boat drifting side-on to the wind.

Dapping, too, where a large bushy fly or a natural insect, such as a daddy-longlegs (crane fly), is allowed to blow out in front of the boat, is also very effective. With dapping, instead of casting, a light floss line and a long rod, in excess of 12 ft (3.66 m), is used so that the breeze takes the fly out on to the water. While it catches all sizes of fish, the method has the reputation of tempting the larger specimens, and each year trout in excess of 10 lb (4.54 kg) are taken "on the dap".

Each year the largest natural brown trout are invariably caught by trolling a large spinner or dead-bait in one of the big Scottish lochs or Irish loughs that are known to hold these large fish. These ferox, as they are known, are highly predatory, forsaking a diet of small invertebrates

ᴬᴮᴼᵛᴱ: A good trout being brought to the net on Tal-y-Llyn in North Wales.

for fish such as perch and, especially, char which inhabit the deep water in these otherwise nutrient-poor lakes. This diet allows the ferox to attain weights of 10–15 lb (4.54–6.8 kg) with specimens up to 20 lb (9.07 kg) occasionally taken on rod and line.

Behaviour and Feeding Habits

Brown trout are highly territorial, particularly in rivers. Once a fish has established a feeding position it will defend it jealously, driving off other trout that come too close. Here the trout is in an ideal position to pick off the adults and nymphs of aquatic insects such as upwings, stoneflies and caddisflies, along with small crustaceans, as they drift downstream

with the current. Even on rivers brown trout have a taste for small fish and are not averse to taking bullheads and minnows, particularly early in the year when other forms of food are scarce.

Brown trout are found anywhere from tiny mountain streams to larger rain-fed rivers and rich, chalk streams. The size that the trout ultimately reach depends greatly on the available food supply and chalk-stream, loch and lough trout, with a plentiful diet of aquatic insects and crustaceans, are generally bigger than those found on rain-fed rivers and streams where natural insects are less abundant.

Rainbow Trout *(Oncorhynchus mykiss)*

Recognition

The rainbow trout is the most important and widely distributed of all the salmonidae species. It is a hard-fighting fish capable of making repeated runs and leaps – a fact which has not gone unnoticed by anglers. Although once known as *Salmo gairdneri*, it has recently been reclassified as *Oncorhynchus mykiss* to show its close relationship with the various Pacific salmon species, such as the coho and chinook.

Most rainbows live and breed entirely in freshwater both in rivers and lakes and, depending on the strain and location, are extremely variable in their colouration. Many wild fish are quite heavily marked with a profusion of dark spots over their body and fins. On our own reservoirs rainbows that have reached the peak of condition on a diet of small invertebrates and fish are bright silver and similar in appearance to steelhead of North America and Canada. Typically though, most rainbows have a dark, greenish-grey back and pale belly with a pink stripe running from the gill plate and along the flanks, the intensity of which increases as the trout comes into spawning condition. Two notable exceptions to this are the golden trout and the blue trout, although both are simple colour morphs of the rainbow developed by fish farmers and stocked in various UK waters.

Habitat and Location

The rainbow trout's original range includes North America, from Alaska down the western seaboard as far as southern California, and Mexico's Pacific coast, Canada and north-east Asia. Also owing to its ease of rearing

and the fact that it tolerates lower water quality and higher temperatures than the brown trout, it has been introduced to many other parts of the world including Europe, Australia and New Zealand, along with South America, Africa and India. Additionally, in certain parts of the world, notably its home range of North America and Canada, there is a sea-run form of the rainbow trout known as the steelhead.

Like the sea-run brown trout the steelhead spends most of the time feeding in the ocean only returning to a river to spawn. Steelhead grow large, up to 20 lb (9.07 kg) or more, and when newly returned to freshwater they are bright silver, extremely strong and one of the most prized sporting fish. They can be caught on a range of tactics including bait, fly fishing and spinning.

ABOVE: A beautifully conditioned rainbow taken on a lure from Hanningfield, a reservoir in Essex.

Behaviour and Feeding Habits

The rainbow trout's diet is extremely varied, and along with a range of aquatic invertebrates and insect larvae, it is not averse to eating larger creatures such as grasshoppers, fish and even mice. In the wild, rainbow trout can grow to 50 lb (22.7 kg) or so, but this is exceptional, and the average is much lower, with a 5 lb (2.27 kg) specimen being a good one. On the smaller put-and-take waters, which often stock big farmed fish, it is possible to catch rainbows in excess of 10–20 lb (4.54–9.07 kg), and the "cultivated" record in the UK stands at over 36 lb (16.33 kg). On reservoirs where the initial stock size is only 1–2 lb (0.45–0.9 kg) a double figure rainbow is the fish of a lifetime, although one water, at Hanningfield in Essex, has produced grown-on fish of over 20 lb (9.07 kg).

Being a cultivated fish, in the UK, there is no specific season for rainbow trout, and a number of waters are open to anglers all through the year. However rainbow trout still come into spawning condition, the female fish becoming dark and full of eggs while the males develop a pronounced kype. In such condition these fish are not good to eat and so some farmers produce triploids, using heat or shock on the eggs to alter their genetic make-up. This produces sterile fish which remain in good condition throughout the year.

Although the vast majority of rainbows caught in the UK are

produced in fish farms, there are a few waters where introduced fish sustain a natural population. The Derbyshire Wye is a prime example where rainbows were first introduced in 1912-13 and have since established themselves, so now "wild" rainbows of up to 2 lb (0.91 kg) or so can be caught in that river along with the brown trout and grayling.

Rainbow trout can be caught on bait, spinner and fly, although, due to restrictions imposed by most fisheries, fly fishing is the most widely used method. On rivers and small lakes normal nymph, wet-fly and dry-fly tactics work well. They also work extremely effectively on the larger reservoirs. However, rainbows are a shoal fish, and it is necessary to locate the depth of the shoal to be successful. In reservoirs some interesting feeding patterns have developed. Although the bulk of their diet comprises chironomid larvae and pupae during early and mid summer, rainbows will feed heavily on daphnia, a tiny animal plankton that proliferates in many of the richer lowland waters.

Rather than picking off the daphnia one by one, the trout swim through the swarms scooping up this living soup and, as it is such a high-protein food source, rapidly put on weight and improve in condition. When rainbows are feeding this way they will often take brightly coloured flies and lures – orange is a great favourite – as long as they are fished at the same level as the daphnia.

ABOVE: The lucky angler plays a rainbow taken at the Avon Springs fishery. Most waters have a day limit of four to eight fish.

BELOW: Playing a rainbow hooked from a boat on the Eyebrook reservoir, near Corby in Northamptonshire.

LEFT: A fry-feeding rainbow from Grafham Water showing the superb condition of many fish that are taken from the rich waters of the lowland reservoirs with plentiful feeding.

Grayling *(Thymallus thymallus)*

Recognition

The grayling cannot be mistaken for any other fish. It is a very beautiful fish with a huge, sail-like dorsal fin, and a silvery-blue streamlined body with delicate violet stripes. Grayling also have irregular dark spots on their flanks, as unique to each specimen as fingerprints are to a human being. As a member of the salmonidae family,

the grayling has an adipose back fin, which is a small fleshy protuberance situated between the dorsal and the top lobe of the deeply forked tail. The head is delicate, being small and pointed, and the mouth contains very tiny teeth with which it grips its food. They also have the scent of wild thyme, hence their Latin name, and make very good eating.

Current Record
British **4 lb 3 oz (1.899 kg)**

Season
June to March.

Distribution
Patchy. Clear, shallow and fast chalk streams in southern England, Yorkshire and the north west.

Natural Diet
Insects, small crustacea, fish fry and water snails.

Top Spots
Southern chalk streams, the Avon, Test and Frome; the Yorkshire rivers and the Welsh Dee.

Top Tip
In best condition in winter in clear water. Fly fish with Red Tag or when trotting; hold back the float occasionally to make the bait rise to just under the surface.

Habitat and Location

The large dorsal is intended to help the grayling to combat very fast flows, and this is the favoured environment of the species. They abound in clear, shallow, unpolluted chalk streams, happily co-existing with trout. Unfortunately, those beautiful fish are very sensitive to water pollution levels and as a result they are not widespread, living in pockets. The southern chalk stream tributaries of the Hampshire Avon and the Kennet, as well as the main rivers themselves, support a thriving population, as do some of the shallow, colder, faster-flowing streams of the north-east and north-west, and grayling are present in the border rivers of Scotland. Elsewhere, particularly in the Midlands, good grayling fishing is very hard to find.

Small to average grayling live in the shallow, fast glides in large shoals, with the bigger fish tending to hang on the creases between the fastest flow and more sedate water. The real specimens, as with other fish, are usually found in steadier, deeper water, where they do not need to expend so much energy and can live a lazier life.

LEFT: **A good grayling being brought to the net, caught on a wet fly in autumn. Grayling are often classed as coarse fish and caught trotting maggots and worms down a swim.**

Size

Grayling do not reach great sizes, and any fish over 1 lb (0.45 kg) in weight is a very worthwhile fish and a 2 lb (0.91 kg) sample a specimen. It is a rare angler indeed who has taken grayling over 3 lb (1.36 kg) in weight, and the current record of 4 lb 3oz, (1.89 kg) taken in 1989, will take an awful lot of beating.

Behaviour and Feeding Habits

The grayling's natural diet consists of small crustacea, nymphs, water snails, fish fry and any spent insects that drift by. They feed on the bottom but are quite happy to feed higher in the water during hatches of nymphs and mayflies. They group up in large shoals and, unlike roach, dace or chub, the coarse fisherman is unlikely to be able to entice them into a swim by regular feeding. Once they colonize an area they stick with it until they are ready to move on. The angler is well advised to spend time checking where they are feeding before contemplating fishing for them.

Grayling feed throughout the year but are at their best in very cold conditions, those clear, icy winter days when perhaps only dace are also willing to feed. In these conditions, they form very tight shoals and individuals tend at times to flash or splash at the surface. These are the signs to look for before starting to fish. Grayling are avid fly feeders, and all the methods appropriate for small river trout take their share of grayling. Leaded nymphs fished singly or a team of rolled nymphs are favourite methods of presentation but in the right conditions they will take the floating fly avidly and in the winter the Red Tag is the traditional pattern to try, fished either wet or dry.

If you want to fish a swim for grayling using coarse fishing methods shoals of grayling will respond to the stimulus of a regular supply of drifting maggots and casters; and trotting a float is the most enjoyable presentation. Initially, the grayling will often feed hard on the bottom but gradually feed at all depths as the competition for the loose feed warms up. This often will not apply to the biggest fish in the shoal, who will hang back and intercept any food item that trickles along the bottom past the rest of the shoal. These bigger fish are lovers of worms, and it is a good idea periodically to swap the maggot for a good-sized worm and run the float further downstream of the normal catching area.

Grayling of all sizes are always looking for aquatic nymphs shooting to the surface, and will often respond savagely to a trotted hookbait made to behave in the same way, by holding back the float so that the bait swings up in the water. Takes to this presentation can be dramatic.

TOP: A dry-fly fisherman plays a good grayling from a very thick bank.

ABOVE: Two good grayling caught trotting.

BELOW LEFT: The huge dorsal fin of the grayling shows clearly in the water.

BELOW: When autumn comes and the leaves start to change colour the grayling fisher comes into his own.

Equipment

Game fishing rods fall into three main groups. Fly rods, spinning rods and bait rods. However, it is fly rods which come in the greatest variety, in a wide range of lengths and line weights designed to fish different-sized waters and fly sizes. They also come in two types. The majority are single handed and used for most types of trout, grayling and, where the water is small enough, salmon fishing too. The second type, which are double handed, are designed primarily for fishing for salmon on large rivers such as the Spey, the Tweed and the Tay. These long powerful rods, up to 16 ft (4.88 m)in length, can cast the heavy lines needed to cover a big river along with handling a large fish in a strong current.

9 ft 6 in (2.9 m) travel rod

Rods

Single-handed Fly Rods

7–8 ft (2.13–2.44 m) Lightweight rods that are used mostly on smaller streams and rivers where long-distance casting is not necessary. They are ideal for dry fly and nymph fishing, where their lightness make them perfect for the light tippets and tiny flies that are needed.

Typically line weights are in the AFTM 3–5 range, although it is possible to find rods capable of casting as low as a 1 weight line for extreme delicacy. For the light-line fanatic, an American rod manufacturer has built the ultimate rod, capable of casting a 0 weight line. It is so light that a line and reel have had to be made especially to match it.

8–9 ft (2.44–2.74 m) Trout rods of this length are normally rated to cast lines between AFTM 5–7. This makes them very versatile, able to cope with a wide range of conditions and water types. Those at the lighter end of the range are ideal rods for dry fly and light nymph work, while those capable of casting a 6–7 weight line are perfect for trout fishing on medium to large rivers as well as lakes and reservoirs.

9½–10½ ft (2.9–3.2 m) These longer rods include the more powerful models used for distance casting on stillwaters or where a river is large and the current strong. At the lighter end of the range they are ideal for fishing anything from a dry fly to heavyweight nymphs, while the heavier rods, designed to cast lines 8–10 weight, are ideal for distance

casting or when big fish are the aim on stocked waters. These rods will fish floating or intermediate lines perfectly, but also have the power to fish fast-sinking lines and big flies so often used on reservoirs.

11–12 ft (3.35–3.66 m) Although the longest single-handed rod used, this type of rod is not necessarily more powerful than those in the 9½–10½ ft (2.89–3.2 m) range. The reason is that it is designed primarily for loch-style

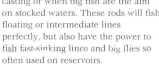

14 ft (4.27 m) salmon rod with reel

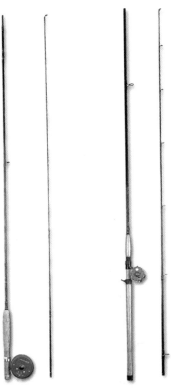

7½ ft (2.29 m) trout rod with ultralight reel

Bait rod with baitcaster reel

fishing from a drifting boat. The technique involves casting a relatively short line, up to 10 yds (3 m) or so, from a drifting boat, and this style of casting requires a more through-actioned rod. As a result, loch-style rods are normally designed to cast lines rated AFTM 5–7.

Double-handed Salmon Rods

11–16 ft (3.35–4.88 m) Unlike the shorter single-handed rods, double handers range from 11–16 ft (3.35–4.88 m). The shorter, lighter models, capable of casting a 6–7 weight line, are designed for fishing a floating line when the river is at summer level and small flies are the most effective. The longer, more powerful rods are designed for when the river is running high at spring or autumn levels and heavy lines and big flies are required to cover the water. Rods such as these, capable of casting 10–11 weight lines, are necessary when large heavy flies, such as metal tube flies, are being fished deep on a sinking line.

Travel Rods

With anglers increasingly prepared to travel to far-flung corners of the globe, multi-sectioned travel rods are becoming more popular. Their appeal is obvious. There is no longer the need to travel with a cumbersome two-piece rod that needs to be transported in a special tube, when a multi-sectioned rod will pack away safely in a suitcase. Today, modern rod manufacture is so good that a rod of five or six sections will perform just as well as one with only two. Many anglers are switching to travel rods for all fishing.

Spinning Rods

Spinning rods come in a range of sizes and weights, depending on the size of fish being sought and the weight of spinner or plug that needs to be cast. Some models of spinning rod are available with a standard reel seat for when using a

8 ft (2.44 m) trout rod with ultralight 6 reel

fixed-spool reel or with a finger which allows the angler a better grip on the rod when using a multiplier.

For light spinning for trout an 8–9 ft (2.44–2.74 m) rod is ideal. It should be capable of casting weights as low as 10 g or less. For sea trout and salmon on small- to medium-size rivers the rod should be 9–10 ft (2.74–3.05 m) and designed to cast weights up to 40 g. For larger rivers you need a rod 10–11 ft (3.05–3.35 m) long capable of casting weights up to 50–60 g with the power to cast large spinners and plugs and hold big fish in fast water.

Bait Rods

For bait fishing on small trout rivers a lightweight coarse fishing or spinning rod is more than adequate, but for worm and shrimp fishing for salmon something longer and more powerful is required. Many anglers use a rod 12–13 ft (3.66–3.96 m) long, designed to cast weights in the 10 to 50 g range. The extra length helps control the bait in its path downstream.

Reels

Game fishing reels can be broken down into three main groups: fly reels, multiplying reels and fixed-spool reels. Fly reels, as their name suggests, are used solely for fly fishing. Multiplying reels are used mostly for spinning for salmon. Fixed-spool reels, on the other hand, are not only used for spinning but are also ideal for bait fishing either with worms or prawns.

Ultralight trout reel

Fly Reels

Unlike other types, a fly reel is only wound when a fish is being played or when line is rewound prior to moving position; otherwise the line is left hanging in coils from where it is repeatedly cast. For this reason fly reels are sometimes considered merely to be line holders. This is a dangerous assumption because when a big fish that is determined to run is

Standard salmon reel

hooked a poorly designed reel is a liability. The simplest and cheapest fly reels have only a simple ratchet mechanism to prevent the spool from running free and the line unwinding unnecessarily. While this is fine for small fish or where a fish cannot run far, for big fish, or where light lines are being used, a smooth free-running drag is essential.

Although uncomplicated in overall-design and construction, most modern fly reels have a sophisticated and very effective drag mechanism. These mechanisms come in a variety of forms but the most common is a disc drag, a circular pressure plate which acts on the spool and which can be increased or decreased in its intensity by a control usually found on the back of the reel. By tightening and loosening the drag, various strength tippets can be used without the constant fear of a break, although the angler should always remember to adjust the drag to the line strength being used before fishing because it is difficult to fine-tune during the fight.

The importance of a smooth, effective drag is at its most obvious when the fisherman is playing a big or hard-fighting fish on light lines. Without one, any jerks and rapid runs made by the fish could easily snap a delicate tippet or leader. Even when strong lines are used for big fish, such as salmon, a drag that will tighten down hard but still allow the line to run out smoothly will make playing the fish a great deal easier while increasing the angler's confidence.

Reel showing the line guard

Most fly reels are single actioned. This means that, unlike a fixed-spool or a multiplying reel, there are no gears, so each full revolution of the handle makes only one turn of the spool. This makes rapid line retrieval a problem and can only be counter-acted by having a large central arbor so that as much line as possible is wound back on every revolution. This is the reason why fly reels should always be filled to their full capacity, the fly line being supported by plenty of backing.

Trout reel

The size of fly reel used depends on the rod and line. The volume of a size 10 double taper, of the type used for salmon fishing, is much greater than a 5–6 weight used for trout, and so the reel has to be correspondingly larger. Also the rods themselves vary greatly in weight, so an 8 ft (2.44 m) brook rod balances best with a tiny 2$\frac{1}{2}$ in (6 cm) diameter reel weighing around 3$\frac{1}{2}$ oz (90 g), while a 15 ft (4.57 m) double-handed salmon rod requires something near 4 in (10 cm) in diameter – weighing in at a hefty 9–10 oz (250–275 g). To make sure the angler has the right size reel for the job most manufacturers give a line capacity with the reel's specification, and this includes the amount of backing that needs to be added first.

Grey Marquis reel

Multipliers and Fixed-spool Reels

A small multiplying reel, a 6500, is the standard for spinning for salmon and big trout, having the capacity to take 250 yds (228 m) of 15–20 lb (6.8–9.07 kg) breaking strain nylon. The smooth, powerful drag mechanism of the multiplying reel is

Multiplier reel

especially important when fishing for large salmon in a fast-running river. It allows the angler to apply great pressure on the fish – to help tire it – but still gives line easily if the fish makes a run. As ultra-long casts are rarely needed the level wind is never removed, as it sometimes is for saltwater fishing. This ensures that the line is always laid smoothly and evenly along the spool, preventing the line from bedding in to itself under the pressure of playing a big fish.

Although fixed-spool reels can readily be used for spinning, for game fishing they are at their most effective used in conjunction with baits such as worms and prawns. Because the line can be fed from the spool much more easily with the fixed-spool reel, it allows the bait to be worked with the current. Some models are particularly good because the spool can be left to run free, allowing line to be paid out until the bait has worked through the area being fished or a fish has actually taken. A turn of the reel handle disengages the bait-runner mechanism, allowing the bait to be rewound or a fish struck.

3010 fixed-spool reel

Fly Lines and Leaders

Originally fly lines were produced from real silk dressed with linseed oil to keep them supple and afloat. Today much of the hard work has been taken out of fly-line maintenance by modern plastic polymers which produce lines needing only the occasional clean to keep them performing at their best.

Fly Lines

Modern materials and manufacturing processes have also produced a further benefit: the ability to create fly lines of widely varying profiles and densities, allowing the fly fisher to present a fly in ways and at depths never before possible.

Fly lines are now available not only in floating, intermediate sinking and medium-fast sinking rates but in

Windcutter fly line

ultra-high density also, with which the fastest sink at a rate of almost 1 ft (30 cm) per second is enough to fish effectively in very deep or fast-flowing water.

For most fly fishing a floating or intermediate-sinking line is the most widely used. Intermediate lines are effective allowing the fly to be fished a few feet below the surface – just where the fish are cruising. Recently, clear lines, such as the "slime line", have become popular.

In addition to the various single densities of fly line there are also sink tips. These lines have a floating belly and running line with a short section of sinking line at the front. They enable a fly to be fished a few feet down in the water while the bulk of the line floats on the surface. The advantage of this is that although the line fishes like a sinker it can still be mended on the surface or allowed to drift on surface currents if fishing a stillwater with buzzers.

The two main profiles for fly lines are double taper and weight forward. Double-taper lines have two tapers of equal length on either end of a central belly. This is the traditional profile, most effective for short- to medium-distance work – up to 20 yds (18.23 m) or so – and where accuracy and delicacy are the main requirements. Weight-forward lines, on the other hand, have most of their weight concentrated in a 12 yds (11 m) belly at the front end of the line. This belly slims down at its rear into much thinner running line. This running line shoots easily through the rod rings, allowing the weight-forward line to be cast long distances. For this reason weight-forward lines are the optimum choice when medium- to long-distance casting is the main requirement. As a compromise, long belly lines with a longer front taper are now manufactured which, over short distances, cast with a delicacy similar to a double taper but which can also be cast much longer distances by launching the belly in the air first, allowing the thin running line to be shot.

For long-distance work a third type of line, the shooting head, is the most effective. Here a short, heavy section of fly line, 10–12 yds (9–11 m) in length, is connected to a slick shooting line such as braided or monofilament nylon. It allows casts of over 40 yds (36.58 m) to be made and is popular for reservoir lure fishing.

Tippets or Leaders

Unlike most other types of line, such as monofilament nylon and Dacron, that require additional weight to cast them, fly lines contain the required weight to load a fly rod. But since the fly line has to be very thick and conspicuous to do this, a finer, more delicate material is needed to link the fly line to the fly in order not to frighten the fish. This is known as the leader or tippet. Leaders come in many forms from straight or tapered monofilament nylon to braided nylon or polypropylene, or special composites such as Poly Leaders: these are available in varying sink rates and act as extensions to the fly line itself.

Most basic of all is a leader of straight monofilament nylon. Where leader turnover is not vital or where it is assisted by a breeze, plain monofilament is a cheap and easy

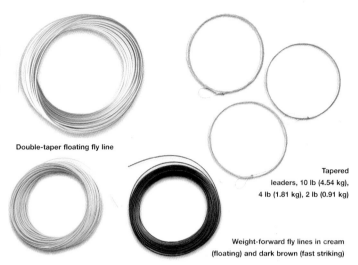

Double-taper floating fly line

Tapered
leaders, 10 lb (4.54 kg),
4 lb (1.81 kg), 2 lb (0.91 kg)

Weight-forward fly lines in cream
(floating) and dark brown (fast striking)

alternative to more complex systems. Also where well-spaced droppers are being used, such as when stillwater nymph fishing or fishing loch-style, it offers the most effective leader construction.

Various breaking strains of nylon are used but for stillwaters 4–6 lb (1.81–2.72 kg) leaders are the most generally used. Although relatively expensive, co-polymer nylon and fluorocarbon are becoming increasingly popular with anglers because they are less visible in the water than ordinary nylon.

For most dry-fly work or where the fly is to be fished on or in the water's surface, a simple tapered nylon leader is ideal. This transfers energy from the fly line through its length, helping the fly to turn over properly even into a breeze. The leader's taper goes from thick at the butt to thin at the tip. An extra 2–3 ft (60–90 cm) of fine nylon tippet is then added at the tip so that repeated fly changes or other damage does not require the replacement of the entire leader.

Braided nylon leaders perform a similar function, though because they are braided some anglers maintain that the energy of the cast is transferred more efficiently to the fly. That apart, the benefit of braided leader is that by altering its density – achieved by adding fine lead or copper wire when it is being manufactured – it can be made either to float or to sink at varying rates. The latter offers great advantages in getting a fly down to fish that are

lying well below the surface while keeping control of a floating line.

Poly leaders are a recent innovation in leader design. They are manufactured as short-tapered lengths of fly line attached by a loop to the tip of the fly line, so offering the best energy transfer of all. They come in a wide range of densities, from floating and intermediate sinking to slow sinking, plus a range of fast sinkers. They can be attached either to a floating or any other density of fly line, providing many alternatives when it comes to fly presentation.

Backing

This is the strong thin line of approximately 30 lb (13.61 kg) breaking strain that is wound on to the fly reel before the fly line. Backing performs a twofold function, keeping the coils of fly line as large as possible – which prevents tangling – and, more importantly, acting as a reserve of line should a hooked fish run out more than the 30 yds (27.43 m) of fly line on the reel.

Backing comes in many forms but the most popular two are braided nylon – not monofilament – and braided polyester. The latter is the most often used because it is cheaper than braided nylon and is also thinner, thus allowing a greater amount to be wound on to the reel. This has advantages when using a small lightweight reel but not where big fish, capable of making long runs, may be encountered; then braided nylon may be the better choice.

Sundries

Along with all the major items of tackle such as rods, reels and clothing there is a variety of other sundry items which, if not vital, are certainly a great help at the waterside.

Landing Net

Having hooked your fish the next task is to land it safely. From the bank it may be possible to beach a played-out fish, but from a boat this is not an option and the answer is to use a landing net.

A landing net has many advantages. For example if you are going to release the fish it can be guided into the net before it is so tired that recovery would be difficult, while if the fish is going to be kept it is less likely to be lost if it is netted quickly. There are many designs for trout and salmon landing nets. For salmon the sturdy, metal-framed Gye net is large enough and strong enough to handle a big fish.

For trout, a lighter model, with a telescopic handle, makes landing a fish easy even from a boat. When choosing a net consider the size of the fish you are likely to catch. Finally, remember that the mesh should be knotless – knotted mesh landing nets are now illegal.

Tackle Bag

This is used to carry all those odds and ends, such as spare reels and fly boxes, which are needed for a day's fishing. They vary in size from spacious ones large enough to hold the multitude of tackle required for reservoir boat fishing to light compact versions used for rivers and streams. Most are made from cotton duck, which is perfectly strong enough, while the fittings vary from brass and leather on traditional models to modern plastic snap locks. Whatever the type of bag, look for one that is

strongly built, preferably lined to keep the tackle dry, and with a wide adjustable shoulder strap.

Fly Boxes

As you build up a collection of flies you need somewhere safe to put them. Fly boxes are the usual places and they come in a wide range of sizes and with a variety of methods for holding the flies in place. For lures and wet flies simple foam-filled boxes made from wood, plastic or aluminium work well. Recently the plastic Fox box with its gripping slots, which prevent moisture rusting the hooks, has become very popular. For dry flies a rigid aluminium box with a number of small compartments, is the best choice because it prevents the delicate hackles being crushed.

Line Tray

If you wade deep while fishing a sinking line you will find that on the retrieve the backing sinks beneath the water's surface to the extent that it makes shooting the line very difficult. Even if you manage it the extra drag will reduce the casting distance. So rather than letting the line simply fall into the water, placing it into a line tray ensures that it shoots easily.

It is worn around the waist and on each pull of the retrieve the line is allowed to fall into it.

Priest

If you intend to dispatch your fish – and on some waters releasing fish is not allowed – it is important to do so quickly. The most efficient method is to use a priest (for administering the last rites). This is a heavy wooden or metal implement used to strike the top of the fish's head. Some priests come with a combined marrow-spoon. These are ideal for finding out what a fish has been eating.

Wading Stick

Fishing for salmon often involves wading in a deep powerful river. However confident you might feel, the use of a wading stick will help ensure you keep your footing even in a strong current. It is used to brace the angler against the flow and help feel for any potholes. Various models of wading stick are available, the most complicated being the collapsible type. The best is a simple, solid stick with a good strong handle and a heavily weighted end to help keep it firmly planted on the river bed.

Boat Seat

Fishing all day from a boat can be uncomfortable. A simple cushion will help but the real answer is to use a purpose-made cushioned boat seat with a back to give plenty of support. Many designs are available that either fit over the gunwales and can be adjusted, depending on the width of the boat, or simply clamp on to the thwart boards. While a fixed seat is quite adequate, one with a swivel, which allows the angler to turn while seated, makes handling the engine or pulling in the drogue far easier.

Bass Bag

If you intend to take fish to eat, it is important to keep them as fresh as possible. A simple method is to use a bass bag. These are made of straw, or other water-absorbent material, and are soaked with water before placing the fish in them. The evaporation of the water produces a cooling effect which helps keep the fish fresh, so they must not actually be left in the water – as on a warm day the fish will slowly poach. A better method is to place the fish in a cool box complete with ice packs. For larger fish, special lined cool bags are available that take the same frozen packs as a cool box.

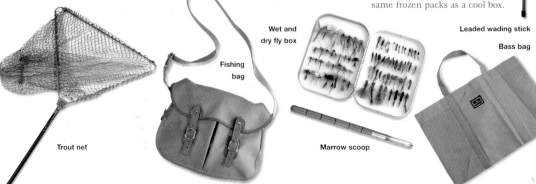

Trout net

Fishing bag

Wet and dry fly box

Marrow scoop

Leaded wading stick

Bass bag

Clothing

Angling is often done in bad weather. Game fish in particular have a requirement for cool, well-oxygenated water and usually take better when the weather is poor. This means that the angler is often fishing in cold and wet conditions. From a boat the situation is even worse; with nowhere to go if the weather turns nasty, the angler simply has to brave it out.

Waterproof Clothing

Fly fishing is an active pursuit, and to be comfortable the angler needs to be kept warm and dry even in the most inhospitable conditions. So, for anyone serious in their fishing it is important that they have the right clothing. At one time waxed cotton was the principal waterproof material, but modern breathable fabrics, such as Goretex and Ventex, are becoming increasingly popular and are now the most widely used. The fact that they are both lightweight and extremely waterproof makes modern breathables the ideal choice for game fishing. They have a number of advantages. For example, their lightness doesn't impede casting and, unlike waxed cotton, they do not become uncomfortably stiff in cold weather. Also the fact that they breathe, allowing sweat to pass out through the membrane while preventing rain from getting in, ensures that the wearer

Waterproof jacket

remains comfortable with none of the dampness and condensation that is so often a problem with other materials such as PVC or waxed cotton.

Waterproof trousers for boat fishing

For boat fishing or when deep wading is not required a three-quarter length coat with a built-in hood is perfect for even the toughest conditions. This design of coat is long enough to keep the angler's back dry even in the heaviest rain and with a suitable fleece underneath will keep the wearer warm, too. This is the length of coat to wear over thigh waders or when fishing from a boat, combined with a pair of waterproof trousers of the same material, to keep the legs dry.

When choosing a waterproof coat look for reputable makes, all of which have good design and properly taped seams to ensure that their products don't leak. It is also important that there is a secure flap over the front of the zip to stop any rain being forced through, plus efficient storm cuffs to prevent any water running down the arms when they are raised while casting.

When deep wading it is advisable to wear a specially designed wading jacket. Again manufactured from a breathable material, these jackets are cut short so that they stay clear of the water. However, as they are much shorter than normal, this style of jacket should always be worn with chest waders. And, as with other waterproof coats, there should be a spacious, built-in hood, preferably with a peak, to prevent rain dripping into the eyes and running down the back of your neck.

Waders and Boots

For fishing either from a boat or when walking in the shallow margins of a lake or river, ordinary Wellington boots are quite adequate. However, many anglers need to wade that bit deeper, especially when fishing from the bank on large lakes and reservoirs or on rivers. Thigh waders are perfect for this task, allowing the angler to wade comfortably in water about two feet deep, giving access to spots unreachable without them. Most thigh waders are made from flexible rubber with a boot attached. Depending on where the angler is fishing they may be cleated – making them ideal for rough ground – studded or felt-soled, which, though smooth, provides the best grip on slippery rocks when they are covered with algae.

For deep wading, so often necessary on rivers when fishing for either trout or salmon, it is vital to use chest waders of which there are three main types. Most commonly used are membrane waders made of PVC or nylon that have a flexible body and legs with an integral rigid boot. They have the advantage that they are relatively cheap, if a little heavy. An advance on the ordinary PVC wader is the breathable wader. These, too, are a membrane but a breathable one constructed to allow sweat but not water to pass through – keeping the

Thigh waders

Chest waders

wearer dry from both sides. Though quite expensive they are becoming increasingly popular and are perfect for summer use or when a lot of walking is involved.

However, when wading for long periods in cold, deep water, neoprene rubber waders are the best choice. They are 3–5 mm thick and made of the same material as divers' wet-and-dry suits. They have tremendous insulating qualities that help keep the angler warm even in the depths of winter. Also, being soft and flexible, they are extremely comfortable suffering none of the pinching that can be a problem with thin, membrane waders. Neoprene waders are available in two types. The first has integral boots, while the second is stocking-foot with additional lace-up boots that look similar to ordinary walking boots. While waders with built-in boots are quick to get on and off, those that use separate boots provide better ankle support – a definite advantage when walking long distances down the river bank.

Safety

Apart from comfort, which is important when wading deep in chest waders, it is vital to consider the safety aspect. Always take great care, especially on unfamiliar rivers, and if you have a ghillie always take his advice over the safe areas to wade. In addition it is important to use an automatically inflating life-jacket should the worst happen. Most important of all, don't wade too deep, especially where the current is strong and, if needed, use a wading stick for support. Even after taking these precautions it is always better to back off into shallower water and cast that bit further than to wade so deep that you lose your footing.

Life-jackets

With game anglers often fishing from boats or wading deep in powerful rivers, safety is very much an issue, and for this reason inflatable life-jackets are becoming increasingly used. Modern life-jackets are a far cry from the old cumbersome foam-filled ones that put off many anglers. Today, automatically inflated jackets are light and unobtrusive, slipping easily over the neck and arms.

TOP: **Flotation waistcoat.**

ABOVE: **A waistcoat specially designed to take the equipment needed by fly fishers.**

A small carbon dioxide cylinder connected to an automatic mechanism is used to inflate the jacket should the angler fall into the water. With a buoyancy of around 150 Newtons the wearer floats easily, face up, even when fully clothed. For those wearing neoprene chest waders more buoyancy is needed and a jacket with 200 Newtons of lift is required to counteract the effect of the waders.

In addition, for those who like to wear a fishing waistcoat, some manufacturers produce combined life-jackets and multi-pocketed waistcoats that are quick and easy to slip on and offer the same buoyancy as the standard life-jacket.

Waistcoats

For anglers who like to walk long distances when they are fishing, a waistcoat or fishing vest takes much of the strain out of carrying all the extra tackle and odds and ends needed at the waterside. Instead of putting all this paraphernalia into a fishing bag and then carrying it around the neck a waistcoat allows enough gear to be carried, but it is evenly distributed around the shoulders thereby causing far less strain. Multi-pocketed waistcoats are available in a wide range of models, from standard cotton ones to lightweight mesh versions which, though having fewer pockets, are ideal when deep wading is necessary and a longer more complicated model would only get wet.

When choosing a fly-fishing waistcoat decide what type of fishing you will be doing most, then find one with enough pockets to carry all you need. This should include pockets for spare spools, fly boxes, leader material etc, plus a large pocket in the back to hold a folded waterproof. If you do a lot of wading or boat fishing it is worth considering a waistcoat with a built-in life-jacket, thus necessitating the purchase of one garment rather than two.

Thermal Fleece

While the system of layering clothing might be new to the angler, it is one long practiced by walkers and mountaineers who need clothes which are light and waterproof but also very warm. These are exactly the same requirements as the angler's, and with more manufactures of angling

Peaked cap

Tweed hat

clothing designing garments with this in mind there is no longer any reason to be cold and wet. A breathable waterproof coat worn over a fleece makes a perfect combination for even the worst weather. Fleeces come in a range of designs from simple single layers, either with a zip front or as a pullover, to those with a Goretex lining, which makes them windproof.

Underwear

For very cold conditions long thermal underwear and a long-sleeved vest of fine silk or Capilene may be worn under trousers or fleece pants along with a rollneck top. This provides the first in a system of layers which trap the air and also draw any moisture away from the body keeping the wearer dry, comfortable and warm.

Gloves

In very cold conditions it is important to keep your hands warm. Fly fishing, in particular, requires constant mani-pulation of the line both to make the fly work properly and to detect takes. With numb fingers this ability is obviously impaired. The only real answer is to use some form of pro-tection such as gloves or mittens, and the best are those specially designed for anglers where the fingertips can

Fleece fishing mittens

above: The well-equipped flyfisher in summer with broad brimmed hat and polarizing glasses.

be left uncovered when fishing, so the line can be easily felt while the rest of the fingers and the hands are kept warm. Although absorbent materials should be avoided, some of the modern ones are so good they provide reasonable warmth even when wet, although two or three pairs can be a boon if you are fishing for salmon early in the year on a really wet day.

Hats

Various types are used by anglers, from the traditional flat cap and deerstalker to wide-brimmed bush hats. For summer wear a light, long-peaked cap to protect the eyes from the sun's glare and help the angler

spot fish beneath the water's surface. With a hood, this style of hat may even be worn during the winter, although in very cold conditions something warm such as the traditional deerstalker with flaps that can be pulled over the ears prevents excessive heat loss.

Polarizing Glasses

As a further safety measure, if you are not a spectacle wearer it is important to wear a pair of polarizing glasses. These not only prevent any possible injury from a fly being cast, but they also stop the sun's reflected glare from the water damaging the eyes. A secondary benefit is that they also help the angler see beneath the surface of the water.

BELOW: Casting for a trout in summer.

Casting

The key to presenting the fly to the fish is the cast and this can take various forms depending on the type of fly fishing you are doing and the area being fished. In fly casting the rod acts as a spring while the fly line provides the weight to load the rod – no leads or other weights are used. The main types of cast used by trout and salmon anglers are the overhead cast, the roll cast, the double haul, and the Spey and double Spey casts, with the horseshoe and steeple casts being used when circumstances dictate. Casting is itself a source of great pleasure and satisfaction and it contributes greatly to the enjoyment of fly fishing.

ABOVE: **Casting a dry fly upstream.**

The Overhead Cast

The standard overhead cast is the basic cast for the beginner to master. It is used over short distances where accuracy rather than distance is important. For a right-handed fisher the angler stands, right or left foot forward according to preference, with 5–6 yds (4.57–5.03 m) of line on the water and the rod held in the right hand, pointing towards the water. Gripping the line with the index finger the forearm is brought smoothly upward until the hand is to the side but just in front of the face. With the wrist remaining straight the rod is now stopped at the 11.30 position so it is upright and slightly behind the angler. (This figure of 11.30

refers to a clock face, with 12 o'clock being directly above the angler's head, and acts as a guide to the correct rod position at any stage of the cast.)

The backward sweep of the rod loops the line out behind the angler and flexes the rod. At this stage it is important not to let the rod drop back too far because this will collapse the cast. With the hand still in the 11.30 position a pause is made to allow all the line to extend fully behind the angler. The pause is crucial and its duration depends on the length of line being cast. Once the line has extended at the back the rod is then brought forward to the 1.30 position. This "loads" the rod and causes the line to loop out in front of the angler. The

rod is then dropped to the 2.30 position, thus allowing the line's momentum to "shoot" any slack out over the water.

If greater distance is needed this process is repeated on each forward stroke with a little line being paid out until the required amount is outside the tip ring. The technique is known as "false casting" and it is used by dry fly fishers to dry the fly and place the cast. The line is then shot as before.

Making an Overhead Cast

1 This angler has his weight on his right foot and has started to drive the line out across the water. Note the tension in the rod as the line starts to come forward.

2 The rod has reached the forward position. The tension has left it and the angler will "shoot" the line trapped by his left hand as the cast extends across the river.

The Roll Cast

The roll cast is the simplest of all presentations. Where a back cast is obstructed it can be the only way of presenting a fly, although accuracy and distance are limited. With the rod pointing down, and a short distance of fly line on the water, the rod is lifted upright then laid back over the shoulder so that the line forms a large loop behind the angler. Once the line has reached this position the rod is swept forward in a single smooth action. The loop of line plus the drag of the line on the water flexes the rod so that by punching it forward and down, the line is made to roll straight out over the water. This gets the fly on to the water and is an ideal method for lifting a sunk line from the water prior to a normal overhead cast.

Making a Roll Cast

1 This cast can be made with trout and salmon rods. Here a trout angler is using a roll cast on a lake.

2 The rod is brought back to the right and then swept up to the vertical position making a loop of line on the angler's right. The rod is then "cut" down to the water and the loop is rolled out across the surface.

ABOVE: Casting an upstream nymph on a north-country stream into the fast water at the head of a pool.

LEFT: Fishing a dry fly on a north-country river. Here the angler has his weight on his left foot and is casting a short line with his cast thrown well up behind him. Accuracy is much more important than distance when fishing for trout in this type of water.

LEFT: The start of a double haul. The line is pulled sharply downwards as it is picked off the water and the left hand is then allowed to drift up to the butt ring. The angler makes another haul as the forward stroke is made; this is quite difficult to time correctly and the reservoir angler must practice until it becomes second nature. The two hauls make the line travel much faster through the air and give great distance to the cast.

The Double Haul Cast

The double haul is the standard technique for long-distance casting with a single-handed rod in which a haul on the line is made both on the forward and back cast. This action generates much greater line speed allowing the line to be shot long distances once the optimum amount of line has been launched into the air. The haul is made with the free hand, which is allowed to drift upward towards the butt ring before making a quick downward haul at the beginning of both the forward and back casts. The line is shot as usual on the forward stroke once 10–15 yds (9.1–13.7 m) of line are outside the tip ring, any loose coils of line on the ground being carried with it. The double haul is the usual technique for reservoir trout fishing because it enables a full fly line, 30–35 yds (27–32 m), to be cast.

Single Spey and Double Spey Casts

When using a double-handed salmon rod and an overhead cast is impossible, the Spey and double Spey casts come into their own. Based on

the roll cast the Spey cast takes plenty of practice to become proficient at it, but most competent salmon anglers should take the trouble to master it. The timing of each stage is crucial as the line must be in contact with the water to load the rod and create the final forward cast. Too late and the line will lift off the water, and the power will be dissipated.

The single Spey is ideal for a strong downstream wind when the angler runs the danger of hooking himself in the back of the neck with the standard overhead cast. The angler faces downstream and raises the rod slightly towards the near bank. The rod is then swept away smoothly out and up, with the butt pivoting at the angler's belt buckle. As the rod comes round to the roll cast position the line will come off the water and be swept upstream with the last 4 yds (3.66 m) touching the water's surface. The rod is then punched forward and high so that the line and fly loop out over the water. It is essential that the fly is drawn upstream so that it is level in the water with the angler. This enables

the angler to change the direction of the line and cast the fly across the river rather than just downstream.

The double Spey is different from the single Spey and is performed over the shoulder of the bank from which the angler is fishing. Fishing from the right bank it is made over the right shoulder and conversely over the left shoulder when fishing from the left bank. It is most useful for changing the direction of a large heavy fly, and an expert can cast a very long way indeed using this cast. If fishing from the right bank the rod is swept slowly back-handed upstream in front of the angler so that the fly comes to rest about 5 yds (3.66 m) in front of the angler. The rod is then rolled out and round downstream in a figure-of-eight movement, and the rod is lifted back up over the right shoulder into the roll cast position. Finally, the rod is punched forward, shooting the line and fly out over the water. It is essential that the loop made in the line is as close to the line as possible, "shaving the cheek of the line", and it is possible to shoot a great deal of line when using this cast. It does, however, take a good deal of practice to perfect.

The Horseshoe Cast

This is a useful cast to use fishing for salmon in a very strong downstream wind if you do not want to use the single Spey cast. When the cast is fished out, lift the fly off the water back-handed, over the left shoulder – fishing from the left bank– and then bring the fly back round over your

The Single Spey Cast

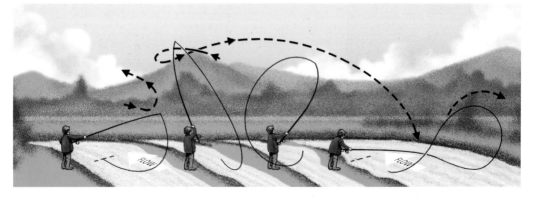

The angler pulls the line upstream until the fly is level in the water. The rod is then lifted over the angler's right shoulder and the loop rolled

out across the river in a continuous movement. With practice this cast can be done quite fast and with a good deal of force.

The angler is making a roll cast to clear the fly before casting again. This is similar to the single Spey but can be made off either shoulder.

right shoulder in one continuous movement. It is not possible to cast a very long way using the horseshoe cast but it makes a neat finish and avoids the fly and line getting wrapped round your neck.

The Steeple Cast

This is a cast to use when you have a very steep bank behind you, or some other obstacle, and you cannot use the single Spey or double Spey cast. It can be made with both trout and salmon rods. With a salmon rod hold the rod out in front of you with your hands rather wide apart on the butt, and the right hand (if fishing over your right shoulder) as far down the rod as you can reach. Raise the rod sharply upwards, throwing the line high into the air behind you. When the line is fully extended bring the rod down and forward, and this pushes the line out over the water. If you are carrying out a steeple cast with a single-handed rod, it is important not to cock your wrist but hold it out stiffly as you bring the rod up. It is surprising how this cast helps you avoid even the most awkward of banks behind you.

RIGHT: The angler is completing a double Spey cast off the right shoulder. The line is just picking up from the water. Experts can cast a long way using this technique.

The Double Spey Cast

The river flows from left to right. The first movement is back-handed, pulling the fly upstream. The rod is then brought over the right shoulder and a loop of line formed on the right. Next, the rod is cut down across the river, shooting the line and fly out across the water. The dotted lines indicate the movement of the rod tip in diagrams both above and opposite.

Salmon Fishing

Salmon fishing has been called the greatest of all sports, and with some justification. Nowadays the Atlantic salmon is under grave threat from netting both on the high seas and in river mouths. Catches in rivers are much reduced, and on many rivers strenuous efforts are being made to implement catch-and-release policies to preserve the spawning stock.

ABOVE: A fine fresh spring salmon from the River Spey, Scotland.

Fly Fishing for Salmon

Salmon can be caught on fly, spinner, worm and prawn, but for the majority of dedicated salmon fishers, fly fishing is the best and most effective way, and on many rivers the rule is fly only. Even on rivers such as the Wye, the famous Welsh salmon river, many beats have now banned the use of spinner and bait.

There are two main ways to fish for salmon with a fly. The first is when the water temperature is cold in the early and late months of the year, below 48°F (9°C): then the technique is to fish with a large fly 2 in (5 cm) or more and to use a sinking line. Later in spring and summer when the water temperature rises above 48°F (9°C) smaller flies fishing on floating lines are the most effective way.

Depending on the river you are fishing the same tackle can be used for each method. Standard tackle when fly fishing for salmon includes a double-handed 15 ft (4.57 m) rod designed to take a 9 to 11 weight line. This type of rod is powerful enough to cover a large river like the Tweed or Spey and works well with either an overhead or Spey cast. In the summer or fishing on smaller rivers, any rod from 12–14 ft (3.66–4.27 m) will be perfectly adequate depending on the water you have to cover.

You need a reel to balance the rod that will hold the line and 200 yds (183 m) of 30 lb (13.61 kg) backing. Modern reels have interchangeable spools, one to hold a sinking line and one to hold a floater. You need a leader of nylon of between 20–8 lb (9.1–3.63 kg) breaking strain, depending on the height of the water and the time of the year that you are fishing, and salmon flies in a variety of sizes from 3 in (7.5 cm) down to size 8 or 10. Salmon have been caught on minute trout flies, and it is a common mistake to fish with too large a fly. Popular modern patterns include Willie Gunn, Ally's Shrimp, Munroe Killer, Stoat's Tail and Tadpole, although there are countless salmon flies and the old patterns are more colourful, with more romantic names, such as Green Highlander, Mar Lodge and Lady Caroline.

Fly fishing for salmon is really a scaled up version of classic down-and-across wet fly fishing. The line should be cast downstream and across the current so that the fly swings enticingly across the pool. When the cast is fished out the angler takes one or two paces downstream and casts

BELOW: Fly fishing for salmon in spring, River Beauly, Scotland.

ABOVE LEFT: Fishing for salmon in summer on the River Spey.

ABOVE: An angler spinning on the River Tay, Scotland, in spring.

again. That way the whole pool is covered systematically. You can leave the line to work naturally with the current or work the fly by pulling in a little line at a time to make the fly dart across the current as if it was a small fish. Takes can come at any time, but most often they occur as the swing begins or at the end when the fly is "on the dangle".

There is something rather special about catching a salmon on the fly. The best chance is when the water conditions are right, the air is warmer than the water and the river has begun to run clear after a spate.

Alternatively, there are three other methods of presenting the fly to the salmon. The first of these is to "back up" a pool immediately after it has been fished in the orthodox manner. When doing this the angler starts at the tail, cast fairly square across the current, and then takes three or four steps upstream, at the same time steadily pulling in the line. This sweeps the fly over the fish in a continuous curve. A good even bank is a great help when attempting this form of fishing.

The other two methods are really summer tactics: the first is to fish with a bushy dry fly, such as a Rat-faced Macdougall, and cast continually over one fish for several hours. This can goad the salmon into taking. It works best when the water is over 60° F (15°C). The other is to "dibble" a large fly down a run, fishing it half out of the water; tubes are now available that will fish at half-cock. Another way of dibbling is to fish with two flies and bounce the dropper on the top of

the water. Fishing with a dry fly, strike as soon as you see the rise, but when dibbling wait till the salmon has taken the fly down before tightening – this requires great self-control.

Spinning

On some rivers when the river is running high spinning is the preferred option. During the early season when the river is still swollen by winter floods, a large spinner such as a Toby, a yellow-bellied Devon Minnow or one of the deadly rubber-tailed spinners can be very effective when fished steadily through a pool. The spinner is cast across and downstream then allowed to sink for a second or two before engaging the reel. How far across stream the cast is made and the weight of the spinner used depends again on the strength of the current. Tobys come in varying sizes and weights up to 28 g. Devon Minnows and Rapalas require additional casting weight in the form of spiral leads or Wye leads. At least one or, better still, two strong swivels should be used to prevent line twist.

Tackle for salmon spinning includes a 10–11 ft (3.05–3.35 m) spinning rod, capable of casting weights up to 2 oz (50 g), and a fixed-spool or multiplier reel loaded with 250 yds (228.6 m) of 15–20 lb (6.8–9.07 kg) nylon.

Bait Fishing

The most commonly used bait for salmon is the humble worm, either large lobworms or smaller brandlings. Depending on just how powerfully the

river is flowing these can be fished either singly or in bunches. The worms are attached to the hook with lead shot or a drilled bullet connected to the line for casting and sinking the bait to the bottom. The most effective and skillful method of fishing a worm for salmon is to cast it upstream and allow it to bump gently along the bottom just slower than the current.

Tackle for worm fishing includes a powerful 12 ft (3.66 m) rod combined with a fixed-spool reel loaded with 250 yds (228.6 m) of 10–15 lb (4.54–6.8 kg) breaking strain nylon. A single size 4 to 8 hook, often with a sliced shank to help retain the worm, is tied to the end with large split shot either pinched on the line or fished as a fixed leger. How much shot is used depends on the strength of the river.

Another effective bait for salmon is shrimp or prawn, although its use is banned on many rivers as it disturbs the water for other forms of fishing. Shrimps are available in a variety of colours, both natural and dyed, with red and purple being the most popular. To fish them they are first straightened out, then a pin is pushed down their middle. A treble hook is then inserted and the whole thing bound together with elasticated thread. Shrimps can be fished in the same way as the worm or, where allowed, fished under a float.

Sea Trout Fishing

There are two main types of sea trout waters. First, those rivers that have large runs of sea trout, and second, some lochs or lakes connected to the sea by a short river that are renowned for their sea trout fishing. Among the best-known sea trout rivers are the Welsh rivers, the Irfon, Teifi and Conway, the West Country rivers, the Torridge and Tamar, and a number of the Border rivers on the west coast of Scotland. The best-known lochs are probably Loch Maree and Loch Hope in Scotland.

ABOVE: A fine fresh sea trout taken from the River Conway at night.

What to Take

There is sometimes no apparent reason why one river will have good runs of sea trout while another has relatively few. All salmon rivers have some sea trout but on some there are so few that they are not worth a special expedition, while a nearby river may have a fair number.

The type of fishery dictates the style of fishing. On most sea trout rivers the main fish are taken at night, after dark, while on lakes and lochs, the main fish are caught in daylight. It must be remembered that in June and July in northern Scotland particularly, night has a short duration.

The tackle required for fishing a river depends very much on its size. Generally, for fly fishing, on a reasonably large river, you will need a 9½–10½ ft (2.9–3.2 m) single-handed

BELOW: A good sea trout is netted on a dark night. A companion is a good idea when fishing at night, particularly on a strange river.

rod capable of casting a 7–8 weight line. A rod suitable for fishing a large reservoir is ideal. The leader should be a minimum of 7–10 lb (3.18–4.54 kg) breaking strain, and you need both floating (or floating with a sinking tip) and slow-sinking or intermediate lines, on separate reels or reel drums. You will need a variety of sea trout flies, not just the old favourites such as Teal, Blue and Silver, and Grouse and Claret, but also any flies that are particularly favoured on the water you are going to fish, and a number of lures, both for fishing on a sunk line after midnight, or cork-bodied floating lures for use on the surface.

As well as rod, reel, nylon and flies, the night fisher for sea trout will need waders, a wading stick, net, a bag for keeping any fish, midge-repellent, scissors, priest, spectacles (if worn), and finally and most importantly a good torch with fresh batteries that is not going to dull to a dim glow at 1.30 am on a dark night.

Night Fishing

Night fishing is not something for the uninitiated, and the beginner is urged to solicit the company of a local or companion who knows the river and the tactics to follow on their first visit. If you are in the position of going fishing alone at night on a new river, it is essential to walk down the river in daylight first, examine all the pools, choose where you hope to fish and then wade the pools when you can see. Also cast to where you think the fish are likely to be and if necessary mark your line with a dab of luminous paint, or check off and memorize the amount of line you

have pulled off to reach the lie. At night sea trout often move up and down streamy runs as they feed or drop back to the flats at the tails of deep pools where they have been lying under cover during the day.

Fish a team of two, not three flies: two is less likely to tangle than three; and fish normal wet fly down the pool to start with. If nothing has happened by midnight, and the regulations of the river allow you to fish on, change to a sunk line and try fishing a sunk lure. Another tactic at night when you can hear the sea trout splashing on the surface is to switch to a floating lure, cast across and down so that it drags across the surface of the water leaving a wake.

Often this is a method that catches the bigger fish. However, it is worth stating that few rivers are the same and local knowledge is invaluable.

Fishing Stillwaters

Fishing on stillwaters for sea trout is very different. The preferred method on many waters is to dap with a bushy fly. You need a longish rod 11–12 ft (3.35–3.66 m) that ideally should be quite soft, a reel, and some floss line. The technique is to cut off a length of about 15 ft (4.57 m) of floss line and then make a series of overhand knots down the line. This just holds the line together a bit which is necessary otherwise the fibres fray too much. Attach a short 4 ft (1.22 m) leader of 7–8 lb (3.18–3.63 kg) with a

dropper to the floss line and attach the floss line to the reel line. Tie the bushy fly on the dropper and a standard sea trout fly, such as a Grouse and Claret, on the point.

When you start to fish, and some wind is absolutely necessary, pull off all the floss line and then let it just blow out in front of the boat, forget about the point fly and bounce the bushy fly along the tops of the ripple in front of the boat. The point fly is only there to anchor the dropper that otherwise can be uncontrollable in a strong wind, although sometimes fish will take the point fly. Fish often come to the dapped fly with a tremendous splash, and it requires nerves of steel not to snatch the fly away too quickly – concentrate on the dapped fly intently and wait for the fish to take it down before tightening.

It is normal for one rod in a boat to dap while the other fishes with a team of wet flies. It is the duty of the wet fly fisher to keep out of the way of the dap, although he should cover any fish that moves to the dap if the dapper fail to connect.

Sea trout can also be caught on a dry fly in still conditions. Cast out and give the occasional twitch, using a team of wet flies. In this situation, a floating line fishing the flies just under the surface is normally best.

Bait and Sea Fishing

In rivers, when the water is high, sea trout can be caught during the day on the fly, and spinning and fishing with worms or maggots is often successful.

Sea trout can also be caught in the sea. This can be very profitable, and the best conditions are places where there are stillwaters close to the sea connected by short streams or burns when the water is low in summer. Then the fish congregate off shore and can be caught by casting with fly or light spinners such as a mepps, during the two hours on either side of high water. It can be quite surprising hooking a good sea trout in the open sea and the main danger is losing it in the weed around the rocks. Another good place is a tidal pool on a river where a worm can be very successful.

Sea trout are fickle creatures. They have been much under threat over the last twenty years, and their numbers have declined markedly; infestation by lice from salmon farms and commercial netting of sandeels have been blamed. Now some famous sea trout waters hardly hold any fish at all. It must be hoped that this situation changes and conservation measures are successful, for hooking and landing a large sea trout at night or having one lunge at the dap is a thrilling experience.

ABOVE: Dapping on Loch Hope, one of the famous sea trout lochs in Sutherland.

BELOW: Fishing a small sea trout river during the day. Sometimes when the small sea trout, usually known as sewin or herling, run in they can be stalked in daytime and caught by fishing a small dry fly upstream. This can be very exciting on light tackle.

Dry Fly Fishing

For many anglers dry fly fishing is the pinnacle of the sport. In bygone days it was regarded as an art so difficult that only a few privileged anglers could attempt it. Nowadays fishing with a dry fly is relatively commonplace and is practised both on rivers and stillwaters. Nevertheless it remains a fascinating way of fishing. To find a rising fish, identify the insect the trout is feeding on and cast to that fish, then watch your fly in breathless anticipation as it floats downstream towards the trout; then to see it rise in the water and take it down off the surface is a wonderful experience, one that is treasured by all anglers.

ABOVE: A blue-winged olive dun on bankside vegetation. This fly hatches in the evening and is one of the best for the evening rise.

River Fishing

Successful dry fly fishing depends on a good hatch of aquatic insects such as upwings or caddisflies, or a fall of terrestrials (land-based insects blown on to the water). When this occurs fish switch from feeding on nymphs and crustacea to taking flies off the surface. The essence of dry fly fishing is to imitate a small creature as it floats on the water. Some patterns such as those incorporating Cul de Canard feathers, which are naturally impregnated with oil, float well untreated but most need an application of floatant to prevent them becoming waterlogged. Floatants come in two main forms, either as a spray or a gel, and are applied sparingly so they do not clog the fly's delicate hackles.

The predominant group of insects of interest to anglers on rivers are commonly called upwings or mayflies. They are members of the family Ephemeridae. There are a number of species, including the blue-winged olive, the medium olive, iron blue and the mayfly, and they make up a large part of the diet of trout and grayling. Trout take them from the surface at two stages in their development. The first is when the nymph first hatches out as a dun, or sub-imago, and floats downstream until its wings have dried and it can fly away. Many duns have greyish wings and olive or pale-straw coloured bodies. After one or two days the duns become sexually mature and change into the imago, or spinner. Males and females mate in the air and the females return to the water to lay their eggs and die. When they have finished laying their eggs they float downstream with their wings outstretched in the form of a cross and are known as "spent". Spinners frequently have reddish bodies, long tails and gauzy wings..

The normal method for fishing a dry fly in a river is to use a single fly on a tapered cast. Accuracy is more important than distance, and the tapered leader, which transfers the energy of the cast and helps it turn over properly, allows the fly to be placed exactly in front of a feeding fish. The successful dry fly fisher spends a great deal of time observing the water, checking the flies that the trout are taking and reading the current to see whether there is any likelihood of the fly dragging and scaring the fish when it is cast.

During the summer months the rise is likely to be to a species of upwinged dun. These olive-coloured flies are quite easy to identify drifting downstream like miniature sail boats. If this proves to be the case, a size 14 or 16 CDC Dun is a good imitation to use. If it is impossible to tell what is causing the activity a more general pattern such as the Adams or the Hare's Ear, again in the same sizes, makes a good starting point.

The next step is to position yourself almost opposite the fish but slightly downstream, making use of any bank-side vegetation to keep out of sight of the fish. The cast should be made so that the fly lands just

LEFT: Fishing the dry fly on the River Avon, Hampshire. The angler has used the bankside vegetation for concealment and is casting at a trout across the river.

upstream and directly in line with where the fish is rising. The fly is then allowed to drift into the fish's vision and, if pattern and presentation are right, the trout gently sips the imitation down. What is important is that the fly drifts with the current like a real insect. If the line drags the fly will skate across the surface and be refused. Casting upstream helps but casting a snaky line, so that there is some slack, ensures that the fly can drift without drag for long enough to fool the fish.

Tackle for river dry fly fishing includes a rod 8–9 ft (2.44–2.74 m) long, teamed with a 4–6 weight floating double taper or long belly fly line. The leader is of tapered nylon 9 ft (2.74 m) long tapering to a 3 lb (1.36 kg) breaking strain tippet. Effective flies include the Adams, Hare's Ear, CDC Dun and Greenwell's Glory.

Stillwater Fishing

Once considered a fringe technique, today dry fly fishing is regarded as one of the most deadly methods on stillwater. Apart from a few specific imitations such as those of the daddy-longlegs (crane fly) and the lake olive, stillwater dry flies look quite different from river patterns. They rely as much on teased out body materials as hackles to keep them floating, and many are designed to sit low in the surface film. Many patterns including the Bob's Bits imitate a hatching

RIGHT: Dry fly fishing on the River Frome, Dorset. Many south-country rivers have a timeless quality with lush green banks and leaves stirring in the breeze.

chironomid midge – the predominant insect on lakes and reservoirs everywhere.

Stillwater dry flies are usually fished, either from a bank or boat, as a team of three, or as a mix with a dry fly on the top and middle droppers and an emerger pattern, such as a Suspender Buzzer, on the point. In calm conditions or when trout are being selective a single fly is effective fished on a short tapered leader with a fine tippet of 4 lb (1.81 kg) breaking strain. The tapered leader allows accurate casting helping to present the fly right in the path of a cruising fish. However the fly is fished, it should be treated with floatant and the leader rubbed with a degreaser to make it sink. This prevents the telltale disturbance caused by a leader trapped in the surface film.

ABOVE LEFT: A good trout rises to a blue-winged olive making the characteristic kidney-shaped whorl in the water.

ABOVE: Fishing a dry fly upstream in fast water. Good eyesight and accurate casting are a great help in these conditions.

For stillwater dry fly fishing a 9–10 ft (2.74–3.05 m) long rod matched with a 6–7 weight forward, floating line provides both distance and accuracy. When fishing a team the leader is 12 ft (3.66 m) of 5 lb (2.27 kg) breaking strain nylon with two droppers spaced 4 ft (1.22 m) apart. Typical fly patterns include Bob's Bits and Hoppers in various colours plus the CDC Dun during a hatch of lake olives. An imitation crane fly or adult damselfly is also effective when the naturals are on the water.

Nymph Fishing

By definition nymph fishing means presenting a fly to a fish beneath the surface, for a nymph is the immature stage of an aquatic insect and spends its life underwater. To be accurate a nymph is the pre-emergent stage of insects such as mayflies, damselflies or stoneflies, which ascend to the surface of the water and there change into the first stage, or sub-imago, of their winged existence. However, fly fishers often use the term nymph more generally, to describe any aquatic invertebrate, be it a nymph, larva, pupa or even a crustacean such as a shrimp.

ABOVE: A natural pond olive nymph starting its ascent to the surface.

Upstream Nymph

The key to fishing a nymph is presenting it as naturally as possible, mimicking the way a real insect moves. On rivers this usually means fishing the nymph upstream and allowing it to "dead drift" with the current. When a real olive nymph or a shrimp is disturbed, rather than swimming it will usually just drift with the current for a short distance until it can regain cover.

It is possible to fish a nymph down-and-across wet fly style, but it is not a way to catch the better fish. To fool the larger, more wily fish the most effective and tested methods are the upstream nymph and the rolled nymph.

In upstream nymphing the line is cast up-and-across-stream so that the flies drift back to the angler at the same speed as the river is flowing.

Also, because the line isn't dragging them around across the current they sink to the fish's level and drift downstream like a real nymph. To keep in contact with the flies, the line must be retrieved – not to feel a take but to ensure that when one comes there isn't too much slack line, and the angler can strike properly.

While the technique of upstream nymphing is straightforward, the real skill comes in detecting takes. Because the line is slack, takes are not going to be felt. In clear, smooth water this is not a problem. By using polarizing glasses to cut out any surface glare, the fish can often be seen taking the nymph – the angler seeing a flash of white as the mouth opens and closes. However where the surface is broken, or where the angle and level of the light makes seeing fish impossible, another method is

required. Instead of looking for a fish the angler watches the end of the line intently. As the line drifts back with the current it does so at a steady, unhindered pace. It is only when the nymph catches the bottom or when a fish takes that the line will stop and drag under the surface. Deciding which is which takes experience, but the best way of determining the difference is that a take usually produces a sudden stab of the line or it moves across rather than with the current. If it is weed or the bottom the line simply draws steadily under. This is not a perfect rule, and usually any twitch or hesitation in the line's drift should be met with a strike.

To make the tip of the fly line more obvious it can be painted with fluorescent orange paint, or a fluorescent orange or yellow braided loop can be used to attach the leader. For fishing at longer range a sight bob, or strike indicator, is a great advantage. Made from a buoyant material such as polystyrene, a sight bob is attached to the leader a few feet above the nymph. It also helps control the depth the nymph fishes.

Rolled Nymph

Similar to the upstream nymph is the rolled nymph. Developed by Czech and Polish anglers, the technique is being used to great effect in the UK for both trout and, particularly, grayling. It involves fishing a team of heavily-weighted nymphs on a very short line, the nymphs being "rolled" along the river bottom almost under

LEFT: Nymph fishing on the River Wye in Derbyshire.

RIGHT: Nymph fishing on the River Avon, Hampshire. Nymphing trout are easy to see in the clear water of the chalk streams.

RIGHT: Nymph fishing on the River Avon, Hampshire. Nymphing trout are easy to see in the clear water of the chalk streams.

the rod tip. Instead of just casting, the angler wades carefully until little more than a rod's length from the area to be fished.

With only a short length of fly line and the leader outside the tip ring the nymphs are flicked directly upstream, and as the current carries them back the nymph on the point sinks until it is tripping along the bottom. As the nymphs drift through the slot being fished the rod follows their progress keeping in contact all the time. When the flies are directly below the angler the rod is lifted or the line retrieved and recast.

Takes can come throughout the drift and are detected either as a draw on the line or more usually by it pausing in its normal drift. The end of the drift is particularly productive and fish will often take when the nymphs are directly below the angler and beginning to rise in the water.

Tackle

Ideal tackle for the upstream and the rolled nymph is a rod 8^{1}/$_{2}$–9^{1}/$_{2}$ ft (2.59–3.05 m) long, rated for a 5 to 6 weight line. The line itself is always a floater, which can be brightly coloured, either orange or yellow, to help detect takes.

For the upstream nymph the leader is 8–10 ft (2.44–2.74 m) long and of tapered nylon. Tippet strength varies depending on the size of nymph being fished and for standard size 12–16 hooks it is 3–5 lb (1.36–2.27 kg) breaking strain. One or two nymphs may be used, the second lighter pattern being fished, either on a short dropper or attached to the bend of the larger, heavier nymph by 6–12 in (15–30 cm) of nylon. Effective patterns include the Pheasant Tail Nymph, Hare's Ear and Iron Blue.

Since the rolled nymph has to get down to the fish's depth very quickly, the patterns used are large and heavily weighted. The leader is also quite short – no more than the length of the rod on to which are tied three nymphs or bugs, two on evenly spaced droppers. Size 10 nymphs are standard for this technique, as are patterns such as the Hare's Ear and shrimp, which are weighted to make them sink.

Nymph Fishing in Stillwaters

Nymphs are also used widely on lakes and reservoirs, and for much the same reason as on rivers – their ability to produce better-than-average fish. Most stillwater trout fisheries in the UK are artificially stocked, mostly with rainbow trout along with a small proportion of brown trout and occasionally some brook trout. On reservoirs and larger lakes the trout are normally stocked weighing about 1 to 1^{1}/$_{2}$ lb (0.45–0.68 kg) and fish larger than this have grown-on by feeding naturally on a diet of crustaceans, insects and small fish.

When fish have been feeding on natural insects for some time they can become quite selective in their diet, and rather than taking any fly or lure drawn past their nose they require a more imitative approach.

The most common natural food for stillwater trout is the larvae and pupae of the chironomid midge. Fishing an imitation, especially of the pupa, is one of the most effective methods of catching fish in stillwaters. Midge larvae live in the bottom silt of lakes and reservoirs, and when pupation occurs these pupae must rise to the surface to transform into the winged adult.

Small vulnerable creatures such as midge pupae make easy pickings, and reservoir trout eat them by the hundred. The pupae can be taken anywhere from the bottom to the

surface, and one of the most successful techniques is to fish three pupae imitations, hanging them from midwater to the bottom. This is done by using a floating fly line and an ultra-long leader, in excess of 20 ft (6.1 m), with two droppers spaced 4–6 ft (1.22–1.83 m) apart. All three patterns should be designed to sink quickly but the heaviest of the three is fished on the point so that it gets to the bottom as rapidly as possible.

The method can be used from either boat or bank, but as it is dependent on moving the flies very slowly the weather needs to be quite calm, especially from a boat, which needs to be anchored to keep it stationary. From the bank, water 8–15 ft (2.44–4.57 m) deep is best, which usually means fishing from a headland or a dam wall where the water is normally deeper close-in to the shore. Once the line has been cast the flies are then allowed a few seconds to sink down through the water before starting the retrieve.

Another method is to fish the nymph just below the surface film when the natural insects are hatching.

RIGHT: A beautiful wild brown trout taken on a nymph. The white line makes the take easier to spot.

Wet Fly Fishing

Wet fly fishing is the traditional method of fishing for trout and grayling in fast-flowing rivers of the north and west of the country where the hatches of insects may be sparser, and the dry fly is more difficult to present to a feeding fish. It is common particularly in the north of England and Scotland where a specific style of wet fly fishing has developed. Many game anglers started fishing for trout with a wet fly in small streams and burns as young children using a team of three flies, casting them across and downstream and waiting for the pluck on the line as the trout intercepted the flies in their path across the river. On stillwaters a number of methods have developed over the years to catch trout in reservoirs as well as the traditional lakes and lochs.

Wet Fly Fishing on Rivers

On rivers the standard method for fishing a wet fly is known as down-and-across. This means that the line is cast downstream at an angle across the flow and involves the angler casting, and allowing the flies to fish round in the current before taking a pace downstream. The process is then repeated so that gradually a stretch of river or a pool is fished thoroughly and every inch of the water is covered.

When fishing down-and-across the flies are fished just under the surface and the angler must try and keep the line as straight as possible so that he or she can strike immediately when a trout rises to the fly or a pluck on the line is felt. The cast is made at an angle across and down the river and

the flies are made to swing across the path of a fish. The method is very effective, especially on rain-fed rivers where the fish are opportunistic in their feeding.

It is important to be in control of the line at all times. In a river that is flowing quickly it is easy to have the flies whipped around in the current far too fast. Fish will still be caught but they will be fewer and almost certainly smaller than if the flies are fished at a steadier pace.

In a river that is moving slowly the line can be cast at less than 45° to the flow and allowed to come round naturally. However, to reduce the effect of a fast current the line should be cast at more than forty-five degrees to as much as ninety degrees, all

ABOVE: Fishing the River Wharfe, Yorkshire, with a wet fly in early spring.

depending on just how fast the river is moving. The speed of the river needs to be judged and the flies made to swing only slightly faster than the current. To help this happen an upstream mend is made. This is done by raising the rod, parallel to the water and placing the line back upstream with the tip of the rod immediately after the cast is made. This helps to take the belly out of the line and makes the flies fish round more steadily.

The effect of the belly on the current is the same as that used by a water-skier. Water-skiers use the fact that they can actually go faster than the boat that is pulling them by swinging across its path. We need to ensure that the opposite happens and that the flies move almost at the same speed as the river – just as any natural food item would. The only exception to this comes right at the end of the swing. With the line almost directly downstream of the angler it can go no further and the flies rise to the surface. As they do they accelerate a little and often a fish will make a grab as its potential food "tries" to escape.

Takes can come anywhere during the cast and are normally felt as a simple tightening of the line. If just a

LEFT: Down-and-across on a typical north country river.

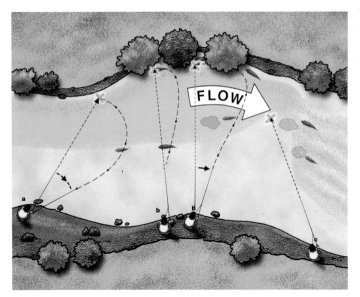

Wet Fly Fishing

The angler at (a) is fishing the head of the pool in the traditional down-and-across manner. If the current is deep enough the flies can be allowed to come right round under the angler's bank before a new cast is made. It is most important to keep the line as straight as possible when fishing in this style.

The anglers at (b) are fishing across-and-down in the Tweed-style and casting again when the flies have travelled a short distance. This method is especially good when fish are feeding under trees on the far bank, as the angler can float the flies down to the fish.

The angler at (c) is fishing the tail of the pool upstream with a team of wet flies to avoid scaring the fish present in the shallower water. When fishing this type of water look out for ripples on the surface: this indicates the presence of larger rocks that the trout will shelter behind. Make sure that all the potential lies are thoroughly covered.

quick pluck is felt and the fish has not taken the fly properly the flies should be allowed to keep working, because the fish will sometimes come back for a second go. A simple lift of the rod is enough to set the small hook if the fish hasn't already hooked itself against the drag of the line.

For normal river wet fly fishing for trout and grayling a rod of around 9–9$^{1}/_{2}$ ft (2.74–2.9 m) long is ideal. It should have a medium-to-through action to absorb the shock of any sudden takes and be capable of casting a number 5–7 line. The smaller and less powerful the river the lighter the tackle can be. Normally a floating line is used, though if the current is particularly fast a sink tip line or a sinking polyleader can be effective because it prevents the flies from skating across the surface.

Although a single fly can be used, it is common practice to fish a team of three on a leader about 9 ft (2.74 m) in length with the flies spaced on droppers 2–3 ft (0.61–0.91 m) apart. The breaking strain of this leader should be about 3–5 lb (1.36–2.27 kg), though it can be lighter if the water is very clear and the fish are proving difficult.

Effective flies for this style of fishing include the Hare's Ear, March Brown, Partridge and Orange, Woodcock and Orange, Snipe and Purple, and Black Spider tied on hooks from size 12 to 16. Usually it is

the smaller, sparser patterns that are most productive. In some rivers, particularly the River Tweed, and the Border rivers, where the angler is fishing large pools, the most effective style is to cast a team of wet flies or nymphs across river, allow them to drift downstream a short distance and then cast again. The flies are not allowed to swing down and across with the current. This is a good method to use when the fish are feeding on hatching nymphs as it allows a natural presentation in the same way as a dry fly. If the flies are drawn in slowly before the next cast is made, then the fish often takes at this point, similar to the "induced take" of

the chalk stream trout when a nymph is drawn past its nose by the fisher.

Wet flies can also be used in the same way in the tails of pools where the water is shallower and the angler would run the risk of scaring the fish if he fished downstream in the traditional manner. A good method is to cast upstream and draw the flies down-and-across over the fish.

BELOW: Fishing the Upper Severn in early spring. The wet fly is at its most productive in the early part of the year when fly hatches are sparser and the trout are starting to come back into condition after spawning. Soft-hackled spider patterns are preferred.

Wet Fly Fishing on Stillwaters

On stillwater the methods of fishing wet flies are a little different from those used on rivers, because without the benefit of a flowing river all the movement imparted to a fly comes from the angler.

Traditional Loch-style

When boat fishing the most popular traditional technique is known as loch style. This method has its roots in fishing for wild brown trout on the lochs of Scotland and loughs of Ireland. The anglers fish from a boat drifting sideways-on to the wind. In such a position the boat provides a stable platform for two anglers and possibly a boatman to work down the wind covering the fish-holding areas of the water. On big, natural lakes the most productive water is often quite shallow, 2–8 ft (0.6–2.44 m) deep, and involves the boat being worked with the oars around the shoreline, the fringes of islands and close to rocky outcrops.

Traditionally loch-style involves "short-lining" in which the angler casts no more than 10 yds (9.14 m) in front of the boat and retrieves a team of wet flies back through the wave. Intrinsic to this technique is working the top dropper on the top of the waves at the very end of the retrieve. It is an effective technique because fish that are following the flies will often take the top dropper fly as it is dibbled by gently lifting the rod.

BELOW: **Wet fly fishing on Rutland Water. This is one of the modern reservoirs that has helped to advance the techniques of wet fly fishing on stillwaters.**

ABOVE: **A Highland loch where the traditional loch-style fishing evolved.**

Fishing Modern Reservoirs

Although traditional loch-style is still widely used the method has been adapted for fishing the lowland reservoirs of England, Wales and Scotland. Instead of just fishing a floating line various densities of sinking lines are used to cover all water depths. Reservoir trout, particularly the rainbows, feed on creatures such as midge larvae and pupae and daphnia – a tiny animal plankton. Daphnia in particular are very sensitive to light, and the sunnier it is the deeper they go. So, in order to catch trout effectively on reservoirs it is important to be able to locate their feeding depth. This is done by fishing a team of wet flies on a sinking line exploring the various levels until takes are forthcoming.

Unless there is obvious activity on the surface the usual method is to start with a fast sinking line such as a Hi-D or a Di-7. Cast out up to 30 yds (27.43 m) in front of the boat, and allow the line to sink before starting the retrieve. By counting down the line can be left longer and longer until the flies hit the bottom, at which point it is obvious that they are working at all depths.

Retrieve rates can be varied from a steady figure-of-eight to a fast strip bringing the flies right up to the boat. At this point it is normal to hang the flies for a few seconds before recasting, because trout will often follow a fly close to the surface before taking, so pulling the line off too quickly will miss these fish. When a take comes it is then a matter of deciding how deep the fish was. If it comes on the first few pulls it is likely that it was close to the bottom, so simply carry on. However, if it was quite close to the boat it could be worth changing to a slower sinking line such as a Wet Cell II or even an Intermediate, especially if the situation repeats itself.

If a hatch of midge takes place and fish can be seen feeding on the surface it is well-worth switching to a floating line. Basically the flies should always be fished at the trout's feeding level – never too deep, never too close to the surface. Although wet flies work from an anchored boat the usual technique is to allow the boat to drift on the breeze – covering a great deal of water and a great many fish. However, in a very strong wind the boat can drift too quickly to fish the flies effectively. In these circumstances a drogue is used.

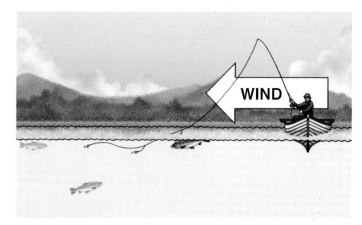

This is an underwater parachute that is towed behind the boat, and its water resistance slows the boat's drift. It is attached halfway along the gunwale, usually by a clamp or a rowlock.

Tackle

Tackle for traditional loch-style fishing includes a medium-actioned rod 10–11 ft (3–3.35 m) long, capable of casting a 6–7 weight line which is usually a floater. Leader length is 10–15 ft (3–4.50 m) of 5–7 lb (2.3–3.2kg) breaking strain nylon. This leader is normally tied with two droppers

spaced 3–4 ft (0.91–1.22 m) apart enabling a team of three flies to be used. For reservoir use the set-up is similar but rods tend to be faster actioned and slightly heavier, especially for sunk-line work. Here a rod of 10–10½ ft (3.05–3.2 m) matched with a 7–8 weight line is the most popular combination. Leaders are normally longer, 12–18 ft (3.66–5.49 m), with the droppers 4–6 ft (1.22–1.83 m) apart, particularly if the water is deep.

Flies include the Silver Invicta, Doobry, Soldier Palmer, Bibio, Peach Palmer, Oakham Orange, Mallard and

ABOVE LEFT: Dibbling the top dropper on a reservoir. Dibbling works best in a breeze when there is a good ripple on the water.

ABOVE: A large brown trout caught fishing a wet fly on a floating line on the Clywedog Reservoir in Wales.

Claret. When constructing a team it is normal to put the slimmer, heavier patterns on the point and middle dropper with the bushier, palmered flies on the top dropper. These bushier flies have more water resistance and work well when dibbled in the surface.

Wet fly fishing from the bank is also effective on lakes, and the basic set-up and flies are similar to those used from a boat. The water is covered by the angler making a cast, retrieving the line then taking a pace. Headlands are usually good places to find fish especially if the wind is blowing across or into them, bringing food within casting distance of the bank. Lure fishing on stillwaters is basically a scaled-up version of modern wet fly fishing. The same floating and sinking lines are used, only they are heavier for casting and retrieving the larger lures.

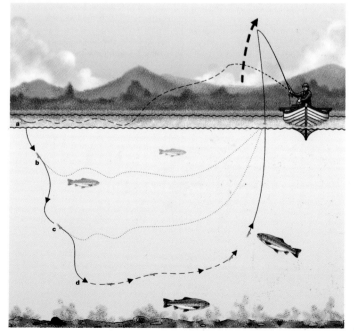

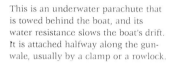

LEFT: The modern style of fishing a team of wet flies on a reservoir designed to find the level of the fish. The angler casts to (a) with a sinking line and then by counting allows the line to sink to various depths (b), (c), and (d), although this technique need not be confined just to three levels. When the flies reach (d) they are drawn up and allowed to hang vertically in the water for a few seconds as trout often follow the flies and take when they are nearing the surface.

Lure Fishing

In most forms of angling, lures refer to spinners, plugs or pirks, but in fly fishing it is the term used for large fly patterns usually tied on size 8 longshank hooks and above. Many lure patterns are very brightly coloured – orange, pink and white are particular favourites, though in contrast the combination of black and fluorescent green is a deadly one, especially during spring and the early summer months. Lure fishing for brown trout and rainbows is usually confined to stillwaters.

ABOVE: The figure-of-eight retrieve.

Lure Fishing on Stillwater

Some anglers regard lures merely as attractors or stimulators of the trout's aggression, but they can play an imitative role too. The most obvious example of this is as fry imitations, patterns designed to suggest coarse fish species such as roach and bream. Trout will often take quite large fish up to 3 in (7.5 cm) or more in length and for an imitation to be effective it must be a similar size to the prey.

Although lures can be fished on heavy wet fly tackle, their large size and air resistance means that they are better fished on specialized rods and lines. Lures may be fished on all densities of line, from floating down to the fastest of sinkers, including Hi-D and Di-7, plus lead core if the fish are in really deep water. Patterns such as floating fry, which imitate a small dying fish hanging in the surface, are best fished on a floater, but other patterns work well fished right down

to the lake bottom. On average, though the most productive depth of water is 8–15 ft (2.44–4.57 m). From the bank 6–10 ft (1.83– 3.05 m) is the optimum depth, but in very hot or cold weather the trout can be much deeper, and some way of reaching this depth of water is needed. If a boat is not an option a reservoir's dam wall is often the place to find the deepest water accessible from the bank and can be the most productive area to fish, both early and late in the season.

From a boat a lure may be fished either at anchor, where the boat is used as a casting platform, or on the drift where it is allowed to follow the wind covering a large area in the search for fish. Drifting may be accomplished either side-on to the wind – similar to loch-style wet fly fishing – or pointing down the wind. Side-on drifting works extremely well when the fish want a slowly moved lure and allows the angler to control

the depth at which it fishes easily. When fish are in the mood to follow right up to the boat it also makes "hanging" the lure possible. This can be a deadly method in which the lure is left to hang static for a number of seconds a few feet below the surface, where this change in pace often entices a following fish into taking.

Drifting with its point down the wind allows the boat to move more quickly, its direction being controlled either by a rudder or a drogue attached to the stern. This technique, often known as Northampton-style, allows two anglers to cast out either side of the boat, letting the line swing round in a large arc before being retrieved. This arc covers a vast area

BELOW LEFT: A reservoir angler chooses another lure from a well-supplied fly box.

BELOW: Reservoir fishing from the bank. Long casting may be necessary.

of water and, by using a fast-sinking line, a large part of the water column can be searched. By using lines of varying sink rates or by counting down before starting the retrieve the lure may be fished at different depths until takes are forthcoming.

As long-distance casting is often necessary from the bank, most lures are fished either on a weight-forward or shooting-head line. The shooting head, constructed from 10–12 yds (9.14–10.97 m) of fly line connected to a shooting line such as braided or plain nylon monofilament, is used where distance is required. In the right conditions this set-up is capable of being cast 40 yds (36.6 m) or more.

Tackle for lure fishing includes a rod 9½–10½ ft (2.9–3.2 m) long capable of casting an 8–10 weight line. Ordinary weight-forward lines may be wound on standard reels designed for 8–10 lines, but for shooting heads a large-diameter model keeps the turns of backing as open as possible and helps prevent tangling.

Retrieve rates should also be varied. In the early season when the water is still cold a slow, steady figure-of-eight retrieve is the most effective. Later in the year when the water has warmed up and the fish are more active a fast strip often works better.

An exception to this is when fishing the Booby, because even during warm weather this buoyant-eyed pattern is most effective when fished extremely slowly, on a fast-sinking line and a 3 ft (0.91 m) leader, along the lake bottom.

Whatever the type of lure, the key is to keep varying the retrieve rate until the effective one has been found. Because of the large size of the flies used, leader strength should be from 6–10 lb (2.72–4.54 kg) breaking strain. Lures may be fished singly or in teams of two or three on a 12–15 ft (3.66–4.57 m) leader with the second pattern on a dropper 4 ft (1.22 m) from the point.

Effective lure patterns include the Cat's Whisker in the original white and fluorescent green plus other colours, the Whiskey Fly, Black Leadhead and the Booby. When trout are taking fry the Deer Hair Fry, Zonker, Minkie and large, white patterns such as a single or tandem Appetiser will catch the most fish.

RIGHT CENTRE: A beautiful silver rainbow caught on a Booby.

RIGHT: Playing a trout on Lough Corrib, the famous trout lough in Ireland, on a fine still day. Conditions do not always have to be perfect for the angler to be successful.

ABOVE: Playing a big trout caught on a lure.

Conservation

Many of the game fish species are under threat. Pressure on our trout and salmon stocks has never been greater. Netting both at sea and in the estuaries depletes the numbers of migratory fish, such as salmon and sea trout, while destruction of habitat and, in particular, spawning sites at the head of salmon rivers, reduces the fish's chance of replenishing its numbers.

Pollution

This also takes its toll. Acid rain, caused by the burning of fossil fuels such as coal and oil, has caused acidification in a number of areas resulting in the lowering of the water's pH. In areas already highly acid, such as peat bogs or coniferous woodland, this can have disastrous results, in some cases rendering the fish unable to breed. This is a real problem both for brown trout and migratory species like the salmon. As a remedy some groups of conservationists and anglers add limestone or powdered lime to the water to increase the alkalinity and make the water more able to support eggs and fry.

Although fly fishers catch a small percentage of any fish population, if they are killed it is still taking away from future breeding stocks. Anglers will often target the larger specimens, and they are thus removing just the fish that are mature enough to reproduce and sustain the numbers. At one time almost all game fish that were caught were killed.

Part of the problem comes from the fact that most game fishing waters in the UK are privately owned. Where salmon and sea trout were concerned the value of a fishery was often gauged by its catch returns, and that meant the number of fish killed. Fortunately an increasing number of fisheries are now beginning to count both killed and returned fish so that there isn't the same incentive for the ghillie to make sure all salmon caught are dispatched to maintain the value of his employer's asset. In fact some are now positively encouraging anglers to return fish to the river or alternatively transport fish caught in spring upstream to the spawning areas. Some rivers operate a strict catch-and-release policy in the early months of the year in an attempt to resurrect the spring run of salmon, and others only allow cock fish to be taken in the autumn, leaving the hens to spawn successfully.

Catch and Release

Today an increasing number of anglers are coming to realize that if

ABOVE: Returning a good brown trout.

they are to have healthy populations of trout and salmon for the future then a more balanced approach is needed. This is catch-and-release fishing. Most of the major game fisheries throughout the world have come to recognize the value of their stocks and now vigorously protect them, making sure that most if not all fish are returned. However, this is only part of the solution because without a concerted effort to conserve spawning areas and prevent habitat destruction, along with the reduction of netting at sea, salmon and sea trout in particular will continue to decline in numbers. Ultimately this has a serious effect on employment and tourism in the sparsely populated north of Scotland in particular.

The decision whether to catch or kill is not as clear-cut as it sounds. On waters with self-sustaining fish populations the argument for catch-and-release is a strong one, but on those where trout are stocked and have no chance of reproducing, releasing the fish once it has been caught does nothing to maintain the species. Indeed the reverse is true, and on small heavily stocked lakes where the natural food supply cannot maintain the biomass of fish they can only lose condition and eventually die of starvation if released.

On the positive side, what catch-and-release also does is instill a greater regard for the quarry. For a fish to be returned unharmed it must be played properly with the correct amount of pressure so that it isn't

LEFT: Bringing a trout to the net on the Kimbridge Water on the River Test, Hampshire. Knotted nets are now illegal.

RIGHT: Returning a brown trout on the River Test. It is important to hold the fish with wet hands facing upstream.

totally exhausted. It must then be held with wet hands, so none of its protective mucus is removed, until its strength returns. In a river, this means holding the fish head into the current so that water flows easily over the gills. In a lake the fish should be supported upright in as deep water as possible. The reason for this is that, especially during the summer, the margins of a lake can become excessively warm and the water deoxygenated. In such an environment a fish is unlikely to recover, and to return it safely it must be returned to the cooler depths where more oxygen is available.

Once the fish is being held upright in the water it should not be released too quickly. Large fish, especially, expend a great deal of energy in the fight and are often exhausted to the extent that they must be properly rested before release. The importance of this rest period cannot be stressed too highly. All too often an angler feels the fish kick and thinking it has recovered, simply lets it go. What happens is that the fish simply heads to the bottom then keels over and dies. Only when the fish has regained its strength and is able to swim off strongly should it be released.

It is also better to keep the fish in the water either by holding it or retaining it in the landing net. Research has shown that when a fish is removed from the water before release its chances of survival are greatly reduced. So if you are not

ABOVE: It is important to return all fish carefully, even undersized trout caught in a wild loch in Scotland.

ABOVE: Many lakes in England have been stocked with rainbows. Here one is being returned carefully.

going to keep a fish, leave it in the water while the hook is being removed. To aid unhooking it is also important to use barbless hooks or hooks with their barbs crushed with pliers. Although hooks treated in this way can result in fish being lost, especially if the line goes slack, it is a small price to pay for ease of unhooking and the reduction in the damage caused to the fish by removing a hook with a barb.

LEFT: Returning a grayling to the water. Grayling are often in poor condition in summer after spawning and are at their best in the autumn.

Flies

Fishing flies fall into two categories: those that are tied to imitate a natural item of the fish's diet and those flies, including nearly all salmon flies, that are intended as attractors, gaudy concoctions that have often caught more fishermen than fish. Fashions in flies change frequently. Twenty or thirty years ago trout flies were tied to mimic the natural insect as closely as possible and salmon flies were works of art with romantic names such as Lady Caroline and Green Highlander. Today patterns of trout flies have become far more standardized, one pattern being used as an imitation of a number of natural insects, while salmon flies are infinitely plainer, and generally more successful.

Wet Flies

Wet flies are designed to sink and often incorporate water-absorbent materials and swept-back wings and hackles to help achieve this. They vary in make up from simple spider patterns to more complicated tying such as the Silver Invicta which has a palmered body hackle and a wing. Although a number are tied to imitate specific insects, either aquatic or terrestrial, the majority are tied as attractors or simply to suggest something alive and edible.

Sooty Olive

This traditional wet fly is a great favourite on the big limestone loughs of Ireland. It imitates the emerging nymphs of the dark lake olives, *Cloeon simile,* which hatch out in prodigious numbers during May and June. It is worth trying on any stillwater where there are hatches of the natural fly.

Zulu

This striking pattern is another traditional stillwater fly and is most effective on either lake or reservoir. It is particularly deadly for wild brown trout and may be fished either on the point or the top dropper of a three fly cast. The Blue Zulu tied with a blue hackle is almost more popular. Use natural seal's fur for the body.

March Brown

The true March Brown, *Rithrogena germanica,* is a fly of freestone rivers. The imitation, with its hare's fur body and subtle shades of brown, is probably even more useful as a general "suggestive" pattern as it resembles different sedges and moths. It works well on either river or lake and used to be a popular salmon fly.

Claret Dabbler

Developed by Donald McClarn for fishing the loughs of Ireland the Dabbler is a great fly to fish as a top dropper fly, and often moves a number of fish even in a big wave. Dabblers are tied in a variety of colours including olive, yellow and fiery brown and are probably taken for sedges by the trout.

Kate MacLaren

The Kate MacLaren is a great fly when lake fishing for brown trout, sea trout and, in its larger sizes, it has taken salmon, too. It is generally fished as a top dropper fly and works especially well when "dibbled" through the tops of waves in rough conditions.

Peach Palmer

With its body of fluorescent peach wool, the Peach Palmer is a modern twist on a traditional wet fly profile. A superb rainbow trout pattern, it is at its best during sunny conditions on a reservoir fished fast on an intermediate or slow-sinking line.

Peter Ross

This is a traditional pattern and is equally effective on river and lake. With its silver and red body and speckled teal wing it resembles a small fish and has caught countless sea trout and wild brown trout. It is slightly less popular now than some years ago.

Gosling

This Irish fly pattern is an imitation of the mayfly, *Ephemera danica,* and is most effective during late May and early June. Although the natural mayfly is yellow the added brightness of a hot orange hackle only makes the Gosling even more deadly.

Doobry

Hailing from the Orkney Isles, the Doobry looks just like a traditional loch fly but was developed quite recently. The design is based on the Zulu with a palmered body and red tag. It is an excellent fly for the top dropper; the black and orange hackles make a great colour combination after rain when the waters of the shallow lochs in the Orkneys are stained with peat.

Oakham Orange

Developed for fishing on Rutland Water, the Oakham Orange is a superb summer fly when the rainbow trout are feeding on daphnia, the tiny plankton that inhabit the lakes and reservoirs of the Midlands. It works well at all depths and can be retrieved at a slow to medium-fast pace. Taff Price's Orange Nymph is another good fly to try when trout are feeding on daphnia.

Dunkeld

This garish fly is a scaled-down version of the fully dressed salmon fly. This version of the Dunkeld is used for trout and sea trout on stillwaters. It is a good general pattern and can be taken as a small fish or sedge pattern. It also works well when the trout are feeding on daphnia when it should be fished quite slowly. It may be tied with a palmered or throat hackle.

Palmered Coch

Based on a traditional imitation of the Coch-y-Bonddu beetle, the Palmered Coch is effective throughout the season especially for wild brown trout. It is at its best fished slowly on a floating line. Although the Coch-y-Bonddu works best during a fall of beetles in June, it will also take fish beneath the surface and is used as an imitation of a number of beetles.

Mallard and Claret

The subtle shades of the body and wing make the Mallard and Claret a great pattern when the sky is overcast. The Grouse and Claret, and Teal and Claret, are similar traditional loch flies that have stood the test of time. It is an effective pattern on both river and lake. It is a popular fly for sea trout at night, although it takes both brown and rainbow trout as well.

Black Pennell

Part of a small range of patterns, including the Claret Pennell. The Black Pennell makes a passable imitation of a midge pupa. It could be held to represent any number of black midges and beetles to be found in stillwaters and many anglers always include a Black Pennell on their cast. This version, with a thicker dubbed body, is an excellent pattern for both sea trout and salmon.

Bibio

An Irish pattern, created by Major Charles Roberts of the Burrishoole Fishery. The Bibio was tied to represent the heather beetle for sea trout fishing. It is now a well-established pattern for lake fishing, effective for brown and rainbow trout. It is a particularly good pattern in the warm weather of August when the natural fly falls on the water.

Kingfisher Butcher

One of a series of patterns including the Silver Butcher and the Bloody Butcher, with its bright-blue tail and orange hackle this is the most colourful of the tribe. It is a favourite fly on Loch Leven, the famous trout loch in Scotland, where Mary, Queen of Scots, was held prisoner. It is a good fly to try when fishing lakes with attractors and resembles a small fish.

Soldier Palmer Muddler

This fly is a hybrid of two classic patterns: the Soldier Palmer, a well-known traditional palmered loch or lake fly that imitated a sedge, and the Muddler Minnow with its deer-hair head, first tied in 1967 by Don Gapen. The combination makes a deadly lake fly for all species, and the Soldier Palmer Muddler is a highly suitable top dropper fly for when there is a good wave.

Teal, Blue and Silver

With its sparkling silver body and slim teal wing the Teal, Blue and Silver bears an uncanny resemblance to a small fish. Along with the Teal and Red, and Teal and Green, it has been a popular fly on Scottish lochs for 200 years. It is a good fly for both lake and river, especially for sea trout, in sizes 8 to 10. It is also effective when blue damsel-flies are on the water.

Claret Bumble

The original bumbles came from Derbyshire and date back to Charles Cotton of *Complete Angler* fame. The modern bumbles were designed by T C Kingsmill Moore for the Irish loughs, and the Golden Olive Bumble and Claret Bumble are the best known. They are effective both for brown trout and sea trout in a good wave. The original blue jay is better as the shoulder hackle.

Silver Invicta

This is the silver-bodied version of James Ogden's classic fly, the Invicta, which has a yellow wool or seal-fur body. The Silver Invicta is a successful lake and reservoir pattern working well throughout the summer. Like the parent fly it is a good imitation of a sedge, or hatching sedge but it is also one to try when trout are taking tiny "pin fry".

Nymphs and Bugs

Nymphs and bugs cover a large group of patterns designed either to give the impression of something alive and potentially edible to the fish or specifically to imitate an aquatic creature such as a shrimp. Others are tied to represent the various stages such as larva, pupa or nymph which make up the life cycles of aquatic insects including midges, damselflies and caddisflies. Many nymph and bug patterns are tied with weighted bodies to help them sink.

Cased Caddis

This heavily weighted pattern imitates a caddis larva complete with its case. It works best fished "dead drift" on rivers or inched slowly along the bottom of a lake. It is a great fly in the early part of the year when trout are low down in the water.

Griffiths' Damsel

Developed by Terry Griffiths, this is a good general representation of an olive damselfly nymph. These are readily taken when the flies are hatching. Fish it with a steady figure-of-eight retrieve on either a floating or intermediate line.

Distressed Damsel

This Charles Jardine pattern is an impressionistic imitation of an olive damselfly nymph. Its long tail of dyed marabou gives it a superb action in the water, and it can be deadly when fished with a steady figure-of-eight retrieve. Opinions differ as to whether trout take the colourful adult fly as well as the nymph, and dressings such as a sunken Camasunary Killer can be effective.

Woolly Worm

This simple bug-looking fly is a good suggestion of something alive and edible. It is best fished slowly along the lake bottom either on an intermediate line or a floating line and a long leader, and may be taken for a caddis larva, damselfly nymphs or leeches. It is a popular fly in the West Country, where it has the reputation for taking large fish. It can be tied in a variety of colours.

Fox Squirrel Nymph

Designed by American fly-tying legend Dave Whitlock, the Fox Squirrel Nymph is a good general pattern and may be taken for a damselfly nymph. Using the fur from a red fox squirrel it works well on either river or lake. In larger sizes it works best when heavily weighted.

Claret Emerger

Emerger patterns, which imitate an aquatic insect as it hatches out at the water's surface, have revolutionized stillwater trout fishing. This Jeremy Herrmann pattern should be fished very slowly just under the surface or allowed to float statically in the surface film.

Mobile Bloodworm

Bright-red chironomid larvae (bloodworms) usually spend their lives concealed in a silt tube. However, when disturbed, they swim with a manic lashing of their body. The soft marabou tail of the Mobile Bloodworm attempts to imitate this movement. They are a staple item in the diet of stillwater trout.

Flash-back Pheasant Tail

The Pheasant Tail Nymph invented by Frank Sawyer is an effective fly in its own right, but add a modern touch of sparkle using pearl plastic tinsel, and you have a deadly variation. The Flash-back Pheasant Tail is effective on both rivers and lakes when the nymphs are hatching.

Ascending Midge Pupa

This imitation of a chironomid midge pupa works well when trout are feeding on the natural, and can be taken at any depth from mid-water to the surface. To imitate the natural pupa it should be fished extremely slowly on the point of a long leader together with a floating line.

Lead Bug

Constructed almost entirely of lead wire, this little fly sinks extremely quickly and is ideal for stalking trout in clear stillwaters. Fished on a floating line and long leader, it should be cast at individual fish and retrieved very slowly. Watch out for takes on the drop.

Stick Fly

Tied to imitate a cased caddis larva, the Stick Fly should be made with an underbody of lead wire to help it sink quickly. A highly competent fly for early to mid season, it works best fished on a floating line and long leader, retrieved slowly along the bottom.

Czech Nymph

This style of nymph has had a huge impact on river fishing for both trout and grayling. It is heavily weighted, sinks very quickly and is fished on a short line in the "rolled nymph" method (see page 220). This is a great fly when the fish are feeding on the bottom and is particularly effective in the autumn. A number of dressings have been evolved to suit this style of fishing. All of them incorporate weight to help them sink.

Longshank Pheasant Tail

The reservoir version of Sawyer's classic Pheasant Tail Nymph, this pattern is tied big on a longshank 8 or 10 hook. The thorax colour may be varied from yellow to orange, green or black. A pearl thoraxed version is particularly good when trout are feeding on pin fry, although the original is a representation of the lake olive nymph. Arthur Cove's version, tied as a buzzer without tails, is a useful stand-by on many lakes.

Prince Nymph
With its peacock herl body this general nymph pattern works well on small lakes and reservoirs. Tied with a weighted underbody it may be fished singly for individual fish or as the point fly of a team of three when it has a chance to sink down in the water.

Shipman's Buzzer
Developed by reservoir expert Dave Shipman, this pattern represents a chironomid midge pupa about to transform into the adult. Greased-up and fished right in the surface film it may be left static, to be intercepted by a cruising trout or retrieved steadily.

Walker's Mayfly Nymph
The late Dick Walker developed this pattern as an imitation of the large pale nymphs of the mayfly, *Ephemera danica*. It works well not only on rivers, where the naturals are to be found, but also on lakes where it is probably taken as a damselfly nymph or hatching sedge. Tied with a heavy lead underbody it is an excellent fly for targeting trout in small clear stillwaters where the individual fish can be spotted.

Montana
Originally an American imitation of a large, dark stonefly nymph, the Montana is now more often used as a general nymph pattern to imitate a number of insects on stillwaters, and is probably taken for a dragonfly nymph. When tied weighted, it is best fished slowly on a floating or intermediate line but it can also work well when retrieved fast with the leader degreased to avoid line wake in calm conditions.

Gold-head Hare's Ear
The Hare's Ear is one of the best traditional representations of the hatching olive nymph. It is normally tied with just a few strands of the hare's fur picked out as the hackle or pale starling wings. Recently fly tiers have added a gold bead at the head of the original dressing, and this glint of gold has been a real attracting magnet for trout and grayling both in rivers and stillwaters.

Classic FM
In this olive version the Classic FM makes a good imitation of a damselfly nymph. Fished on a floating or intermediate line with a slow figure-of-eight retrieve, the marabou tail works superbly and stimulates the movement of the original as it rises to the surface. Even if damselfly nymphs are not hatching this fly gives the impression of something edible and has been used with success on many waters.

Skinny Buzzer
Reservoir trout eat midge pupa in vast numbers. This pattern imitates the profile of the pupa extremely well and, being slim, cuts through the water quickly to go down to the trout's feeding level. As with all buzzer patterns, fish this ultra-slow on a floating line and long leader.

Shrimp
This pattern imitates the small freshwater shrimp, *Gammarus pulex*, which is to be found in large numbers on both rivers and lakes. It is tied with a heavy lead underbody to help it sink quickly and easily and is best fished quite slowly along the bottom.

Dry Flies

Dry flies are intended to float on or in the water's surface. Many, particularly the modern ones, are tied with buoyant or water-repellent materials such as polypropylene, Antron or deer hair to prevent them sinking. A large proportion of dry fly patterns, especially those designed for use on rivers are imitative rather than impressionistic, tied to represent specific aquatic insects such as mayflies, caddisflies and various species of olives.

CDC Caddis
The soft, downy texture of Cul de Canard is perfect for tying the wings of a variety of insect imitations. Here the CDC provides the roof-wing profile of an effective adult caddis pattern that is fished on the surface. Most caddis patterns work best early in the year and are fished on or near the bottom.

Klinkhammer Special
Hans Van Klinken came up with this original-looking and highly effective pattern. Tied parachute-style, where only the hackle and wings float, it was designed to imitate an emerging caddis. It is deadly on rivers for both trout and, particularly, grayling when naturals are hatching.

Shadow Mayfly
This bushy dry fly bears little resemblance to a real mayfly. However, the combination of palmered grizzle hackles for the body and red game hackle points for the wings produces a simple pattern that is extremely effective during a mayfly hatch, when it is often taken rather than more realistic patterns.

Yellow Humpy
A buoyant fly, the Humpy is designed for fishing in turbulent water for it is a superlative floater and is easily visible in rough water. When it is cast upstream it should be allowed to bounce back on the riffle when the trout come at it extremely quickly. A great pattern for freestone trout.

Adams
An American design and probably the most popular dry-fly pattern used by anglers today. The Adams is superb on all types of water, especially on rivers. It is a great general pattern and particularly effective during a hatch of medium olive duns. There is a detailed description of tying this fly on page 246.

Bob's Bits

This simple stillwater dry fly is the brainchild of Bob Worts. With its teased-out seal fur body, the Bob's Bits sits low, right in the surface film and is deadly during a midge hatch when it imitates the hatching insect trying to break through the surface film. It is tied in many colours: red, orange, olive and black.

Sparkle Dun

This is a variation on the Comparadun, a very effective pattern for difficult trout when they are taking duns off the surface. The Sparkle Dun not only has a tail of Antron but also a polypropylene wing to help it to float, and there is no hackle, to ensure the overall profile is as lifelike as possible.

Parachute Grey Duster

The Grey Duster is an immensely popular dry fly on both rain-fed rivers and chalk streams. This is the parachute version where the hackle is wound on a small post on top of the hook. This allows it to fish right in the surface film, emerger-style, imitating the emerging nymph.

Foam Beetle

A simple little pattern tied on a size 16 to 18 hook, the Foam Beetle sits low in the water. It is a great pattern to try on finicky trout either on river or lake. This is definitely one to try when fish are taking small terrestrials in a flat calm, on those evenings when one fish will be a triumph. Fish it very slowly indeed.

Pheasant Tail

A simple, impressionistic fly, the Pheasant Tail is an effective pattern on all types of river. Its overall profile makes it one to try when trout are taking duns, but when it is sparsely dressed and fished right in the surface film. It is an excellent imitation of the olive spinner for the evening rise.

Mayfly Spinner

With its outstretched wings this imitates the spinner of the female mayfly as it lies trapped in the surface film when it has laid its eggs. At this stage it is taken eagerly by trout that, at times, appear as if they have been waiting all day. There are a number of patterns, and it is a good idea to have several available in the fly box. Change the fly if the first pattern does not work.

Blue Damselfly

Although this fly will spend most of its time in the fly box, when trout are taking adult blue damselflies in the summer it is one of the best patterns to try and certainly the most successful. High summer, when the naturals are patrolling the lake margins, is the time to give this a cast and it should be fished to imitate the quick flight of the natural insect.

Red Tag

This is a classic grayling pattern, some 150 years old, and it is particularly effective on rain-fed rivers. It is a great fly for the winter months, when the river is low and clear after the first frosts, and may be tied and fished either dry or wet.

Hare's Ear

Any fly pattern incorporating mottled brown hare's fur is going to be effective. This tying is no exception, working extremely well both as a general pattern and during a hatch of olive duns, particularly in the first months of the year.

CDC Dun

Cul de Canard is a wonderful material for all kinds of dry fly wings, but it is probably most effective for imitations of olive duns. Here it is used for the CDC Dun, a superb pattern for both lake and river. The clipped thorax hackle keeps the pattern as sparse and as realistic as possible, and it is one of the first patterns to try.

Elk-hair Caddis

Al Troth's Elk-hair Caddis is a simple robust imitation of an adult caddis or sedge fly and is effective when used for both. With its buoyant elk-hair wing and palmered body it floats well and may be drifted with the current when fished on a river or twitched to mimic the movement of the natural, fishing in the sedge hatch on lakes.

Claret Hopper

Although called a Hopper this fly has nothing to do with grasshoppers. Instead it is an extremely popular stillwater dry fly that is at its most effective during a hatch of large brown midges. It is tied in a range of colours including claret, orange, olive and black. There are over 400 species of midges $\frac{1}{8}$–$\frac{3}{4}$ in (3–20 mm) long, so the problems of imitation for the angler is obvious. When the trout are feeding on midges it can pay to try a number of different patterns if the first is not accepted.

Royal Wulff

The Wulff series of flies, with their V-shaped hair wings, was invented by the late Lee Wulff, one of the most celebrated American anglers. The Grey Wulff and White Wulff are often used on chalk streams when mayflies are hatching. It is a style of tying incorporated into many patterns, and this – the Royal Wulff – is a version of the classic Royal Coachman and makes a superb general river pattern. The Coachman is said to have been invented by a Royal coachman over 150 years ago and represents a white-winged sedge.

Greenwell's Glory

Originally tied by Canon Greenwell for fishing the River Tweed, on the Scottish–English border, the Greenwell's Glory is still a fine imitation of small- to medium-sized olive duns. It is fished upstream and allowed to drift drag-free with the current. The Greenwell's Nymph is also effective.

Black Gnat

Tied to imitate a specific insect, the *Bibio johannis*, the Black Gnat can be used to suggest a wide variety of small black creatures. It may be tied in a range of hook sizes from 12 down to 22. The smaller sizes are particularly deadly when trout are feeding on tiny black midges or smut (black insects).

Daddy-longlegs (Crane Fly)

This is an imitation of the daddy-longlegs or crane fly, a terrestrial insect most often seen during the cool damp months of autumn. The Daddy has a reputation for enticing the bigger fish and is often used when dapping on lakes and lochs. Otherwise it is recommended that it is fished on a floating line and allowed to lie stationary on the water. There are a number of patterns: the most popular uses knotted pheasant tail fibres to represent the trailing legs of the natural insect.

G&H Sedge

If you need a really buoyant sedge pattern, then this is the one to choose. The G&H Sedge uses spun and clipped deer hair to form the roof-wing profile of the sedge and works equally well on rivers and lakes. In larger sizes it even works for salmon when they can be induced to take a dry fly. Sedges emerge at dusk and on a river can provide the most exciting half hour of the evening rise before darkness falls. They are equally prolific on stillwaters and lochs.

Hairwings

Normally tied on large hooks hairwings include many of the lures and flies used for salmon fishing on rivers and trout fishing on reservoirs. Normally used as a wing, hair is a tough material and works well on patterns designed to fish where the current is strong and would flatten softer feathers. Although some artificial hair is now used, bucktail, stoat and squirrel's tail are the most popular and are available in a wide range of natural and dyed colours.

Goldie

This was developed by Bob Church for big Rutland Water brown trout. The Goldie can be tied either on a single longshank hook or two, in tandem, if a really large lure is need. It is best fished on a fast-sinking line from either a boat or the bank. It is reminiscent of the popular black-and-yellow tubes used for salmon in spring and autumn.

Whiskey Fly

This hot-orange lure is a real killer during the summer months when trout are taking daphnia – a tiny animal plankton. Fish feeding on daphnia will often go mad for orange flies, and the Whiskey Fly fits the bill. It works best when fished quite fast on an intermediate or normal sinking line. Let the line sink before starting the retrieve.

Sweeney Todd

A Dick Walker pattern, the Sweeney Todd is a good early season fly on reservoirs and small stillwaters. The fluorescent magenta aiming point, at the throat, was intended to stimulate the trout into taking the fly near the head, thereby reducing the number of missed takes. It has been one of the most successful lures for many years.

Mickey Finn

This colourful hairwing uses fine mylar tubing to create a sparkling body. It is a popular reservoir pattern for the summer and originated in America. It is at its most effective in the summer months when the water temperatures are high and it is taken by rainbow trout. Like most lures it should be stripped fast through the water.

Woolhead Sculpin

This is a modern imitation of a sculpin or bullhead, a small bottom-dwelling fish most commonly found on rivers. It has a habit of fooling the larger, more predatory trout. The fly is very similar to the Muddler minnow, another imitation of the sculpin.

Blackie

Originally a reservoir lure, the Blackie is also a highly effective fly when sea trout are lying deep. It works best after midnight, fished on a fast-sinking line to get right down to the fish. It is tied either on two hooks in tandem or with a flying treble.

Deer-hair Fry

Trout will often specifically target small coarse fish as they float dying near the surface. This buoyant design, which uses spin and clipped-deer hair for its body, imitates this phenomenon superbly and should be fished almost static on a floating line.

Zonker

The Zonker uses a strip of rabbit fur still on the skin as a highly mobile wing and tail. In its natural grey form it is a fantastic fly to use when trout are feeding on fry. Tied in other colours, such as white, black and pink, it is a fine general lure pattern.

Streamers

For mobility and action there is little to beat feather as a winging material, and streamers and feather-winged patterns are extremely effective on many types of water. Although cock hackles were once the most commonly used material, they have been almost entirely superseded by marabou. This soft, ultra-mobile feather is now used to produce the wings and tails on a large number of patterns for reservoirs and small stillwaters, because combined with a weighted body or head, it provides the fly with an almost irresistible action.

Leprechaun
Devised by Peter Wood the name, not surprisingly, comes from its bright-green colour. An effective pattern during bright summer days when there is a lot of algae in the water.

Muddler Minnow
This is the tying of Don Gapen's original Muddler, created to imitate a small fish. The technique of spinning and clipping a deer-hair head is now used in a range of lures and imitative patterns.

Dawson's Olive
Although basically a lure, the subtle combination of varying shades of olive gives this fly a very natural appearance, and it may be taken as a damselfly nymph or other creature. Fished slowly on a floating or intermediate line it works on all types of stillwater. Watch out for takes on the drop.

Junglecock Viva
The is a scaled-down version of the original Viva, named by its creator after the Vauxhall car. Tied on a double hook and with Junglecock eyes, it is a great point fly for sunk line fishing out of the front of a drifting boat. The action of the boat works the fly and takes fish in all conditions and a variety of waters.

Idiot-proof Nymph
Not a nymph at all, the IPN uses a soft marabou tail plus a weighted Fritz body to deadly effect. It is tied in a wide range of colours, including black, olive, orange and pink, and can be fished on either a sinking line or as a floater with a long leader. Either way it is a lure worth trying for stocked rainbows.

Black Leadhead
A superb pattern on all types of lake and reservoir the Leadhead, with its mobile tail and weighted head with its painted fish eye, produces a ducking/diving action when it is retrieved that trout cannot resist. It can be tied in a range of colours with black, white and orange among the most successful.

Mrs Simpson
This New Zealand pattern uses layers of pheasant body feathers for the sides. It is best fished slow and deep on lakes. It is a passable imitation of a dragonfly nymph and may be taken as such by trout.

Mylar Fry
A good imitation of a fish, the Mylar Fry works well when trout are feeding on tiny roach fry and sticklebacks. It is best to fish this lure slowly on a floating or intermediate line.

Concrete Bowl
This pattern was tied specifically for fishing on large man-made reservoirs, a number of which are simply concrete bowls. Black and green is a deadly colour combination for lake trout, and this lure is no exception.

Medicine Fly
This Hugh Falkus pattern was designed specifically for sea trout on rivers. It is tied light and slim for when the river is running low and clear during the summer. The body may be either fine silver tinsel or just silver paint.

Yellow Booby
Love it or hate it, the Booby is a devastatingly effective pattern when the trout are feeding hard on the bottom. It should be fished on a fast-sinking line with a short leader of about 3 ft (0.91 m) and retrieved very slowly. Boobies are available in a variety of colours all of which can work well including yellow, white, black and green.

Orange Cat's Whisker
The original version of the Cat's Whisker has a white marabou wing and tail plus a fluorescent green body. The profile is now tied in a range of colours and the version illustrated here is the all-orange one. Usually fished on a sinking line the Cat's Whisker is often taken on the drop as the lure descends through the water.

Ace of Spades

This twist on the Black Chenille lure uses a matuka wing capped with bronze mallard to produce a dense profile. The Ace of Spades works well early on in the season, and should be fished slowly along the bottom using a sinking line. It was invented by David Collyer and is effective in dark water.

Black Rubber Legs

The kicking action of the rubber legs is one that stillwater trout find difficult to resist. This pattern is deadly on all types of water. The pattern should be weighted and fished with a twitchy retrieve to accentuate the leg movement on either a floating or intermediate line. This stimulates the fish to take.

Appetizer

Bob Church tied this reservoir pattern back in the early 1970s specifically to imitate roach fry. It proves effective to this day, tied on either a single longshank hook or two in tandem if the trout are taking larger fry. Fish it on a sinking line from either bank or boat, although a slow sinker is best in shallow water.

Haslam

This is a traditional feather-winged pattern that is extremely popular in Wales for both salmon and sea trout. It is normally tied on size 6 and 8 salmon hooks and may be fished on a floating, intermediate or sink-tip line depending on the water conditions and temperature. It works best in the summer.

Minkie

A superb fry imitation, this Dave Barker pattern uses a mobile strip of grey mink fur as its wing. It is most effective when fished slowly, on a sinking line, around weed beds and other areas which hold shoals of coarse fish fry that the trout chase after in summer when the fry have just hatched.

Hairwing Salmon Flies

Old-fashioned salmon flies were tied with many feathers as their wings. They remain objects of great beauty. Nowadays a salmon may be caught on one occasionally, but they are generally just used as a last resort. Modern salmon flies even those based on old patterns, are simpler in design and easier to tie. Many use hairwings as this gives them more life in the water. All should be tied in a variety of different sizes to cope with different water levels.

Hairy Mary

A popular salmon fly similar in colour to the feather-winged Blue Charm. It may be tied on single and double hooks as well as tubes and Waddington shanks. It is a fly that is most often used in the summer when the salmon are taking smaller flies in duller colours fished on the surface with a floating or sink-tip line. It is a good fly for grilse.

Garry Dog

This bright fly is tied either on doubles and trebles or, in larger sizes, on tubes and Waddingtons. On some rivers it is used all the year round but it is generally a fly for the autumn or spring when yellow-and-black and plain yellow colours seem to work best. It is also successful in the evenings when fish will take a fly a size or two larger.

Executioner

This handsome-looking fly, with its flash of red and silver and junglecock cheeks, hails from the River Kent in Cumbria. It was originally tied as a sea-trout fly but it has proved an excellent fly for salmon as well. It works well in the summer and is usually tied on smaller-sized hooks. Fish the Executioner on a floating or sink-tip line.

Stoat's Tail

This all-black fly with just a hint of sparkle is probably the most popular salmon fly of all. It may be tied on single, double and treble hooks, and if a particularly large fly is required, on either a tube or Waddington shank. In its smaller sizes it is also very good for sea trout. A Silver Stoat's Tail with a silver body and black wing is also good.

Willie Gunn

This is a superb fly for either spring or autumn salmon fishing and may be tied on either tubes or Waddington shanks. The most effective sizes are from 1¹⁄₂–3¹⁄₂ in (4–7.5 cm) long. It is made up of yellow, orange and black hair tied on top of each other, often on a copper tube when a sinking fly is required.

Mini Tube

When the water is clear and low, salmon often respond best to tiny patterns. A Mini Tube should be fished on a floating line and is a fly for summer fishing. It may be tied in a range of colours, although blue and black are the most useful and it can be very small indeed. It may be difficult to get small enough trebles.

Ally's Shrimp

This versatile pattern was developed by Alastair Gowans, one of the best salmon anglers, and is one of the most popular salmon flies in use today. It works right through the season in various water conditions. Its long-tail style is said to imitate the natural shrimp of the sea and has now been copied in a number of other patterns.

Munro Killer

An extremely popular salmon pattern, the Munro Killer has an ultra-long wing of mixed bucktail to give it plenty of fish-attracting movement. It is a highly effective fly throughout the season and particularly in the autumn when the leaves are turning colour and salmon seem to prefer orange-coloured flies.

Baits

There are a number of ways of catching game fish other than with a fly. When water conditions dictate, the use of artificial baits such as spinners and plugs or even natural ones, including worms and prawns is perfectly legitimate, depending on the regulations that apply to the water you are fishing. A number of salmon rivers may be "fly only" or fly only during certain months of the year, and similar restrictions may apply to trout lakes and reservoirs. Although frowned upon by some, bait fishing for trout and salmon does work. In ordinary water conditions it can sometimes be very effective. However, when the river is high and coloured and fish are not responding to a spinner, let alone a fly, it can be the only method of catching fish.

ABOVE: Large salmon flies have much in common with minnows.

Natural Baits

If you are fishing on a river that permits the use of baits either all the year round or when certain water conditions prevail, then there are two main natural baits to try.

Worms

Although various baits can be used, including maggots and more natural ones such as caddis grubs, the two most popular are worms and shrimps.

Worms are effective for trout, grayling, sea trout and salmon. For trout and grayling a single worm or a bunch of small worms, such as brandlings or gilt tails, is perfect. However, for sea trout and salmon the use of two or more large lobworms is usually more effective. They can either be fished with a spinning rod with the aid of a bubble float, if allowed, or cast gently upstream with a fly rod and allowed to rumble down the river bed.

Shrimps and Prawns

These are the saltwater variety of baits preserved and dyed various colours such as red and purple. Shrimps can be extremely deadly, and on a number of rivers their use is prohibited. They also have the reputation of causing a strong reaction in the salmon. Either they take it forcefully or are unsettled by them and bolt out of their lie, so many anglers frown upon the use of shrimps. However, in big heavy water the much larger prawn can sometimes prove the only method of catching a fish so, where allowed, it is a worthwhile method in difficult conditions. Both are prepared in similar ways. First they are straightened and a sharp-eyed needle is inserted through from head to tail. Then the hook is attached and the whole thing bound with elasticated thread to keep it together.

Artificial Baits

Artificial baits for salmon and trout consist of a large variety of spinners and spoons. Some are more popular than others.

Rubber Tails

Rubber Tails, or Flying Condoms as they are less politely known, have taken salmon spinning by storm and in their various colour combinations are now the most widely used

LEFT: A successful angler nets a small salmon caught on a spinner.

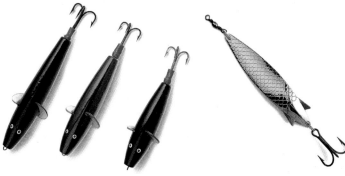

Minnows in various sizes

Toby

Rapala sinking lure

spinners in the UK. They come in a variety of types with either a plain or beaten metal blade or with a small revolving minnow at the front. Whichever type, they all have one thing in common: a soft vibrating rubber tail which salmon find irresistible. Rubber tails come in a choice of weights from 7–20 g and in a variety of colours, such as red and gold, red and silver, black and gold, and yellow and gold.

Toby

Once the most commonly used spinner for salmon, it is manufactured by a Swedish tackle company and produced in a range of sizes, weights and colours. Copper, silver and gold are particular favourites although a zebra pattern and the multi-coloured Toby Flash are also very effective. For heavier water there is also the Toby Salmo range, a broader, heavier spinner at 30 g, as well as a super-lightweight version available only in blue and silver at 8 g for use in summer conditions.

Devon Minnows With the profile of a small fish, the aptly named Devon Minnow is a great favourite among salmon anglers. Devons come in a wide range of sizes and colour combinations. Black and gold, blue and silver, and brown and gold are particularly effective, the darker colour always being on the minnow's back. They are available in sizes ranging from 2–3^1/$_2$ in (5–8.9 cm) and in weights from 8 to 20 g.

The closely related quill minnow, being much lighter than the Devon, is most effective in clearer, slower-moving water. Here the lightness of the minnow works superbly even in the reduced flow rate and is ideal for

catching trout and sea trout when the river is low.

Rapalas

Various models of Rapala are becoming increasingly popular for salmon fishing. Their darting action makes them much more lifelike in the water than the traditional Devon Minnow although they are considerably more expensive. The most popular models in the range are the Original Floating and the Countdown in blue, gold and brown although the newer Husky Jerk with its superb action and built-in rattle has become extremely well-liked.

ABOVE: **A fine fresh spring salmon taken on a Devon minnow.**

In larger sizes the diving action of the Countdown, the Shad Rap and the Husky Jerk makes them extremely effective when trolling on big lakes for salmon and brown trout, particularly in the early months of the year.

Mepps

For spinning in clear, shallow water there is little to beat the Mepps. In its smaller sizes it works well for trout and in larger sizes for trout and salmon. With their weighted body and revolving metal blade Mepps come in sizes ranging from the tiny size 0, which can only be cast without extra weight on the lightest of rods, up to size 5 which is more than adequate for salmon.

Weights

Not all spinners and baits are heavy enough to be cast without extra weight. Split shot or drilled bullets are commonly used for bait fishing; it is easier to fish them in the rocky, tackle-hungry pockets where fish hold. For spinning more specialized weights, the Hillman Anti-Kink Lead and the Wye Lead are often used. Remember though to use lead-free weights.

Swivels

When using any type of spinner it is important always to use at least one swivel to prevent the line from twisting. While ordinary barrel swivels are perfectly adequate for salmon fishing or when trolling for large brown trout, ball-bearing swivels are far better. Although more expensive the advantages of ball-bearing swivels over the standard type are that they are not only extremely strong, but they are able to revolve even under the pressure exerted by a big fish.

Fly Tying

Tying threads

While all the flies you will ever need can be purchased, there is something extremely satisfying about catching a fish on a fly that you tied yourself. On a practical level the ability to tie flies enables old favourites or new patterns to be created with a specific hatch or set of conditions in mind. This not only brings the angler one step closer to understanding how fish behave, but it also contributes to the evolution of fly tying.

Tools

For many experienced fly fishers the ability to tie flies and to fish go hand in hand. And even for the novice, with a little practice and a bit of practical advice, the ability to tie simple but effective flies is only a short time away. The first step is to select the right equipment.

Vice

The most important tool of all is the vice. This fits on the tying bench and grips the hook firmly between metal jaws, allowing the tyer enough room to apply all the various materials. When choosing a vice it is vital to ensure that the jaws really can grip both large and small hooks securely. Rather than choosing the cheapest vice, go for something reasonably priced instead. Preferably it will be a lever-operated model that allows the tyer to exert the right amount of pressure by depressing a cammed lever to the rear of the vice.

Fly-tying vice

Scissors

At least one pair of sharp fine-pointed scissors is needed both to prepare materials and to trim off any excess or wayward fibres. It is better to have two pairs, however. The first can be used for cutting tinsel or other tough materials, such as wool or quill, while the other can be kept for trimming hackle fibres etc.

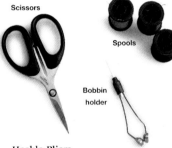

Scissors

Spools

Bobbin holder

Hackle Pliers

This small sprung-wire tool grips hackles and other fine materials between its jaws, allowing them to be wound easily without being damaged by the fingers. Make sure that the hackle pliers you choose have rubber-covered jaws to prevent them cutting delicate hackles.

Bobbin Holder

The bobbin holder helps the tyer apply the tying thread, while keeping waste to a minimum. It also provides additional weight which allows the thread to be left hanging while still retaining enough tension. This prevents the materials already applied from unravelling. Always choose a spigot bobbin holder, preferably one with a ceramic tube. The ceramic is extremely hard and smooth, and never damages the thread, unlike the old-fashioned metal ones.

Whip-finish Tool

With its sprung metal arms, the whip-finish tool is a great help to those who find the task of whip finishing – completing a fly – difficult merely using the fingers.

Dubbing Needle

This simple little tool is used for teasing out dubbing materials, freeing any trapped fibres, hairs or feathers and applying varnish.

Materials

Next come the materials, all the furs, feathers and other bits and pieces which actually make up the various fly patterns. Not surprisingly the selection is vast. However, when beginning fly tying it is better to choose just a few of the most popular materials and get used to using those before becoming more adventurous.

Tying Thread

This is the fine, strong thread which holds the fly together. Originally natural silk was used, but today man-made rot-proof products, such as nylon, are the most popular. Tying thread comes in a wide range of colours, although black, brown and olive are the most used.

Tinsels

Tinsel

Tinsel provides a fly with sparkle and comes either in a flat strip, as a round thread or as a wire. Once metal, modern tinsels are either coated or

Chenille

made from plastic to prevent tarnishing. Silver and gold are the traditional colours but pearl lurex is very popular in modern patterns.

Wool

With its coarse texture wool is ideal for winding or for teasing out and dubbing on to create a chunky body. It can also be used for tails. Wool comes in a wide range of colours, both plain and fluorescent.

Olive cock cape

Natural and dyed cock capes and saddle patches

Chenille

French for "caterpillar", chenille certainly has a worm-like appearance and is usually wound along the hook to create a dense succulent body. It comes in a wide range of colours and diameters, and can be used for lures right down to small nymphs.

Cock Hackles

These feathers come from the neck of a domestic chicken and are used for tails, wings and, most commonly, for the hackles of wet and dry flies. Cock hackles come in a wide range of natural and dyed colours.

Marabou

This downy feather comes from a domestic turkey and is available in plain white plus a whole range of dyed colours, including fluorescents; however white, black and olive are the most popular. The texture of the marabou gives it a superb pulsing action and it is used widely in tying reservoir lures and tadpoles.

Coral marabou feathers and Superfloss

Marabou feathers

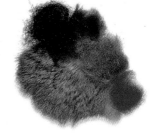

Hare's fur and dubbing materials

Dubbing

Many furs, such as hare, rabbit and seal, are used for dubbing. They come in a vast range of natural, dyed and blended colours and may be used for the bodies of wet flies, dry flies and nymphs. Man-made products, such as Antron and polypropylene, are also widely used, particularly for dry flies.

Floss

Floss is available in a wide range of colours and is normally wound along a hook to a create slim, tapered body. Silk was the original material but rayon, which winds flat and smooth, is very popular today. Recently, stretchable products have become more widely used.

Feather Fibre

Many types of feather, such as pheasant tail, ostrich and goose quills, are used either plain or dyed to create soft, natural-looking bodies in a variety of nymph and dry-fly patterns. Sections of wing quills from either the mallard duck or starling are also used for the wings of wet and dry flies.

Hooks

Fly hooks come in a range of sizes and types from the minute size 24 for tying the smallest of dry flies right up to 3 in (7.5 cm) Waddingtons used for salmon. Between these two extremes the most popular hook patterns for trout and grayling flies include round bend wet fly in sizes 10–16, lightweight dry fly in sizes 12–18 and longshank hooks in sizes 4–12. For salmon the hooks are larger, from size 4–10, and these can be either singles, doubles or trebles. If a really big fly is needed a tube or a Waddington shank combined with a treble hook allows flies up to 3 in (7.5 cm) or more to be created.

Getting Started

Once you have obtained a good range of tools and materials it is time to put them to use. Before getting to grips with all the intricacies of tying flies it is a good idea to learn a few simple techniques such as how to fix the hook in the vice and how to start off the tying thread. Also, what is often forgotten at this stage but is extremely important, is how to finish a fly off securely. There is little point going to all the effort of tying a fly if, after you have added all the materials, you cannot stop the thread unravelling and the fly falling to pieces.

Fixing the Hook in the Vice

The first step when tying a fly is to fix the hook in the vice. The object is to secure the hook so that it doesn't move as you wind the thread but there is enough of it showing to allow easy application of the materials.

Most fly-tying vices have jaws where the gap can be altered by turning a knurled wheel just in front of the lever. This allows various sizes of hooks to be gripped securely. To fix the hook, insert the bend of the hook in the jaws and depress the lever firmly with the free hand. If after depressing the lever fully the hook is still loose, turn the wheel so that the gap decreases slightly. Adjust the gap a little at a time until it is small enough so that the jaws grip the hook firmly when the lever is fully depressed.

Once the gap is adjusted correctly it is time to position the hook. There are various ways of doing this but the best is to have just the bend of the hook gripped by the jaws with all of the shank and the point of the hook showing. Some fly tyers advise having the point of the hook masked by the jaws to prevent it snagging the tying thread and breaking it while you are tying. This can happen and it is a nuisance when it does, but masking can damage the hook which is more serious, and it is better to have as much of the hook showing as possible as this makes it easier to tie in all the materials you need.

1 Offer the hook up to the jaws and see if it fits, so that the hook is held firmly in the vice.

2 If the gap is incorrect adjust the jaws with the knurled wheel until it is slightly greater than the thickness of the hook.

3 Depress the lever fully to grip the hook firmly. If necessary you can loosen the jaws slightly to adjust the hook's position.

4 Ensure that the shank of the hook is horizontal and only the bend is masked. You can then apply the materials more easily.

The Whip Finish

With the tying thread in place you are now almost ready to tie a fly. But first you must learn how to finish off. It may sound back-to-front but without learning how to finish off a fly securely all your efforts will be wasted – your creation will simply fall to bits when being cast.

The best and most secure way of accomplishing this is with a whip finish. Here the thread is wound over itself to form a loop which is drawn tight, thus holding the loose end of the thread secure. Either fingers or a special whip-finish tool can be used to create a whip finish. Here a tool has been used since it is the most commonly employed method, especially for novices.

The whip finish is normally made once all the materials have been added and a small head formed. However for ease of illustration the sequence uses a bare hook and floss rather than normal tying thread.

Starting the Tying Thread

With the hook fixed firmly in the vice and in the correct position it is time to apply the tying thread. Tying thread is used to hold all the other materials in place so it is the first thing to be fixed to the hook. Tying thread is normally run on at the hook's eye and then taken down the shank where the first materials are caught in and secured at the tail of the fly.

The method is to loop the tying thread over the shank and, while holding the loose end taut, wind the other end of the thread over it and the hook shank. This puts the thread under friction and secures the loose end in place. It is important to prevent the thread slipping off as you wind it in. It sounds quite easy but it can be a little tricky for the beginner so this is a technique worth practising. To help illustrate the correct procedure thicker floss which is more visible, rather than tying thread, has been used to illustrate this sequence.

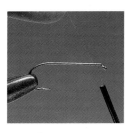 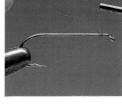 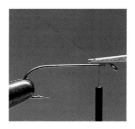 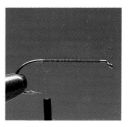

1 Loop the tying thread over the shank holding the loose end of the thread above with the thumb and forefinger of your left hand and the bobbin end, which will be wound round the hook, below in your right.

2 Holding the thread taut using a bobbin holder, begin to wind the thread down the shank so that it covers the loose end. Five or six turns will be enough to prevent the thread from unravelling from the hook.

3 Cut away the excess loose end with sharp scissors before continuing to wind the thread down to the bend of the hook. Some tyers apply a dab of clear varnish to the hook to help to hold the fly together.

4 Wind the thread down the shank to a position opposite the hook point. Ensure that the thread turns are closely butted and flat so they form an even base for the materials that are to follow them.

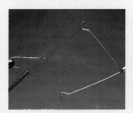  

1 Assuming the fly has been completed, take hold of the tying thread and loop it over both hooks of the whip-finishing tool so that it makes a triangle.

2 Flip the tool over. This will form one turn of the whip finish and make one turn of the loose end of the tying thread on the hook.

3 Repeat the process four or five times adding an extra turn of the loop over the loose end every time. This will create a firm whip finish.

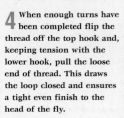 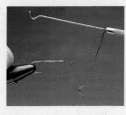 

4 When enough turns have been completed flip the thread off the top hook and, keeping tension with the lower hook, pull the loose end of thread. This draws the loop closed and ensures a tight even finish to the head of the fly.

5 Finally, remove the lower hook and pull the thread tight. The head of the fly can now be varnished to prevent the thread wearing. Some of the following fly patterns have coloured heads.

Tying Sequences

Nymph: Pheasant Tail Nymph

The Pheasant Tail Nymph is a traditional nymph pattern invented by Frank Sawyer on the Hampshire Avon and is effective on both rivers and lakes. It can be tied in a variety of sizes to suggest a wide range of small invertebrates. This version differs from the original, having a hare's-fur thorax instead of plain pheasant tail fibres.

This pattern demonstrates how to tie a feather fibre body, build a simple thorax common to all nymphs and rib the body of a fly.

Hook: **size 16 wet fly–size 8 longshank**
Tying Thread: **brown**
Tail: **cock pheasant tail fibres**
Rib: **copper wire**
Body: **cock pheasant tail fibres**
Thorax cover: **cock pheasant tail fibres**
Thorax: **hare's fur over copper wire**

1 Fix the hook in the vice, catch in the tying thread and run the tying thread down the hook shank to a point opposite the barb.

2 Select four well-coloured cock pheasant tail fibres and catch them in so that the tips project past the bend to form the tail.

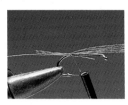

3 At the same point catch in 2 in (5 cm) of fine copper wire. This will form the rib. Secure this with the tying thread.

4 Wind the tying thread back up the shank towards the eye in neat touching turns. Stop two-thirds of the way along.

5 Take hold of the pheasant tail fibres and now wind them over the shank in close turns so that there are no gaps. Secure the ends with the thread.

6 Wind the copper wire over the body in four or five open, evenly spaced turns. These should be wound in the opposite spiral to the pheasant tail.

7 Secure the end of the rib before cutting away the excess feather. Then, catch in another slip of pheasant tail fibres just where the body ends.

8 Wind the end of the copper wire over the remaining shank building a distinct lump. This both forms the thorax and adds extra weight to the fly.

9 Wax the tying thread then take a pinch of hare's fur and dub it with a finger-and-thumb twist on to the tying thread. You only need a little.

10 Wind the dubbed fur over the copper wire to form the thorax of the nymph. Allow plenty of hairs to stick out. These mimic a real nymph's legs.

11 With the thread just behind the eye draw the pheasant tail fibres over the back of the thorax and secure them in place with the thread.

12 Remove the excess feather and build up a small head. Complete the fly with a whip finish and secure the head with a drop of varnish.

Hackled Dry Fly: Red Tag

A simple but deadly pattern, the Red Tag is a great favourite with many anglers fishing for trout and grayling. It is the traditional fly to use for grayling in the winter. It can be fished either wet or dry but the latter method is most commonly used.

This tying sequence illustrates how to tie in a wool tail, a peacock herl body which is used in a number of dressings and a collar hackle common to the majority of dry flies.

Hook: **size 12–18 light wire dry fly**
Tying Thread: **brown**
Tail: **red wool**
Body: **peacock herl**
Hackle: **natural red game cock**

1 Fix the hook in the vice and run the tying thread on down to the bend in touching turns, creating a solid base for the body. Cut away the excess tying thread.

2 At the bend, catch in a tuft of red wool to form the tag. Position the wool on the top of the hook and allow the waste end of the wool to lie along the hook shank.

3 Select three or four strands of peacock herl and catch them in at the base of the tail. Secure the waste ends along the shank, winding the tying thread back up the hook.

4 Twist the peacock herls together and wind the rope over the shank to form the body. The herl on the peacock fibre will stand out to form the body. Tie them in at the head.

5 Trim off the excess herl and select a natural red game cock hackle with fibres slightly longer than the hook gape. (A natural red game hackle is actually brown.)

6 Remove any broken or downy fibres from the hackle base and catch it in just behind the eye leaving a short section of bare stem. Make certain it is secured properly.

7 Take hold of the hackle tip with a pair of hackle pliers and wind on three or four full turns to form the collar hackle at the head of the fly. This is the way to put on all hackles used when tying dry flies.

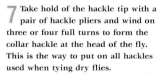

8 Secure the hackle point with the tying thread before removing the excess. Build a small neat head and complete the fly with a whip finish and a dab of clear varnish. Trim the red tag at the tail if necessary.

Winged Dry Fly: Adams

The Adams, which is an American pattern, is probably the most popular dry fly pattern in use today. Although it imitates no particular insect, the use of mixed red game and grizzle hackles produces a superb impression of a natural olive making the Adams highly effective especially during a hatch of olive duns.

The sequence shows how to tie a hackle fibre tail, hackle point wings and a mixed collar hackle.

Hook: **size 12–22 light wire dry fly**
Tying Thread: **black**
Tail: **mixed natural red game and grizzle cock hackle fibres**
Body: **muskrat or grey rabbit**
Hackle: **mixed natural red game and grizzle cock hackles**
Wing: **grizzle hackle points**

1 Fix the hook in the vice jaws and run the thread down to the bend. Catch in natural red and grizzle cock hackle fibres at the tail. Slip one turn of the thread under the tail to cock it.

2 Select two well-marked grizzle cock hackles. They should be of equal size and with no broken fibres. Wider feathers further up the cape are the best.

3 Having taken the thread close to the eye, strip the hackle fibres from the stems to leave two short tips. These should be slightly longer than the hook shank.

4 With the hackle tips placed together, curves apart, catch them in with the tying thread over the bare stems. Make sure that the feathers lie on top of the hook shank.

5 Lift the feather tips to the vertical. Run the tying thread around their base to secure them in place. Extra turns behind the tips will ensure that they stay in the correct position on the hook.

6 To ensure that the tips stay slightly apart draw the bare stems back between them and secure them along the hook shank. This also makes doubly sure that the tips stay in position.

7 Take the thread down to the tail. Take a pinch of muskrat or grey rabbit fur and apply it to the thread. Using a gentle finger-and-thumb twist, dub it on to the thread. It can help to apply wax to the thread.

8 Having created a fluffy, tapering rope, wind it up over the shank in close turns. Stop just short of the wings to leave enough room for the hackles that have to be wound on to the fly last of all.

9 Select two well-coloured cock hackles – one of natural red game, the other of grizzle. Ensure that they have the same fibre length and that they are not damaged in any way.

10 Remove any soft, downy material from the base of both hackles to leave a short section of bare stem. Use this bare section to catch in the hackles at the base of the wings.

11 Keeping both hackles together grasp the tips with a pair of hackle pliers. Carefully, so the feathers don't separate, wind them first behind, then in front of the wings.

12 Secure the tips of the hackles at the eye before removing the waste. Build a small neat head, and then complete the fly with a whip finish and a dab of varnish as before.

Winged Wet Fly: Invicta

The Invicta is a classic winged wet fly and is most effective during the summer months on lakes and rivers. Tied large it makes a good sea-trout pattern for loch fishing but it is at its best when used for brown and rainbow trout on reservoirs and lakes. It is especially successful during a hatch of sedge flies as it is an excellent imitation of hatching sedge pupa.

This pattern illustrates how to tie a dubbed body, a palmered hackle and a wet fly wing.

Hook: **size 14–8 medium-weight wet fly**
Tying Thread: **brown**
Tail: **golden pheasant topping**
Rib: **fine oval gold tinsel**
Body: **yellow seal fur or substitute**
Body Hackle: **red game cock hackle**
Throat Hackle: **blue jay**
Wing: **hen pheasant centre tail**

1 After fixing the hook in the vice run the tying thread to a point opposite the barb. There, catch in a golden pheasant crest feather plus 2 in (5 cm) of fine gold tinsel.

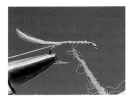

2 Take a pinch of yellow seal's fur or a man-made substitute such as Antron. Dub it on to the tying thread with a simple finger-and-thumb twist. This will form the body of the fly.

3 Add the fur thinly to create a fine but fluffy rope. That done, wind the rope along the shank towards the eye. Ensure that there are no gaps and that the effect is even.

4 Once the body has been wound select a natural red game cock hackle with fibres slightly longer than the gape of the hook. Judge this by bending the hackle against the hook as shown.

5 Prepare the hackle by stripping off any down or broken fibres from the base to leave a short section of bare hackle stem. Catch this hackle in just behind the eye of the hook holding it securely in place.

6 Take hold of the hackle tip with the pliers. Wind the hackle towards the tail in open, even turns. Ensure that no fibres are trapped. This technique is called palmering and is used on many traditional patterns.

7 Once this body hackle has been wound to the base of the tail take hold of the fine gold tinsel and make one turn over the hackle tip holding it in place. Make sure the tinsel is flat and without kinks.

8 Continue winding the gold tinsel up over both the body and hackle towards the eye. The turns should be evenly spaced and are intended to lock the hackle turns in place. It is easier to do than it appears.

9 Secure the rib at the eye with thread turns before removing the excess tinsel and feather. Take a pinch of blue jay and catch it in under the body as a throat hackle.

10 Take a slip of golden pheasant centre tail three times the width of the intended wing. Fold one edge to the centre of the slip then fold it in half to form the wing.

11 Offer the wing up to the hook and secure it in position with thread wraps. The first turns of thread should pull directly downwards to prevent the wing from twisting.

12 Remove the excess feather before building a neat head and casting off the thread with a whip finish. Complete with a drop of clear varnish to the head.

Hairwing: Garry Dog

This brightly coloured hairwing salmon fly is one of the most popular patterns and on some rivers is fished right through the year. It may be tied, as here, on a double hook or on a single or treble. It is even tied, when a very large fly is needed, as a tube fly or Waddington up to 3 in (7.5 cm) in length.

The sequence shows the methods for tying a golden pheasant crest tail, a floss body, a throat hackle and the basic hair wing. This is used in many salmon flies.

Hook: **sizes 10–4 1–3 in (2.5–7.5 cm)**
Waddington shank or tube
Tying Thread: **black**
Tip: **round silver tinsel and yellow floss**
Tail: **golden pheasant topping**
Rib: **oval silver tinsel** Body: **black floss**
Hackle: **dyed blue guinea fowl**
Wing: **dyed yellow hair with a little
dyed red hair underneath**

1 After fixing the hook in the vice, by one point only, run the tying thread down to a position opposite the barb. Catch in 2 in (5 cm) of fine round silver tinsel.

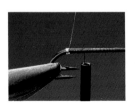

3 In front of the tip catch in 2 in (5 cm) of golden yellow floss. Wind on three turns ensuring each is flat and that there are no gaps. Secure the loose end and remove the excess.

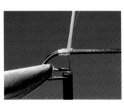

4 Select a well-coloured golden pheasant crest feather. Choose one with a nice curve and no twists. Catch it in as a tail allowing the waste ends to lie along the shank as shown.

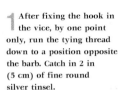

2 Take hold of the tinsel and wind it for three close-touching turns to create the tip. Secure the loose end of the tinsel with thread wraps and remove the excess.

5 At the front of the tail catch in 3 in (7.5 cm) of oval silver tinsel leaving the waste end along the shank. Wind the tying thread to a point just behind the eye and catch in 6 in (15 cm) of black floss.

6 Take hold of the floss and begin to wind it down the shank. Allowing the floss to flatten as it is wound will help create a smooth body. Continue winding the floss to the base of the tail.

7 Once the tail has been reached begin to wind the floss back to its catching-in point. Wind the floss so that each turn overlaps slightly to create a tapered effect over the body of the fly.

8 Secure the loose end of the floss at the catching-in point and remove the excess. Take hold of the oval silver tinsel and wind on five evenly spaced turns to make the rib. This can be done using hackle pliers.

9 Take a dyed-blue guinea fowl feather and tear off a bunch of fibres. Ensuring that the tips are level, catch the fibres in beneath the hook so that they fall just short of the hook points.

10 Remove the butts of the hackle and take a bunch of dyed yellow hair and a second smaller bunch of dyed red hair. Place them together so that the tips are in line, red beneath yellow.

11 Estimate the wing length. It should be just longer than the hook. Cut the butts of the wing to size and catch the prepared wing on top of the shank just behind the eye.

12 Secure the hair in place with tight thread turns. Build a small neat head, completing with a whip finish. Finally, add a coat of black varnish to the head to finish the fly.

Featherwing: Olive Goldhead

The Olive Goldhead is often a deadly pattern for stillwater trout. The use of soft mobile marabou for the tail produces a sinuous effect in the water that trout find difficult to resist. Although tied in olive in this sequence, patterns of this type may be produced in a whole range of colours, from black to yellow, to white and orange, whatever you want to create.

The sequence shows how to apply a gold bead and to tie a marabou tail, a chenille body and a partridge hackle.

Hook: **size 12–8 medium weight wet fly**
Tying Thread: **olive**
Tail: **dyed olive marabou**
Rib: **fine oval gold tinsel**
Body: **olive chenille**
Hackle: **dyed olive partridge**
Head: **3 mm gold bead**

1 Before fixing the hook in the vice, slip a 3 mm gold bead over the point. Push the bead up to the eye and wind on turns of fine lead wire to form a short underbody.

2 Run on the tying thread just behind the bead and use it to secure the lead wire in place. As a further precaution a drop of strong glue may be added to the turns of lead.

3 Take a plume of dyed olive marabou and tear off a generous pinch of the fibres. Ensure that all the tips are in line. Any which are not can simply be pinched off.

4 Run the tying thread down the shank to a point opposite the barb. Offer up the tuft of marabou, catching it in as a tail with tight turns of thread.

5 The short gap in the underbody allows the tail butts to be attached without creating unnecessary bulk. That done, catch in 3 in (7.5 cm) of fine gold tinsel at the base of the tail.

6 Take 2 in (5 cm) of olive chenille. With the tips of a pair of scissors gently remove the herl from a short section of the core of the chenille. Catch the chenille in by this bare core at the tail.

7 Wind the tying thread up to the rear of the gold bead. Then, taking hold of the end of the chenille with a pair of hackle pliers, wind it, too, up to the bead in touching turns as shown.

8 Secure the loose end of the chenille with a few turns of thread before removing the excess. That done, wind the gold tinsel up to the bead in three or four evenly spaced turns up the body of the fly.

9 Select a dyed olive, grey partridge body hackle. Choose one with fibres approximately twice the length of the hook gape. Make sure the feather has no broken fibres.

10 As the partridge feather has a thick stem it must be caught in by its tip. Stroke the fibre back away from the tip and catch it in just behind the gold bead.

11 Grasp the end of the partridge hackle with a pair of hackle pliers. Make only two full turns – the effect should be quite sparse. Don't wind in to the thick stem.

12 Secure the loose end of the hackle with turns of thread and remove the excess. Finally cast off the thread using a whip finish at the back of the bead to complete the fly.

Tying Knots

The knots below illustrate a variety that are commonly used by coarse, sea and game anglers. Beginners should practise first with string since this is easier to handle than nylon.

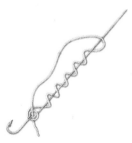   

Mahseer Knot
This knot is well used among specimen anglers and in particular, those travelling abroad. As the name suggests, it was originally used by Mahseer anglers in the giant fast-flowing Indian rivers. A good all-round knot for tying hooks to line, swivels or joining two lengths of line together.

Palomar Knot
This is a popular knot for many anglers, especially among carp anglers who often use this knot when tying hooks on to braid rather than nylon. The knot causes the minimum strangulation and is therefore kinder to lines, particularly braid lines which can part if too much friction is applied.

Four-turn Water Knot
The water knot is well used by coarse, sea and game anglers and offers a good, strong, reliable knot for joining two lengths of line together. In game fishing circles it is widely used for creating droppers when fishing a team of flies, while the coarse angler will often use it to create a paternoster link.

Five-turn Sliding Stop Knot
A stop knot can be created from heavier line or coloured power gum, to act as a marker when distance fishing. Its most common use though is as a stop when float fishing in deeper water. Tied on the line above the float at a set depth, it stops the float sliding any higher up the line.

Uni Knot
This knot is extremely versatile and has a good following among anglers who prefer to use braided mainlines. It is used by sea anglers where the tying of large hooks to heavy-duty line is required. It is also a good knot to use with standard mono lines and offers a great strength when used for tying on hooks.

Double or Full Blood Knot
Most commonly used for joining two lines together. A good knot for the coarse angler who needs a knot to join a lower breaking strain hooklength line to the mainline. As it is a strangulation knot it should be wetted before pulling down tight. This will help to prevent friction burns on the line.

Spade End Knot
Used mainly by the coarse angler, this knot is very useful for tying on spade end hooks. Although many continental anglers are able to tie tiny hooks like 24s by hand, there is in fact a gadget known as a hook tyer that will produce this knot for you in a fraction of the time it takes you to tie it.

 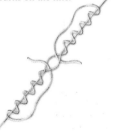  

1 Start with a 360° degree circle in the line with the loose end pointing away from the bend of the hook. The hook should lie over the line.

2 Wind the outside of the loop over the hook shank about seven to eight times. Pull the ends to tighten, and the line will be whipped into place.

Shock Leader Knot

This knot has been specially developed to join a heavy leader to a lighter mainline. It is a much-used knot for the beach angler who is casting long distances. A length of heavier line, usually 50lb (22.68 kg) is joined to the mainline. This leader will then take the brunt of the cast and stop the lighter mainline from breaking.

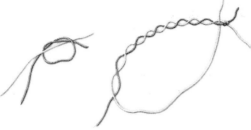

1 Tie an overhand knot in the heavier leader and pass the lighter line through the knot alongside the protruding gap.

2 Pull the overhand knot in the leader as tight as possible, then wrap the tag of the lighter main line around the leader a minimum of six times, but not more than ten. Next, thread the tag back through the first wrap formed, the one right up against the overhand knot.

3 Form the knot, first with gentle pressure on the mainline against the leader, then with equal pressure as the knot closes.

4 The finished knot should be pulled firmly to ensure the 'creep' has been taken up. The tag should be trimmed.

Locked Half Blood Knot

This knot is used for tying on hooks or swivels to the line. It is a firm favourite among sea and coarse anglers for the joining of eyed hooks. Sea anglers often use this for tying down swivels. Being a sort of strangulation knot, it needs wetting with saliva before being tightened down, to prevent friction burn.

1 Thread the line through the eye of the hook or swivel and twist the tag and mainline together. Complete three to six twists.

2 Thread the tag back through the first twist. The heavier the weight of the line, the fewer twists you will need to use.

3 Pull the line, (but not too tightly) to begin with, so that the knot starts to form.

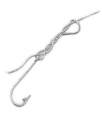

4 To lock the knot, thread the tag through the open loop which has formed at the top of the knot.

5 Pull the knot up firmly and test the knot to see that it holds. Trim off the surplus tag.

Double Overhand Loop

This simple but effective loop is most commonly used to accommodate a loop-to-loop hooklength. It can also be used to house a swivel or weight, by simply slipping the loop through and over the swivel or lead.

1 Form a loop at the end of your line.

2 Tie an overhand knot with the loop.

3 Add another wrap to the knot.

4 Close up the knot tightly and the loop is ready. This knot is also used when joining a cast to a mainline.

Grinner Knot

This knot is used by many anglers to attach the fly to the leader. It is very secure, and with practice it is easy to tie. There are a number of knots used by anglers to do this, Tucked Half Blood Knot, Turle Knot and Double Turle Knot being some of them.

1 Take the line through the eye of the hook, take it over the line and then make an overhand knot.

2 Add three or four turns to this overhand knot, depending on the thickness of the line you are using.

3 Pull both ends to tighten the knot, moistening it with saliva to prevent any line burn.

Loop Knot

This is a similar knot to the Grinner, and the first stages of tying the knot are the same. However, once the first overhand knot has been tied the turns are added around the mainline. This makes a good strong knot, but it is not quite as neat as some others.

1 Take the line through the hook and then tie an overhand knot.

2 Take three or four turns around the mainline above the overhand knot.

3 Pull both ends of the line to tighten the knot securely in place.

Surgeon's Knot

This is a good knot when you have to use to join two lengths of line of different strengths. It is used by sea anglers when joining a shock tippet to a main line. The only problem with this knot is that it can be difficult to tighten properly.

1 Lay the ends of the two lines to be joined side by side. Make sure you have allowed enough line.

2 Make four overhand turns, carefully keeping the two lines as level as possible.

3 Pull steadily and slowly on all four ends to tighten the knot properly. This can be difficult.

The Needle Knot

Needle and Nail Knots are the best ways of attaching a leader to a fly line. Their main advantage is that they form a straight knotless link with the line that runs no risk of catching in the top ring of the rod. They also enable the angler to add a thick length of nylon to the fly line to assist in tapering the cast and presenting the fly more accurately to the fish. There are a number of versions of this knot, all of which are relatively easy to tie with practice. The version shown here is one of the simplest.

1 Heat a thin needle. Push the point of the needle up the core of the line.

2 Thread the nylon on the needle and push the needle out at the side.

3 Take the needle a short distance down the line and push it right through.

4 Pull the nylon through and then bring the needle back and repeat stage 3.

5 Make the second hole nearer the end of the line as shown. Thread the nylon through.

6 Tie a figure-of-eight knot at the end of the nylon to act as a stop and pull the knot tight.

Acknowledgements

The publishers wishes to thank the following individuals and suppliers for their help and the loan of equipment and material for photography:

Dave Ellyatt
Drennan International Limited
Bocardo Court
Temple Road
Oxford OX4 2EX
Tel: (01865) 748989

Mike Ashpole
Ashpoles of Islington
Green Lanes
London N16
Tel: (0171) 226 6575

Mr Brian Frattel
Farlows
5 Pall Mall
London SW1Y 5NP
Tel: (0171) 839 2423

Martin Ford
27 Willesden Avenue
Walton
Peterborough PE4 6EA
(01733) 322497

Andrea Barnett
Hinders of Swindon
Ermin Street
Stratton
St. Margaret
Swindon SN3 4NH
Tel: (01793) 333900

Lyn Rees
Shimano (UK) Ltd.
St. John's Court
Upper Forest Way
Enterprise Park
Llansamlet
Swansea SA6 8QR
Tel: (01792) 791571

Fishing suppliers:
Lawrence Short
Trace Ace
PO Box 236
Chatham
Kent ME4 6LF
(01634) 848839

Tony Caton
Gemini Tackle Co.
Gemini Works
Mill Lane
Caistor
Lincolnshire LN7 6UA
(01472) 852966

Relum
Carlton Park Industrial Estate
Kelfale
Saxmundham
IP17 2NL
(01728) 603271

PICTURE CREDITS

The publishers would like to thank the following people for their kind permission to reproduce pictures in this book:

Jacket: Front cover, Tony Miles – bl; Martin Ford c & r. Front flap: Barry Ord-Clarke – l; Bruce Vaughan – r. Back cover: Martin Ford – t & bl; T. Miles – cl, t & bl. Back flap: T. Miles – l.

Inside: Martin Ford & Dave Barham pp. 5 bl; 6 bl; 16 b; 19 c; 35 c; 37 tr; 86 tr; 96 cl & r, bl & r; 102 tr; 104 bl; 107 tr; 109 b; 110 b; 124–5; 127 r; 140; 141 tr; 142 l; 144; 145 tl; 146 tl; 147 bl; 149; 148; 149 cl, cr & br; 150; 151; 152 c; 154 bl; 153 c & bc; 156 c; 158 tc & bl; 159; 160 tr; 162 tc & br; 168; 169; 170; 171 tc; 172; 173; 174; 175 tr; 178; 182; 184; 185; 186 tl. Peter Gathercole – pp 2; 188–89; 190; 191; 192 b; 193; 194 cr & bl; 195; 196; 197; 198 bc; 199; 200 bl; 201 br; 209 br; 210; 211; 212; 213; 214; 215; 216; 217; 218; 219; 220; 221; 222; 223; 224 bl; 225 tr; 226; 227; 228; 229; 238 bl; 239 bc. Graham Marsden pp. 21 tr; 74 br; 123. Tony Miles – pp. 5 tl; 12; 13; 14 b; 15; 18–19; 19 tr; 20b; 21 b; 22 b; 23; 27 tr & b; 29 t; 30 b; 34 bl & br; 35 t; 36 b; 37 tl & cl; 38 b; 39; 42 c; 43 tl & br; 45 tl & br; 63 br; 64 br; 67 br; 70 tl; 82 bl; 83 bl; 86 t & c; 87 b; 88 b; 91 cr; 92 tr; 98 b; 100; 101; 111 t; 116 bl; 117; 118; 119; 120; 121; 122; 201 tr. Barry Ord-Clarke 209 tl. Bruce Vaughan – pp. 6; 9; 116 tr; 224 tr. John Wilson – pp. 1; 5 bl; 8 cr; 10–11; 17; 24 c & b; 25 t & b; 26 b; 27 tl; 28 b; 29 c; 31 tl & c; bl; 33; 40 b; 41; 42 tr; 43 tc & br; 46 br; 48 c; 49 cr; 50 t; 51; 53 tl; 55 tr; 57; 91 t; 126; 127 tl; 149 tr; 201 bl & cr.

key: r = right, l = left, t = top, tl = top left, tr = top right, tc = top centre; c = centre; b = bottom, bl = bottom left, br = bottom right, bc = bottom centre.

Index

Page numbers in **bold type** refer to main species entries.

A

Aberdeen hook 164, 171
Abramis brama see bream
aerator pump 145
anchored bait 90
Anguilla anguilla see eel
Atlantic salmon 12, 114, 190–1, **192–3**, 214–15, 238
autogreaser 80
Avon float 68, 73, 75, 103

B

backing 205
bait
 anchored 90
 boiled (boilies) 52–3, 54–5, 58, 59, 87, 96
 coarse fishing 42–59
 colouring and flavouring 56–7
 deadbait *see* deadbait
 dense bait 84
 essential oils 56
 exploding plugs 99
 floating 54, 55, 86–91
 fly fishing 91
 game fishing 215, 238–9
 groundbait *see* groundbait
 jerk bait 114, 115
 live *see* live bait
 mass 49
 off-the-shelf 55
 particle 48–9, 55, 58, 79
 paste 46–7
 prebaiting 58, 59
 processed 44–5
 propbait 114
 sea angling 140–58
 sea trout fishing 217
 synthetic paste 47, 56
bait boat 59
baitcaster reel 202
bait dropper 59, 70
baiting cone 59
bait pump 144
bait rocket 55, 59
bait rod 202–3
bait soak 55
bale arm 161
barbel 12, **14–15**, 45, 46, 51, 56, 58, 59, 61, 63, 83, 84, 99, 100, 101, 117, 118, 119, 123
Barbus barbus see barbel
bass 126, **130**, 145–8, 150, 151, 153, 154, 156, 158, 159, 160, 168–73

bass bag 206
beach-buddy 165
beachcast 166–7
beachcaster 160
beads 165
bedchair 64
Belone belone see garfish
birds 90
bite-off 92
bivvy 64
bleak 51
Blicca bjoerkna see bream, silver
bluebottle meat fly 43
boat fishing 126–7, 152
boat seat 206
bobbin indicator 69
boiled bait (boilies) 47, 52–3, 54–5, 58, 59, 87, 96
boilie punch 71
bolt rig 70, 93–5
 feeder 94–5
bomb link 90
bouncing 83
brandling worms 238
bread bait 44, 49, 54, 55, 56, 58
bread paste bait 46
bread punch 44
breakaway lead 164–5
bream 11, 12, **16–17**, 45, 46, 58, 63, 75, 80, 82, 93, 107, 120, 122, 123, 126
 black **139**
 red 147
 silver 16, 17
bullhead 51
bull huss 170
bung 103, 104–5
bung remover 105
bung retractor 104
bush 103
butt indicator 69, 90

C

Carassius carassius see carp, crucian carp 12, **18–19**, 46, 54, 56, 58, 61, 65, 80, 81, 83, 84, 86, 88–90, 120, 122
 common 16
 crucian 16, **24–5**, 51, 76, 80
 fishing abroad 123
 leather 16
 mirror 16
 "wildies" 16
carp float 68
carp groundbait 55
carp hook 87
carp rod 60, 61, 160, 175
casters 42–3, 49

casting
 game fishing 210–13
 shore fishing 163, 166–7
catapult 59, 71, 79, 104, 109
catfish 12, **20–1**, 51, 63, 83, 86, 123
centrepin reel 61
chair, folding 64
cheese paste 46
Chelon labrosus see mullet, thick-lipped
chenille 241
chub 11, **22–3**, 44–6, 50, 51, 54, 61, 83, 84, 86, 87, 91, 99, 101, 114, 115, 117, 119
chub rod 61
clip swivel 165
closed-face reel 61
clothing 62, 207–9
cloud bait 58
coalfish **132**, 152, 154, 156, 169, 175
coarse fishing
 abroad 123
 bait and groundbait 42–59
 equipment 60–71
 fly fishing 91
 locating fish 116–23
 species 14–41
 summer 116
 surface fishing 86–7
 winter 116, 117–19
cockles 42, 57, 148
cod **129**, 140, 143, 144, 146, 147, 151, 155, 157, 169, 170
codling 126
Conger conger see eel, conger
connector (pole fishing) 103, 104–5
controller 89
 surface 72, 87
cool box or bag 50, 53
counterbalance 70–1
courge 145
crab 153, 164
 hermit 151
 peeler 140–1
crease swim 118
crimp 84
crystal float 68
crystal missile 68
Cyprinus carpio see carp

D

dab 126, **133**, 150, 153, 164, 168, 169
dace **26–7**, 65, 83, 86, 91, 99, 117
dapping 115, 197

deadbait 50–1, 57, 61, 78
 dense bait 84
 freelining 84–5
 spinning 110
 wobbled 110
deep hooking 78
dense bait 84
Devon Minnow 239
dibbling 225
Dicentrarchus labrax see bass
disgorger 33, 65
distance rig, one-hook 176
diving plug 114
dogfish 126, 143, 159, 168, 169, 170
 greater-spotted 138
 lesser-spotted **138**
 spurdog *see* spurdog
double haul cast 210, 212
double-rubber balsa 68
Dover sole **138**, 164, 168
down-and-across 222–3
drag system 161
driftbeater 68
drifter 68
drift float 68, 80
drifting 226
drogue 224–5, 226
dropper 205, 224, 225
dubbing 241
dumpy slider 68

E

eel **28–9**, 46, 50, 51, 84, 86, 168, 169, 171
 conger 126, **128**, 142, 151, 159, 170
electronic alarm 68, 69
Esox lucius see pike
essential oils 56
estate lakes 780
estuary fishing 170–1
exploding plugs 99

F

feathers 152, 155
 fly tying 241
featherwing 249
feature finder float 72
feeder fishing 82, 94–5, 99
ferox 197
figure-of-eight retrieve 226
fishmeal paste 47, 52
fixed-wire lead 164
flapper 142–3, 170
Flectolite 153, 154
flick tip 102
floatant 80, 86
floater loop 90
float feeder rig 79
float fishing 72–82, 160
floating bait 54, 55, 86–91
floating plug 112–13, 114, 154
float legering 78–89
float rod 61, 160

NOTES

NOTES

NOTES

NOTES

NOTES

NOTES

NOTES

NOTES